S0-AHT-223

Italian Immigrant
Radical Culture

Italian Immigrant Radical Culture

The Idealism of the Sovversivi *in the United States, 1890–1940*

Marcella Bencivenni

CABRINI COLLEGE LIBRAR
610 KING OF PRUSSIA ROAD
RADNOR, PA 19087

NEW YORK UNIVERSITY PRESS
New York and London

#688559428

NEW YORK UNIVERSITY PRESS
New York and London
www.nyupress.org

© 2011 by New York University
All rights reserved

References to Internet websites (URLs) were accurate at the time of writing.
Neither the author nor New York University Press is responsible for URLs
that may have expired or changed since the manuscript was prepared.

Library of Congress Cataloging-in-Publication Data

Bencivenni, Marcella.
Italian immigrant radical culture : the idealism of the sovversivi
in the United States, 1890–1940 / Marcella Bencivenni.
p. cm.
Includes bibliographical references and index.
ISBN 978-0-8147-9103-5 (cl : alk. paper) — ISBN 978-0-8147-0944-3 (ebook)
1. Italian Americans—Politics and government—History—19th century.
2. Italian Americans—Politics and government—History—20th century.
3. Radicalism—United States—History—19th century. 4. Radicalism—
United States—History—20th century. 5. Italian Americans—Intellectual
life—19th century. 6. Italian Americans—Intellectual life—20th century.
7. Italian American literature—History and criticism. 8. Giovannitti,
Arturo M., 1884–1959. I. Title.
E184.I8B46   2011
973'.0451—dc22   2010048336

New York University Press books are printed on acid-free paper,
and their binding materials are chosen for strength and durability.
We strive to use environmentally responsible suppliers and materials
to the greatest extent possible in publishing our books.

Manufactured in the United States of America

10 9 8 7 6 5 4 3 2 1

Contents

Acknowledgments

The idea for this book began almost a decade ago at a graduate seminar class at the City University of New York. Up to that point my research interests had focused primarily on early-twentieth-century American cultural radicalism. As I was studying the group of rebels of New York's Greenwich Village, I came across an Italian poet, Arturo Giovannitti. Naturally I became curious about him and decided to find out more about his life and his relationship to American radicalism. I had the good fortune to count among the CUNY faculty the late Philip V. Cannistraro, one of the pioneers of Italian American studies. His guidance was fundamental to this project. Indeed, without him this book would not have been written. Not only did he help me conceive the project, but he also kindly offered his time, expertise, and support.

I am also greatly indebted to Nunzio Pernicone, who after Cannistraro's passing became my most trusted mentor. He carefully read the entire manuscript in its various stages, sharing with me his research and unsurpassed knowledge of Italian American radicalism and offering invaluable advice and support throughout the long journey of completing the book. Michael M. Topp also provided useful criticism, pushing me to think more deeply about culture and identity politics, thus helping to improve the book significantly. I also owe thanks to Marie Anne Trasciatti for reading and commenting on chapter 4, and Salvatore Salerno for generously sharing his research and lending me his files and art collection on the Paterson (New Jersey) anarchists. I must also extend my most sincere appreciation to a larger cohort of scholars who have provided both inspiration and encouragement: most notably, Donna Gabaccia, Jennifer Guglielmo, Jerry Meyer, Fraser Ottanelli, Marta Petrusewicz, and the late Rudolph J. Vecoli and Paul Avrich.

This book has also benefited greatly from the critical reading of several colleagues who have become some of my closest friends. Carol Giardina, Hilary Hallett, Carol Quirke, and Ernest Ialongo offered plenty of suggestions and criticism in the early stages of writing. Evelyn Burg, Jacob Kramer, Carol Quirke, and Dan Wishnoff continued to offer their feedback throughout this book's completion. I am deeply thankful for their attentive readings and insightful comments, and even more for their friendship. Not only did they offer significant scholarly criticism, but they also provided crucial support and encouragement when I needed it most. Their comradeship made it possible to transform the frustrating and sometime alienating process of writing this book into an enriching communal experience.

I also thank Joel Wurl, Daniel Necas, and Haven Hawley for their assistance at the Immigration History Research Center in Minneapolis and for granting me permission to publish archival material from the IHRC collection. As well, I thank Kees Rodenburg at the International Institute of Social History in Amsterdam and the entire staff of the New York Public Library, where I spent endless hours reading microfilms of Italian radical papers. Special thanks also go to Steve Fante, the grandson of Fort Velona—the subject of the book's last chapter—for his willingness to share information on his grandfather and for lending me some great photos.

I am also very grateful for various funding I received as I worked on this project: the E. P. Thompson scholarship from the Graduate School of the City University of New York, a grant from the Davis-Putter Scholarship Fund, and a grant from the National Italian American Foundation, all of which enabled me to complete my initial research. Three grants from the Professional Staff Congress–City University of New York (PSC–CUNY) Research Award Program while at Hostos Community College were crucial to expanding my research and getting released time from teaching to complete the book.

Finally, I am obliged to New York University Press for believing in this project, particularly to Matthew Frey Jacobson for his enthusiastic endorsement and to my editor, Eric Zinner, for his patience. My appreciation also extends to assistant editor Ciara McLaughlin and managing editor Despina Papazoglou Gimbel for their indispensable assistance.

I reserve the last paragraph for the most important persons in my life: my parents, Benito and Marisa, who have given me unwavering love and support; my brother, Egidio, and my sister, Natalia; my husband, Lucien O'Neill, who provided moral support as well as editorial advice throughout the years I spent working on this project; and my newborn son, Philippe, who fills my heart with joy every day in ways I never imagined. This book is for them and in memory of Philip V. Cannistraro.

Introduction

On January 11, 1912, mill workers in Lawrence, Massachusetts, began a three-month strike to protest a cut in their already thin wages. This "crusade for bread and roses," as the strike was soon called, became one of the most celebrated working-class protests in American history. For the first time, unskilled immigrants of many different nationalities overcame ethnic differences and scored a significant victory against American industrial manufacturers.

The Lawrence strike had an enormous impact on the American public consciousness, bringing attention to the atrocious living conditions of unskilled workers and the social divisions that plagued American industrial society. Overnight, the strike also catapulted Italian immigrant workers into national prominence. Italians constituted the largest single ethnic group of Lawrence's polyglot population, and they played a decisive role in the strike. Providing both leadership and mass militancy, they introduced the American labor movement to new tactics of direct action that reflected their native traditions of struggle and resistance. As local reporters of the strike noted, "angry" Italians "rushed the gates, broke open the doors, damaged the escalators, pulled girls from their work, cut off the electric drive, stopped the machines throughout the mill, and threatened to kill any person daring to put the machinery in motion."[1]

Historians have by now written detailed accounts of the Lawrence strike and other labor conflicts of the period, recognizing the crucial contributions of Italian workers and leaders.[2] Scholars of Italian American history have also increasingly documented how these struggles were part of a larger transnational radical movement and subculture that constituted a significant presence in the Italian immigrant community and the American Left until World War II.[3]

Thanks to these pioneering works, we know that Italian Americans possess a vibrant if "lost" radical past. As early as 1882, Italian immigrants founded a socialist club in Brooklyn, New York. Radical organizations then multiplied and spread across the United States, from large urban cities to smaller industrial and mining areas. By 1900 there were thirty official Italian sections of the Socialist Party along the East Coast and countless independent anarchist and revolutionary groups throughout the nation, replete with alternative newspapers, social clubs, and schools. The heart of this movement was a transnational generation of social rebels or *sovversivi*—as they were collectively called in Italian—that included anarchists, socialists, syndicalists, and, after World War I, anti-fascist and communist refugees.

During the past decade, there has been a surge of interest in the *sovversivi's* radical world. Scholars, however, have directed their attention almost exclusively to the organizational and political aspects of the Italian immigrant Left, analyzing the movement principally through its labor constituency and its official documents. This book, in contrast, focuses on the movement's cultural and literary dimension—the way traditions, institutions, literature, and art fused with and sustained political work. Adopting an interdisciplinary approach that combines immigration, radical, and cultural history, it documents the wide spectrum of Italian immigrant radical culture in the United States and examines the many forms it took.

I use the term "radical" to encompass the whole range of class-based ideologies associated with the European political Left: anarchism, socialism, syndicalism, and communism. These political ideologies had significant doctrinal differences but had the same goals: to overthrow capitalism, emancipate the workers, and establish social and economic equality. "Radical" in this sense has a strictly political, ideological meaning. My definition of "culture," on the other hand, has a broad and contextual connotation, embracing both a literary and an anthropological meaning. It refers to the general process of intellectual and artistic developments, but it also describes a particular way of life, a worldview, or *mentalité*.[4]

This study basically re-imagines the *sovversivi's* cultural world—their milieu, beliefs, and artistic expressions. On one level, it tells the history of their movement and their activities. On another, it analyzes the institutions and cultural forms they developed: the press, literature, poetry, theater, and iconography.

Italian immigrant radicals came to America with values, beliefs, and mores that influenced their activities in the United States. Besides creating political parties, groups, and unions, they engaged in a wide range of cultural and recreational activities that shaped and defined their political culture. They formed evening and Sunday schools that drew on the Italian socialist experience of *Università Popolari* (people's universities). They created countless educational circles and self-organized radical bookstores that made hundreds of books and pamphlets (both nonfiction and fiction) available to workers. They had their own orchestras and dramatic societies that sponsored weekly performances in local bars, circles, or hired halls. They arranged special dances, concerts, picnics, and annual festivals such as the *festa della frutta*, a peasant custom held each autumn to celebrate the fall harvest. In place of traditional national and religious holidays, they established their own revolutionary celebrations, such as May Day, the international workers' day. They sponsored conferences and lectures; published newspapers; and produced hundreds of pamphlets, poems, social dramas, drawings, and cartoons.

This rich oppositional culture was at the heart of Italian immigrant radicalism. Cultural events, institutions, and literary works came to occupy a special place in the life of Italian radicals, sustaining and spreading their values, entertaining their communities, and bolstering the movement's organization and strength. Some initiatives were extremely successful, attracting thousands of Italian immigrants and raising hundreds of dollars for radical endeavors. This book contends that it was through these cultural venues, in addition to official doctrines or party policies, that radical leaders expressed and carried their political ideology beyond the narrow confines of the workplace.

Radicalism has typically been studied and measured through traditional forms of political participation and activism such as union and party membership or voting. But to understand radical experiences fully, we need a broader definition of the "political." We must move away from the workplace as the central paradigm of working-class identity and acknowledge, as the historian Robin Kelley has urged, the "importance of the cultural terrain as a site of struggle."[5] Scholars have produced many such cultural histories about the radical experiences of blacks or other ethnic groups such as the Jews, Germans, and Finns.[6] But the study of culture has yet to transform—and displace—popular perceptions of the Italian American experience.

The underlying premise of this work is that class alone cannot explain the *sovversivi*'s radicalism. Their politics were rooted in cultural as well as social experiences—shaped by their ethnic identity and immigrant experiences as well as by their internationalist credo and commitment to a working-class revolution. Their radicalism, in other words, embodied a complex system of traditions, institutions, and values that immigrants brought with them from Italy and adapted to new American circumstances.

For all the recent proliferation of studies on the Italian radical diaspora, there is still a need for a synthesis that brings together the various shades and components of the movement. Historians so far have focused on five distinct components of the Italian American Left: the anarchist movement, the Italian Socialist Federation, the unions, the anti-fascist movement, and, to a lesser extent, the communist presence. Collectively their works point to the enormous richness and sectarianism of Italian American radicalism. But their emphasis on and preoccupation with the exceptional elements of each one of the Italian American leftist groups have obscured their common culture and roots. Without denying or diminishing the movement's political fragmentation, this book shows that despite their ideological differences, the *sovversivi* shared the same cultural traditions, the same ethical values, the same dreams and hopes. This common vision, I suggest, was an integral aspect of the movement. Not only did it provide the main source of aspiration, but it also encapsulated a distinct "way of life," a sensibility based on communal Italian traditions and working-class solidarity.

In recovering the *sovversivi*'s culture, this book underscores the important role of literature and art as forms of both self-expression and propaganda and, more generally, the centrality of culture and the intellectual vanguard in the formation and development of radical ideologies. The *sovversivi* are a perfect example of what Antonio Gramsci has called "organic" intellectuals. They fulfilled a crucial role as "constructors," "organizers," and "permanent persuaders" of their community. They provided crucial leadership among their co-nationals; mediated between the Old and the New World, and, above all, articulated through various cultural apparatuses the feelings, experiences, and hopes of Italian workers in America.[7]

Yet, with the exception of a few biographical studies of "great men" like Carlo Tresca, Sacco and Vanzetti, and Vito Marcantonio, the cadre of the Italian American Left remains little known.[8] Important leaders such as the poet Arturo Giovannitti, the cartoonist Fort Velona, the playwright Alessandro Sisca, and the union organizer Antonino Crivello, or radical women like the syndicalist Bellalma Forzato-Spezia and the anarchist poet Virgilia D'Andrea, are almost completely forgotten—their memory erased by Americanization, their papers and writings consigned to a few archives. However, they were once revered within the Little Italies and the American labor movement, serving important social functions as "ethnic brokers" of the immigrant communities and producers of a lively radical subculture.[9] One of the purposes of this book is to rescue these untold stories and forgotten voices from historical oblivion.

Complementing the emerging scholarship on Italian immigrant women's activism, this study also addresses gender issues, providing examples of radical women's leadership as well as radical men's ambiguous views toward the woman question.[10] My goal, however, is not just to make the world of Italian immigrant radicals more visible. In keeping with broader currents in the field of radical history, I examine and interpret cultural sources that have escaped the attention of scholars, such as plays, poems, short stories, and cartoons. Not only do these cultural sources disrupt stereotypes, but they also provide unique insights into the human side, the emotions, and the worldview of the *sovversivi*, as well as their conflicting views about class, gender, and ethnicity.

I am especially interested in how Italian immigrant radicals expressed their political beliefs through culture; what themes they privileged; what institutions they established; and how their cultural production informed their radical politics. Indeed, a basic question permeates this study: What can we learn about Italian immigrants' radicalism from what they produced and wrote?

The book's organization reflects the colorful and multifaceted nature of Italian immigrant cultural radicalism and generally adopts a thematic format. Building upon existing scholarship, chapter 1, "Italian American Radicalism: Old World Roots, New World Developments," offers a general overview of the Italian radical movement in the United States. It begins by mapping the social and political scene in Italy after the struggle for unification in 1861, focusing particularly on the rise of anarchism and revolutionary socialism. It then turns to the United States and the emergence of the Italian immigrant radical movement from the first anarchist and socialist clubs at the turn of the nineteenth century, when the great Italian immigration began, to the fight against fascism and the movement's eventual decline after the 1930s.

The second chapter offers a collective profile of the *sovversivi*, as well as a discussion of their organizations and cultural life. It examines their role as ethnic leaders, the institutions they established, and their worldview. The subsequent chapters explore the most significant cultural forms by which the *sovversivi* expressed their political ideas, each illuminating one particular dimension of the Italian immigrant radical culture.

The large number of Italian radical newspapers points to the fact that a critical portion of the *sovversivi*'s ideological struggle took place in the pages of the press. Chapter 3, "A Literary Class War: The Italian American Radical Press," examines this crucial institution. Surveying more than fifty radical newspapers, ranging from anarchist to socialist, communist, and anti-fascist, it provides an overview of the press and a discussion of the main themes, programs, and debates contained in its pages.

The *sovversivi* recognized the importance of leisure and built vibrant institutions that entertained the immigrant workers while educating them to revolutionary ideals. Chapter 4, "Politics and Leisure: The Italian American Radical Stage," looks at the most popular and effective of these recreational activities: the radical stage. Focusing on several plays that have survived, it discusses the use of drama as a medium of political propaganda and, simultaneously, as a form of popular entertainment and artistic self-expression.

The next two chapters enter more specifically into the literary realm, looking at Italian American radicalism through the lenses of fiction. Chapter 5, "Italian American Literary Radicalism," offers a reevaluation of the Left cultural tradition in Italian Americana, bringing attention to the role of literature and cultural traditions in the making of Italian immigrant radical politics. Recovering hitherto neglected radical texts, it examines two popular literary forms: the novelettes, or short stories, and poetry. Written by radical intellectuals or self-taught workers, these narratives provide—like the plays—unique insights into the emotions and values of Italian radicals.

The sixth chapter, "Arturo Giovannitti: Poet and Prophet of Labor," delves deeper into the *sovversivi*'s poetry by discussing the figure and work of Giovannitti, one of the most charismatic figures of the Italian American Left, who achieved national prominence as the leader of the famed 1912 Lawrence strike and as one of America's best poets.

The final chapter, "Allegories of Anti-Fascism: The Radical Cartoons of Fort Velona," explores the visual culture of the Italian American anti-fascist movement, specifically focusing on the radical cartoons and caricatures of the artist Fort Velona.

The Conclusion discusses the significance of these cultural forms, showing the many ways in which culture informed and sustained the activities of Italian radicals. By retrieving the texts and arts of Italian immigrant revolutionaries, I hope, this study will contribute to a more rounded history of the Italian American radical experience and encourage the development of further studies that examine culture and politics in their simultaneity.

Italian American Radicalism

Old World Roots, New World Developments

Old World Roots

The story of Italian American radicalism begins with the massive emigration of Italians who entered the New World between 1880 and 1920. More than five million—four-fifths of them from the southern regions and the islands—migrated to the United States during this period. Italians became the largest nationality of the "new immigrants" from southern and eastern Europe, constituting more than 20 percent of the total immigration population. The great exodus of Italians was the result of economic, social, and political pressures. Like other European countries, Italy experienced a severe agrarian crisis in the 1870s, resulting largely from the expansion of the American economy. To make things worse, the South was also plagued by a series of calamities that occurred between the end of the nineteenth century and the beginning of the twentieth century: first the epidemics of malaria and cholera (1884–87) followed by the spread of phylloxera in the vineyards, then the volcanic eruptions of Vesuvius and Etna (1906), and finally the earthquakes of 1908, which destroyed much of the Sicilian province of Messina and part of Calabria. The extraordinary growth of the population from eighteen million in 1801 to thirty-two million in 1901 and increasing political unrest also contributed significantly to massive emigration.[1]

With the important exception of a small portion of artisans and craftsmen, such as barbers, tailors, shoemakers, and masons, the great majority of Italian immigrants entered the American labor market as wage earners, and as unskilled, manual workers. Between 1899 and 1910 only 0.5 percent of all emigrants from Italy were listed as professionals; 5 percent were artisans, and 83.9 percent were *contadini*, land-poor peasants who generally lived in small villages under pre-modern social and economic conditions.[2]

Their rural origin was a significant factor in their reception in the United States and their adaptation to the new environment. To Anglo-Saxon Americans, the looks, habits, and cultural traditions of the new immigrants appeared backward, primitive, and ultimately inferior. Italians were seen as not only of a lower stock, but also frequently as not "white." Employers, for example, "referred to South Italians as 'black labor' as opposed to the 'white men' of Northern Europe."[3] Similarly, U.S. immigration officials used "South Italian" as a separate designation that put Italians in a middle ground within the racial order of white-over-black. As Matthew Jacobson has pointed out, "it was not just that Italians did not look white," but "they did not *act* white."[4] Popular magazines and newspapers, for example, warned repeatedly that southern Italians were "by nature" emotional, bloody-minded, treacherous, and vengeful—a view that was encouraged and reinforced by sensational accounts of "Black Hand" criminality, the material of vaudeville comics, and nativist propaganda.[5]

Discrimination toward Italians in America was of course neither as systematic nor as harsh as the racism experienced by people defined clearly as nonwhites, like African Americans, Asians, and Mexicans. As Thomas Guglielmo has argued, Italian immigrants by virtue of their "color status" were "on arrival" granted important political and legal privileges such as the right to naturalize, to live in certain neighborhoods, to apply for certain jobs, and to intermarry, privileges that were instead regularly denied to people of African or Asian descent.[6]

Yet as scornful epithets like "Dago," "Wop," and "Guinea" indicate, Italians did suffer from extensive ethnic hostility. Anti-Italian feelings emerged more dramatically in the South and Midwest, where American mobs lynched Italian immigrants on at least a dozen occasions. The most infamous lynching occurred in New Orleans on March 14, 1891, when eleven Italians were killed by a mob after a jury acquitted nine of them of the charge of murdering the local chief of police. Justifying the mob's actions, the *New York Times* published an editorial that powerfully encapsulated general perceptions of Italian immigrants at the time. "There can be no doubt that the mob's victims were desperate ruffians and murderers," the editorial read. "These sneaking and cowardly Sicilians, the descendants of bandits and assassins, who have transported to this country the lawless passions, the cut-throat practices and the oath-bound societies of their native country, are to us a pest without mitigation."[7]

Even American labor officials exhibited nativist prejudices, casting Italian immigrants as "undesirable" and "injurious." By the 1890s, when southern Italians began to arrive in large numbers, American trade unions rallied in support of legislative restrictions against them, arguing that new immigrants (mostly Italians and Slavs) were undercutting the American workers' standards of living. To Samuel Gompers, the president of the American Federation of Labor, Italian workers were nothing more than unorganizable wage cutters, incapable of appreciating the value of unionism because of their rural background and culture.[8]

These negative perceptions profoundly affected Italian immigrants' adjustment to American society, as well as their response to labor organization and struggle. Samuel Baily in his comparative study of Italian immigrants in New York and Buenos Aires shows that racial discrimination was an important variable in the assimilation process. In Argentina, Italians adjusted rapidly and successfully to the new environment; they also made up about 40 percent of the organized workers and provided the most important leadership in the labor movement. By contrast, Italians in the United States were notoriously slow to assimilate into and reluctant to participate in American mainstream unions. Baily argues that the reasons for this discrepancy lay in distinct economic, political, and social conditions, as well as in the host societies' different perceptions of the Italians. Argentinians saw the Italians, who emigrated there mostly from the northern regions of the peninsula, as better than and "superior" to the darker indigenous population and welcomed them as bearers of "civilization" and "whiteness." The U.S. establishment, instead, considered Italian immigrants members of an inferior race that threatened to corrupt the dominant Anglo-Saxon stock and culture, and consequently restricted opportunities for them, instigating in turn among Italian workers diffidence and resentment toward American institutions.[9]

Sweeping generalizations and stereotypes about pre-modern cultures in general, and southern Italians in particular, also resonated in early scholarly studies of Italian immigration and American labor. Until the 1980s, when social historians brought new attention to minorities and other marginalized voices, many scholars uncritically accepted the view of southern Italians as a homogeneous peasantry—an undistinguished mass of conservative, subservient, and apathetic "amoral familists." According to this perception, which was first advanced by the sociologist Edward Banfield in the 1950s, southern Italians were incapable of collective and political action because their entire worldview revolved around and was limited to the nuclear family.[10]

Centuries of foreign rule, political oppression, and economic mismanagement had indeed convinced the *contadini* that states were inherently oppressive and corrupt—a sentiment aptly captured by the still popular imprecation *"governo ladro"* (thief of a government). Skeptical of institutionalized power and authority, they naturally learned to rely mostly on themselves and their immediate clans, creating an intricate interlocking web of patronage and mutual obligations.[11] However, as an increasing number of revisionist works have shown, this did not prevent them from organizing themselves, cooperating with fellow workers, or understanding the principles of unionism and socialism. In fact, one can find many examples of Italian peasants participating actively in strikes and revolts, just as there is ample evidence of peasant solidarity and cooperation. Donna Gabaccia has also noted that the *contadini* were, in their own way, intensely class conscious. Many Italian folk proverbs, for example, divided the world starkly into two antagonistic classes—the rich and the poor—clearly expressing "the exploitative interdependence between the two groups."[12] The level of injustice was such that in the words of Carlo Tresca, one of most important Italian immigrant radicals, "You did not need to read Karl Marx to be convinced that society as it stood had to be changed."[13]

Moreover, new studies on southern Italy indicate that Italian rural society was not fixed, immutable, and static, as traditionally described. The life of the *contadini* was actually characterized by great mobility, job flexibility, and social activism. The seasonal nature of the Italian rural economy, based on olives, nuts, citrus, grain, and wine harvests, encouraged constant moving and migrant flows. Similarly, off-season unemployment drew peasants to work as masons, joiners, blacksmiths, shoemakers, weavers, and spinners, often hundreds of kilometers away from their homes. This phenomenon of "coming and going" was indeed so intense that, according to Andreina De Clementi, it constituted "the major system of temporary emigration of western Europe."[14]

Rural life was characterized not only by mobility but also by unrest, conflict, and rebellion, manifested mostly in the form of *jacqueries*, riots, banditry, and brigandage, as discussed by Eric Hobsbawm in his classic study of pre-modern social revolt.[15] By the late nineteenth century, as Italy underwent industrialization and modernization, these traditional types of spontaneous protest evolved into more organized struggles aiming at a fundamental political, economic, and social change. Italy achieved unification in 1861, but the *Risorgimento*, as the movement for national independence was known, brought neither the political stability nor the economic prosperity Italians were longing for. The newly established state failed to develop the infrastructure and social reforms so desperately needed, especially in the South. Conditions of life throughout the peninsula actually worsened after the agrarian crisis of the 1870s, and so did popular resentment at the state. The result was a gradual awakening of working-class consciousness and a surge of organized activism, discernible in the growth of mutual aid societies, workers' leagues, chambers of labor, cooperatives, and strikes.

Already in 1868, following the imposition of a tax on flour, violent protests and demonstrations occurred in the northern province of Verona and rapidly spread to the rest of Italy. Flour millers shut down their mills while peasants broke into municipal buildings and public offices shouting: "Down with the city administration and the city taxes: we want to pay, but when we can!" The protests were eventually suppressed by the police: 257 demonstrators were killed, 1,000 wounded, and almost 4,000 arrested. Its failure notwithstanding, the revolt against the flour tax showed that the peasants and mill workers were not "potatoes in a sack," incapable of organization or revolt. In fact, in the following decade, from 1870 until 1880, they carried out 465 strikes (one-fifth of them in the textile industry) demanding wage increases and general welfare for the workers.[16]

The gradual rise of literacy also contributed to the promotion of greater class consciousness. Before Italian unification only 21.8 percent of the total population over five years of age could read and write. After 1861, however, public schooling became mandatory, and illiteracy decreased steadily. According to governmental statistics, by 1911 the Italians who could read and write numbered 18,322,866, or 58 percent of a total population of 34,671,377.[17]

But an even more important factor in the rise of working-class organizing was the circulation of new radical ideas embodied first by republicanism, then anarchism, and eventually socialism. Republicanism emerged out of the Italian political movement for national unification led by Giuseppe Mazzini. Combining republican values, egalitarianism, and inter-class cooperation, Mazzini's program of national unity inspired Italians to fight not only for the country's unification but also for the "moral improvement" of the nation and the progress of the entire humankind. Mazzini's unrelenting opposition to caste, privilege, and inequality and his emphasis on universal suffrage and education contributed powerfully to the development of the Italian labor movement.[18]

It was in the spirit of Mazzini's collectivism and cooperation that Italian workers formed the first *Società di mutuo soccorso* (mutual aid societies) in Piedmont during the 1850s. These institutions were self-help organizations that provided legal, medical, and educational assistance to their members. By 1895, there were 6,725 mutual aid societies spread throughout Italy; 1,597 of them were in the South, which at that time had 37 percent of the country's population. Each society was autonomous, but all of them were animated by a spirit of comradeship and class solidarity.[19]

Although not strictly labor organizations, the mutual aid societies provided a model for emergent workers' leagues and cooperatives, which in turn led the way to chambers of labor based on the French anarcho-syndicalist *bourses de travail* and modern trade unions such as the *Confederazione Generale del Lavoro* (CGL, 1906) and the *Unione Sindacale Italiana* (USI, 1912). These working-class organizations functioned as important centers of political propaganda and helped significantly to spread socialist ideas, develop a sense of solidarity among workers, and promote social and economic reforms.[20]

But after Italy's unification and Mazzini's death in 1872, anarchism supplanted republicanism as Italy's revolutionary vanguard. The Russian anarchist Mikhail Bakunin arrived in Italy in 1864 and attracted many converts, including a large number of intellectuals, especially in Naples and in the region of Emilia-Romagna. Bakunin advocated immediate social revolution and the destruction of power and authority in all their forms, including the state. His anti-statism naturally found fertile ground in Italy, where localism and distrust of government were, and to some extent still are, strong. Bakunin also attacked Mazzini and Marx for their neglect of the peasantry, insisting that the revolution should start from the country, not the cities. His stress on the role of the peasantry to carry out the social revolution, as well as his emphasis on spontaneous and voluntaristic revolt, fit perfectly the Italian situation and also explains his popularity in other European rural areas—most notably Andalusia, Spain's southern region. By 1874 anarchists were the leaders of the anti-authoritarian wing of the Italian section of the International Workingmen's Association (the First International), claiming more than 30,000 members.[21]

In the following decade, however, anarchism began to decline as a result of internal dissent and governmental repression, and it was eventually overshadowed by the rise of socialism. Socialist ideas made their first inroads in Italy in the late 1870s as Marxist works were translated into Italian; by the 1890s, socialism became the Left's predominant radical force. Among the most important disseminators of Marxism were Antonio Labriola, probably the most important Italian Marxist theoretician, and Filippo Turati, the main founder of the Italian Socialist Party, which was formed in August 1892 following the Congress of the Italian Workers' Party in Genoa. The new party made rapid strides. After one year it had 131,000 registered members and included 270 workers' associations.[22]

Out of this radical milieu emerged the *Fasci dei Lavoratori* (literally, bundles of workers), a leftist movement launched by Sicilian socialists in 1889 that rapidly spread into rural areas, eventually claiming a membership of more than 300,000 farm and sulfur workers. The *Fasci* led a series of violent uprisings, including a three-month-long strike in 1893 against landowners and state taxes in western Sicily. Eventually, the *Fasci* movement was crushed. Pressured by the frightened gentry, Prime Minister Francesco Crispi imposed martial law and launched a six-year-long period of violent repression that imperiled not only the labor movement but civil liberties as well. All leaders were arrested, more than 1,000 Sicilians were deported to penal islands, 100,000 voters were disenfranchised, and socialism, in all forms, was declared illegal.[23]

Yet the riots and demonstrations of the 1880s and 1890s had important political repercussions: They awakened the political consciences of thousands of men and women and increased their dissatisfaction with the liberal government. In the political elections of 1895 the Socialist Party obtained twelve seats in the legislature and the number of socialist workers' associations continued to grow, soaring from 270 in 1892 to 442 in 1896.[24]

Contrary to general assumptions, the peasantry was not untouched by these events. As Rudolph Vecoli has pointed out, radical ideas "were penetrating even into the heart of the deep South" thanks to military service, emigration, and the teachings of propagandists. The Italian labor movement in the late nineteenth and early twentieth centuries also attracted many peasants in the southern regions, especially in Sicily, Puglia, and Campania. In 1901, agricultural workers constituted 23 percent of the 661,478 official members of Italian unions and chambers of labor—the highest percentage of all European countries. The peasants, as Denis Mack Smith has suggested, were potentially the most rebellious element in Italian society.[25]

Migrant Italians did not leave their traditions of voluntary associations, militancy, and protest behind. They often came from precisely the most militant towns and continued to be politically active wherever they settled. Many, as we will see, had already been important leaders and organizers in Italy. As they migrated, they carried their ideologies and experiences of insurrectionism and unionism into their new communities, developing and sustaining through correspondence, newspapers, and itinerant lectures close ties with their comrades back home in Italy as well as in other Italian communities abroad. This ongoing connection, as Ernesto Ragionieri first suggested, resulted in the "internationalization" of the Italian working class, or, to use a more contemporary term, a "transnational" radical movement and culture that sought to shape the course of political events in both Italy and the United States. Indeed, as other historians have documented, Italian American radicalism had roots in ideas and developments originating on both sides of the

Atlantic and was informed by both ethnic and class allegiances. Its history must, therefore, be understood as the product of a reciprocal interaction between Old World experiences and New World developments.[26]

Most of the leaders of the Italian American Left had already embraced socialist dreams in Italy, but thousands of Italian immigrant workers were radicalized by their experience in America, particularly by their exposure to ethnic discrimination and economic exploitation. Images of a "wonderful new life" and a "land of plenty" where everybody could prosper gripped the imagination of Italians, sending them across the Atlantic. Life in the New World, however, proved to be full of privation, loneliness, and backbreaking toil. As one immigrant from Buffalo, New York, lamented in 1909 to his wife back in Italy: "What disillusionment . . . we who believed we could improve our condition by coming to America. Everywhere I see injustice and inequality. I am sorry to say that this country is worse than Europe for any man with a heart who wishes to live honestly."[27]

Immigrant disappointment was a major catalyst toward radical ideologies. The story of Bartolomeo Vanzetti, the anarchist executed with his comrade Nicola Sacco in 1927, offers perhaps the best example of the way in which the harsh economic and social conditions of life in North America radicalized immigrants. Before his arrival in the United States in 1908, Vanzetti had shown little inclination toward radical activities and ideas. He converted to anarchism largely as a result of the discrimination and exploitation he faced in the "promised land." Like thousands of others, he emigrated at the age of twenty with great expectations and hopes, but, as he wrote in his autobiography, he soon encountered "all the brutalities of life, all the injustice, the corruption in which humanity struggles tragically." In anarchism he found a new ideal, a community, and a culture that gave his existence new purpose and meaning. He learned that "class consciousness was not a phrase invented by propagandists but was a real, vital force"; he grasped "the concept of fraternity, of universal love"; and he dreamed of a day when there would be "a roof for every family, bread for every mouth, education for every heart, the light for every intellect."[28] He was not alone in endorsing this dream.

New World Developments

The Italian community in the United States grew steadily after 1880. That year's census counted only 44,230 foreign-born Italians, but in 1900 the number had increased to 800,000. By 1920 about four million Italian immigrants lived in the country—400,000 in New York City alone.[29] Italian immigrants gravitated toward large cities, such as New York, Boston, Philadelphia, Chicago, and San Francisco; industrial towns in the northeastern coast; and mining settlements in Pennsylvania, Ohio, West Virginia, and Illinois. It was, therefore, in these areas that they established the most vibrant and long-standing radical communities.

Radical ideas were propagated in the *colonie italiane*—as the Italian immigrant communities were then called—by charismatic political exiles fleeing from the harsh governmental repression that followed the uprisings of the *Fasci Siciliani* and the infamous *Fatti di Maggio* of 1898—a series of riots and labor protests in Milan, Puglia, Marche, and Sicily that were violently suppressed by the police, resulting in the deaths of 80 workers and the injury of 450.[30]

Political emigration had already occurred during the Italian nationalist struggle, but the tumultuous events of the 1890s caused an unprecedented exodus, forcing thousands to escape long prison sentences or *domicilio coatto*—confinement. Virtually every famous Italian anarchist theorist visited the New World at the turn of the twentieth century.[31] The first to arrive was the Neapolitan Francesco Saverio Merlino (1856–1930), the movement's foremost intellectual and theorist. He remained in America only one year, from 1892 to 1893, but during this time launched two important anarchist publications—*Il Grido degli Oppressi* (1892–94) and the English-language *Solidarity* (1892–98)—that gave great impetus to the anarchist movement in the United States.[32]

The anarchist poet and playwright Pietro Gori (1865–1911), also known as the "gentle anarchist" and the "knight of the Ideal," followed in 1895. Born in the Sicilian town of Messina, he achieved a first-rate education, graduating in law from the University of Pisa. As a student there, he joined the anarchist movement and soon became one of its most important and beloved leaders. Between 1894 and 1902 he lived in exile and spent one year in the United States. Despite the brevity of his sojourn he gave as many as 400 lectures throughout the country and along with the Catalan anarchist Pedro Esteve established *La Questione Sociale* (1895–1908) in Paterson, New Jersey, which became one of the most influential organs of anarcho-syndicalism in America. A powerful and persuasive speaker, he also composed many literary works and songs, including three volumes of poetry and five social dramas.[33]

Two other notable anarchists, Giuseppe Ciancabilla (1872–1904) and Errico Malatesta (1853–1932), arrived in the United States in the late 1890s. Ciancabilla was the first theorist of anti-organizational anarchism among Italians, opposing all forms of institutionalized power and calling for direct and, if necessary, violent action. He remained in America from 1898 until his sudden death in 1904, helping spread anarchism westward through his newspapers *L'Aurora* (1899–1902) and *La Protesta Umana* (1902–4), as he moved from Paterson to Spring Valley (Illinois), then Chicago, and finally San Francisco.[34]

Unlike Ciancabilla, Malatesta was an advocate of organizational anarchism, supporting the creation of a united revolutionary working-class movement. According to the famed Russian-American anarchist Emma Goldman, who had met Malatesta in London in 1895, "his name was one of the best-known and best-beloved in Latin countries." Disembarking in America in 1899, Malatesta soon won many converts, especially among the founders and readers of *La Questione Sociale*, which he edited briefly upon his arrival. Even though he departed from America a year later, his legacy left a powerful mark on the Italian American anarchist movement.[35]

While none of these great anarchist figures remained permanently in the United States, their presence and propaganda, as well as their international reputations, provided a strong foundation for the embryonic anarchist movement, developing close transnational ties between comrades in the Italian American communities and Italy. Their ideas were reinforced by a second group of anarchist refugees who arrived in the United States after 1900, including Carlo Tresca, Luigi Galleani, Maria Roda, Raffaele Schiavina (alias Max Sartin), and, after the rise of fascism, Aldino Felicani, Armando Borghi, and Virgilia D'Andrea. Not only did these anarchists stay longer in America, they also became more involved in, and influenced by, American events. Of them the figure who had the strongest impact on the Italian American anarchist movement was Luigi Galleani (1861–1931).

From a middle-class family, Galleani was born in Vercelli, near the northern Italian city of Turin. Originally trained as a lawyer, he eventually abandoned practicing law, turning his energy to radical activism. His writings, defiant speeches, and central role in working-class organizations soon brought him to the attention of Italian authorities, who arrested him several times, eventually condemning him to confinement at Pantelleria, an island off the coast of Sicily. With the help of the French anarchist Elisée Réclus, he escaped, traveling first to Egypt, then London, and, finally, landing in the United States in October 1901. He originally settled in Paterson, New Jersey, where he assumed the leadership of *La Questione Sociale*. But a year later, after being charged with inciting riots during a strike by Paterson's silk workers, he moved to Barre, Vermont, where immigrant marble workers from Massa Carrara, Tuscany, had established an anarchist haven in 1894. Here he launched his own newspaper, *Cronaca Sovversiva*, which became the most influential organ of Italian anarchism in America, distributed also in Europe, South America, and Australia. For sixteen years, until his deportation in 1919, Galleani's fierce and eloquent voice roared throughout the pages of *Cronaca* calling for "propaganda of the deed"—the overthrow of capitalism by insurrectionary violence and armed retaliation. He also rejected all forms of government and organization, including labor unions, which he believed would inevitably become as corrupt as the system they opposed. His breed of anti-organizational anarchism dominated the Italian American anarchist movement and inspired one of the most extreme and dedicated groups of militant revolutionaries in the United States, including among others Nicola Sacco and Bartolomeo Vanzetti. In 1922, after Galleani was deported, his disciples founded *L'Adunata dei Refrattari* in New York; it remained a powerful, if lonely, voice of anarchist protest until 1971.[36]

By the early twentieth century, Italian socialist leaders also began to arrive in America. For example, Paolo Mazzoli, the editor of a socialist newspaper in Modena, helped to establish the Socialist Italian Party of Pennsylvania in 1893; Giusto Calvi, a socialist leader from Liguria who became deputy for the Italian Socialist Party in 1905, launched the newspaper *Avanti!* in Philadelphia in 1895; and Bernardino Verro, one of the most renowned heroes of the *Fasci Siciliani*, came to the United States in 1898 to organize Italian workers in Buffalo, New York, and nearby towns. Upon his return to Italy, Verro was elected mayor of his native town, Corleone, in 1914 and was killed by the Mafia a year later.[37]

Other socialist leaders like Camillo Cianfarra, Dino Rondani, Gioacchino Artoni, and Giacinto Menotti Serrati were also crucial in planting the roots of the Italian socialist movement in the United States. Meanwhile, thousands of quarry workers from Tuscany, weavers from Piedmont, peasants from Reggio Emilia, and artisans from Sicily who had participated in the uprisings of the late nineteenth century began to arrive en masse in the United States, providing rank-and-file support for the emergent socialist movement. By 1900 there were thirty official Italian sections of the Socialist Party throughout the East Coast (two in New York) and countless independent circles in the West, the Midwest, and the Northeast. "Their activities," wrote the Italian American socialist Mario De Ciampis in his first-hand account of the Italian immigrant revolutionary movement, "were already remarkable in 1896, consisting of incessant propaganda, organization of cooperatives, and formations of circles wherever they could gather some comrades." On November 7 of that year, Italian socialists in Pittsburgh founded the newspaper *Il Proletario*, which remained the major organ of Italian revolutionary socialism in the United States for several decades.[38]

By the beginning of the twentieth century, thanks to the ideas and experiences brought by visiting radical leaders and rank-and-file militants, Italian immigrants possessed a rich radical political culture that, paralleling that of the motherland, covered the entire spectrum of class-based radicalism—socialism, syndicalism, anarchism, and, later on, communism. The ultimate objective of these ideologies was similar: overthrow capitalism, emancipate the workers, and realize economic and social equality. But serious disagreements existed about the goals of the revolution and the tactics to be adopted vis-à-vis the state. Socialists advocated the political seizure of state power by an avant-garde, disciplined, and centrally organized workers' party. In contrast, anarchists considered the state incompatible with liberty. Therefore, they rejected every form of authority and advocated total abstention from politics, including voting, election to public office, and membership in political parties. Syndicalists represented a middle ground between the two. Opposed to electoral politics, they called for direct action in the form of general strikes, sabotage, and revolutionary insurrection.[39]

Quarrels originating in Italy over issues of doctrines and tactics were transported to American soil, creating often insurmountable barriers among local radical groups. Personal rivalries over the leadership of the Italian immigrant Left also weakened the movement, fomenting feuds, hostility, and suspicions. However, taken as a whole, Italian immigrant radicals constituted an important minority among their co-nationals in the United States and exerted an influence within the American labor movement in general and the Italian community in particular, far greater than their number would suggest.

The Anarchist Movement

One of the most distinctive aspects of Italian radicalism in the United States was the early strength and influence of anarchism and revolutionary syndicalism relative to socialism, particularly in the Northeast. While anarchists in Italy lost ground after 1892, they persisted in America until World War I. Not only did anarchism last longer in the American communities than in Italy, but it was also more popular among the Italians than among any other immigrant group.[40]

The popularity of anarchist ideas in the *colonie italiane* derived in part from the early influence of anarchism in Italy and the important role of anarchist emigres in America. But it also rested on the specific nature and conditions of Italian immigration. Unlike other immigrants, the Italians did not come to America with the intention of settling permanently. Most of them planned to return to their native towns as soon as they had accumulated enough money to buy land in their villages, and in fact between 1900 and 1920 about half did repatriate. For this reason, they remained largely indifferent to American politics, language, and customs—an attitude strongly encouraged by the discrimination they encountered within American society and mainstream labor unions.[41]

Moreover, by 1910 less than 25 percent of Italian immigrants were naturalized and eligible to vote; consequently, the majority of Italians had no voice in political and legal reforms. This lack of voting rights also helps explain why socialism did not eclipse anarchism among Italian workers in the United States, as it did in Italy. Anarchism and syndicalism, which rejected electoral politics and espoused direct revolutionary action, were in many ways more compatible with the needs of these "birds of passage" eager to improve their conditions as soon as possible. The methods of struggle of anarchism and syndicalism—sabotage, strike, spontaneous and direct action—were also closer to the forms of protest and the radical traditions of the *contadini*.[42]

Anarchists banded together in autonomous groups by names evoking "libertarian" and revolutionary values such as "*I Nuovi Viventi*" of Spring Valley, Illinois; "*I Liberi*" of New Britain, Connecticut; "*I Risorti*" of Paterson, New Jersey; "*La Falange*" of Brooklyn, New York; "*Gruppo Autonomo*" of East Boston; "*Demolizione*" of Latrobe, Pennsylvania; "*Gruppo Libertà*" of Needham, Massachusetts; and "*Risveglio*" of Ybor City, Florida—to name a few.[43]

These groups represented the nuclei of Italian anarchist activism in the United States. Evidence from survived newspapers and existing oral histories suggests they were active and widespread. Each circle held weekly meetings, usually in the evening or on Sunday, for self-education and debate. As we will see in the following chapter, they also frequently sponsored public lectures and study groups, as well as cultural events such as plays, dances, and picnics.

The movement, in the words of one activist, was small, but "very convinced and solid." Most groups had between twenty and forty members, but a few—such as "*Il Gruppo Diritto all'Esistenza*" of Paterson or the "*Bresci Group*" of East Harlem, named after Gaetano Bresci, the anarchist immigrant who assassinated Italian King Umberto I in 1900—counted a few hundred comrades and lasted almost two decades, until the fierce repression of 1917–20. William Gallo, the son of Firmino Gallo, a silk weaver and one of the most prominent anarchists in Paterson, maintained that "there were about three or four hundred anarchists [there], practically all of them Italians." According to one anonymous source, the movement reached its highest point right before the outbreak of World War I with about 10,000 active militants throughout the nation.[44]

As Paul Avrich and Nunzio Pernicone, the two main authorities on Italian American anarchism, have documented, Italian immigrant anarchists were divided among anarchist-communists, anarcho-syndicalists, and anarchist-individualists. The vast majority, however, were followers of the anarchist-communist brand popularized by the Russian Peter Kropotkin. Anarchist-communists accepted Marx's critique of capitalism but rejected his program for social change through the establishment of a socialist state. Government, whether socialist or bourgeois, was for them always the expression of power and centralized authority, and therefore inherently oppressive and repressive. To ensure liberty, in their view, the state had to be abolished and society reorganized along federalist lines, with local and regional confederations of voluntary associations.[45] "What we want," explained *La Questione Sociale*, "is a society with neither kings nor governments, a social state in which people are free to do as they choose. Neither slaves nor masters, neither rulers nor ruled, but all free, all equal: in a word anarchy." Anarchist-communists assumed that, once free from any chain and legal obligation, people would, without compulsion, dedicate their energies to pursuing their own interests in conjunction with those of the community. "From everyone according to his/her strength and to everyone according to his/her needs" was the formula of anarchist-communism.[46]

While sharing the notion that real social change could be reached only through social revolution, anarchist-communists were split into *organizzatori* and *anti-organizzatori*—that is, advocates and opponents of formal organization. In the United States, this division was exemplified by *La Questione Sociale*'s group of Paterson, New Jersey, and Carlo Tresca's *Il Martello* on the one side, and Luigi Galleani's *Cronaca Sovversiva* and its successor, *L'Adunata dei Refrattari*, on the other. The first two groups believed in the need to organize workers and cooperate with unions and other movements committed to improving the conditions of the working class. They supported, for example, the Industrial Workers of the World (IWW), the revolutionary union founded in 1905, and encouraged strikes against silk manufacturers in Paterson and other industrial towns. In fact, as Salvatore Salerno has argued, *La Questione Sociale*'s group, *Diritto all'Esistenza*, leaned toward the principles of industrial unionism well in advance of the IWW's inaugural convention. Many of its earliest articles favored a model of revolutionary unionism similar to that advocated by the French union *Confédération Générale du Travail*

(CGT), urging workers to adopt tactics such as general strikes, direct action, and sabotage in their struggles against industrialists and manufacturers.[47]

In sharp contrast, the *galleanisti*, as the followers of Luigi Galleani were known, embraced the anti-organizational line, distinguishing themselves with their extremism and unrelenting opposition to all forms of structured organization, including labor unions. For Galleani, any form of organization was "a harbinger of authoritarianism"; hence, he vehemently rejected participation in parties, unions, and even anarchist federations.[48]

Although Italian anarchists in the United States were predominantly anarchist-communist in orientation, other views were represented as well. Anarchist-individualists, inspired by the ideas of the German philosopher Max Stirner, popularized in his book *The Ego and His Own*, were also a visible if small section of the anarchist movement. Rejecting communism and any form of collective organization, anarchist-individualists emphasized personal freedom and individual action over everything else.[49] Enrico Arrigoni (alias Frank Brand), the editor of *Eresia* (1928) and one of the best-known individualists, who lived illegally in the United States from 1924 until his death in 1986, explained that "for us freedom is the greatest good, and with freedom we make no compromises." Individualism was considered the most natural aspect of human nature and, consequently, the founding principle of society. More than a theory to propagate, it was "a way of conceiving individual life and living it highly." Socialism, with its emphasis on collectivism and association, was impossible to realize because "what guides and rules life is not, and will never be, oneness but distinction, difference, and variety among single individuals, single interpretations, and single actions."[50]

Anarchist-individualists also rejected rigid, orthodox doctrines and dogmas and stressed instead the ever-changing and dynamic aspects of life. As Massimo Rocca (alias Libero Tancredi), the editor of *Il Novatore* (1910–11), declared: "[W]e are intellectually heterodox to any formula and affirm an independent opinion of individual revolt and revolution of class, which goes beyond the narrow organizational roads of syndicalism; ignores future utopias; and negates any socialist and humanitarian tendency. . . . We believe neither in religion nor in science, neither in heaven nor earth, but in energy and life."[51]

Anarchist groups tried occasionally to overcome their differences and band together. The most ambitious effort to achieve unity was made at the end of 1939, when Italian anarchists, by now dying out, convened in New York City for a general conference meant to establish "harmony" within the movement and launch a new anarchist paper, *Intesa Libertaria*. But the project failed miserably and *Intesa* suspended publication after only four issues. The *galleanisti*—led by Raffaele Schiavina, who edited *L'Adunata dei Refrattari* from 1928 until its closing—boycotted the conference. Carlo Tresca and his followers cooperated at first but soon backed out under mounting polemics with the *Gruppo Berneri*.[52]

For four decades, anarchism remained a visible force of the Italian American Left, but two other ideologies—revolutionary socialism and syndicalism—would eventually vie for the support of Italian workers.

The FSI and Italian Labor Unions

As the historian Michael Topp has documented, the spread of revolutionary socialism and syndicalism was in large part the result of the activities of the *Federazione Socialista Italiana* (FSI)—the Italian Socialist Federation. Founded in 1902 by Giacinto Menotti Serrati, who had arrived from Italy to assume the directorship of *Il Proletario*, the FSI intended to bring together the numerous Italian socialist circles that had sprung up in the northeastern United States and coordinate their activities and resources. Within a year of its founding, the FSI counted forty-five sections with at least one hundred official members.[53]

The creation of the FSI was a direct response to American developments. Until 1901 the American Left was represented by the Socialist Labor Party of Daniel De Leon. That year, however, Eugene V. Debs's party, Social Democracy of America, merged with a secessionist wing of the Socialist Labor Party led by Morris Hillquit to form the Socialist Party of America (SPA).[54] The split posed a delicate question for Italian immigrant socialists: Which of the two parties should they join, the older Socialist Labor Party or the newly formed SPA? Considering both parties politically timid and xenophobic (significantly enough, the SPA did not have foreign-language federations until 1910), Serrati suggested that his members withhold their affiliation and establish instead their own federation, focusing on issues specific to their community.[55]

Despite efforts to unite Italian immigrant socialists, the FSI was torn between reformist and revolutionary socialists, a struggle paralleling that of other socialists in Italy as well as in Europe and America over whether social change should be achieved through gradual reforms and parliamentary democracy or through social revolution.

The founding of the IWW in 1905 marked a turning point for the FSI and Italian American radicalism. Scholars have not been able to determine whether Italian socialist leaders were present at the first convention of the IWW. Italian workers, however, showed great enthusiasm for the new organization, and at its second congress in 1906 the FSI voted to affiliate to the IWW, eventually embracing revolutionary syndicalism as its official ideology at the Utica congress in 1911. Bruno Cartosio has suggested that Italian attraction to the IWW stemmed in part from the nativist attitudes of the American Federation of Labor, which excluded unskilled workers and was also openly hostile to trade workers from southern and eastern Europe. But he also noted that a second important factor accounting for Italian support of the Wobblies—as IWW members were commonly known—reflected their doctrines and tactics, which were very similar to those advocated by anarchists and syndicalists.[56]

Indeed, the rise of the IWW paralleled the emergence of revolutionary syndicalism in Europe and was profoundly affected by it. Based on the ideas of Georges Sorel in France, syndicalism was theorized in Italy in the early twentieth century by Arturo Labriola, Enrico Leone, and Paolo Mantica through newspapers such as *Avanguardia Socialista* and *Divenire Sociale*. Striving to offer a coherent ideological alternative to reformist socialism, syndicalists stressed the primacy of working-class action and unions as instruments of revolutionary struggle. Generally from the South, Italian syndicalists also accused the Italian Socialist Party of focusing too exclusively on the northern proletariat and ignoring the plight of southern Italians. By 1904 syndicalists enjoyed considerable support among Italian workers, so much indeed that in September of that year they were able to organize the first general strike in Italy, paralyzing the country for four days.[57]

The driving force behind the spread of revolutionary syndicalism among Italian immigrants in the United States was Carlo Tresca. A native of Abruzzo, where he was born on March 9, 1879, Tresca embraced socialism at a young age, becoming at twenty-two the secretary of the Italian Railroad Workers Union and the editor of the local socialist newspaper *Il Germe*. In 1904, he decided to emigrate, like other rebels, to escape a prison term stemming from his political activities—the first of thirty-five arrests. He settled in Philadelphia and at the request of the FSI assumed the editorship of *Il Proletario*. Tresca by now had ideologically shifted toward revolutionary syndicalism—a shift that culminated into anarcho-syndicalism by the early 1910s. He rejected political activity aimed at seizing state power and insisted that capitalism could be overthrown only by the workers' own revolutionary organizations. Only the methods and actions of syndicalism—sabotage, strikes, boycotts—and a truly revolutionary consciousness could bring material gains for workers. His campaign to propagate syndicalist ideas was very successful: Under his leadership, the circulation of *Il Proletario* increased from 4,000 to 5,600 and the FSI's sections grew from thirty to eighty with more than a thousand members.[58]

But the FSI's affiliation with the IWW widened the tensions between the reformists and the revolutionaries, eventually leading the moderate wing to withdraw from the organization. The leader of the Italian reformist faction was Giuseppe Bertelli, a professor from Empoli, Tuscany, active in the Italian Socialist Party. Bertelli arrived in the United States in 1906 to assume the editorship of *Il Proletario*, after Carlo Tresca had left his post to establish his own newspaper. After a few months, he became convinced that the FSI was too isolated and that Italian immigrant workers could fight successfully for their rights only if they integrated into the American socialist movement and worked through the established American labor unions.[59]

His campaign to bring the FSI under the aegis of the American Socialist Party was ultimately unsuccessful. The bulk of FSI members were revolutionary syndicalists who did not believe in conventional politics and were skeptical of institutionalized parties. Hence, they resisted rather than embraced assimilation and integration. The insularity of the FSI also reflected the close influence of Italian politics and events. As Michael Topp has noted, the FSI was in many ways an organization with more intense connections to the Italian Left and to Italy than to the American Left and the United States. Its leaders and members, explained Topp, "continued to view their class ideas through the prism of their ethnic identity, remaining closely in touch with and deeply affected by Italian political culture."[60]

Frustrated, Bertelli left the FSI in 1908 and moved to Chicago, where he launched *La Parola dei Socialisti*. Two years later he formed another Italian Socialist Federation organized as a section of the SPA. As Elisabetta Vezzosi has documented, this federation counted about a thousand supporters, including resourceful men such as Arturo Caroti, Emilio Grandinetti, Alberico Molinari, Girolamo Valenti, and Gioacchino Artoni, who played crucial roles in the Italian American labor movement as strike leaders and union organizers. In the early years, however, reformist socialism remained concentrated mostly in Chicago and other cities of the Midwest, while the Italian communities in the Northeast continued to be dominated by anarchism and syndicalism.[61]

The period from 1910 to 1919 marked the pinnacle of Italian immigrant radical activities. The new ties to the IWW ended the isolation of the FSI and catapulted Italian radicals such as Carlo Tresca and Arturo Giovannitti, the leader of the 1912 Lawrence strike, into national prominence. By 1910, Italians represented a vital segment of the American multinational labor force, constituting up to 20 percent of the workers in coal mining; 10 percent of those in iron mining; more than 10 percent of those in the textile industry; and more than 20 percent of those in the garment industry. As labor historians have recently documented, Italians participated vigorously in these industries' labor struggles, providing both leadership and mass militancy.[62]

Not only did Italian immigrants partake in large numbers of strikes, they also introduced new elements of struggle into the American labor movement, drawing from their hometown traditions of resistance. During the 1912 Lawrence strike, at the suggestion of Italian radicals, strikers formed the first moving picket lines in U.S. history and organized a "children's exodus," sending their offspring to the homes of sympathizers in nearby towns so that they would be relieved from caring for them—a method that was frequently used in Italy and Europe to support strikers. Having faced frequently vicious police repression in their own country, Italians were also generally more militant, tenacious, and confrontational than other workers, often urging their colleagues and peers to oppose violence with violence, reprisal with reprisal.[63]

As more and more Italian immigrants engaged in strikes, the unions became another important center of radical activism. The history of the Amalgamated Clothing Workers of America (ACWA) and the International Ladies' Garment Workers' Union (ILGWU), founded in 1900 and 1914 respectively, offers perhaps the best example of the desire and determination of Italian workers to unionize. In the mid-1910s, Jews accounted for almost 40 percent and Italians slightly more than 30 percent of the garment industry labor force, but the leaders and overwhelming majority of employees of these unions were Jewish. As the number of Italian workers in the garment industry increased, Italian organizers demanded their own locals, contending that it would be easier to reach out to their *paesani*, who did not understand English and did not trust outsiders, through separate and autonomous unions. After six years of negotiations and assurances to union leadership that they were capable of organizing, Italians secured their own locals. Paramount among these were Local 63 of the ACWA, led by Augusto Bellanca, and Locals 48 and 89 of the ILGWU. Representing the Italian cloakmakers, Local 48 was created in 1916 under the leadership of Salvatore Ninfo, a Sicilian immigrant who had arrived in New York in 1899. Local 89 became instead the union of Italian dressmakers. It was formed in 1919 and run by the imperious Luigi

Antonini, a newcomer from southern Italy who began working as a presser in New York and eventually became vice president of the ILGWU.[64]

These institutions unionized hundred of thousands of Italian workers. Their success rested largely on the charismatic influence and talents of their socialist leaders: Emilio Grandinetti, the Bellanca brothers, Luigi Antonini, Arturo Caroti, and Fort Velona. Mostly from the South, these leaders were acutely aware of the distinct sensibilities and values of their fellow workers and appealed to a shared sense of Italian ethnic identity to convince them to join the unions. For example, they made use of village ties to foster class solidarity, overlapping class consciousness with ethnic consciousness. Similarly, they played on family values and respect to promote loyalty toward the union, urging workers "not to dishonor your name and that of your family by committing treason against your fellow workers" and warning them of "the social ostracism that [awaits] any Italian scab." Indeed, as the labor historian Steve Fraser has put it, Italian union organizers won the trust of Italian immigrant workers and bound them to the unions by cultivating *personalismo*, a brand of politics based on informal patronage and one-on-one relationships with the workers.[65]

A major achievement of these Italian locals was the unionization of women, who represented 84 percent of the workers in the dress and shirt-waist industries by 1913. Italian female workers were initially reluctant to join the unions. Gender roles in the Italian family were clearly defined: The man was the head of the family and its breadwinner while the woman was confined to the role of mother and housekeeper. Catholicism played a crucial role in reinforcing these social expectations, teaching women to be submissive and virtuous.[66] As recent works suggest, however, these gendered norms should not be overstated. Carol McKibben and Diane Vecchio, for example, have showed that Italian women's lives did not fall into a neat separation of public and private spheres. Italian women were not passive victims of a patriarchal culture but made important economic and social decisions inside and outside the home, often working in a variety of posts as agricultural laborers, factory workers, midwives, and small-business operators. As Jennifer Guglielmo has demonstrated, they also participated in labor strikes and created political clubs that often operated independently of formal organizations—and independently of men.[67]

Italian radicals, as we will see in chapter 3, generally overlooked women's activism and expressed little concern about their status in the workforce. However, as more Italian women entered the garment industry, labor leaders increased their attention to the plight and needs of female workers. Starting in 1909, Italian American unionists created institutions specifically devoted to organizing Italian women—such as the Women's Mutual Benefit Association, which offered girls medical benefits but required that they attend a monthly meeting, or the Italian Girls' Industrial League, which educated its members about trade unionism. To attract more Italian American women to the labor movement, in 1913 Luigi Antonini and Alfonso Coniglio also launched *L'Operaia*, a working-class paper geared particularly to the education of Italian female workers. The union's consistent efforts eventually paid off. By 1914, some 76,522 Italian women had joined the unions in New York. This triumph derived especially from the empowerment of women members themselves. Radicalized by their desperate working and living conditions, women such as Angela and Maria Bambace, Tina Cacici, and Laura di Guglielmo proved crucial in drawing their co-workers and neighbors into the labor movement through workplace committees, house visits, and educational programs. Thanks to their mentoring and organizing efforts, thousands of Italian women participated alongside Italian men and other immigrant workers in the strikes of the late 1910s, distinguishing themselves on picket lines, at strikers' meetings, and on committees. Some of them, police rolls reported, proved to be "exceedingly energetic and bellicose."[68]

The "new unionism" of the mid-1910s, with its emphasis on organization, ethnic cooperation, and practical ends, helped break down the insularity and isolation of Italian radicals. It also tried, albeit unsuccessfully, to reduce the factionalism among the various groups and provide a common ground for cooperation and interaction. Anarcho-syndicalist Carlo Tresca, revolutionary socialist Arturo Giovannitti, and communist Antonino Capraro, for example, all initially endorsed the new unions and helped them to thrive. It was in this spirit of cooperation that in 1919 radicals of all stripes collaborated to found the Italian Chamber of Labor in New York. Inspired by the enormous success of the *camere del lavoro* in Italy, which after World War I had more than two million members, the Chamber sought to unite existing Italian labor organizations in the New York metropolitan area but failed to forge a united front as reformist socialists and communists vied for control.[69]

At the end, unions allowed Italian radicals to forge connections with other ethnic groups and win lasting improvements that elevated the economic and social well-being of their members. At the same time, however, as Charles Zappia has argued, they moved Italian Americans away from the language of revolutionary socialism toward more mainstream and pragmatic forms of political activism and organization, reflecting an increasing Americanization of original Italian politics.[70]

Postwar Reaction and the Anti-Fascist Movement

Along with the rest of the American Left, Italian American radicalism sharply declined after World War I, weakened by strong internal dissent over Italian participation in the conflict and the impact of systematic governmental repression. Italy's declaration of war on Austria-Hungary in 1915 compelled radicals to confront their relationship to nationalism and *italianità*, provoking among many "a crisis of conscience as their leftism collided with their patriotic sentiments."[71] Socialists and anarchists remained generally firm in their opposition to the war, but the interventionist debate had a disastrous effect on the FSI. Following the example of eminent Italian revolutionaries such as Arturo Labriola, Paolo Orano, and Benito Mussolini, several Italian American syndicalists and anarchists succumbed to nationalistic propaganda and masculine rhetoric, putting their ethnic identity before their class internationalism.[72] This split opened a wound within the Italian Left and the Italian American Left that contributed to the rise of fascism.[73]

An even more serious blow, however, was inflicted by the "Red Scare" of 1919: the anti-radical hysteria that gripped the United States after the triumph of the Russian Revolution. Fearing that communism would spread to American soil, the U.S. government launched a massive repression of radicals and dissenters from 1917 to 1921. More than 6,000 suspected radicals were arrested and several hundred foreigners were deported under such draconian laws as the Espionage Act (1917) and the Sedition Act (1918), which threatened up to twenty years in prison and fines up to $10,000 for anyone interfering with the draft, encouraging desertion, obstructing the sale of Liberty Bonds, discouraging recruitment, or speaking, writing, and publishing anything against the government, Constitution, flag, or uniform of the United States.[74]

Irreparable damage was done: Radical headquarters were shuttered, newspapers suppressed, hundreds of militants assaulted, arrested, and sentenced to prison. Along with other socialist organizations, the Italian Socialist Federation was severely crippled by the Red Scare and disbanded in 1921. Like other radical papers, its organ, *Il Proletario*, was denied mailing privileges and its top members were arrested and in some cases deported.[75] Italian anarchists, whom American authorities considered largely responsible for a rash of bombings that occurred between 1914 and 1919, were prime targets of the anti-radical crusade. On April 14, 1917, federal agents invaded the office of *L'Era Nuova* in Paterson, New Jersey, arresting its editor, Ludovico Caminita, and suppressing publication of the newspaper soon afterward. Two months later, in June 1917, and then again in February 1918, they raided the headquarters of *Cronaca Sovversiva* in Lynn, Massachussets, securing more than 3,000 names and addresses of readers and subscribers, leading in turn to about a hundred arrest warrants. Charged with conspiracy against the United States, in 1919 Luigi Galleani, "the bugbear of American authorities," was indicted and deported along with at least eight of his most dedicated followers.[76]

Among those caught up in the FBI roundups were also Nicola Sacco and Bartolomeo Vanzetti, arrested in 1920 on charges of robbery and murder of two employees in a small shoe factory in South Braintree, Massachusetts. The following year they were tried, found guilty, and, although the evidence against them was contradictory and inconclusive, sentenced to death. As in the case of previous fellow radicals who were victims of governmental oppression, Italian American radicals responded quickly, forming a defense committee and winning the support of labor organizations, the SPA and the American Civil Liberties Union. But despite worldwide sympathy, on August 23, 1927, the two Italian anarchists were put to death by electrocution.[77]

In this climate of fear and repression, unions also lost momentum and power nationwide. From a high of more than five million in 1920, labor union membership declined precipitously in succeeding years, with the only exceptions being the garment workers' and miners' unions.[78] The success of the Russian Revolution, however, helped revitalize the movement, giving radicals new hope and faith. Many members of the FSI and the IWW embraced communism and, on November 6, 1921, organized the *Federazione dei Lavoratori Italiani d'America* (Federation of Italian Workers in America), a section of the American Labor Alliance. Located at 81 East 10th Street in New York's Greenwich Village, the federation aimed at "uniting all avant-garde elements of the Italian subversive movement in the United States."[79] Among its founding members were Antonino Capraro, Ignazio Camarda, Antonio Presi, Frank Bellanca, Flavio Venanzi, and Taddeo Cuomo. The official organ of the new federation was *Alba Nuova* (1921–24), which led the way to the founding of the communist daily *Il Lavoratore* (1924–31).

Soon, however, all the energies of the Italian American Left were directed toward a new and unexpected war: the crusade against fascism and its leader Benito Mussolini. As the late Philip Cannistraro has documented, Italian fascists began organizing in the United States as early as 1921 when Agostino De Biasi, editor of the nationalist newspaper *Il Carroccio*, founded the first *Fascio*, or fascist organization, in New York City. As the *Fasci* began to multiply, in 1925 Mussolini created the Fascist League of North America (FLNA) to coordinate and impose control over their activities. According to Ignazio

Thaon di Revel, the president of the FLNA, by 1927 there were one hundred *Fasci* throughout the United States with around 14,000 members, mostly recruited from the lower middle class with a high percentage of war veterans and second-generation Italian Americans.[80]

Mussolini closed down the FLNA in 1929, worried by the alarm that expanding fascist activities were causing in the American press, particularly after the publication of Marcus Duffield's article "Mussolini's American Empire" in *Harper's*. This, however, did not mean the end of fascist activities in the United States but simply a shift in the regime's policies. In place of the *Fasci*'s aggressive tactics, Mussolini adopted a more cautious program of cultural propaganda. Working in unison with the local business elite, the clergy, and the Italian consulate, he quickly gained control of institutions like the Dante Alighieri Society, the *Casa Italiana* of Columbia University, the Italian Historical Society, and the Order of the Sons of Italy, as well as that of mainstream newspapers. It was principally through these institutional agencies, rather than political venues, that the masses of Italian Americans became exposed to fascist rhetoric.[81]

While it is impossible to determine exactly how many Italian Americans fell under the spell of fascist demagoguery, scholars concur that admiration for Mussolini was quite widespread. In 1940 the anti-fascist historian Gaetano Salvemini estimated that "out-and-out" fascists represented 5 percent of the Italian American population (that would mean approximately 250,000 out of the almost five million Italians living in the United States at that time), and that sympathies for Mussolini amounted to an additional 35 percent.[82]

But not all Italian Americans succumbed to "Mussolinianism."[83] Ironically, Il Duce's rise to power offered disillusioned radicals a new *raison d'être*, compelling them to reorganize their forces in the name of democracy and freedom. A vigorous opposition, coming from the whole spectrum of the Italian American Left and representing, according to Salvemini, about 10 percent of all Italians living in the United States, arose as soon as Mussolini came to power in 1922.[84]

The Italian American anti-fascist resistance greatly benefited from the arrival of political exiles, or *fuorusciti*, as they were commonly called in Italian. Among these migrants were rank-and-file activists and leaders who had experienced fascist violence first-hand, as well as a number of distinguished scholars, journalists, and politicians. Much of the leadership of the Italian American Left in the 1920s and 1930s came from their ranks. Vincenzo Vacirca, Serafino Romualdi, Vanni Montana, and Giuseppe Lupis were among the first to arrive and to generate support for both socialism and anti-fascism. Anarchists Armando Borghi and Virgilia D'Andrea, who arrived in 1928, joined the small but forceful cadre of *L'Adunata dei Refrattari*, helping keep alive the flame of anarchism. Communists Vittorio Vidali (also known as Enea Sormenti), Ambrogio Donini, and Giuseppe Berti became the dominant personalities of the Italian Federation of the Workers' Party of America (later renamed the American Communist Party). Finally, a group of liberal intellectuals, including Gaetano Salvemini, Max Ascoli, Count Carlo Sforza, Giuseppe Borgese, and Luigi Sturzo, began to arrive in the mid-1930s.[85]

This latter group represented the cream of Italian intelligentsia. Salvemini, for example, enjoyed an international reputation as an historian and was offered the chair of Italian Civilization at Harvard University in 1933, a post he held until his return to Italy in 1947. Ascoli was an eminent scholar too. A professor at the University of Rome, he came to New York on a Rockefeller Grant in 1931 and, after his fellowship expired, obtained a permanent position at the New School for Social Research. Sforza and Sturzo were esteemed statesmen who combined anti-fascist sentiments with democratic sympathies. Together, these *fuorusciti* played a crucial role in generating American support for anti-fascism. They brought greater respectability and visibility to the resistance, and, thanks to their access to American academic and intellectual circles, they were able to forge crucial alliances with American intellectuals.[86]

But the most significant contributions to anti-fascism came from the old cadre of radicals who had led Italian immigrant workers before the war—Arturo Giovannitti, Girolamo Valenti, Fort Velona, and above all Carlo Tresca, whom fascist authorities dubbed the "*deus ex machina* of anti-Fascism." Italian labor unions also played a crucial role, subsidizing anti-fascist activities, organizing large anti-fascist rallies, and propagating anti-fascism through radio programs and union activities.[87]

On April 10, 1923, under the auspices of the Italian Chamber of Labor, Italian radicals gave life to the Anti-Fascist Alliance of North America (AFANA). Claiming a total of 150,000 members, the organization elected Frank Bellanca as chair, Arturo Giovannitti as general secretary, and Salvatore Ninfo of Local 48 as treasurer.[88] Although AFANA soon disintegrated under the weight of ideological and tactical divisions, the escalation of fascist violence and terror eventually forced the anti-fascists to intensify their efforts.

The murder of Italian socialist deputy Giacomo Matteotti by fascist agents in June 1924 spurred great indignation and horror throughout Italy as well as abroad, threatening to bring down Mussolini. The radical press dedicated large attention to the case, fiercely denouncing Mussolini's involvement in the murder as well as the regime's oppressive and terrorist methods. But in the end Matteotti's murder did not undermine the power of fascism in Italy, nor in America. On January 3, 1925, in the most important speech of his career, Mussolini assumed full responsibility for Matteotti's death and, unleashing a "second wave" of violence, declared the dictatorship.[89]

As Mussolini consolidated his regime, Italian American radicals exhibited greater combativeness. For the second time, they sought to put their differences aside and forge a united front against fascism. Thanks mainly to the joint efforts of Carlo Tresca and Vittorio Vidali, AFANA was resurrected on October 1925 and relocated to the Rand School, at 7 East 15th Street in New York. Despite the regime's constant efforts to crush the opposition and the radicals' own divisions, the anti-fascist resistance continued to grow. In addition to rallies and demonstrations, radicals sponsored newspapers, tours, and conferences exposing the connection between Mussolini and Italian and American prominent businessmen; they organized all-out campaigns against the visits of fascist diplomats in the United States; and on several occasions they waged guerrilla warfare against local Blackshirts—fascist paramilitary groups so called because they wore black uniforms—disrupting fascist parades, attacking their headquarters, and often fighting them hand-to-hand in the streets.[90]

Clashes between the anti-fascists and the Blackshirts escalated after 1925, claiming altogether a dozen lives and culminating in two causes célèbre: the Greco–Carillo trial and the Terzani affair. Calogero Greco and Donato Carillo were two anti-fascists accused of murdering two fascists during a Memorial Day parade in New York in 1927. Athos Terzani was another anti-fascist activist charged with the killing of Antonio Fierro, a young anti-fascist shot during a clash with the pro-fascist American Khaki Shirts, in 1933. In both cases, the charges were clearly fabricated by Italian American fascists in collusion with U.S. authorities, but the *sovversivi* were able to unmask the conspiracy, and all defendants were eventually acquitted.[91]

The struggle against Mussolini became "an all-consuming passion" of the Italian American Left, but the power and strength of pro-fascist forces was in the end far superior, assisted as they were by Mussolini, his emissaries, and American authorities, who generally considered anti-fascists to be dangerous Reds.[92] If radicals were unable to stop the process of "fascistization" of the Little Italies, as Rudolph Vecoli has termed the rapid spread of pro-fascist sentiments among Italian Americans, they certainly slowed it down. Perhaps more important, they were able to bring fascism into the national spotlight, unmasking the connection between the rise of fascism in Italy, postwar reaction, and intensified nativism in the United States. Through their incessant propaganda and heroic resistance they eventually awoke American opposition to Mussolini, pointing out the danger his regime posed to world democracy and peace. In doing so, they paved the road for the broader anti-fascist struggle that came with the creation of the Popular Front in the mid-1930s, when leftist groups of various denominations joined forces against fascism and Nazism.

The Great Depression and Communism

The continued fight against fascism notwithstanding, by the 1920s the Italian American Left had begun its irreversible decline. Despite the persistent influence exercised by Carlo Tresca and the small cadre of *L'Adunata dei Refrattari* in the New York metropolitan area, anarchism had lost its base of support. The number of syndicalists and revolutionary socialists also declined dramatically. The Italian section of the Socialist Party of America counted only around 400 official members by 1929. Economic hardship and widespread unemployment made it particularly difficult for old radicals to sustain their activities and publications. The only radicals who managed to increase their strength were the communists, who numbered around 1,000 by the mid-1920s and, after declining during the end of the decade, peaked again by the mid-1930s.[93] Their relative influence is also reflected in the composition of the anti-fascists who fought in the Spanish Civil War. Fraser Ottanelli's research indicates that more than half of the 300 Italian American volunteers who joined the Abraham Lincoln Brigade and the Brigata Garibaldi to help Spanish Republican forces defeat fascism were communists.[94]

But even the communists were a negligible number considering they represented a mere 1 percent out of the 51,000 registered members of the American Communist Party (CPUSA) in 1938. However, as in the case of previous radical ideologies, support for communism in the Little Italies was fluid and should not be assessed through official party membership only. Italians, for example, joined in larger numbers the Garibaldi-American Fraternal Society, the Italian section of the International Workers Order (IWO)—a pro-communist benefit organization established in 1931 that provided unemployment benefits, sick leave, and life insurance, as well as cultural and educational activities, for its members. As Gerald Meyer has documented, the Garibaldi Society had 11,000 members organized into 130 lodges; it was the IWO's sixth-largest ethnic section and represented 6 percent of the Society's total membership.[95]

Readership of Italian-language communist newspapers also suggests a wider base of support than official party figures indicate. *L'Unità Operaia* (1932–38) had a weekly circulation of about 5,000 copies, and its successor, *L'Unità del Popolo* (1939–51), reached approximately 10,000 copies in 1940. Other radical newspapers such as the socialist *La Parola del Popolo*, the anarcho-syndicalist *Il Martello*, and the anarchist *L'Adunata dei Refrattari* also continued to publish throughout the 1940s and up to the 1970s, despite the declining numbers of their political groups. Their survival attests to the regular presence of a small but steady contingent of radicals and radical sympathizers who continued to "fan the flames of discontent."[96]

But the movement's leadership and power had increasingly shifted toward mainstream unions and social democracy. Despite their initial support for the Russian Revolution, by the mid-1920s Italian American unions distanced themselves from communism and embraced more moderate ideological positions. For example, when communists gained control of AFANA in 1926, Locals 89 and 48 withdrew their support from the organization and established the Anti-Fascist Federation for the Freedom of Italy. In 1935, Luigi Antonini officially left the Socialist Party when Norman Thomas, whom he considered too radical, was elected its president. Like Antonini, most Italian union leaders had become increasingly accommodationist. They no longer sought to overthrow capitalism, the government, and other forms of oppression, as they had done in the 1910s. Rather, they focused on ameliorating working conditions through state reforms, community institutions, and labor bargaining.[97]

The Great Depression briefly revived radicalism and opposition to capitalism, stimulating labor and working-class protest to an unprecedented degree.[98] By then, Italian Americans constituted a significant portion of the labor force in the garment industries, as well as other mass-production industries such as the automobile, steel, radio, and rubber goods sectors. Hundreds of thousands of them joined the Congress of Industrial Organizations (CIO) and participated in the labor struggles of the period on a larger scale than ever before. But as Rudolph Vecoli has accurately noted, "they did so for the most part as members of a multiethnic working class" rather than as a distinctive Italian American radical movement.[99]

The expansion of education and the rise of mass consumption transformed second-generation working-class culture, engendering, in Michael Denning's words, a "Cultural Front" that crossed ethnic, racial, and class lines.[100] Important Italian American radical writers and artists like John Fante, Pietro Di Donato, Ralph Fasanella, Carl Marzani, and Louis Fraina were products of this new multi-ethnic laboring culture. Famous Italian American radical politicians also emerged out of this popular frontism. Peter Cacchione, for example, represented the Communist Party as a New York City councilman for three consecutive terms (1941–47); Vito Marcantonio served as a radical congressman representing East Harlem from 1934 to 1948; and Fiorello La Guardia was elected mayor of New York for three terms from 1934 to 1945.[101]

The leaders of this generation, however, were remarkably different from the immigrant radical leaders of the early twentieth century. They had been politicized in the Italian American settlements rather than in Italy and were fully familiar with the world of American politics. For these reasons, they were able to transcend the ethnic barriers that had limited the influence of the earlier leaders within the larger American society. But while different, their radicalism was nurtured and sustained by the traditions and culture of militancy that their forefathers had brought with them from Italy. It is to this culture that we must now turn.

The *Sovversivi* and
Their Cultural World

Italian American Leadership: The Prominenti *and the* Sovversivi

Bringing attention to the important role of ethnic leadership in shaping immigrant life, the late John Higham noted that immigrant leaders "focus the consciousness of an ethnic group and make its identity visible. . . . [They] create the structures of the ethnic community; they produce (or confirm) its symbolic expressions; they exemplify the style that enables the group fully to experience itself."[1] Traditionally, the Italian American leader was thought of as someone who had wealth and power in the community: a "prominent man." The *prominenti* or *padroni*, as these leaders began to be called in the *colonie italiane*, essentially replaced the Old World *signori* in America.[2] They ran the immigrant banks, mainstream newspapers, employment agencies, saloons, and boarding houses and were often presidents of the many Italian societies that arose in the United States.

In terms of social status, the *prominenti* were not unlike the leaders of other immigrant groups, but only a few of them could be considered leaders in the sense described by Higham. They were certainly the most visible and influential element of the Italian immigrant communities; as such, they served an important role as intermediaries and "powerbrokers," using their political connections and wealth to deliver patronage to the community. But they were far from exemplary, inspirational, or "programmatic" leaders. Envisioned leadership should implement strategies, goals, and programs for the betterment of the group it represents, combatting prejudice and discrimination, for example, or elevating the group's socioeconomic level. Instead, the real focus of the *prominenti* too often was to advance their own interests at the expense of the poorer Italians.[3]

There were of course among them honest men who provided critical advice and guidance to the uprooted immigrants, but generally speaking, as the anti-fascist exile Gaetano Salvemini lamented, they were "parasites of one sort or another . . . who have always lived off the poor."[4] Serving as middlemen between the immigrants and American society, they charged exorbitant fees for all their services—such as securing jobs for the newly arrived; supplying transportation, shelter, and food; writing letters for the illiterate; extending loans to the needy; sending remittances to Italy; or translating consular documents. The radical newspapers, as we will see in the next chapter, abound in stories of swindles, extortions, and even deaths perpetrated at the expense of the Italian workers by these local *padroni*, and even American journalists occasionally denounced such appalling practices.[5]

Like the *prominenti*, the Italian priests who migrated to America had significant influence, but, with a few exceptions, they were men of mediocre quality, and, as Rudolph Vecoli has argued, "not a few were mercenaries, if not worse." Indeed, the Catholic Church failed to provide guidance and organizational structure for the Italian immigrants in the United States, as it had done for other European nationalities like the Irish and the Polish. The American Catholic hierarchy sneered at feisty Italian religious practices with their Madonnas, patron saints, and processions and excluded Italians from the organized Church, confining them to church basements. Even after Italians built Our Lady of Mount Carmel Church in Harlem with their own hands in 1884, they were restricted to worship in its "lower church" until 1919. Suspicious of priests and institutional religion, Italian immigrants found American Catholicism with its rigid rules and practices incompatible with their colorful system of beliefs and traditions. As a result, Italian parishes and parochial schools emerged slowly and, until World War II, social-service activities sponsored by the Catholic Church in Italian communities remained scarce.[6]

Despite their marginal social status, it was the radical leaders or *sovversivi*, as they were generically called in Italian, who functioned as the real strategists and spokesmen of the *colonie italiane*, furthering the interests of their co-nationals and promoting goals that, though essentially class based, benefited in the long term the vast majority of Italians in the United States. The *sovversivi* offered an alternative political leadership, promoting ideas that were totally at odds with the traditional beliefs of the majority of Italian immigrants and that were intended to challenge the hegemony of both American capitalists and Italian bosses. They were, to use Gunnar Myrdal's classic formulation, "leaders of protest" or, in the words of Elisabetta Vezzosi, "radical ethnic brokers" who helped to mediate between the immigrant community and American society, welding together issues of class, nationalism, and ethnicity.[7]

The *sovversivi*'s role is perhaps best described by what Antonio Gramsci in his influential writings on culture termed "the organic intellectuals." Gramsci pointed out that every social group "creates together with itself, organically, one or more strata of intellectuals which give it homogeneity and an awareness of its own function not only in the economic but also in the social and political fields." Perhaps more important, Gramsci posited that all men are potentially intellectuals, thus challenging the mechanistic understanding of the relationship between workers and intellectuals that dominated early Marxist cultural theory. As he wrote:

> There is no human activity from which every form of intellectual participation can be excluded: *homo faber* cannot be separated from *homo sapiens*. Each man, finally, outside his professional activity, carries on some form of intellectual activity, that is, he is a "philosopher," an artist, a man of taste, he participates in a particular conception of the world, has a conscious line of moral conduct, and therefore contributes to sustain a conception of the world or to modify it, that is, to bring into being new modes of thought.

This, however, does not mean that anyone can fill "the function of intellectuals." What distinguishes the "true" intellectuals for Gramsci is the social function they perform as active participants in practical life—as "constructors," "organizers," and "permanent persuaders" of distinct social groups. These "organic" intellectuals are defined not by their profession or social status but rather by the role they play in articulating and organizing the ideas and aspirations of the class they represent.[8]

The *sovversivi* fulfilled exactly this function. They became strategists, spokesmen, and local community builders, providing guidance, bridging the Old and New worlds, and directing through various cultural apparatuses the feelings, needs, and hopes of the workers. As Nunzio Pernicone put it, they "functioned as the militant vanguard of Italian immigrant workers against the American capitalists who exploited them at the workplace, and against the Italian elite who lorded over them within the *colonie italiane*."[9]

For almost half a century they worked to enlighten the minds of Italian immigrant workers, to make them aware of their class interests and rights, and to inspire them toward a more democratic and higher form of human life. Their dedication, passion, and struggle for social change have enriched the lives of both Italian immigrants and American workers; the following discussion is intended to restore them—and their subculture—to their rightful roles in both Italian American studies and the history of the American Left in the twentieth century.

The Sovversivi: A Social Profile

The Italian American radical cadre was composed of an immigrant generation of writers, artists, editors, and political organizers who had grown up in the turbulent years following the unification of Italy. This group included anarchists and socialist political emigres, educated and self-taught immigrants who were radicalized in America and, after World War I, a large number of antifascist and communist refugees. Italian authorities referred to them generically as "*sovversivi*" (subversives) and from 1894 to 1945 carefully monitored and recorded their activities both in Italy and abroad. The resultant archival collection, known as *Casellario Politico Centrale*, contains about 160,000 files of such radicals, 6,000 of which refer to activists in the United States.[10]

Unfortunately, there are no figures for the rank-and-file militants. Other factors, such as the high mobility of Italian immigrants as well as the attempts of radicals to conceal their activities and views, make it impossible to quantify exactly the *sovversivi*'s strength. However, recent scholarship indicates that Italian radical enclaves existed and flourished throughout the United States. Nunzio Pernicone has estimated that in New York City—the largest and most active of the Italian radical communities in the United States—there might have been 10,000 Italian activists by the 1920s, or about 2.5 percent out of a population of about 400,000 local Italian residents. Though small in proportion to the rest of the Italian American population, they undertook, in the words of Paul Buhle, "the monumental task of community and factory organization with an unexcelled vigor."[11]

The three most important Italian radical leaders in the United States were the anarcho-syndicalist Carlo Tresca, the revolutionary poet Arturo Giovannitti, and the ultra-anarchist Luigi Galleani. But there were many others—like the playwright Riccardo Cordiferro; the cartoonist Fort Velona; the socialists Vincenzo Vacirca and Girolamo Valenti; the communists Antonio Capraro and Vittorio Vidali; the labor organizers Antonino Crivello, Emilio Grandinetti, Frank Bellanca, and Arturo Caroti; as well as women like Maria Roda, Bellalma Forzato-Spezia, and Virgilia D'Andrea—who, though forgotten today, were revered in the Italian American communities of the early twentieth century.

Contrary to assumptions that Italian immigrant radical leaders came prevalently, if not exclusively, from the northern cities of Italy, the *sovversivi* in the United States were in large part children of the South. Donna Gabaccia has calculated that Sicilians constituted as much as one-third of the Italian labor leaders working within the various branches of the American unions, particularly the Amalgamated Clothing Workers of America (ACWA). But unlike their destitute southern countrymen, the majority of the radical leaders were educated men of middle-class or upper-class origin. Moreover, unlike the *contadini*, who were forced to migrate in search of *pane e lavoro* (bread and work), they came to the New World to escape governmental oppression or to follow their dreams.[12] They looked to the United States, in the words of Tresca, "as the wanderer in the desert looks for a drop of water when thirst grabs him by the throat." "I went on fighting in the small town," he wrote, "but dreaming of a better, bigger field of action; looking forward . . . toward America, the land of the free."[13] In effect, many other revolutionaries saw America's extraordinary industrial growth as an ideal ground for radical activism and experimentation. Especially after the struggle for the eight-hour day and the Haymarket Affair, leftists became convinced that capitalist development in the United States would inevitably lead to class conflict and revolution, out of which a new socialist society would emerge.[14]

The *sovversivi* were generally born in the decade between 1870 and 1880 and came to the United States between 1900 and 1910, during the peak of Italian immigration. They tended therefore to be young, with a median age of twenty-five. The *fuorusciti* who came after the rise of Mussolini, however, were typically much older. While they tended to be concentrated mostly in the northeastern cities and Chicago, the *sovversivi* moved whenever and wherever needed by the movement to give lectures, organize strikes, provide leadership, or fulfill jobs as editors of radical newspapers. Consequently, regardless of where they had originally settled, they were known to Italian workers throughout the United States and were widely admired and respected. Some also traveled back and forth between the United States and Italy, bringing the latest ideas and strengthening transnational links between radicals on both sides of the ocean.

Some were single when they emigrated, but they all eventually married and had children. Their domestic and sentimental life, however, remains somewhat of a mystery. Even though we know of cases in which their wives were involved in the movement, the *sovversivi* tended to be reticent about their personal lives.[15] Carlo Tresca, for example, never mentioned in his autobiography his marriage to Helga Guerra, his daughter Beatrice, or his long and turbulent relationship with Elizabeth Gurley Flynn. Similarly, Arturo Giovannitti, the poet laureate of the movement, rarely spoke or wrote about his family life but was described by his son, Len, as a tyrannical father and husband. For all their talk about emancipation and equality, when it came to gender it is fairly obvious that the *sovversivi* regarded politics as a male, public sphere and family as a female, private sphere. They were also notoriously known as womanizers. Although this was a characteristic by no means limited to Italian radicals, among the *sovversivi* infidelity was not only tolerated but often discussed in terms of prowess and pride. As Michael Topp has argued in his study of the Italian Socialist Federation, Italian immigrant leftists put enormous emphasis on masculinity, using assertions about virility and sexuality to bolster their comrades' courage and determination to fight.[16]

The vast majority of the *sovversivi* were artisans and professionals who had received their education in Italy prior to their emigration. Luigi Galleani, for example, was a lawyer; Alberico Molinari, Semplicio Righi, and Matteo Siracusa were prominent physicians; others, like Arturo Giovannitti and Carlo Tresca, came from privileged families of professionals and landowners. Once in the United States, they generally pursued careers as journalists, editors, and labor organizers.

The leadership of the Italian American Left, however, was not exclusively from middle-class background. Many important organizers—such as Efrem Bartoletti, Gioacchino Artoni, Giuseppe Cannata, Alfonso Coniglio, and Fort Velona—came from the ranks of the working class and made their living as miners, factory workers, or day laborers. They were among the hundreds, perhaps thousands, of Italian immigrants who broke the barriers of illiteracy, often attaining astonishingly high levels of intellectual sophistication.

Forced to quit school at the age of thirteen to help his father, Bartolomeo Vanzetti, among others, gained an impressive and far-reaching education on his own in America. He read incessantly history, science, and political theory; novels by Hugo, Tolstoy, and Zola; Dante's *Divine Comedy* and the Bible; and above all the works of the great anarchists—Kropotkin, Reclus, Malatesta, and Merlino. And he did so, as he wrote, "while doing work all day, and without any congenial accommodation . . . by a flickering gas jet, far into the morning hours."[17]

Equally telling is the story of Gioacchino Artoni. Born in 1866 into a poor family in a small village near Reggio Emilia, like Vanzetti, he was forced to drop out of elementary school and work to supplement his father's meager income. He emigrated to the United States in 1896 in search of better opportunities, but, like others, he encountered many difficulties. A father of seven, he worked first as a miner in Pennsylvania, then as a textile worker in Paterson, New Jersey, and eventually as an organizer of the ACWA. Despite his limited education, "Papà Artoni," as he was affectionately called by his comrades, developed an early passion for learning and went on to become one of the most effective socialist orators and labor organizers in America. As his friend Arturo Meunier said on the occasion of Artoni's death in 1937, though he was born from nothing, with an instruction that did not go beyond elementary education, scourged by misery and illness, with a numerous family to support, buried in the bowels of the mines—this outcast, who should have been a victim of his own destiny, found the strength to educate himself, to study the social question, to read incessantly, and to grasp the multiple problems of the proletariat.[18]

Indeed, the self-educated worker was one of the most interesting products of the radical movement of the late nineteenth century—the worker with little formal education who, stirred by the positivistic and socialist revolutions of his time, developed a tremendous passion for learning, dedicating his leisure time to reading and studying.[19] It is also important to recall that although many *sovversivi* were already involved in revolutionary struggles in Italy before emigrating, a few of them, along with thousands of Italian immigrant workers, embraced radical ideologies only after settling in the United States, in response to the economic exploitation, ethnic discrimination, and political marginalization they experienced. Arturo Giovannitti, for one, developed a revolutionary consciousness after encountering the brutal reality of industrial and urban life in America instead of the "promised land" he expected to find.

As noted in the previous chapter, the *sovversivi* were irremediably divided over issues of doctrine, the state, the role of unions, and their relationship with the American and the Italian Left. Despite frequent calls to unity and collaboration, there also existed bitter rivalries among leaders and political groups that prevented de facto political accord. Yet, as Richard Oestreicher argued in his case study of working-class life in Detroit, fragmentation and solidarity in the early labor movement were not mutually exclusive: Differences in ethnicity, traditions, cultures, and ideologies coexisted with working-class values of cooperation, equality, and social justice.[20] In a similar way, for all their differences of political theory and temperament, the *sovversivi*— as even their collective noun suggests—shared a distinct worldview, a sensibility based on communal traditions, solidarity, and values. To understand the nature of their radicalism, we must in a sense, as Paul Buhle has long suggested, understand this mentality.[21]

At the risk perhaps of generalizing, we can identify five crucial elements of the *sovversivi*'s social vision: a passionate commitment to the humanist principles of liberty, equality, and social justice; a belief in education as a key to emancipation; a deep love for humankind and life; an exceptional sensitivity toward human suffering and oppression; and a disarming idealism and messianic faith in the "Ideal." I argue that these collective values and principles—this *mentalité*—reflect an important ethical dimension of Italian immigrant radical culture which has been overlooked by the factionalism that split the movement. Indeed, their ideological differences—which no doubt weakened the movement—notwithstanding, Italian radicals all shared the same dream: the establishment of brotherhood and social equality for every man and woman on earth. The *sovversivi*, in this respect, were foremost romantic revolutionaries who grieved for the plight of the poor and who struggled to remake the world in their own image. In the words of the poet Arturo Giovannitti, they believed:

> That a great day shall come, O Master, when,
>   Even as from a putrid clod a flower,
> So in thy heart shall bloom the love of men,—
>
> A day when sweet and noble tasks shall hallow
>   These charnels where thy slaves now drudge
>   and plod,
> And thou no more a groveling swine shalt wallow
>   Amid the puddles of their sweat and blood[22]

This "common ideal" was an integral aspect of their radicalism, surfacing repeatedly in their speeches as well as their writings. Class alone does not explain the *sovversivi*'s activism, determination, and courage. Socialism, anarchism, syndicalism, and communism were for them more than political doctrines; they were part of a larger *Weltanschauung*—a theology rooted in a deeply internalized web of social values, traditions, and institutions. "Anarchism at the bottom is an ethical philosophy," declared Valerio Isca, an Italian socialist who converted to anarchism after the executions of Sacco and Vanzetti. "When a man realizes that it is immoral to exploit another man and immoral to oppress another man, and when he refuses to do so," he explained, "that man has become an anarchist, as far as I am concerned."[23]

Italian radicals aspired not only to political and economic changes, but, to borrow Eric Hobsbawm's comments on Andalusian anarchists, "they were for a new moral world." Like the "prophetic minority" of Jewish radicals described by Gerald Sorin and other revolutionaries of their time, the *sovversivi* shared an ethic of social justice and equality that sought not only to emancipate the working class, but also to create a new culture and society.[24] As Luigi Nardella, an Italian American communist, said regarding Luigi Galleani in 1977: "[he] told people *how* to live and that was important."[25]

The *sovversivi*'s vision drew largely upon three European traditions: the Enlightenment, with the rationalist and humanist thought that evolved from it; internationalism; and millenarianism. The Enlightenment—particularly its emphasis on science, progress, and education—provided the main intellectual framework, internationalism the main dream, and millenarianism the main driving force.

Although present to some extent in all revolutionary movements, millenarianism, "the hope of a complete and radical change in the world," found a classic expression in places like southern Italy and Andalusia, Spain, because of their pre-modern conditions. For the oppressed peasants, socialism and anarchism represented essentially a "new religion" that gave voice to their vengeance and aspirations. This prophetic element was crucial in mobilizing and organizing them. Radicals effectively channeled the peasants' hatred for the rich and privileged *signori* into an attack upon the system. "A single speech by [Nicola] Barbato or by [Bernardino] Verro," wrote an Italian historian referring to the rapid growth of the socialist *Fasci* in Sicily during the 1890s, "was sufficient to arouse minds out of the lethargy of centuries." What struck a responsive chord among the *contadini* was the hope that a revolution would come to stamp out all wrongs and create a new world without poverty, hunger, or injustice. As Italian officials noted in 1910, "the peasant (listening to the Socialist preaching) was struck by it and believed in truth that a new religion had come, the true religion of Christ, which had been betrayed by the priests in alliance with the rich. And in many villages they abandoned the priests. . . ." This millenarian character is clearly manifested in the *sovversivi*'s literary writings, which abound in religious symbols and terminology.[26] This is not to say, however, that their radicalism was the expression of Old World "primitive" and archaic forms of revolt. While millenarian in outlook, the *sovversivi*'s ideas were a conscious, rational response to both the socioeconomic destabilization of nineteenth-century Italy and their increasing disillusionment with life in America.

The *sovversivi* were also deeply moved by the national struggle for Italian unification. Children of the *Risorgimento*, they idolized the revolution's heroes and their noble fight for freedom, democracy, and equality. As Tresca recalled in his autobiography, many of them had childhood memories of the Italian war for independence:

A wave of discussion was sweeping Italy and everybody was talking about *liberty, change,* and *fight.* The tradition of Garibaldi was still alive. We were hearing from our fathers the most wonderful tales about their struggles in Garibaldi's ranks, about their march on Rome for the sake of *Free Thought*. Free thinking was in vogue. All in all the country was astir with political unrest.

These stories colored the *sovversivi*'s imagination, creating an idealized past of their country and stimulating their desire for action and leadership.[27]

From the *Risorgimento* the *sovversivi* also inherited an intense anti-clericalism that remained a steady note through their entire political lives. The cause for Italian unification assumed a profound anti-religious character as the Catholic Church, which controlled Rome and the surrounding regions known as the Papal States, resisted change and tried to maintain its supremacy over the national state. In 1864, Pope Pius IX decreed his *Syllabus of Errors* in which he publicly condemned the separation of state and church and the whole liberal outlook, further exacerbating anti-clerical critics. Giosuè Carducci, the poet of the *Risorgimento* par excellence and 1906 Nobel laureate, echoed the feelings of many Italians when in his controversial *Inno a Satana* (Hymn to Satan, 1865) he derided the Church as an enemy of freedom of speech, as well as an obstacle to intellectual inquiry and economic and social progress.[28]

Like Carducci, the *sovversivi* openly espoused free thought and called for the secularization of culture. In both their speeches and writings, they fiercely attacked religious dogmata, exposed the misdeeds of the Church, and openly insulted the priests, often driving them out of their posts. Their hatred for the Church and their vilification of religion became so legendary that they gained a reputation as *mangia preti* (priest eaters).[29]

From the recollections of friends, the *sovversivi* emerge as people of noble character—good at heart, honest, gentle, generous, and peaceable by nature. Commemorative profiles published after their deaths emphasized their "immense sense of responsibility," their "spirit of abnegation for the workers," and above all their "profound devotion to the Ideal of human redemption." But their sentimental humanism should not obscure the fact that they were also dedicated revolutionaries who believed in the use of insurrectionary violence and armed retaliation if necessary. As Carlo Tresca explained, "War is war. A strike is an episode of the class struggle. It is a legal weapon used by organized workers prompted, in their action, by common danger, aspirations or want, and is always confined to a demand for better working conditions or more pay."[30] Their struggle was not directed against American capitalism alone. As we will see in the next chapter, with equal, if not greater, intensity they fought against the *prominenti* who controlled the political and social life of the Italian colonies.

The Sovversive

The Italian radical movement was male dominated, but, as recent works by Donna Gabaccia, Jennifer Guglielmo, and Franca Iacovetta, among others, have documented, there were a considerable number of women activists. In fact, hundreds of women's names can be found in the pages of the radical press beneath political articles, short stories, and poems. Women's names also pop up in the subscription lists of radical newspapers, though in smaller numbers than men's. As early as March 14, 1893, the anarchist publication *Il Grido degli Oppressi*, for example, listed nine women out of a total of sixty-six new subscribers. Editors also consistently noted the participation of women in radical cultural events, such as lectures, plays, picnics, and dances.

Unfortunately, lack of additional sources makes it difficult to go much beyond the names of most of these women. Existing information, however, suggests that women made important contributions to the radical movement and culture. While they did not generally join political groups and unions until the late 1910s, they were active on a local level, particularly as community organizers and fundraisers of solidarity campaigns. As police files suggest, some of them—most notably the anarchists Maria Roda, Virgilia D'Andrea, and Ernestina Cravello; the labor organizer Angela Bambace; and the syndicalist Bellalma Forzato-Spezia—also managed to achieve positions of power and leadership.[31]

Paul Avrich came across women's activism even in the most extreme radical fringes. Gabriella Antolini (1899–1984), an affiliate of Luigi Galleani's ultra-revolutionary anarchist school, risked her life to take a bag full of dynamite by train from Steubenville, Ohio, to Chicago in January 1918. The dynamite served to prepare a bomb in retaliation for the arrest of eleven *galleanisti*, including Mary Nardini, dubbed "the queen of the anarchists" by the press. Discovered by the train's porter, Antolini was convicted of federal crimes and sent to the Missouri State Penitentiary at Jefferson City for fourteen months, where she befriended the famous anarchist Emma Goldman and the socialist Kate Richards O'Hare, both of whom had been convicted under the Espionage Act for hindering the war. After she was released, she lived for a time in Detroit and then went back to New England, where she worked as a seamstress. In 1993, the sculptor Siah Armajani created two ten-foot-high steel gazebos to commemorate Antolini and her brother Alberto for the Storm King Art Center in Mountainville, New York.[32]

Women also organized their own separate propaganda groups, in which they discussed not only socialism and anarchism but also feminism. As early as the 1890s, Italian women in New Jersey, New York, Boston, and Spring Valley (Illinois) had formed distinctive female clubs to bring forth the emancipation of women, such as the anarchist group *Emancipazione della donna*, the *Gruppo femminile di propaganda*, and the women's group Luisa Michel, named after the French socialist heroine of the 1871 Paris Commune.[33]

Ideologically, the Italian immigrant women who became politically active in the United States tended, like the men, to favor revolutionary socialist and anarcho-syndicalist ideas. This inclination derived, as noted earlier, from the greater influence and strength of the anarchists, as well as from the anarchists' use of direct forms of protest that were better suited to the needs and radical traditions of Italian immigrants. But anarchism appealed more to women also because of its distinctive message of liberation and its uncompromising egalitarian and humanistic vision. As José Moya wrote regarding female participation in the Argentine radical movement, "anarchism contained a gender ideology that was in many respects more liberationist than that of contemporary mainstream feminism."[34]

Women's radicalism grew out of the same causes as the men's: exploitation, oppression, and discrimination. But many immigrant women who became politically active in the United States were also initially radicalized by their families. Both Gabriella Antolini and Maria Roda grew up in intensely anarchist milieux. Antolini's family, as noted by her son Febo, was an "anarchist family": Her father and older brothers, Alberto and Luigi, were subscribers to Galleani's *Cronaca Sovversiva*, and her first husband, August Segata, whom she married when she was not yet sixteen, was also known as "a rank socialist and anarchist." By the time she was seventeen, she had joined the group *I Liberi* of New Britain, Connecticut, and was participating in all its activities, including lectures, picnics, and theatrical performances. She quickly became an "adored" figure in the movement, trusted and respected by her comrades. Her status in the movement was obviously enhanced by her part in the dynamite conspiracy of 1918, and above all by her staunch refusal to cooperate with the police following her arrest. After her release from prison she became active in the Sacco-Vanzetti Defense Committee, and in the 1940s she joined the group *Libertá* of Needham, Massachusetts, which had been formed in 1925 to reorganize Italian anti-organizational anarchists after the governmental repression that followed World War I. She remained a devoted anarchist until her death in 1984.[35]

Maria Roda, the youngest and probably the fiercest of the Italian immigrant *sovversive*, shared a similar background. Her father, Cesare Balzarini Roda, was a textile worker and, according to police records, one of the most active and "dangerous" anarchists of Como, the Rodas' native town. As a result of her upbringing, Maria Roda was a self-proclaimed anarchist already in her teens and in 1891 was sentenced to five months in prison for seditious acts. She crossed the Atlantic a couple of years later to join her family, which had migrated to Paterson, New Jersey, to work in the silk industry. As soon as she arrived she threw herself into anarchist activities. On July 15, 1893, her name appears among the subscribers of *Il Grido degli Oppressi*, and on December 30 she published there a long article entitled "What the Anarchists Want" summarizing her political credo. Anarchists, she explained, "want in the first place the destruction of authority, private property, religions, and family." Instead of private property, she clarified, anarchists want common ownership for the social good; instead of religion they demand progress and science; and instead of the current family, based on material interest and hypocritical conventions, they call for free unions based on mutual love and respect. After specifying that anarchists ultimately want a better life for all, she concluded the article with a defiant promise of victory. "In spite of your gallows, your axes, your lead, and all your infamous laws," she warned her bourgeois enemies, "you will not prevent us from throwing you back in the gutter from which you came."[36]

In Paterson, Roda met Pedro Esteve, the Catalan anarchist who helped establish *La Questione Sociale* along with Pietro Gori. They fell in love, married, and, while raising a family of nine, worked incessantly to organize local anarchist groups and to assist the struggles of workers throughout the United States. Slender, with brown eyes and brown curly hair, Roda became immensely popular among Italian and non-Italian anarchists alike, hypnotizing hundreds with her eloquence and beauty. Even Emma Goldman fell under the spell of this young woman, "the most exquisite creature" she had ever seen.[37]

But whereas the most defiant women emerged from the anarchist ranks, it was in the unions that Italian women's activism flourished most. Angela Bambace is probably the best example of a large group of successful women organizers. Her involvement with the labor movement began in 1917 as a young sewing machine operator, when she joined, along with her sister Maria, Local 89 of the International Ladies' Garment Workers' Union (ILGWU). At the union meetings, they listened to socialist orators and labor organizers and became aware of the importance of unionism. It was at one of these meetings that Maria Bambace met her husband, the Sicilian Nino Capraro, a communist and organizer for the ACWA.[38]

Both sisters helped to organize the strike of the waistmaker workers in 1919, enduring the first of many arrests. They visited the homes of nonstrikers and spent many hours talking to families about the importance of unity and solidarity. Their knowledge of "the old way" and their ability to speak to workers in their own language won many converts. By 1927, Angela Bambace, a divorced mother involved with the anarchist Luigi Quintiliano, had become one of the most active garment union organizers. Demonstrating great ability and leadership, in 1956 she was elected vice president and member of the general executive board of the ILGWU. She was the first woman to reach such a position.[39]

The stories of these women and their writings offer compelling evidence of a female radical world. As we will see in the next chapter, women published their own articles, poems, and pamphlets, trying to break down the general indifference toward, and often open hostility against, the "woman question." They attacked men's authority and privilege and developed sophisticated critiques of conventional gender norms and patriarchy. But they did so without putting the issue of women's liberation above all else. Unlike other countries like the United States or Britain where women's struggles emerged as autonomous movements, in Italy the rise of feminism coincided with the growth of the left-wing movement and remained closely tied to the larger class struggle. Socialists, in particular, effectively connected women's oppression to the capitalist system, assuming that the abolition of social inequality would bring in its wake freedom for women as well. Ultimately, then, the main focus of Italian radicalism remained the same for both sexes: the overthrow of capitalism and the creation of a better and more just world.

The Radical Milieu

Just as the *sovversivi* created various political groups, so too they developed an extensive and elaborate social infrastructure that contributed to produce a distinctive subculture and community. Among the most vibrant and militant centers of radicalism were the anarchist community of Barre (Vermont), comprising stone and marble cutters from the northern Italian city of Carrara; the anarcho-syndicalist community of silk workers in Paterson (New Jersey); and the Latin community of Ybor City (Florida), where Italian workers in the cigar industry joined forces with Cuban and Spanish radicals.[40] Distinct radical neighborhoods also existed in all principal industrial cities and mining states such as Pennsylvania, Ohio, Illinois, Colorado, and Montana, where Italians settled in great numbers. New York City boasted the largest and most active of such radical settlements. East Harlem and lower Manhattan, particularly the area stretching from 8th to 23rd streets and Second to Fifth avenues, epitomized the heart of Italian immigrant radicalism, hosting a great number of socialist schools, social centers, newspapers, and radical cafés.

Scholars have noted the tendency of Italian immigrants in the United States to establish stable and insular communities with intense social relationships and ethnic, fraternal, and cultural societies that re-created the life of the Old World. Radical conclaves conformed to this pattern. Most Italian radical organizations, affinity groups, and unions had their offices and newspapers in the same districts. It is not difficult to imagine, as Nunzio Pernicone has described it, the *sovversivi* crossing "paths on a daily basis, chatting on street corners, visiting each other's offices, and eating dinner together." This "togetherness" was reinforced by cafés and restaurants that served as important centers of socialization, political debate, and intellectual conversation. A common meeting place in New York was John Pucciatti's Spaghetti House on 12th Street at Second Avenue (now simply John's)—"the favorite meeting place of free thinkers of all nationalities," said one newspaper ad—where for one dollar radicals could discuss politics while enjoying an appetizer, some pasta, an entrée, and a bottle of wine. Other popular hangouts in the city were Albasi's grocery and the Vesuvio's restaurant in East Harlem.[41]

The *sovversivi* generated a multitude of subsidiary institutions through which to disseminate their message, carrying the revolutionary "Ideal" beyond the confines of the factories and the unions into their neighborhoods. These institutions included the press, clubs, informal schools, and dramatic societies. Chapters 3 and 4 will discuss in detail the *sovversivi's* radical press and stage; the following pages focus instead on the educational institutions and the leisure-time activities they sponsored: lectures, dances, concerts, picnics, *feste*, and processions. Drawing upon the left-wing political and cultural milieu of the nineteenth century, these traditions became an integral part of the *sovversivi's* radical world. They contributed to create and sustain a rich social and cultural life for the movement at a local level, serving several important functions. First, they operated as a base for propaganda and recruitment. Second, they provided the opportunity for people who sympathized with socialist ideas but did not necessarily belong to any political group to be active participants in the movement. In fact, while only a tiny fraction of the Italian immigrants were official members of parties and organizations, thousands partook in the *sovversivi's* cultural activities on a regular basis—attending lectures and schools, socializing at parties, and protesting at rallies. Even though many had no clear theoretical political ideology, they were receptive to radicalism because of their opposition to misery, exploitation, and corruption.

In addition to being the main conduit through which revolutionary ideas reached the wider immigrant community, cultural and social events helped to promote unity and solidarity among the movement's members, strengthening the relationship between the leaders and the rank-and-file as well as their commitment to social change. Finally, educational and recreational activities also provided courage, resources, and support, bolstering the organization by displaying its strength and power to the outside world.

Circoli

By the end of the nineteenth century, socialists and anarchists in the United States had developed myriad educational, social, and cultural centers, like the International Working People's Association (IWPA)'s Workmen's Circles or the Germans' *Artbeiter Ring* and *Sonntagschule*.[42] The *sovversivi*'s own version of such institutions were the *circoli*—small clubs affiliated with anarchist, socialist, or communist groups with the goal of advancing knowledge and working-class consciousness among the Italian immigrants. The radical press is filled with announcements of such organizations. Typical of them were the *Circolo di Studi Sociali*, dozens of which flourished throughout the country; the *Circolo di Cultura Moderna*, established in 1916 in Harlem to encourage the spread of culture among Italian workers; and the *Circolo Educativo Operaio*, born in the 1920s to propagate communism among youth.[43] Another important literary circle, the Mario Rapisardi Literary Society, so called in honor of a famous Sicilian poet of revolt, was founded on February 6, 1921, "to awaken the workers' minds and to promote awareness of their rights and might through knowledge."[44] Countless *circoli* with similar goals were duplicated across the United States, from the early migrations of the 1890s throughout the 1910s and 1920s and even, although less frequently, during the 1930s. They became the intellectual nucleus of the movement—the main basis for education, recruitment, and propaganda.[45]

Each club typically sponsored weekly meetings, social gatherings, debates, and endless lectures that were regularly publicized in the radical papers. Most of them focused on political and social themes, but many others dealt with cultural and educational topics such as "Art and Revolution," "What Is Religion," "Women and Family," and "Zola and Tolstoy."[46] The weekly meetings were usually small and restricted to the club's members, but larger gatherings, open to the wider community, were held, usually on Sundays. The *New York Times* reported that Sunday meetings sponsored by the Bresci Group in the basement of the building at 301 East 106th Street in Harlem "drew as many as 150 people."[47] Similarly, Joseph Moro recalls that when he invited Galleani to speak in Taunton, Massachusetts, against the war, as soon as word spread that he was going to give a speech "a huge crowd gathered from all over, and we had an all-night party and dance."[48]

These cultural events usually took place at the groups' headquarters, in labor unions halls, or *Case del Popolo*—People's Houses. Members, however, also frequently held educational meetings in their homes. Bruno Coniglio, the son of Alfonso Coniglio, a well-known anarchist in Tampa, remembers that his family always had people coming in. "Twice a week they would come over and my father would teach them what little he knew. . . . [W]ell, then others did the same thing."[49]

The *circoli* also provided access to literary material through self-organized "*librerie rosse*"—red bookstores. For example, Angelo Massari, an immigrant working in the cigar industries in Tampa, recalled in his autobiography that at the *Circolo di Studi Sociali* he had joined in 1902, he had the opportunity to "read pamphlets, newspapers, books, and all kinds of sociological literature," in addition to "attending all the lectures and debates that the two groups, socialists and anarchists, organized."[50]

The libraries' collections included a large assortment of inexpensive books and pamphlets, ranging from social novels and dramas to propaganda booklets and anti-clerical tracts. One of the richest and most popular was the *Biblioteca Sociologica* of the anarchist group *Diritto all'Esistenza* of Paterson. It included at least 200 titles grouped under various headings according to the main topic. Most of the books were the works of renowned international literary and political figures such as Zola, Tolstoy, Dostoyevsky, Hugo, Gorki, Lenin, Marx, Kropotkin, Bakunin, Gori, and Malatesta. But many others were written by local literati and printed by small publishing houses such as the Avanti Publishing Company or the Casa Editrice Il Martello.[51]

In the cigar industries in Florida, Italians had access to these readings also thanks to the widespread use of *los lectores*, professional readers hired and paid by the workers to read to them newspapers, political tracts, and novels for several hours a day while they were working in the factories. As Gary Mormino and George Pozzetta have documented, this practice had begun originally in Cuba in the mid–nineteenth century and was brought to Florida by Cuban immigrants working in the cigar factories during the 1880s. Quickly, several Italians, including some women, became regular readers.

For the little-educated workers, they represented an enormous source of information, knowledge, and, often, political conversion. Alfonso Coniglio, talking about the role of the readers, said, "Oh, I cannot tell you how important they were, how much they taught us. Especially an illiterate like me. To them we owe particularly our sense of the class struggle." The readers' influence went well beyond the factories. The information they disseminated was carried into the wider community via a series of informal networks. Immigrant Frank Giunta explained that when workers went home they shared with their families what they had learned that day. "Each evening," he reminisced, "my sister would come home and give us verbally what had taken place. We stuck around the family table some thirty minutes or so after supper to hear my sister give us the episode of the day and the news she had heard from the lector."[52]

Giri di Propaganda

Immigrants were also exposed to political theories and propaganda thanks to pre-organized lecture tours known as *giri di propaganda* through which charismatic radical leaders traveled across the Italian communities scattered across the United States to deliver speeches or engage in political debates. The speaker held forth usually for about an hour; the lecture was followed by a discussion and then food, music, and dancing. Some *giri di propaganda* lasted one or a few weeks, but others went on for months. Pietro Gori gave as many as 400 lectures within the year he stayed in the United States. Thanks to this networking, radical leaders could bring their message to even the most remote Italian immigrant outposts. Carlo Tresca, among others, played a crucial role in spreading revolutionary ideas among Italians in industrial and mining areas of New Jersey, Connecticut, Massachusetts, Vermont, Pennsylvania, Ohio, and Illinois and even in some large wineries in California.[53]

Propaganda tours also played a central role in connecting the radical immigrant world and reinforcing transnational ties among radical groups and workers. First, they helped the *sovversivi* keep in touch with one another and forge alliances with radicals of other nationalities; second, they contributed to the effort to popularize radical ideas and recruit new members; finally, they served as an associative force for the community, pulling workers together around common problems and needs.

Many immigrants heartily welcomed these events, regarding them as special opportunities to enter the world of knowledge and deserving therefore of the utmost respect and consideration. Unfortunately, in most cases it is impossible to establish exactly how many people attended, but newspapers often suggested that they drew large crowds, including women. *La Questione Sociale*, for example, took proud notice of the enormous success of Pietro Gori's lecture "Women and Family" in 1895 and the "overwhelming" presence of the "gentle sex." Similarly, *Il Lavoro* wrote that 300 people attended a lecture by Girolamo Valenti, "The Social War," at Clinton Hall in New York on March 3, 1917.[54] Some people went to these lectures out of genuine political interest, but many others attended simply out of curiosity for the guest speakers. Immigrant workers revered the orators, considering them heroes of the working class and luminaries who, in the words of Vincenzo Farulla, a Sicilian immigrant who became active in an anarchist movement in the Boston area, "expressed what I wanted to say but couldn't because I did not have the words."[55]

When Tresca undertook a lecture tour in California in 1915 to talk against the war, a comrade noted that "he left our workers in a state of emotional frenzy and with the desire to hear him speak again as soon as possible." In the Italian Swiss Colony winery, the company's guards tried to expel him but several hundred workers deterred them, demanding to hear him speak. Tresca's friend Luigi Parenti commented, "Never would I have thought that comrade Carlo Tresca's propaganda tour of California could have aroused so much enthusiasm even in localities where until today our propagandists have never visited."[56]

Bartolomeo Provo (1898–1993), a factory worker, amateur artist, and self-declared hobo, became an anarchist on the eve of World War I after hearing a lecture in Springfield, Massachussetts, by Costantino Zonchello, the editor of *Il Diritto* and later *L'Adunata dei Refrattari*. Provo recalled, "I saw a leaflet announcing that Costantino Zonchello was going to speak on 'The Italians in America.' I attended the lecture and was very enthusiastic about it. I went over to talk to him. . . . He suggested that I subscribe to *Cronaca Sovversiva*, so I did. That was in 1915. I was not even eighteen years old. And since then that was it. . . . I am now ninety-two—I am glad that I have always been an anarchist. I have never seen a better or nobler idea."[57]

Catina Willman (1899–1991) had a similar experience. Born Caterina D'Amico in Sicily, she emigrated to the United States with her parents and lived in Brooklyn. When she was a teenager she "heard Galleani speak at an open air meeting" and was so moved that overnight she converted to anarchism. "I liked what he had to say and the way he said it," she explained. "He spoke directly to my heart. I became an anarchist and took part in picnics, amateur theatricals, and other activities." In the 1920s she was active in the anti-fascist movement and the Sacco-Vanzetti Defense Committee, and for several years she was the companion of Armando Borghi, the anarchist anti-fascist exile.[58]

As Nunzio Pernicone has remarked, the propaganda tours not only affected the people who attended the lectures; they also profoundly touched the *sovversivi* who gave them. By going to remote mining and manufacturing towns, radicals saw for themselves the grim conditions of industrial life. The brutality and exploitation endured by immigrant workers reinforced their commitment to fight capitalism and their faith in the goodness of their cause. In an article published in *Il Proletario* in 1906, Tresca described his horror at discovering the working conditions of Italian miners in western Pennsylvania. After his lecture, the miners brought him to see the furnaces where coal was transformed into coke for factory use. Tresca described the scene as "a living hell" and concluded that after seeing what he saw none would "repeat the lie that work ennobles; rather, as a reproach to capitalism, they would say that work brutalizes and kills."[59]

Università Popolare

The *sovversivi* understood that two of the major obstacles to organizing their fellow immigrants were their poor education and the hegemonic power of the priests and the *prominenti*. In order to succeed, they believed, they had to liberate Italians from their superstitions, their provincialism, and their servility toward the boss. As the editors of *Il Proletario* put it in 1902, "the book and the newspaper are the most potent means to hasten the triumph of workers' rights." Much of the *sovversivi*'s energy was expended therefore in a massive campaign to educate the immigrant masses and combat the influence of the local elite.[60]

This campaign took a variety of forms, from newspapers, leaflets, and lectures to clubs, libraries, and schools. The most ambitious expression of the *sovversivi*'s educational creed was the *Università Popolare*, an informal school created to support the educational needs of working men and women. Its roots go back to Great Britain during the 1870s, with the creation of the University Extension program, which aspired to make higher learning accessible to everyone. From England, the campaign for popular education spread quickly to other European countries—Austria, Germany (*Wiener Arbeiterbildungsverein*), Holland, France (*Coopération des idées*), and then Italy.

The main goal was to offer people basic instruction and disseminate knowledge in science, literature, and art through conferences, lectures, debates, and the diffusion of pamphlets and books. These educational efforts reflected important changes in Western thought—the expansion of scientific knowledge and positivistic thought, the increasing secularization of education, and the rise of the working-class movement—which helped promote the idea that education was a universal right, essential to the moral, intellectual, and social advancement of the whole of humankind. The people's universities became a peculiar project of the Italian Left, but they also won the support of various segments of the middle class, including intellectuals, politicians, public employees, journalists, and teachers. In this sense, they were the expression of two mounting demands: one liberal, which saw education as a way to foster progress in society, and the other radical, which considered education a vehicle of working-class empowerment.[61]

After a year of intense debate and preparations, Turin launched the first *Università Popolare* in November 1900; in the course of the following years the initiative had reached all major Italian cities, including those in the South and the islands. Each school was independent and self-regulated: Some were affiliated with the working-class movement, others with existing public institutions; some were free of charge while others were reserved to paying members. All, however, shared the same objectives: popularize positivist learning, combat ignorance and prejudices, instill love for knowledge among the masses, and elevate the moral and social conditions of the working classes. The *Università Popolare* had enormous success at its opening: In its first year of life the program in Turin counted 700 students, Genova had 1,500, Rome 1,340, Venice 1,226, and Milan 10,000. Their numbers declined after the first three years because of internal divisions as well as the schools' failure to develop curricula that held the interests of the workers. But the *Università Popolare* played, nevertheless, a crucial role in keeping alive the debate over the role and future of education and the need for educational reforms.[62] The school's main organ, also called *Università Popolare*, founded in Mantova in 1901 and directed by the anarchist Luigi Molinari until 1918, was particularly instrumental in popularizing a "libertarian" pedagogical approach, insisting on the need for laic, scientific, and nondogmatic education.

The *sovversivi* launched the first *Università Popolare* in the United States on February 21, 1903, at the Entre Nous Lyceum in New York City. Carlo Tresca, among others, helped found one in Philadelphia in 1908 and another one in Pittsburgh in 1909. He described the response of the workers at the inauguration where he was asked to deliver a speech as "the greatest and warmest reception I ever received from people assembled in a hall."[63]

Funds for these initiatives were obtained from self-imposed membership fees and from voluntary contributions of supporters. Members were expected to pay a monthly fee of 20 cents to meet basic expenses, such as the rental of the classroom and the publication and distribution of the school programs and books. However, as in the case of other radical initiatives, most of the money actually came from fundraising events.[64]

As in Italy, the curriculum of the *Università Popolare* in the United States was wide-ranging and did not focus exclusively on politics; lectures covered health and medical issues, scientific theories, and art and literature. But while the topics were not necessarily radical, the approach was unmistakably rational and secular. The main function of the *Università Popolare* in the *colonie italiane* was indeed to counter the influence of the Catholic Church and the *prominenti*. The school's inaugural lecture, for example, focused on Charles Darwin's theories of evolution. The featured speaker was Giacinto Menotti Serrati, who had recently arrived in the United States to edit *Il Proletario*. *La Questione Sociale* reported that eighty people were present at the grand opening. The newspaper later complained that the program failed to arouse the interest of the general public, but it also noted that the existing members attended all classes assiduously and enthusiastically. Indeed, although the *sovversivi* constantly lamented the apathy of Italian immigrants, the *Università Popolare* continued to operate throughout the 1910s. For instance, an ad published in *Il Lavoro* announced the implementation of courses of the *Università Popolare* in Italian and English at various public schools in Manhattan and Brooklyn, under the auspices of the ACWA. It also noted the enormous success of a course called "Socialism and Eloquence" given by Vincenzo Vacirca at the Rand School, which met for two hours, from 8 P.M. to 10 P.M., once a week for three months.[65]

The *sovversivi* also became passionate advocates of the *Escuela Moderna* (Modern School) advanced in 1901 by the Catalan anarchist Francisco Ferrer. Unlike the *Università Popolare*, the Ferrer schools were openly revolutionary and experimental in both methods and objectives. Their goal was to destroy the myths and moral laws of the old regime and promote a libertarian culture based on free thought, love, solidarity, and reason. Ferrer was eventually arrested on charges of sedition and executed in 1909, but more than fifty Modern Schools were created throughout Spain in the following years.

The idea of the Modern School also had a lasting influence among anarchist and socialist circles in both Europe and America. Anarchists across the United States, for example, organized more than twenty Modern Schools. The first and most influential was the Francisco Ferrer Center at St. Mark's Place in New York City. Founded in 1910 by a group of prominent anarchists, it lasted until 1918. The school began with only nine students but eventually grew into one of the most important cultural centers of New York's radical movement, with lecturers of the caliber of Emma Goldman, Jack London, Lincoln Steffens, Margaret Sanger, and famous art teachers like Robert Henri and George Bellows.[66]

By the time of World War I, the *sovversivi* had founded at least three Ferrer schools in the United States—in Paterson, Boston, and Philadelphia—along with hundreds of other free-thought schools and circles. Rudolph Vecoli found that the campaign for *"libero pensiero"* bore fruit even in remote outposts such as Cle Elum, Washington; Thurber, Texas; and Bear Creek, Montana. Particularly successful were Sunday and evening schools that offered free classes in various subjects, ranging from English to economics, literature, and political science.[67]

The legacy of the movement for popular education established by the *sovversivi* could be seen well into the 1920s. A case in point is the Leonardo Da Vinci Art School, organized in 1923 in New York by a group of artists headed by Onorio Ruotolo, a distinguished sculptor loosely affiliated with Italian radical circles. Originally located in the Church of St. Mark's at 288 East 10th Street, the Leonardo, as it was fondly called, offered classes in Fine and Applied Arts to poor students of all races free of charge. In a few years, the school rapidly expanded, produced excellent artwork, and won a considerable reputation. Enrollment grew from 75 to 600 students in 1934, and The Friend of Italian Arts Association was organized for the support of the school.[68]

Picnics, Feste, *and Dances*

As recent studies have argued, entertainment was an important aspect of the radical movement of the nineteenth and early twentieth centuries. German, Jewish, and Finnish immigrants all developed oppositional cultures embodied in ethnic and working-class traditions that included plays, dances, picnics, and processions. The *sovversivi* too engaged in a wide range of recreational activities that promoted a vision of solidarity and unity and at the same time enriched the social life of the immigrant community. These events, as Bruce Nelson noted in his social study of Chicago's anarchists, also offered the opportunity for different crowds to mingle together. Unlike unions or political groups whose members were occupationally or politically homogeneous, leisure-time activities transcended divisions "by mixing skilled, unskilled and petty proprietors together; old and young, apprentices and journeymen, recent immigrants and older settlers," as well as men and women.[69]

Music occupied an important role in these events. Plays, lectures, parades, and picnics—all included concerts by radical groups' orchestras performing famous opera compositions, international working-class hymns like the "Marseillaise" or the "Internationale," and Italian revolutionary songs like "*Bandiera Rossa*" (red flag) or "*Lugano Bella*," written by Pietro Gori in 1894 on the occasion of his expulsion from Switzerland, where he was in exile. Each song sought to nurture revolutionary consciousness, educating, inspiring, and emancipating workers. As the scholar Dieter Dowe has written, "the function of the workers' songs lay not only in strengthening feelings of solidarity, satisfying emotional needs and expressing a protest against oppression; it also confidently proclaimed the certainty of victory."[70]

The importance of music in the cultural world of the *sovversivi* is also reflected by the fact that their libraries included songbooks with revolutionary titles such as the *Canzonieri dei ribelli, Canzoniere rivoluzionario, Canti anarchici rivoluzionari,* and *Nuovo canzoniere sociale.* Similar to the IWW pocket-size *Little Red Song Books,* they were sold to workers for a few cents or given as a present to new members of radical groups or subscribers of radical newspapers. Not only were lyrics one of the main weapons used to popularize revolutionary ideas, they were also extremely successful. Richard Brazier, a songwriter and member of the Spokane branch committee, which put together the first IWW song book in 1909, admits that what first attracted him to the IWW "was its songs and the gusto with which its members sang them." "Songs are easily remembered but dull prose is soon forgotten," argued the supporters of the first red song book. "Our aim and principles," they added, "can be recorded in songs as well as in leaflets and pamphlets—in some cases even better. For songs will be more apt to reach the workers than dry-as-dust polemic."[71]

Dances were also extremely frequent and popular. Italian immigrants' love of dancing was legendary. Despite their long hours of work and their miserable living conditions, they always found occasions to get together and have fun. As Bartolomeo Vanzetti recalled in his autobiography, "In the evenings the sordidness of the day was forgotten. Someone would strike up a tune on the violin, the accordion or some other instrument, and some of us would dance."[72]

Like other radicals, the *sovversivi* held smaller, local dances on a weekly basis and larger, more formal ones on major holidays, such as the Fourth of July and New Year's Eve, or to commemorate important revolutionary anniversaries. Anarchist William Gallo recalled that the Piedmont Club of Paterson organized a dance "every Saturday, with music played by a little orchestra." He played the guitar; his brother Henry the violin; his brother-in-law, Spartaco Guabello, the mandolin; while his mother acted in the plays, which were all "about the life of the poor and how they were oppressed."[73]

Local unions also had their own separate annual galas and concerts. Radical papers announced these *serate speciali*, as they called these special entertainments, on their last pages, giving often specific information about the evening program. Tickets for these concerts and balls cost about 25 cents and were typically free for women. According to newspapers' reports, as many as 400 to 500 people attended, dancing, drinking, and playing all night. *Il Grido degli Oppressi*, for example, reported that the *Serata di famiglia* that took place on November 30, 1894, in Paterson, New Jersey, attracted 400 Italians and lasted until 4:00 A.M.[74]

These cultural events became a regular part of immigrant life. They were an essential form of entertainment and fundraising. Virtually all radical newspapers relied on these social activities to fight deficit and raise money for radical causes. Anarchist Attilio Bortolotti remembered that "almost every Saturday there was a dance and a *recita* [performance] to send a few dollars overseas." And he added, "There's where I learned to put my hand into my pocket and pull out as much as I could, usually four or five dollars, a tidy sum in those days."[75] Besides helping radical newspapers, the collected amount was often devolved to assist political prisoners, war victims, or the family of an arrested or deceased comrade. Anarchists, for example, went out of their way to provide financial assistance to the wife and two daughters of Gaetano Bresci after he was executed for killing King Umberto I in 1900. Police intervened twice to prevent such a benefit evening from taking place—on November 11, 1900, at Germany Hall in New York City and on February 9, 1901, at the Brooklyn Atheneum—but the Italians were still able to raise thousands of dollars.[76]

Another common occasion for socializing and raising funds was the picnic. Again, radical newspapers of the period are filled with picnic ads. *La Questione Sociale* informed its readers that the *Circolo di Studi Sociali* of West Hoboken, New Jersey, would hold a "libertarian picnic" on July 15, 1906, to raise funds for radical newspapers. The invitation specified that "music will cheer the feast" and that the price of the ticket, 25 cents, "includes five drinks or snacks." It also admonished workers to attend, encouraging them to bring along families and friends. More than twenty years later the picnic was still a regular feature of Italian immigrant radicalism—a fact suggesting the continuity of radical traditions. The newspaper *Libertas*, for example, announced in its August 1927 issue the organization of the "Eighth International Picnic" under the auspices of the IWW for the benefit of *Il Proletario*. As indicated in these ads, picnics lasted a whole day and included games such as sack races, target firing, and pull-rope; concerts; dancing; poetry; and raffles with special gifts such as cameras, watches, books, yearly subscriptions to radical newspapers, and even revolvers.

Another standard event that drew large crowds was the *festa della frutta*, a traditional Italian peasant festival that was held annually in the fall with elaborate decorations of fruits and vegetables to celebrate the season's harvest. When *La Questione Sociale*'s group gave such a feast in October 1906, the paper noted its overwhelming success despite terrible weather. "The Italian colony," it wrote, "did not disappoint us, crowding the beautiful hall filled with all kinds of fruit trophies symbolizing a better and healthier future." Like the picnics, the feast included performances, music, games, and raffles.

These family events were a regular feature of the nineteenth- and early-twentieth-century labor movement. They were occasions for propaganda and fundraising, but they also satisfied the recreational and emotional needs of the workers. For southern Italians they also represented a special link to their native cultures and places. The *contadini* spent most of their time outdoors in their native villages and deeply missed their countryside and the direct contact with nature. Picnics and dances became for them, as for other workers, "eagerly anticipated opportunities to flee a home or a boarding-house, to dress up, to take the children, to see friends, to hear an orchestra or choir, and to dance until late into the night."[77]

May Day

Like other radicals, the *sovversivi* established their own alternate holidays that celebrated their values in place of traditional national and religious ones. Conventional celebrations like Christmas, the Fourth of July, September 20 (the anniversary of the capture of Rome), and Columbus Day were replaced by revolutionary anniversaries: May 1 (the international day of labor), November 7 (the anniversary of the Russian Revolution), November 11 (the anniversary of the Haymarket execution), and March 18 (the anniversary of the Paris Commune). Every year on these dates they published special issues embellished with drawings and poems and held massive demonstrations, rallies, and meetings followed by theatrical performances, dances, and concerts.[78]

But the quintessential radical event for Italians, as well as for other immigrant workers in the United States, was the celebration of May Day, the international working-class holiday. As Eric Hobsbawm has argued, May Day was "an invented tradition," born out of the desire of the Left to claim rituals of its own, in opposition to those created by the state—such as the institutionalization of public ceremonies and official holidays, the production of public monuments, and the use of national symbols such as uniforms, parades, bands, and flags.[79]

The origins of May Day are by now well known: Its roots go back to 1886 in the United States when workers led by the Knights of Labor and various anarchist groups organized a series of demonstrations demanding the eight-hour day, culminating in the famed Haymarket tragedy and the execution of five anarchists. Four years later the International Socialist Congress, meeting in Paris, designated May 1 as the international holiday of the workers of the world in honor of the five anarchist martyrs and the fight for the eight-hour day. Ironically, May Day in America was soon supplanted by Labor Day, a state-sanctioned celebration observed the first Monday of September. But, as scholars have noted, the tradition of May Day remained alive and well among immigrants, as an expression of working-class internationalism and solidarity.[80]

Writing about May Day observances among Italian immigrants in the United States, Rudolph Vecoli noted that by the early 1900s May Day had taken "a precise form with its prescribed rituals, symbols and rhetoric, modeled after the celebration in Italy." Contrasting sharply with the orderly and disciplined labor parades in America, May Day for Italians was a day of mass protests, demonstrations, and strikes characterized often by violence and confrontations with the police. Reports of Italian immigrants marching defiantly through the streets of American cities carrying socialist and anarchist flags, singing revolutionary anthems, and displaying banners with slogans such as "neither God nor boss" or "*Demolizione*" shook American elites and even most American socialists.[81]

Reporting on the Labor Day parade of 1895 in Philadelphia, the *New York Times* noted that "when the parade was formed today, one of the Italians carried a red flag at the head of the line and frantically moved it amid the cheers of the throng of 1,000 persons." The police intervened, promptly arresting the flag bearer and using their clubs "freely" to subdue the protesting crowd. Yet, to the dismay of the police, after the arrest another Italian, Angelo Picozzi, "pulled a red flag from his pocket and waved it in the face of the police." His action, it was noted, "pleased the crowd, and cheers for the flag and for anarchy rent the air, followed by hooting of the police." A similar incident took place during a May Day demonstration in Detroit in 1909 where Italian socialists displayed their own emblems despite the explicit ban of the local commissioner, who had told them that only U.S. flags were allowed. "The parade leaders," noted the *New York Times*, "undaunted, unfurled their red banners, but the officers seized them. The Socialists fought hard but were overpowered, and several were taken to Headquarters."[82]

Despite its confrontational character, May Day among Italians was also infused, like their radicalism in general, with a millenarian spirit linking the heroic struggles of the past with the promise of emancipation in the future. Articles published in special issues of radical newspapers dedicated to May Day are filled with a rhetoric meant to inspire and stir the workers, as in this plea by Carlo Tresca:

> Come O May, and in the powerful chorus of robust voices which calls you, may the downtrodden, may the weak of today hear clearly the bell that you ring to call them together; come O May, harbinger of peace, of justice, of love and make each slave a free man.[83]

Celebratory articles about May Day also absorbed intense religious symbolism and language. As *La Questione Sociale* put it, workers awaited May Day—often referred to as the "workers' Easter"—as a "*dio liberatore*," a redeemer, expecting as if on this day "an occult force would arise from the bowels of the earth to destroy the capitalist class and bring to the suffering proletariat comfort and freedom."[84] References to religious language became indeed so common and widespread that some newspapers eventually complained that despite their anti-clerical mission, tributes to May Day were starting to seem like "a rosary where Jesus' name was replaced with that of Karl Marx."[85]

The *sovversivi*, particularly the anarchists and the syndicalists, also frequently lamented the demise of May Day's "original physiognomy and fiery character" with the passing of years. They reminded Italian workers over and over that *Primo Maggio* was not meant to be a *festa*, a day of leisure and fun, but a manifestation of *lotta*, an expression of the strength, unity, and determination of workers to rebel against their oppressors and overthrow capitalism—a day of unyielding militancy, as it had originally been in 1886.[86]

Despite the *sovversivi*'s admonishments, the militant and spontaneous character of May Day eventually gave way to a more indulgent celebration, combining merrymaking and good cheer with working-class slogans and iconography. Celebrations typically included talks on the origins and significance of May Day, commemorations of the Haymarket martyrs, readings of revolutionary poetry, dramatic performances (a favorite was Pietro Gori's *Primo Maggio*), singing of socialist songs, as well as food, drinks, games, and, of course, dancing.

Closely associated with the arrival of spring, May Day became also an occasion for picnics and outdoor celebrations. As photographs of crowds of Italian immigrant men, women, and children with musical instruments, bottles of wine, and copies of radical newspapers attest, May Day became a family event. Women were strongly encouraged to attend (entry was typically free for them), and their presence was always proudly remarked on by radical newspapers and celebrated as a victory over clerical influence. In 1907, organizers from Boston's Dorchester section, among others, noted that despite fears that the *festa* "would take place without the intervention of the female sex . . . this time the *corvi* [crows, i.e. priests] got the worst of it, and to our great astonishment we saw the girls wearing red ribbons."[87]

But even though May Day receded into a *festa*, the *sovversivi* continued to use its symbolic force to reiterate their calls for practical action and spread the message of working-class solidarity and unity. May Day indeed became one of the few occasions for Italians to join forces with other ethnic groups—marching with them on the streets, listening to the speeches of various labor leaders in different languages, and sharing with them music, food, and dancing. A good example of such a display of solidarity took place in 1922 when the Italian Chamber of Labor co-sponsored an international May Day meeting with several other organizations, including the American Civil Liberties Union, the Socialist Party, the United Labor Council, and the Workers' Party. The ad published in *Alba Nuova* urged Italians to "observe May Day," "to proclaim their solidarity with the workers of the world," and "to join your voice—in this day of redemption, hope, and struggle—to the voices of thousands of other brothers of different nationalities." The meeting took place at Park Circle in Harlem and included renowned orators in both Italian and English.[88]

But how successful were May Day and the other "invented" traditions in promoting the *sovversivi*'s "Ideal" among Italian American workers? No doubt, they fell short of the *sovversivi*'s expectations. Radicals did not hide their disappointments and frustrations, denouncing in their newspapers, with regret and sometimes disgust, what they perceived as the indifference of the immigrants. Many obstacles were cited as explanations for their inability to win over the masses: high mobility rates, widespread intention among immigrants to go back to Italy and consequently frequent repatriations, conflict and competition with other ethnic groups, poor education, and persistent regional divisions that fragmented the immigrant community.[89]

Available evidence, however, suggests that the *sovversivi*'s campaign did bear important fruit. Rudolph Vecoli, for example, found various letters published in radical newspapers attesting to the participation of Italian workers in radical cultural events not only in large cities but also in remote small towns and mining camps in Montana, West Virginia, Iowa, and Wyoming. Radical institutions, traditions, and events created indeed an autonomous cultural and social space—or, in the words of Benedict Anderson, an "imagined political community" that gave Italian workers a sense of belonging and kinship. They tried to serve the needs of Italian immigrants, offering a way to express their dissatisfaction and aspirations stemming from their life in America. As Vecoli put it, they "greatly boosted workers' morale because the participants experienced their collective identity and potential power. As such they were important catalysts in the construction of a working class consciousness."[90]

Despite their struggles for freedom, equality, and social justice and their devotion to the cause of the poor and the oppressed, the *sovversivi*'s dream of revolution remained unfulfilled. But we should not underestimate their role in the Italian American communities and the American labor movement. As others have pointed out, the *sovversivi* undertook the formidable task of politicizing, educating, organizing, and inspiring the masses of Italian workers in America.[91] To disseminate their message they created schools and educational circles; gave thousands of lectures; published pamphlets, poems, and newspapers; and organized feasts, picnics, and processions. This rich cultural and social life was not unique to the *sovversivi*; it reflected the emergence of a working-class subculture of opposition shared by many other radicals and workers of their time. But the *sovversivi* fused it with distinctively Italian values and traditions—the intense personal relationships and conviviality; the love of good food, drinks, and fun; the spontaneity and defiance of struggle; the fierce anti-clericalism and masculine ethos—that gave their counterculture a flavor of its own.

A Literary Class War

The Italian American Radical Press

The book and the newspaper are the most potent means to hasten the triumph of workers' rights.

Il Proletario, May 17, 1902

An educated worker is always, inevitably always, a revolutionary worker.

Il Grido della Folla, May 20, 1916

In January 1888 members of the Italian socialist-anarchist-revolutionary group Carlo Cafiero—named after a famous nineteenth-century Italian anarchist hero—met in their office at 108 Thompson Street in New York City to launch a journal that would "express and give voice to [their] ideas."[1] *L'Anarchico,* as the paper was called, was the first of nearly 200 radical Italian-language newspapers produced in the United States from the late nineteenth century through the World War II period—the third-largest figure in the nation after the German and Jewish presses. Almost one-third of these newspapers were published in the New York City metropolitan area, but the Italian radical press, like Italian immigrant radicalism itself, had a wide geographic distribution, including almost every state, smaller industrial and mining towns, as well as the great cities.[2] Much of what we know of Italian American radicalism comes from the contents of these periodicals. Their general characteristics and themes, as well as the main debates they generated in their pages, are the focus of this chapter.

The importance of the press to study the Left is today well acknowledged. As Bruce Nelson succinctly put it, newspapers served as "the movement's public face."[3] Existing photographs of Italian immigrant workers displaying copies of radical publications during May Day celebrations and picnics attest that newspapers were an important source of identity and self-expression, providing a sense of shared community and purpose. Indeed, more than any other document, the press captured the whole of the *sovversivi*'s world, conveying not only their political ideas but their entire culture. As Nunzio Pernicone put it, it was their "real institutional base," playing several crucial roles and functions.[4] To start with, newspapers represented the primary medium of communication for hundreds of Italian comrades throughout the United States and across the Atlantic, providing an essential transnational network of regular contacts and information for radical leaders, organizers, and workers. Besides being the *sovversivi*'s principal nexus, the press also served as the movement's financial center, raising funds for solidarity campaigns such as strikes, arrests of comrades, or international working-class struggles, often with impressive results.[5] But above all, the press was an instrument of political propaganda and theorizing. Its primary purpose was to create a forum of political discussion and education. As the communist paper *Alba Nuova* stated in 1921, radical editors sought "to awaken the workers' minds and promote consciousness of one's rights and might through knowledge."[6] To this end, they published articles on political theory and ideology and covered local and international news, with special attention given to strikes, revolutionary upheavals, and political repression.

Ideologically, the Italian immigrant radical press never constituted a united front. Paralleling the doctrinal differences of the movement it represented, it encompassed radical papers of every stripe. Socialists, syndicalists, anarchists, communists, labor unions—all had their own separate organs of information and propaganda, all claiming to represent the true interests of the working class. Not only was the press ideologically split, but radical editors also spent much of their energy in never-ending polemics and vitriolic attacks against one another.[7]

The Italian American radical press also had the highest publishing birth and death rates of any other ethnic press: About half of its publications lasted less than two years. Aldino Felicani, a noted anarchist and editor who organized the Sacco-Vanzetti Defense Committee, recalled that when a group wanted to start a publication, "we just announced that our paper would come out on such and such a date and that we needed money to publish it. That was sufficient to bring us enough money to publish the paper." But while this form of financing helped produce many papers on short notice, it seldom assured a long life.[8] This precariousness reflected in turn three objective problems: the elevated mobility of Italian immigrants and widespread return migrations that slowed the formation of a stable working-class community; the disproportionately high costs of publication and distribution in comparison to the destitution of Italian workers; and, finally, governmental suppression.[9]

In his pioneering study on the immigrant press, the sociologist Robert Park has called radical publications "mendicant papers"—papers that "are either regularly supported by the parties and societies they represent, or [that] are constantly driven to appeal to the generosity of their constituency to keep them alive."[10] Money was indeed a continual source of worry for Italian radical papers. From inception, they were constantly on the verge of economic failure. Even the most successful newspapers operated in "a state of perennial deficit" and regularly threatened to suspend publication because of a lack of funds, particularly in times of widespread economic recession and unemployment such as the Panic of 1907 or the Great Depression.[11]

Appeals for the workers to renew their subscriptions, pay up, or send contributions appeared in almost every issue. After the second year of publication and a circulation of 3,000 copies, the editors of La Questione Sociale, the leading anarchist paper of Paterson, New Jersey, confessed that despite the support of many comrades, it could not sustain a weekly publication. "The typographer, the press, the post office," they explained to their readers, "they are not satisfied; in fact they could not care less about the praises you send to the editorial office; what they want is dollars, and they do not joke."[12]

When the deficits soared to alarming figures, the sovversivi turned to sottoscrizioni straordinarie (ad hoc contributions) and fundraising events such as picnics, dances, or theatrical performances. These initiatives, as we saw in the previous chapter, were generally greeted with enthusiasm by the workers. But even when Italians responded favorably, the collected amounts were generally inadequate to cover mounting expenses and debts, often leaving newspapers with no choice but to suspend publication.

Economic hurdles and political factionalism also seriously undermined the possibility of creating a long-term influential daily, like the legendary Yiddish-language Forward (1897–1983), that could serve as a cohesive voice of Italian working-class interests. As Mario De Ciampis has recounted, in the early twentieth century Il Proletario, the organ of the Italian Socialist Federation, attempted to become a daily but could not sustain the costs of publication.[13] Similarly, Il Lavoratore, the Italian official voice of the American Communist Party, was published as a daily at its inception in 1924, but the initiative quickly succumbed for lack of additional funds. Of all the papers published by the sovversivi only the anti-fascist Il Nuovo Mondo and its successor La Stampa Libera managed to appear on a daily basis for several years. All the others had a weekly, biweekly, or monthly circulation.

Part of the problem was that the sovversivi limited or rejected advertisements. To them, ads connoted commercialism and threatened the editorial—and thus the ideological—integrity of the paper, as advertisers could be subject to external pressures. Unlike mainstream papers, which were often subsidized by consular offices and prominent businessmen, the radical press had limited external sources of income. Thus, their survival depended almost exclusively on newsstand sales, the contributions of sympathizers, and, especially, on subscriptions, often encouraged with special gifts such as books, prints, or pens. Considering that the audience was almost exclusively working class, often including the poorest section of the immigrants, it is not surprising that funds for publishing were always in short supply.[14]

In addition to lack of funds, the *sovversivi* were often forced to suspend their publications by the American government. Because the distribution of radical papers depended almost entirely on second-class-mailing privileges, abrogation of mailing licenses became the most common method used by the authorities to shut down radical publications, especially during World War I.[15] As specified by the Espionage Act of 1917, foreign-language radical papers had to submit "true" English translations of articles dealing with political issues to local post offices, and if they did not comply they were "permanently denied the use of the mail."[16]

Between 1917 and 1919, federal agents ransacked the editorial offices of many Italian radical papers, confiscating subscription lists and literature, damaging printing equipment, as well as arresting, and in some cases deporting, their directors. *Il Martello*, among others, "was confiscated many times, so many," recalled Tresca, "that I would confound myself if I tried to count them now."[17] The *sovversivi* therefore had often no alternative but to discontinue publication or, whenever possible, resume their journalistic activities under new mastheads, formats, and places of publication.[18] *Il Proletario* is perhaps the best example of such irregularity. Founded in Pittsburgh in 1896, during its fifty-year history the paper relocated five times, constantly changing its format and periodicity, and counting so many different editors that a list of these individuals reads like a *Who's Who* of the Italian immigrant Left.[19]

Despite these odds, the *sovversivi* established newspapers that endured many years and, in the words of Italian authorities, were "very widespread and reach[ed] even the small mining and industrial centers where no other Italian newspaper has known how to penetrate."[20] About one-third of them lasted for ten to fifteen years and one-tenth for more than fifteen years, including *Il Proletario* (1896–1946), Carlo Tresca's *Il Martello* (1916–46), the reformist socialist *La Parola del Popolo* (1922–82), the anti-organizational anarchist *Cronaca Sovversiva* (1903–19), and its successor *L'Adunata dei Refrattari* (1922–71).[21]

Newspapers typically expressed the life and ideas of distinct radical groups, unions, or communities, but a large number were "one-man papers," the enterprise of single individuals, who usually supported themselves with their writing, supplemented by lecturing and organizing. This was the case, for example, of Carlo Tresca, who published and edited three newspapers: *La Plebe*, *L'Avvenire*, and *Il Martello*. The papers followed Tresca's own life, relocating as he moved from one city to another, interrupting their publication as he was arrested or in financial distress, and resurrecting under a new name when they were suppressed by governmental authorities.[22] Another example is *Cronaca Sovversiva*, which reflected almost entirely the ideas and program of its editor, the anti-organizational anarchist Luigi Galleani.[23] The list of "one-man papers" could go on and on, reflecting the *sovversivi*'s inflexible commitment to their "Beautiful Ideal."[24]

In addition to standard newspapers, the *sovversivi* also frequently resorted to *numeri unici* (single issues) and *numeri d'occasione* (special issues) to commemorate radical anniversaries or to bring attention to urgent events, such as strikes or arrests. The Italian branch of the IWW of Brooklyn, New York, spawned, for example, two important publications; the first one, *Risorgimento*, was published in May 1920 on the occasion of the Russian Revolution, and the second, *Libertas*, in August 1927, two days before the execution of Sacco and Vanzetti. Examples abound of other journalistic "calls to arms," attempting to awake and inform Italian workers. While it was not always successful, this intense publishing activity set the stage for important debates within the Italian American radical community, ranging from class struggle to feminism, religion, nationalism, and race relations, that helped define the *sovversivi*'s identity.

Circulation

Italian radical papers followed the layout of traditional newspapers of the early twentieth century, with four to eight pages and a large folio size if weekly, sixteen pages or more with a smaller format if monthly magazines. Their price ranged from 2 to 5 cents, slightly more expensive than the commercial dailies that sold for 1 cent on weekdays and 3 cents on Sunday—a difference that reflected and was a consequence of the *sovversivi*'s categorical refusal to accept ads.[25]

Most newspapers' circulation remained restricted to a few thousand readers. Yet, there were others like *Il Proletario* or *Il Martello* that averaged 5,000 to 8,000 copies (with peaks of 10,000) and were distributed in Italian immigrant communities across the United States and in Europe as well. The communist press was particularly influential in the late 1930s, achieving a circulation of 7,000 copies with *L'Unità Operaia* and peaking at 10,000 with *L'Unità del Popolo.*[26] As early as 1923, *Alba Nuova*, the first Italian American communist paper, claimed 6,000 subscribers and a circulation of nearly 20,000 copies.[27] The anti-fascist dailies *Il Nuovo Mondo* and *La Stampa Libera* had the largest circulation of all papers, selling between 25,000 and 35,000 copies.

There is no question that in comparison with the commercial press, which reached hundreds of thousands, the figures for the radical papers are rather small—although not smaller than those of other ethnic groups of the same period, with the only exception being Jewish papers. These data, however, effectively challenge the conservative and acquiescent image that is usually associated with Italian immigrants, confirming the existence of a vigorous radical subculture. Philip Cannistraro and Gerald Meyer have speculated that in New York City in the 1920s the radical press as a whole accounted for perhaps as much as one-third of the city's Italian-language circulation.[28]

Actual readership of radical newspapers was probably appreciably higher than what circulation figures suggest. Given the poverty of the Italian immigrants, radical papers were usually shared by neighboring families and workers and were also read aloud in the factories, homes, and other gathering places; thus, even illiterate workers were exposed to political propaganda and radical ideas.[29]

Style and Aesthetics

Art played a significant role in defining radical papers. Graphic logos, revolutionary slogans, and drawings helped to give newspapers an easily recognizable meaning for their working-class readers.[30] Italian radicals carefully chose subtitles to identify the political orientation of their papers and clarify party affiliation. They also used revolutionary mottoes and aphorisms by literary figures like Zola, Hugo, Tolstoy, and Rousseau to illustrate their ethical beliefs and moral values along with their political ones. Slogans like "Neither slaves, nor masters / Neither oppressors, nor oppressed," for example, anticipated the bellicose character of anarchist publications, which called for the destruction of existing political, religious, and economic institutions. By contrast, Marx's historic motto, "Workers of the world unite!" or revolutionary labor slogans like "For organization and class struggle" were typical of syndicalist and communist papers, which stressed direct action and unity.

Like other leftist publishers, the *sovversivi* also frequently used graphic logos to characterize their papers. The symbols used were those typical of international labor and working-class struggle: hammers, sickles, scythes, torches, broken chains, working men, and sunrises. Metaphors of rebellion, these images became a constitutive part of proletarian art and culture and were naturally adopted by Italian radical papers to assert their alliance with workers. The masthead of *Il Proletario*, for example, pictured a worker with a sickle in the act of hoeing the ground, while right below the title appeared a rising sun irradiating energy and light, evoking hope for a better tomorrow. Similarly, the masthead of *La Questione Sociale* featured an old but strong man hammering swords, with a lion and a sheep peacefully sleeping at his feet. As the editors explained, the picture "reproduced the giant of rebellion, who transforms a bunch of swords into an instrument of work with his powerful muscles—those swords that serve today to oppress thousands of workers for the caprices of bloody kings and emperors who rule the world."[31] The image of the animals, traditionally at war and now miraculously together, symbolized, in this case too, the hope for a more just and peaceful world.

In general, a vigorous masculinity pervaded the iconography of radical papers, exemplified by the virility and strength of working-class men's bodies. Images of male workers dominated Italian, as well as other nationalities', leftist papers, identifying work and revolution as essentially male. However, as more Italian female workers began to enter industries in the late 1910s and gain political visibility, new representations of women began to appear in radical papers. For example, the masthead of *L'Operaia* (1913–19), the organ of Local 25 of the International Ladies' Garment Workers' Union (ILGWU), featured a sensual bare-breasted woman, wrapped in an ancient Roman toga, holding a burning torch in her left hand and a pamphlet of Local 25 in her right hand. The image still betrayed traditional conceptions of womanhood as feminine, delicate, and sensual. But the mere fact that a woman was used for the masthead of a labor newspaper signaled a new sense of female empowerment.

Other graphic logos were more sophisticated: the anti-fascist *Il Veltro* (1924–25) featured a greyhound, accompanied by the verse "*Verrà che la farà morir di doglia*." The symbol and the lyric referred to an early passage of the *Divine Comedy* wherein Dante in his imaginary descent into the inferno is scared by a she-wolf and rescued by the Roman poet Virgil, who foretells him:

Molti son li animali a cui s'ammoglia,	She mates with many living souls and shall
e più saranno ancora, infin che 'l Veltro	yet mate with many more, until the Greyhound
verrà, che la farà morir con doglia.	arrives, inflicting painful death on her.
Questi non ciberà terra nè peltro,	That Hound will never feed on land or pewter,
ma sapienza, amore e virtute,	but find his fare in wisdom, love and virtue;
e sua nazion sará fra feltro e feltro.	his place of birth shall be between two felts.[32]

In Dante's verses the symbolic value of the greyhound is not clear. Literary critics have speculated that it might stand for Christ, or for a religious or political figure of the time. In the case of Giovannitti's paper, however, the allegory is self-evident: Fascism represents the wolf, while the greyhound is the working class, the force that will crush all human greed and vices and finally establish a world of love, wisdom, and virtue.

Il Veltro's iconography also reveals the literary sophistication and inventiveness of the *sovversivi*, who drew frequently from popular, classical, and religious Italian literature to advance the cause of revolution.[33] *Il Veltro's* editors skillfully used Dante to counter fascist nationalist propaganda and to evoke a sense of *italianità* that was rooted in Italy's finest literary and artistic traditions.

Italian American radical papers also frequently featured dramatic artwork by famous Italian artists such as Gabriele Galantara and Giuseppe Scalarini or talented Italian immigrants such as Onorio Ruotolo, Ludovico Caminita, and Fort Velona. Satires of clericalism, big business, and fascism were the most common themes. A number of magazines, such as *Il Fuoco* (1914–15), *Vita* (1915), *La Guardia Rossa* (1918–21), or the single-issue *Rinascimento* (1920), also included bold, colored covers by Italian and leading American graphic artists such as Art Young, Robert Minor, and John Sloan.

In his analysis of IWW culture, Salvatore Salerno pointed out the importance of art expressions as "means of unifying workers" and "disseminating knowledge" of industrial unionism. In a similar way, the use of slogans, logos, cartoons, and drawings in the Italian radical press reflected the *sovversivi's* attempts to link art and revolution by creating a language and symbolism that reinforced their message of revolt and solidarity.

Contents: General Themes and Topics

The radical press hardly constituted a unified front. Yet for all their disagreements, radical papers covered similar themes and were concerned with similar issues. All, for example, aimed at educating, informing, and emancipating the immigrants. Whether fighting for the triumph of socialism, anarchism, or communism, radical editors emphasized education and knowledge as the precondition for revolutionary organizing and activity. "The workers' most important conquest, the conquest of all conquests," explained the playwright Riccardo Cordiferro, "is the conquest of the book."[34] Not only did radical papers publish informative articles about politics, they also talked about literature, science, and practical day-to-day issues of immigrant life, like hygiene, nutrition, birth control, alcoholism, and children's education. As the editors of *Il Proletario* pointed out, "we don't simply want to launch a socialist paper" but also "a paper that, beyond the politics of parties and class struggle, carries out a daily act of purification and moral recovery."[35] It was in this same spirit that a group of concerned physicians, including Ettore Tresca, Carlo's older brother, founded *La Parola del Medico* in 1916. Devoted entirely to health education, the paper featured articles on diet, medicine, and diseases in an effort to instruct immigrants about proper medical practices and thwart the influence of fraudulent doctors.[36]

Perhaps more important, radical papers were united by the same struggles: First, they all conducted a fierce muckraking campaign against the so-called *camorra coloniale* (colonial mafia), the triumvirate of wealthy Italian businessmen, consular officials, and priests; second, they mobilized against war, imperialism, and fascism; finally, they helped promote women's emancipation and racial equality. By embracing these unifying battles, the press helped cement a common culture that bound together Italian radicals and workers even if it exposed the ideological diatribes that divided them.

The Struggle against the Prominenti

Of all the wars fought by the radical press, the most pervasive was the campaign against the world of the *prominenti*. As we saw in chapter 2, these powerful men ruled the Little Italies by monopolizing jobs and controlling established institutions. Radical newspapers especially exposed their ruthless practices as employment agents by publishing stories of Italian workers who were abused, exploited, forced to work under horrific conditions through threat and intimidation, or recruited as scabs under false contracts. For example, on June 5, 1892, the anarchist paper *Il Grido degli Oppressi* reported that twenty-five Italian workers went to the mines in Pennsylvania, lured by an ad promising them $1.50 a day. When they arrived, they found seventy-five workers, mostly Italians and Greeks, all working for 75 cents. They were kept under control all the time and when they refused to work on Sunday they were forced at gunpoint to return to the mines.[37]

Several years later, in 1906, *Il Proletario* published a letter by an immigrant denouncing the inhumane conditions of work in Virginia, where Italians were sent by employment agencies with false promises. "Workers are deprived of the most basic rights," he wrote; "there is no freedom whatsoever; and those who run away, if caught, are subjected to the brutality of the *aguzzini*—the bosses' private armed guards."[38] Unfortunately, stories like this were not rare. While Italian immigrants performed the hardest jobs—mining; building bridges, railways, and roads; or shoveling the snow away—the Italian bosses became richer and richer at the expense of the poor Italian workers. As *Il Grido degli Oppressi* sadly commented, "The worst enemy of the Italian people are the Italians."[39]

The campaign against the world of the *prominenti* was not limited to exposing their thievery. Italian radicals seized every opportunity to denigrate and mock their posts as well, particularly the Italian consulate and the commercial press. Described as "the greatest den of *cafoneria coloniale*" (colonial vulgarity), the consulate was one of the most corrupt Italian American institutions. The consuls, pointed out the *sovversivi*, did nothing to put an end to the exploitation of the workers by the local bosses and bankers or to improve the living conditions of the Italian immigrants. Instead of helping immigrants, the consuls were a mere extension of Italy's "parasitic bureaucracy." Carlo Tresca compared them to "hyenas always on the warpath for fresh blood," exacting extremely high fees for immigration documents, selling their favors to the best buyer, and cooperating with Italian authorities to spy and combat radicalism.[40]

These polemics often ended in court. Following repeated accusations against his office and his person, Consul Naselli of Philadelphia filed a suit against Carlo Tresca and Giuseppe and Giovanni Di Silvestro in 1905 under libel charges for a series of allegedly defamatory articles published in *Il Proletario* that year. Naselli's prosecution asked $15,000 for damages, using copies of *Il Proletario* that contained articles against the state and governmental authorities to predispose the jury negatively against the defendants. Eventually, the judge reduced the amount of the damages to $1,000, but the defendants were sentenced to three months in prison.[41] Court decisions were often harsher: Italian consuls were very influential and benefited from the protection of *prominenti* who in turn had connections to American authorities. Yet, despite the dangers of conviction, radical editors did not give up, continuing to expose the "dirty" role of the consuls and other *padroni*.[42]

The *sovversivi* also systematically denounced mainstream Italian-language newspapers, blasting vitriolic attacks against their publishers and editors, particularly Carlo Barsotti and Agostino De Biasi of *Il Progresso Italo-Americano* and Luigi Barzini of *Il Corriere d'America*.[43] In the 1930s, the main enemy became instead Generoso Pope. An immigrant of poor background and education, Pope began to work in construction and within a few years rose to foreman, superintendent, and eventually owner of the Colonial Sand and Gravel Company, the nation's largest supplier of building materials. His enormous wealth enabled him to purchase *Il Progresso*, *Il Corriere d'America*, and *Il Bollettino della Sera*, using his influence to spread fascism among the immigrants.[44]

As with the consuls, the *sovversivi* made such men the targets of constant offenses, accusations, and satire. Called the worst imaginable names— "cancerous plagues," "rotten rubbish," "kings of *cafoni*"—and compared to obnoxious beasts such as asses, pigs, or chameleons, they embodied what the *sovversivi* hated most: selfishness, opportunism, falsehood, and greed. As one writer put it, they were "common people with no morals or conscience. . . . Every day there emerge new ones like poisoned mushrooms. They are all the same: they belong to the category of the cheats and thieves."[45]

For the *sovversivi*, the press was supposed to be an instrument of political information, education, and ideological debate. Mainstream papers, instead, were an expression of conservatism and colonial bossism that pursued self-interest at the expense of the workers.[46] As Giacinto Menotti Serrati pointed out in a letter to his comrades, "The Italian immigrant working class will never achieve consciousness of its interests as long as there exists a press hungry for dollars, flattering and false, which corrupts the workers' character and disfigures their mind and heart."[47] Indeed, as George Pozzetta has noted, mainstream papers often worked against the best interests of their readers. Motivated by profit, they used as their principal model sensational tabloids, flooding their columns with lurid details of murders, kidnappings, and passionate crimes. Fifty percent of their publishing space was devoted to ads paid for by medical imposters, real estate swindlers, and unscrupulous employment agents.[48] Gino Speranza, a successful lawyer and reformer, lamented the poor quality of the Italian American commercial press, referring often to *Il Progresso* as a "blackmailing journal."[49] Even *La Follia*, a popular nonradical humorous publication, made fun of the editors and contributors of mainstream newspapers, exposing their intellectual mediocrity, materialism, and even their grammatical errors.

Anti-Clericalism

The radical press found itself also at constant war with the Catholic Church. The *sovversivi*, as we saw earlier, were staunch anti-clericals. In line with Marx's belief that religion is "the opiate of the people," they considered institutional religions an opportunistic invention of the dominant classes to justify social inequalities and keep the masses enslaved.[50] "The church," pointed out *Il Grido degli Oppressi*, "pretends to deplore the abuses and injustices of the world, but at the same time preaches resignation, submission, and passive acceptance of one's own destiny."[51] Workers' liberation, declared Serrati, cannot be God's work but the result of class organization and struggle. "What the workers need," he continued, "is not prayers but action, not humbleness but determination, not resignation but struggle."[52]

Anti-clerical invective filled the pages of radical newspapers, admonishing against the evils of religious propaganda, particularly the pernicious effect of Catholic influence over women.[53] To prove their point, the *sovversivi* exposed the Church's historic crimes and demystified the theoretical incongruities of dogmata such as the theory of creation, the Immaculate Conception, the existence of hell and heaven, and the existence of God itself, countering them with scientific explanations.[54] As Carlo Tresca declared during a debate with Reverend Petrarca in front of "an enormous crowd" in Milford, Massachusetts, "We socialists, at least the majority, are positivists . . . we don't believe in the existence of a supernatural being, and reject every prejudice, every religious belief."[55]

The illustrated review *L'Asino* (1892–1925), founded in Rome by Guido Podrecca and Gabriele Galantara, is the most evident example of Italian anti-clerical feeling. Claiming a circulation of more than 100,000, *L'Asino* won international admiration in the early twentieth century along with the French magazine *Assiette au Beurre* and Germany's *Simplicissimus* for its provocative illustrations and superb satire.[56] When Father John A. Di Pietro arrived on a Catholic mission to Ybor City, Florida, in 1905, he regretted to inform his superiors that Italians there were largely indifferent to religion, noting that "every week about 70 copies of the most infidel, anarchical, and lascivious paper published in Italy [*L'Asino*] are distributed among them."[57] *L'Asino* was eventually denied entry to the United States in 1908 on the grounds that it contained pornographic material, but it was so popular among Italian immigrants that a special edition of the paper was promptly issued for distribution in America.[58]

Radical papers countered religious traditions with the promotion of a secular culture. One article in *L'Asino*, for example, proudly reported that workers of the village of Clivio, in the northern Italian city of Varese, had created a lay kindergarten, so that children would not be exposed to the "lies" of the Church.[59] The newspaper also launched the idea of anti-clerical marriages, encouraging readers to boycott religious weddings and endorse civil unions. To this end, it published communiqués of men and women looking for anti-clerical soulmates, and, under a column titled "Examples to Emulate," it proudly announced the births of "socialist babies," who instead of "being contaminated" by "holy water" were baptized to the rhythm of revolutionary songs and given libertarian names such as Libero (free) or Alba (sunrise). Similar columns appeared also in Italian American radical papers. *L'Avvenire*, noted Nunzio Pernicone, had a column called "In the Black World" that chronicled the misdeeds of the priests; another one, "Without Priests," publicized the stories of Italian comrades who refused to christen their children, raising them instead as "champions of free thought."[60]

Radical papers in the United States especially criticized the celebration of religious festivals, such as the feast of "the Madonna del Carmine" or of regional saints, with their processions, simulacra, and rituals.[61] Barefoot, holding candles and banners, and reciting prayers, thousands of immigrants, mostly women, regularly marched along the streets of the *colonie italiane*, often for miles and miles.[62] For the *sovversivi*, such folk traditions were unacceptable reminiscences of a medieval world, the product of ignorance, fanatical bigotry, and superstition. Often sponsored by the local parishes, these religious rituals, radicals believed, perpetuated and reinforced passive perseverance. Radicals detested especially the idea that immigrants would spend thousands of dollars on fireworks, banners, and other decorations, instead of using this money for more serious and urgent needs. To emphasize what they saw as the absurdity of these religious cults, radical papers used sarcasm, humor, and open contempt. For example, in 1903 *Il Proletario* printed an "open letter" to the "Dear Madonna del Carmine, c/o Eternal Father— Heaven," in which the author questioned the Madonna's miraculous powers and wanted to know if she was the best and most powerful of all Madonnas.[63] The letter was signed by Gaetano Mirtillo, but it is difficult to tell whether it was authentic or was rather a deliberate joke to ridicule immigrants' religious creeds. In any event, its publication exemplified the literary inventive-

Padre e marito... spirituale.

— Ma don Giordano! Se non la
smettete chiamo la mamma!
— Non occorre, carina! C'è già
stata prima di te!

Figure 3.1
"Spiritual father and husband,"
L'Asino, January 8, 1905, 7.
"Father Giordano," cries the
woman, "if you don't stop I am
going to call my mother." "It
will not be necessary," replies
the priest; "she has already gone
through it before you."

ness of the *sovversivi*, who often resorted to satire and other forms of popular
culture to expose what they perceived as the naiveté of Italian immigrants.

The *sovversivi* also used any chance they had to discredit and attack the
priests—the *maiali neri* (pigs in black), as they called them. They warned
Italian parents against the priests' perceived incompetence as teachers, in
some cases publishing, as did *La Fiaccola* of Buffalo in 1910, statistics that
demonstrated the alleged shortcomings of Catholic schools.[64] But their
favorite tactic to disparage the clergy was to expose the priests' sexual misconduct. One vignette published in *L'asino* shows a priest pinching a young
woman (fig. 3.1). "But Father Giordano!" she protests, "if you don't stop I am
going to call my mother." "It will not be necessary," says the priest; "she has

already gone through it before you." Another one pictures a woman in the act of taking the communion at Mass whispering to the priest: "My husband will not come home tonight . . ." "I will see you at midnight, then!" replies the delighted priest (fig. 3.2).[65]

In one case, Carlo Tresca managed to publish in his newspaper *La Plebe* a compromising photograph of a priest, Reverend Di Sabato of Connellsville, Pennsylvania, "on a sofa with his head nestled comfortably against the breast of his lovely housekeeper, whose left arm embraced him around the neck." Tresca was of course sued for libel, but was able to prove the authenticity of the picture and further dishonor the priest by bringing to court an unwed mother who identified the priest as the father of her child. Di Sabato eventually lost the libel case, but Tresca was nevertheless found guilty of libeling the priest's housekeeper.[66]

Figure 3.2
"Communion of . . . thought," *L'Asino*, June 18, 1905, 6. "My husband will not come home tonight," whispers the woman to the priest. And he replies: "I will see you at midnight, then!"

The *sovversivi*'s hatred of priests, however, was not motivated by ideological reasons alone. The Roman Catholic Church proved to be a major bulwark against the radicalization of Italian immigrant workers, combatting all forms of radical activity and countering radical propaganda with its own. Under pressures from the Church, for example, the American police raided several radical bookstores in 1908, on the grounds that they were selling anti-clerical literature. Among the most notable victims of such repression was the owner of the Vanni bookstore in New York's Greenwich Village, who was arrested because some of his books were deemed sacrilegious and immoral. Especially in the 1920s, with the advent of fascism and the signing of the Lateran Accords between Mussolini and Pope Pius XI in 1929, the Catholic Church in the United States worked side by side with *prominenti* and consuls to silence the *sovversivi*.[67]

Ironically, while Italian radicals saw atheism as a liberating force that would finally bring "Truth and Light," they simultaneously borrowed religious terms to describe their own political devotion to the "Ideal." Similarly, while the priests were demonized, Jesus was glorified as a rebel and outcast: "Christ was born poor and died poor," wrote *Il Proletario*; "the priest may be born poor but dies rich." "Christ taught the religion of love and tolerance," it went on; "the priest has imposed Catholic faith through wars, torture and Inquisition." And again: "Christ died on the cross for the redemption of the poor; the priest wants handcuffs and bullets for the slaves of work."[68] Indeed, as we will discuss in chapter 5, for all their anti-clerical scoffing, Italian radical writings were pervaded by an intense religious sensibility, consistently projecting "Christianized" images of the revolution and its martyrs.

Anti-Nationalism, Anti-Militarism, and Race

Along with religious institutions, Italian radical papers also vilified the practice of erecting monuments, organizing banquets, and participating in nationalistic parades to commemorate Italy.[69] These events, argued the *sovversivi*, were a strategy of Italian authorities to spread patriotism among the immigrants and prevent workers from questioning the policies of the Italian government and local *prominenti*. The *sovversivi*, however, made it clear that they opposed not love of country and its culture but rather the belief that people should accept uncritically and blindly whatever actions the state deemed appropriate. As Elisée Réclus, a French anarchist and contributor to *La Questione Sociale*, explained:

It is certainly a commendable thing to love one's homeland, its people, its art and letters. . . . But the name of patriotism is a façade to hide something completely different. . . . It is not enough to love one's country, to speak the native language and to love the culture . . . but it is necessary to march at the sound of the drums and trumpets, to throb with pride at the view of the national flag, sustaining it even when it is wrong. . . . And, above all, a good patriot must hate anyone who lives beyond the national frontier.[70]

Implicit in this critique was the belief that patriotism threatened working-class internationalism, promoting racial hatred and ethnic divisions that would only benefit the ruling class. Like other internationalists, the *sovversivi* disclaimed the relevance of any particular state, pursuing an idealist vision of global humanity and egalitarian universalism that, they believed, could be realized only through a proletarian revolution.

Discussion of nationalism escalated during Italy's invasion of Libya in 1911 and, above all, during World War I, when patriotic fervor pushed almost 300,000 Italian Americans to serve in the U.S. army and 65,000 to return to Italy to fight.[71] Among other commentators, James Warbasse, an eminent Italian American socialist doctor, reminded workers that

the patriotism imposed on them is nothing but shabby provincialism; that the racial prejudice instilled into their minds since birth is nothing but blind hatred without any rational foundation; that religions are meant to make them superstitious and passive slaves of authority; and that all these creeds are fomented by the same powers that make and want wars.[72]

Combining anti-nationalist with anti-militaristic principles, several new libertarian papers, such as *Vita* (1915), *Il Grido della Folla* (1916), *La Riscossa* (1916–17), and *L'Anarchia* (1918–19), were launched with the goal of countering the jingoist propaganda exerted by mainstream media and the state and uniting workers against their real enemy—capitalism. While they were short-lived, these publications show the *sovversivi*'s continual efforts to resist the conservative policies of the American and Italian governments and to uphold their internationalist, anti-militarist, and anti-imperialist principles despite mounting political repression. "Let's give back an aspiration to the proletarian movement and a goal to the revolution," read *Il Grido della Folla*'s opening editorial. "We don't want to be oppressed or exploited any longer. This society stinks. Let's demolish it. Let's raze it. Let's destroy capitalism. Let's annihilate the church. To arms!"[73] The call to arms was not metaphorical—all readers who subscribed to the paper would receive a revolver as a gift.

Evidence shows that in addition to nationalism and militarism, Italian radicals also opposed racism and contemporary racial theories based on consanguinity, ethnography, and biology. Their papers, as Rudolph Vecoli and Salvatore Salerno have noted, showed a remarkable empathy for "the barbaric treatment of blacks" and "the crimes committed by the white race" against indigenous people in the name of "civilization."[74] In a bold article published in 1892, *Il Grido degli Oppressi*, for example, labeled Christopher Columbus "a pirate and adventurer," arguing that, far from being "Italy's great glory," his discovery of America marked the beginning of Europe's "colonial politics," launching "a series of terrible massacres and usurpations against the native people and the Africans."[75]

Unlike American socialists, who virtually ignored the plight of blacks, Italian radicals offered in their papers detailed reports of some of the most brutal lynchings in the history of the American South, openly attacking the U.S. government for denying African Americans equal rights, legal protection, and human dignity.[76] The *sovversivi* did not hesitate to defend also Chinese immigrants. In an article discussing the "true" motive behind the Chinese Exclusion Act of 1882, *Il Proletario* rejected contemporary stereotypical views of the Chinese as an "inferior" and "un-assimilable" race that was "depressing salaries," insisting that such views were meant to divide workers and further the interests of the capitalists.

For the *sovversivi*, racial theories, like nationalisms and religions, were an instrument of the dominant class to pit people against one another, promoting hatreds and preventing class solidarity. As Ludovico Caminita, an anarchist editor and writer, explained in his essay "Odio di razza?" racial hatred was "the result of conflicting economic interests deriving from specific circumstances created by the bourgeoisie to maintain its class dominion."[77] The real solution, as the title of an article published in 1909 put it, was "not racial struggle but class struggle." "The worker, the oppressed—whether Chinese, Russian or any other nationality," explained another writer, "is our brother, just as it is our enemy the boss, the oppressor, even if he is from our same town."[78] The *sovversivi*, in other words, essentially dismissed race and ethnicity as categories of identity, insisting that class interests represented the true source of bonding and the "only mainspring of proletarian progress."[79]

But as in the case of religion, the *sovversivi*'s attitudes toward nationalism and race were far more complex than their words suggest. Despite their sincere empathy for the plight of blacks, their language also evoked deeply internalized racial images and stereotypical views of Africans as savages and cannibals that were often used as desultory metaphors to describe the state of southern Italy or Italian immigrants themselves. The debate over the Italian invasion of Libya in 1911 is a case in point. Radicals unanimously condemned the war as an imperialistic venture under the guise of a "civilizing mission," contending that it was ludicrous to believe that Italy could "civilize" another country when she had failed to provide for the basic needs of her own citizens, particularly in the South. But, as Michael Topp has discussed, in making their point they manifested considerable contempt for their own southern co-nationals, who were portrayed as backward and barbaric, likened to "cannibals in central Africa" and seen as "more closely related to the chimpanzee than they are to Adam and Eve."[80]

Despite their professed anti-patriotism, Italian radicals also maintained a close connection, and emotional attachment, to their home country, drawing on their shared sense of *italianità* to appeal to their fellow workers and to respond to the racial affront and discrimination they experienced in America. Indeed, as other scholars have argued, their politics were constantly informed by personal, cultural, and political ties to Italy. *L'Unità del Popolo*, for example, underscored its internationalist ethos by quoting not Marx but Garibaldi: "Be united, o People, be united, and you shall be free." The paper's editor, Gino Bardi, also sought to challenge fascist claims that the Left was un-Italian by connecting the struggle of anti-fascists to the republican tradition of the *Risorgimento* and citing as an example Giuseppe Mazzini's famous internationalist creed: "I love my fatherland because I love all fatherlands."[81] The *sovversivi*, indeed, sought constantly to affirm the distinctively national yet universal appeal of the struggle of the *Risorgimento*, countering the imperialistic image of Italy with the vision of a nation embodying a great egalitarian, libertarian, and artistic tradition.

The Woman Question

In keeping their commitment to advance the cause of freedom and equality, radical papers also took up the defense of women's emancipation, stressing the need to mobilize and organize female workers. As early as the 1890s, *Il Grido degli Oppressi* and *La Questione Sociale* featured articles of a feminist nature, many written by women themselves.[82] The plea of the anarchist Maria Roda published in the September 15, 1897, issue of *La Questione Sociale* was probably the most powerful of these early calls to feminist action. Addressing her fellow working women, she wrote: "Let our men—who suppress our will, who do not allow us to think and act freely, who consider us inferior to them, who impose on us their authority, as fathers, brothers and husbands, and, believing to be stronger than us, trample us, oppress us, and sometimes even hit us—let our men know: we want freedom and equality too."[83]

In another powerful manifesto published a few years earlier, another anarchist woman named Alba emphasized that "we, as women, more than anybody else should be revolutionaries." "Not only are we oppressed and despised like men," she explained, "we are also haggled and weighted as *carne da piacere* [flesh for pleasure]." Hence, she concluded, "we should be the first to support the anarchist-socialist-revolutionary movement because it only can bring peace to our hovels and free us from the yoke of the capitalist, the priest, the state, and the husband too."[84] Expressing a similar sentiment, Virgilia Buongiorno, a member of a feminist club of Paterson, noted that "from centuries and centuries" women had been denied the same rights and duties as men. The solution, she argued, was for women to join the anarchist struggle "for the most complete emancipation of suffering humanity" and the demolition "of all the false prejudices that infest the world."[85]

Radical women denounced sexism, but they also blamed their "sisters" for being vain, superficial, and interested only in mundane affairs and gossip. As they explained, their frivolity and coquetry reinforced men's views of women as intellectually inferior and represented a major obstacle for women's emancipation. "How can we gain the respect of men," wrote a woman by the name of Titì in 1906, "if all we worry about is how we look?"[86] Some also considered women partially responsible for their own oppression, complaining that they were too submissive. Ersilia Grandi, an anarchist exile who moved to the United States with her lover, Giuseppe Ciancabilla, in 1898 and remained active in the movement throughout her life, made it clear that women's emancipation should begin with and be made by women themselves. Liberation, she explained, would come only when women realized "how to conquer freedom and escape the social environment that suffocates them, whether in the family, in intimate relations, in today's hypocritical conventions, or in public life."[87]

These arguments were part of a wider international debate on the "woman question" that developed in conjunction with the women's suffrage movement in Britain, France, and North America during the mid–nineteenth century.[88] In Italy the woman question became a subject of intense discussion after unification. In 1864, Anna Maria Mozzoni (1837–1920), the first and one of the most acclaimed Italian feminists, published *La donna e i suoi rapporti sociali* (*Woman and Her Social Relationships*), in which she described the oppressive condition of women in Italy, criticizing the Italian Civil Code of

1865 for sanctioning women's legal inferiority to men. Largely based on the Napoleonic Code, the new laws still deprived Italian women of the right to vote, to hold any public office, and to control and dispose of their income. Inspired by the egalitarian and libertarian ideas of the *Risorgimento*, Mozzoni believed that women were "oppressed by institutions" and went as far as to argue that "a legal husband is, for a woman, intellectual castration, perpetual minority, the annihilation of her personality." In 1881 she helped to found the *Lega promotrice degli interessi femminili* (League for the Promotion of Women's Interests) in Milan to further the cause of women and raise awareness of their problems.[89]

Other women quickly joined her. In 1868 Gualberta Alaide Beccari (1842–1906), the daughter of Girolamo Beccari, a leading patriot of the Italian struggle for unification, launched *La donna*, a periodical dedicated to women's issues to which Mozzoni was a regular contributor. Another important feminist paper, *L'Italia femminile*, was established in 1899 by Emelia Maraini, a socialist teacher, and the writer Sibilla Aleramo, best known for her 1906 autobiographical novel *Una donna* (translated into English as *A Woman at Bay*), which recounted her oppressive marriage and her desperate struggle to win independence.[90]

By the early twentieth century, Italian feminists had intensified their campaign to free women of traditional oppression: In 1908 the First Congress of Italian Women was organized, followed two years later by the National Committee for Women's Suffrage. Despite these milestone events, the legal and civic status of Italian women did not improve much. Even though women's suffrage was discussed twenty times in the Italian Parliament between 1863 and April 1918, women gained the right to vote only in 1945, after the fall of the fascist regime.[91]

The debate over women's oppression in Italy reverberated in the Italian immigrant radical communities in the United States. Radical papers frequently reprinted Mozzoni's writings and published pieces by female immigrant contributors that exposed, as one of them put it, "the miserable status that we, women, occupy before society."[92] Starting in the early 1910s, articles on working-class women, their rights, and their struggle appeared regularly in the radical press. Some papers also featured regular columns called "*La pagina della donna*" (the woman's page), aimed at discussing "the wide and complex problem of the modern woman" and promoting a new image of her "as a social and rational being, instead of confining her, as unfortunately still happens in the Italian press, to the subject of erotic and adulterous *letterume* [rotten literature]."[93]

One of the most important Italian feminist theorists to emerge in the United States was the syndicalist poetess Bellalma Forzato-Spezia. Echoing Mozzoni's views, she argued that the major obstacle to women's emancipation rested in the rigid Italian family structure and traditional gender divisions. In her articles, she also identified religion, with its emphasis on women's acquiescence and submission to men, as a strong deterrent to organizing female workers. Stressing education as the key to their enfranchisement and liberation, she urged women to break free from the hegemony of the priest and the Catholic Church and to attend union meetings and other political gatherings instead of the Mass.[94] She also discussed the woman question in relation to the law, showing how it discriminated against women on the assumption that they were "incapable," "irresponsible," and "weak."[95] These views, she pointed out, were conveniently construed by men to keep women submissive, but she warned: "We worry about the same problems you do. . . . The freedom and justice that you love, we love them too."[96]

Radical women's efforts to challenge traditional gendered views, however, did not necessarily meet with the approval of their male comrades. Instead of encouraging female political activism, the *sovversivi*, radical women complained, typically ridiculed their attempts. For instance, when women of the *Gruppo Femminile Luisa Michel* in Spring Valley, Illinois, requested that rules of membership for the Prosperity Club, an all-male anarchist saloon, be changed to include also women, the men rebuffed them. As the paper *L'Aurora* reported through a letter describing the ensuing polemic, women, according to the majority of male members, "should be excluded because they are women," and "if [they] want a club . . . they should create their own."[97]

Similarly, the founders of the feminist group *Emancipazione della Donna* of Paterson sadly commented in 1902 that, after years of intense organizing, they could not fully count on radical men. In an open letter to their *compagni* they denounced men's scorn, demanding respect and support for their work of propaganda. "Our faith and modest intentions have been appreciated by many good male comrades who have assisted us with great, brotherly encouragement," they noted. But they added, "our *compagni* have been reluctant to defend us from the angry persecution of many eternal malcontent men who see in our intents nothing but pride, in our actions nothing but mistakes, in our words nothing but orthography, rewarding us with their malice, their jokes, their never ending arrogance."[98]

In theory the *sovversivi* recognized gender oppression. "If the woman occupies an inferior place in society today," the editors of *L'Aurora* admitted, "it is because we condemn her to it. . . . It is we who force her to mind only the cooking, laundry, sewing and housecleaning."[99] Radical newspapers published plenty of articles condemning the subordinate conditions of women or, as Alberto Guabello put it, their "double slavery: by government and by man."[100] *Il Grido degli Oppressi*, among others, wrote as early as 1892:

> There is nothing more unjust than the inequality between men and women, established and maintained by artificial means. . . . All tends to keep women in a state of economic and moral dependence on men: their limited or inexistent education, the types of jobs more or less servile to which they are destined, the lower salaries, and finally prostitution, which awaits them whenever they have no other means to support themselves.[101]

But while many radical men expressed solidarity toward women's demands, their attitudes were filled with contradictions. To some extent, they understood that women's traditional roles had to be reconsidered and men themselves had to change the way they treated their wives and daughters. "Whereas yesterday women used to be servants," argued Giovannitti, "today they must be equal partners."[102] Anarchists concurred: "We, real champions of universal freedom," declared A. Ferretti in *La Questione Sociale*, "want the woman to enjoy maximum liberty, just like a man. We want her to stop being a slave of man and become his comrade instead." *Il Proletario* further encouraged Italian men to see women as their companions and treat them with respect. "Let's start by destroying the tyrant that is within us," it declared; "it is not enough to call [our woman] *compagna*, we must recognize her as such."[103]

But for all their emancipated beliefs about gender equality and their promises to treat women on a par with men, the *sovversivi* rarely put into practice their noble ideas. "There are many men who claim they are free thinkers, socialists, or anarchists," noted Titì, "but within the family they are the opposite of the propagandist, the apostle, the emancipated individual."[104] As the historian Jennifer Guglielmo has documented, many other women expressed similar frustrations with the men in the movement who "routinely positioned themselves at the center of the revolutionary culture," ignoring, marginalizing, or, worse, ridiculing women's activism.[105]

Italian leftists seemed also incapable of appreciating women's direct contributions to the labor movement. Although Italian women played a vital role in the Lawrence strike of 1912, Italian syndicalists failed even to recognize their participation, much less the implications of that participation.[106] The *sovversivi*'s prejudices against women are particularly evident in their private

Figure 3.3
Labor organizer Angela Bambace (1898–1975) and her lover, anarchist Luigi Quintiliano (1893–1970). Angela Bambace Papers, Immigration History Research Center, University of Minnesota.

lives. When labor organizer Angela Bambace in 1919 married Romolo Camponeschi, her father's choice as a suitor and husband, she had to suspend her union activism. Her decision to return to work and to resume her political activism in 1925, breaking away from the traditional role of wife and mother, eventually led to their divorce. During the legal litigation for the custody of their children, her husband effectively used her political radicalism as evidence of her unfitness as a mother, and she lost the custody of the children.

After Bambace fell in love and moved in with Luigi Quintiliano, an anarchist who had emigrated from Rome in 1910, things did not change much (fig. 3.3). Despite his libertarian ideas, Quintiliano too resented her political involvement and demanded her unconditional attention.[107]

Quintiliano's contradictory behavior—a radical outside, a despot at home—was not anomalous. While often admired by his contemporaries for his sensitivity and devotion to the workers, and despite his frequent references to gender equality in his speeches and writings, Arturo Giovannitti verbally abused his wife.[108] Carlo Tresca abandoned his wife, Helga Guerra, and daughter for Elizabeth Gurley Flynn but was chronically unfaithful to her too, including an affair with Flynn's younger sister Sabina while the three shared an apartment in Greenwich Village.[109]

Among other publications, the socialist labor newspaper *Il Lavoro*, as Bènèdicte Deschamps has discussed, is a perfect example of the ambiguity that existed among the *sovversivi*, and socialists in general, toward the woman question.[110] Founded in 1915 in New York City as the Italian voice of the newly founded American Clothing Workers of America (ACWA), *Il Lavoro* aimed primarily at spreading unionization among Italian workers. From its start until its demise in 1932, the paper carried an intense propaganda to mobilize Italian women, who by 1911 constituted half of the female workers of New York City's garment industry and between 25 and 33 percent of the nation's clothing industry.[111] But while the editors welcomed women as partners who should attend meetings and sustain the union, they were quite reluctant to champion unconditional suffrage for women or total equality between genders. *Il Lavoro*, argued Deschamps, supported feminism as long as the movement did not question the specificity of the respective genders or attempt to set women against men.[112]

Similarly, in one of the few articles trying to define "feminism" explicitly, *Il Fuoco* published an article by Isabel Bass, an American, stating that "feminism is not a movement intended against men, but towards the development of the woman—her intelligence, her body, her social horizon—so that she can become a true companion of man."[113] Like *Il Fuoco*, most Italian radical papers never completely separated the woman question from the issue of working-class struggle or unionism. Women's oppression for them remained linked to class, not gender, inequality.[114]

This position was popularized above all by the German socialist August Bebel. In his book *Die Frau und der Sozialismus* (*Women and Socialism*, 1879), he associated women's oppression with capitalism, concluding that the overthrow of the latter would eventually bring in its wake social emancipation for women. Translated into Italian in 1896, Bebel's argument found large support among Italian socialists, effectively delaying the development of an autonomous movement for women's emancipation in Italy. Even communist papers continued to oppose feminists' attempts to frame the problems of women in the context of the "sex struggle," persisting in viewing female liberation as something to be worked out with male comrades. "The Communist Party," wrote *Alba Nuova* in 1924, "must not organize women in independent organizations. Rather it must include them in local political organizations as members with rights identical to those of men, allowing them to participate in all directive organs and giving them access to all positions within the party."[115]

Socialist men were often also openly hostile to working women. Echoing the views of the Italian socialist and gynecologist Tullio Rossi-Doria, who argued that female work outside the home went against biology, many socialists considered female industrial work a threat to the family as well as to men's employment in that it would lead to decreased salaries and job competition.[116] Emphasizing women's alleged innate qualities—"their unique concerns as mothers," their "greater sensitivity," and their "maternal altruism"—men argued that the natural and most suitable place for women was the home and that their special contributions to the socialist cause lay in their roles as mothers and educators of tomorrow's generation.[117] "If there is one noble, sublime, holy I would say, mission in our society," wrote *La Questione Sociale* in 1897, "this is certainly the mission of motherhood." "No one better than the woman," echoed *L'Operaia* sixteen years later, "can carry on such an important act of redemption; no one better than her can preach the gospel of human brotherhood, adding to the sweet word the charitable work of social philanthropy."[118]

Indeed, it was difficult even for Italian radical women to liberate themselves from the idea of domesticity and their traditional roles of wives and mothers.[119] Her radicalism notwithstanding, Bellalma Forzato-Spezia, in a pamphlet titled *La donna nel presente e l'educazione dell'infanzia* (Contemporary women and childhood education), talked about the importance of family education and the revolutionary role of motherhood in shaping the ideas and characters of children. Echoing what Caroline Waldron Merithew would call "anarchist motherhood," she argued that women were, as mothers, in the unique position to sustain the revolution by passing on to their children their vision of a just and egalitarian society. "Come with us!"—she urged her fellow female comrades—"Give us in your children some rebels, some demolishers, some avengers, some barricade heroes. . . . And then, we will finally crush the bloody bulwark of private property, and, on its smoking ruins, we will hoist the red gonfalon of a new civilization based on liberty and universal justice!"[120]

Maria Roda agreed. In an article written to "mothers," she called attention to the maternal duty to teach children "the path to Truth." Combining education with emancipation, she argued, would give mothers a unique opportunity to fight bourgeois values and promote instead the noble ideals of anarchy. "You will not teach them to adore a god who does not exist, which is a lie," she admonished; "instead of god you will teach them to admire Nature." She also told women to teach their children to love all peoples rather than one's country and to educate them to free love rather than impose on them the legal marriage based on material interests. More important, she went on, mothers should teach their children, boys as well as girls, to be fiery and dignified, standing up for their rights against the capitalist who exploits them daily.[121]

Articles instructing mothers how to become revolutionary teachers could be found in the pages of many radical papers.[122] The notion of a woman's "special role" in raising her children was of course neither new nor distinctive of Italian immigrant feminism. Linda Kerber in her pivotal study of American women in the early republic showed that after the Revolution the mother in the United States came to be seen "as the custodian of civic morality"—who would nurture "public-spirited male citizens" and guarantee "the steady infusion of virtue into the Republic."[123]

Like the American postrevolutionary maternalists, Maria Roda, Bellalma Forzato-Spezia, and other Italian immigrant feminists, both socialists and anarchists, essentially used motherhood as a rationale that would permit them to gain power and claim a larger political role within a revolutionary movement that was dominated by men. In mining towns like those studied by Merithew in northern Illinois, labor was "gender-segmented." Women were barred from coal mining, but their unpaid labor—cleaning, washing laundry, cooking, and watching their children—was essential to the survival of the community. The development of "anarchist motherhood," as Merithew reminds us, shows that Italian women's resistance often took place "in contexts well beyond the point of production."[124]

Many Italian immigrant radical women also seemed uncomfortable accepting more modern views of womanhood. Fearing the dissolution of old values, and particularly family disruption, a female contributor to *Il Lavoro* confessed her difficulties in embracing the "new feminism" of the early twentieth century and urged her *compagne* to "not give up our femininity" and "to remain women despite all the political fights, the social avant-garde, and the progress we have made."[125] On the one hand, radical women, and men, admired American women's lifestyle, particularly their economic independence, their education, and their modernity, understanding that these were essential to women's liberation. On the other hand, they were concerned about the impact that these "libertine" customs could have upon the integrity of Italian family values. "There is no doubt," wrote "*Sora* (sister) Maria" for *Il Nuovo Mondo*, "that the position of the woman and wife in America is infinitively superior to that of Italian women." American women, she explained, are confident, emancipated, and respected by their men; as a result, their conjugal relationships are based on honesty and equality, rather than on gender oppression. But, noted the writer, not all these changes are good. "The woman's emancipation," she clarified, "has taken place at the expense of maternity."[126]

As Virginia Yans-McLaughlin has suggested, the emphasis of radicals on motherhood and their reluctance to seriously challenge conventional gender roles reflected both the pervasive sexism of Italian men and the persistence of traditional family attitudes and practices.[127] As late as 1937, *L'Italiana*, an educational monthly published by the Eleonora Duse Italian Women's Club in Rochester, New York, insisted on identifying Italian women with the domestic realm. Although the paper supported socialist and progressive ideas, its subtitle left no doubt as to what was perceived as the woman's real mission; it read: "A magazine of the Italian woman—*the true* friend of the family" (emphasis mine).

But even if radical efforts produced little change in the family status of Italian women, these efforts succeeded in making women for the first time the subject of public debate and political concern. Female emancipation and politicization did eventually occur, but only gradually. By 1919, when Local 89 was established, many women not only were active union members but also held important administrative posts.[128]

The Anti-Fascist Crusade

After Mussolini became prime minister in 1922, the fight against fascism became the top priority of the Italian American radical press. Existing newspapers of various tendencies, such as *Il Proletario*, *Il Lavoro*, *Il Lavoratore*, and above all *Il Martello*, increasingly concentrated their journalistic warfare against Il Duce and his propaganda. In many ways their fight was an extension of the class struggle that the *sovversivi* had waged against the *camorra coloniale* since the 1880s—and in many cases their enemies were also the same individuals.[129]

As Mussolini's influence grew, new papers joined old ones with the specific goal of combatting fascism. The first of them, *Il Veltro*, was launched in New York in May 1924 by the Italian Chamber of Labor and edited by the Chamber's secretary, Arturo Giovannitti. Its main goal was to reconcile the movement's internal divisions and focus its energy strictly on the anti-fascist campaign. The paper featured sophisticated articles on the political nature of fascism and the condition of Italy under Mussolini's regime written by a broad range of contributors, including socialists Carmelo Zito, Girolamo Valenti, and Frank Bellanca; communists Antonino Capraro and Raimondo Fazio; and social-democrat intellectuals of the caliber of Amedeo Bordiga and Don Luigi Sturzo. It is not clear why such an ambitious paper stopped publishing in 1925, but it may be that the highly theoretical nature of its articles disaffected Italian American workers or unions stopped financing it.

That same year, however, a group of socialists and union leaders in New York founded *Il Nuovo Mondo*, the first anti-fascist daily to appear abroad.[130] The timing of *Il Nuovo Mondo* reflected the *sovversivi*'s growing concerns with Italian events: "Today in Italy," blasted the opening editorial, "even the Mutual Aid Society is a crime, freedom of thought and of press, other than that blindly associated with absolutism and murder, is a crime; the working-class cooperative is a crime, just as it has become a crime to belong to any political party that oppose Fascism, even the liberal or democratic ones." *Il Nuovo Mondo*, promised the editors, intended to stand up against this wanton tyranny and fight with inflexible determination on behalf of the civil rights of the Italian people and for the liberation of the working class. It was going to be to Italian working immigrants what the daily *Forward* was to Jewish workers: "an instrument of justice and education, of freedom and emancipation, of responsibility and guidance."[131]

Located at 81 East 10th Street, between Third and Fourth avenues, a block notoriously known as "the citadel of Italian American anti-Fascism," *Il Nuovo Mondo* quickly grew into the most important organ of anti-fascism in the United States.[132] Its success rested in part upon the support provided by the unions' subsidies and private advertisements, but especially upon the editors' intention of creating a paper for a general audience, rather than for the members of a specific party only.

To appeal to a large readership, *Il Nuovo Mondo* adopted the style of mass-market metropolitan dailies with a tabloid format and a wide range of general features. In addition to articles about political ideology, it covered international political news with a strong emphasis on Italian developments, labor news, and union bulletins. A whole page was devoted to crime news and current events of the city of New York, while the last page featured serialized popular literature. Also, in stark contrast to other Italian American radical papers, *Il Nuovo Mondo* accepted private advertisements.

Transcending the extraordinary array of political ideologies and personalities of the Italian American Left proved, however, much more difficult than the editors had anticipated. Mutual suspicions and quarrels between the communists and social-democrat union leaders increased throughout 1926, eventually resulting in a decisive split.[133]

Besides internecine divisions, *Il Nuovo Mondo* had to also face the Italian government. As early as December 1925, the editors denounced the attempts of the Italian ambassador to the United States to suppress the publication and have its editors prosecuted for their hostile writings against Mussolini.[134] Retailers were threatened, packages containing the copies of the newspaper were confiscated, and the consulates pressured merchants to discontinue their advertising. As if this were not enough, on November 2, 1926, Blackshirts plundered the paper's printing office, wrecking two composing machines.[135] This persistent boycott campaign eventually produced the desired effect: Torn by dissension and bereft of funds, in 1931 the paper passed into the hands of the leaders of the Sons of Italy—a mutual aid organization established originally in 1905 to protect the interests and rights of Italian immigrants that in the 1920s became Mussolini's biggest supporter.[136]

Anti-fascists, however, did not surrender and founded a new daily called *La Stampa Libera.* Edited by Girolamo Valenti (1892–1958), a Sicilian-born socialist and labor organizer who arrived in the United States in 1912, *La Stampa Libera* continued publication until 1938, an extraordinary run considering the economic hardship of the Great Depression and the continual harassment by the fascist regime.[137] An excellent writer and lecturer, Valenti carried on systematic attacks against Mussolini in both the Italian-language and the American presses, unmasking the fascist infiltration of Italian American cultural institutions such as the *Casa Italiana* and the Order of Sons of Italy and the key role played by the *prominenti* in disseminating fascist propaganda through their press.[138]

Il Nuovo Mondo and *La Stampa Libera* were the most enduring and effective organs of anti-fascism, but by no means the only ones. A score of new newspapers sprang up in response to fascism.[139] Among the most original was *La Scopa* (1925–28), a satirical weekly published by the Anti-Fascist League of New Jersey and edited by the dilettante poet Francesco Pitea (see chapter 5). While the tone of most anti-fascist publications was intensely dramatic and polemical, *La Scopa* used satire and humor to expose the dangers posed by Mussolini and his nationalist rhetoric. Its masthead, for example, depicted a worker with a broom in the act of sweeping away all fascist dirt, symbolized by animalistic images of *Il Duce* and his emissaries. Other regular features included poetic invectives against Mussolini and the *prominenti*, comic cartoons, and a column called *"eventi del giorno"* (today's events), which mocked new fascist measures and policies.

Another ambitious anti-fascist paper was *Nazioni Unite*, published in New York City from 1942 to 1946 by a group of Italian intellectual exiles, including Gaetano Salvemini, Massimo Salvadori, and Max Ascoli. Like earlier anti-fascist papers, the purpose of this new journalistic venture was twofold: to discredit fascism and to halt the "fascistization" of the Little Italies, making clear that "love of Italy" did not equal "support of Fascism."[140]

Dismantling decades of pervasive fascist propaganda emanating from the Italian consulate, Italian American cultural institutions, and the mainstream press, including American sympathetic treatment of Mussolini, proved in the end impossible. But while they were unable to stop fascism, radical papers played a crucial role in conceptualizing the anti-fascist struggle and informing Italian Americans on crucial issues facing Italy and Italians.

The radical press accomplished other important goals as well. It was instrumental in promoting education among working-class Italians. In opposition to the commercial press that often worked against the best interests of the immigrants, the *sovversivi*'s papers showed a genuine concern for the welfare of their co-nationals. Lofty ethical standards, a noble sense of mission, and a high quality of writing testified to their belief in the educational value of the press. Through their papers, they fought countless battles to defend the workers' rights and combat discrimination, illiteracy, bossism, social injustice, economic inequality, and fascism. These campaigns brought direct benefits not only to the workers but also to the ethnic group as a whole, and they remain today a valuable evidence of the worldview and dreams of a small but passionate group of radicals.

Politics and Leisure

The Italian American Radical Stage

In 1896, the anarchist poet Pietro Gori, who had just arrived in the United States, published a one-act skit entitled *Primo Maggio* (May Day), which he had written a few years before in an Italian prison. The play told the story of Ida, a young peasant woman who leaves her village and family behind to follow a mysterious stranger to "the country of Love and Truth . . . where the land belongs to all; . . . where freedom is the only law and love the only bond; . . . where misery is unknown and equality guaranteed to all."[1]

Symbolically set on International Workers' Day, the play carried a strong message of liberation and solidarity dramatizing hope, victory, and empowerment for working people. The famous aria of Verdi's opera *Nabucco*: "*Va pensiero, sull'ali dorate . . . ,*" which most Italians knew by heart, opened and closed the play. But Gori reset Verdi's lyric, written originally as a lament of the Hebrews for a home of their own, to new words honoring "the great flowering ideal"—the anarchist and socialist dream of a future earthly paradise where inequality and injustice have been banished. The song begins with an invocation of May, "sweet Easter of the workers," and quickly moves into an exhortatory call for action, a cry meant to stir and galvanize the workers, as evident above all in these two stanzas:

Disertate, o falangi di schiavi,	O phalanxes of slaves, run away from
dai cantieri, da l'arse officine;	The worksites, the parched workshops;
via dai campi, su da le marine,	Flee from the fields, from the swelling seas,
tregua, tregua all'eterno sudor!	Put aside never-ending toil!
Innalziamo le mani incallite,	Let us raise our calloused hands,
e sian fascio di forze fecondo;	Let us join together in a growing force;
noi vogliamo redimere il mondo	We want to redeem our world
dai tiranni de l'ozio e de l'or.	Tyrannized by both sloth and gold.

Compelling music and rhetorical sentimentalism made Gori's *Primo Maggio* an instant classic both in Italy and the United States, where it was performed time and time again, especially on the occasion of radical holidays with Gori himself often playing the guitar, singing, and acting in it during his brief American sojourn. As Robert D'Attilio has suggested, both the play and the song were instrumental in popularizing May Day among Italian immigrant workers.[2]

Gori's success derived largely from the inspirational nature of his plays and the choice of themes dramatizing the immigrant experience. For example, *Senza Patria* (Without Country), another popular play written by Gori in 1899, evoked the ordeal of Giorgio, an impoverished *contadino* who had fought in the Italian war for unification but after becoming increasingly disillusioned with the newly formed state decided to emigrate in search of bread and work denied to him at home. While articulating the pain of abandoning one's country, the play also questioned the meaning of patriotism. When Anita, Giorgio's daughter, tries to convince her boyfriend to leave with her and her father for America, he hesitates, pointing out that he has a duty to serve in the military. "Isn't our country like our mother?" he asks. "A good mother does not simply give birth to her children," replies Anita, "but must also raise them with love." Forced to leave their homeland in search of a better life, migrants, the play suggested, become *i senza patria*—"those without a country"—anti-citizens belonging to a single moral community rather than to a distinctive nation. By disclaiming the relevance of any particular state, Gori in effect gave expression to the internationalism of his time—a sentiment captured above all in the final scene, wherein Giorgio, by now ready to leave, declares with fervor to the audience that there is "only one country, the world; and only one family, the human race."[3]

Gori's plays were among the earliest examples of a rich theatrical culture that was simultaneously the product and the expression of the *sovversivi*'s radical milieu. The theater occupied a very special place in the world of Italian American radicals, supporting their communities, entertaining the workers, and helping to promote radical causes. Like the Left theater of the Popular Front, the *sovversivi*'s stage was "the real cultural center of the radical movement." Next to the press, it represented the most powerful vehicle for political propaganda and education, as well as the primary source of funding for radical papers and other political activities. For, as Irving Howe said, "the theatre was the art form that reached everyone in the immigrant world."[4]

Starting from the late nineteenth century until the 1930s, throughout the United States the *sovversivi* organized "red" theatrical groups known as *Filodrammatiche rosse* with the goal of "spreading the modern ideals of social justice and solidarity through the theatre."[5] The first of them, *La Cosmopolita Operaia*, was formed in Paterson, New Jersey, as early as 1895. At least seven Italian radical theatrical groups functioned in New York City during the first two decades of the twentieth century—the *Filodrammatica dell'Unione Socialista*, the *Filodrammatica sovversiva*, the *Compagnia Drammatica Sociale*, the *Circolo Filodrammatico: "L'avvenire,"* and the dramatic companies "Peppino Capraro," "Enrico [Henrik] Ibsen," and "Germinal." Radical amateur societies sprang up in other small towns as well, like the *Filodrammatica Sovversiva* of Providence, Rhode Island; *I Liberi* of New Britain, Connecticut; and *Arte e Libertà* of Lynn, Massachusetts, which "put [on] hundreds of plays, complete with prompter's box and homemade scenery."[6]

The formation of these groups and their activities were regularly announced in the last pages of the radical newspapers. The available evidence supports three conclusions. First, amateur dramatic companies were widespread and could be found virtually anywhere anarchist or socialist groups operated. Second, theatrical activities were frequent; hardly a week went by without the staging of a play. Third, like the dances and picnics discussed in the previous chapter, radical performances drew large audiences and must therefore be understood as a significant aspect of the *sovversivi*'s culture.

Readers' correspondence on the back pages of radical publications conveys indeed great satisfaction with the outcome of actual performances. A worker from West Hoboken, New Jersey, reported in *Il Grido degli Oppressi* that *Il processo scandalo o gli anarchici di Roma*, a play about police repression against anarchists staged at the Dramatic Hall on July 29, 1892, had been a "triumph," generating $27.50 on behalf of the newspaper.[7] Other financial reports published in the labor press confirm that theatrical events were rather successful, collecting on average between thirty and fifty dollars and occasionally as much as one hundred dollars a night. Admission varied from 5 to 10 cents in the early twentieth century and increased to about 50 cents after World War I, but it usually remained free to children and women. While it is impossible to establish exact turnouts, by comparing earnings and ticket prices we can estimate that between 300 and 500 people, and sometimes as many as 1,000, per night went to see these performances—a very high number if we consider that it matches the figures of the audiences of mainstream performances of the same period.

Paul Avrich's interviews of Italian American anarchists offer further evidence of a rich and vibrant theatrical culture that continued to enliven the *sovversivi*'s radical community well into the 1940s and 1950s. Attilio Bortolotti—in the words of Emma Goldman "one of the biggest men we have in our movement"—reported that in Toronto, where he had emigrated in 1920, the *Gruppo Libertario* had organized a *filodrammatica* that "put on works by Pietro Gori, Gigi Damiani and others." Similarly, Oreste Fabrizi, an Italian socialist–turned–anarchist who came to America after the rise of Mussolini, recalled that in Somerville, Massachusetts, there was a *Filodrammatica* associated with the *Circolo di Cultura Operaia* at the *Casa del Popolo* at 26 Mansfield Street and that it also had "lectures and picnics for la *stampa nostra* [our press]."[8]

Although constantly referred to by other scholars of Italian American radicalism, the *sovversivi*'s dramatic groups and their performances have never been studied. Cultural historians have documented the theatrical activities sponsored by the American labor movement and other ethnic radical groups, such as the Jews, Latvians, and Finns, but the radical component of the Italian American stage has been completely ignored. The specialists in the history of the Italian American theater, Emelise Aleandri and Maxine Schwartz Seller, do not even acknowledge the existence of the *filodrammatiche rosse*, assuming, erroneously, that Italian radicals did not have any interest in arts and letters.[9]

But as this book documents, the *sovversivi* engaged in a wide range of cultural activities and generated hundreds of literary and artistic works that, as some scholars have recently recognized, were as sophisticated as and often better written than many mainstream productions.[10] Among the most prolific playwrights were many well-known figures of the Italian American Left: most notably Riccardo Cordiferro, Arturo Giovannitti, Vincenzo Vacirca, and Ludovico Caminita. With the exception of Cordiferro, who was a fulltime writer and professional playwright, these people wrote in their spare time, in addition to organizing the workers, lecturing, publishing, and editing radical papers. That despite their limited time and financial resources they managed to also compose plays and dramas makes their achievements all the more remarkable.

Radical plays were staged in the *sovversivi*'s social clubs, in unions' auditoriums, in cafés, on picnic grounds, or, in case of special occasions, in hired halls of local theaters. Performances tended to be very long, lasting from 8:00 P.M. until midnight. Plays were never staged alone. Like the American vaudeville, the *sovversivi*'s stage included a wide variety of material such as songs, poems, monologues, dancing skits, raffles, and games like the popular *tombola* (bingo). A grand ball usually concluded the evening. As Irving Howe, discussing the Yiddish theater, has pointed out, "remembering how hard it had been to earn their few pennies, audiences liked to feel they were getting a 'full' evening."[11]

Like the Jewish spectators described by Howe, Italian immigrants also participated actively in the performances they attended. On one occasion, *La Questione Sociale* remarked on the enormous enthusiasm generated by the dramatic performance of *The Cage*, a naturalist play by the French novelist Lucien Descaves (1861–1949), presented at the Social Theatre of Paterson on April 29, 1899, in celebration of May Day. "We could not have wished for a better outcome: huge crowd, splendid recitation, and excellent financial return," it noted. And then it added: "We would like to report above all the profound impression the performance made on the audience, which applauded energetically the most salient scenes, as well as the Neapolitan farce and the choir of revolutionary songs that followed the drama."[12] In sharp contrast to Anglo-Saxon American audiences, which, as noted by Lawrence Levine, had become increasingly "dignified and quiet" by the late nineteenth century, the Italians sang, wept, laughed, cheered the hero, or hissed the villain. They demanded that songs be repeated or new acts be added to prolong a show they were enjoying. When they did not like the play, the director or the producer would often hastily fix the story, improvising new scenes and events to please the audience.[13]

As in the case of other cultural activities sponsored by the *sovversivi*, the receipts of these performances were generally used to subsidize radical groups, newspapers, or solidarity campaigns for political prisoners. Hence, many of the actors involved in the staging were volunteers from the radical community, including many women. Nicola Sacco's wife, Rosina, regularly acted in the plays put on by the radical theater group of Milford, Massachusetts. Sacco proudly remarked that she was "a fine actress" and that together they used "to arrange for dramatic performances and to raise money for all sorts of causes." Jeanne Salemme, an anarchist active in East Boston, also took part with her husband, Joseph, in the performances organized by their club on Maverick Square. And so did many other *sovversive*, such as Fiorina Rossi in Needham, Elvira Catello in East Harlem, and Ernesta Cravello, Ersilia Cavedagni, and Ninfa Baronio in Paterson.[14]

Theater, indeed, as Jennifer Guglielmo has written, offered women "a sanctioned way to move somewhat freely beyond their families" and be active in the movement. Some women even formed their own orchestras and theater groups and occasionally wrote and produced plays that enacted their ideas on women's emancipation, such as *La figlia dell'anarchico* (The anarchist's daughter) by Nena Becchetti, which centered on eight immigrant women—four mothers and their daughters—staging the pain and poverty under which they, and so many other immigrants, lived.[15]

The function of the *filodrammatiche rosse* did not differ much from that of other theaters. A primary role was to provide an opportunity for Italian immigrant workers to socialize and escape the hardships of daily life, coloring their tedious week with a touch of drama and excitement.[16] But, as in the case of other radical theaters, the stage was seen not only as spectacle but also as an important shaper of public opinion and a crucial catalyst in the making of social consciousness. As Colette Hyman and other drama scholars have recognized, the workers' theater reflected essentially an effort "to use working people's leisure hours as a terrain for political education" and "to develop and sustain among working people and their allies the solidarity necessary for bringing about social and political transformation."[17]

The Italian American radical stage was also born essentially as a social and cultural force intended to mold the opinions of the audience and to awaken their political and social consciousnesses. Hence most of the productions were "problem" plays containing a strong indictment of capitalist society and focusing on social issues and problems peculiar to the Italian American community, such as the *padrone* system, ethnic discrimination, and economic hardship.

It is difficult to prove whether political performances effectively succeeded in mobilizing audiences, but one can nevertheless sense the intense emotions they must have evoked.[18] As the following story of Joseph Moro illustrates, radical plays, with their message of vengeance, redemption, and emancipation, did strike a responsive chord among the exploited and disillusioned workers. An Italian immigrant from the Abruzzi region, Moro came to America in 1911, at the age of sixteen, and settled in Stoneham, Massachusetts, working as a shoemaker. Raised within an intense Catholic milieu, he was initially a very religious boy—a "mystic," as he put it. But in 1912 he attended a picnic organized by the *Galleanisti* near Wakefield, Massachusetts, and overnight converted to anarchism. "I found the place just in time to see *Calendimaggio*, a play by Pietro Gori," he said. "I was deeply moved. It inspired me so much that in twenty-four hours I gave up all my religion, all my former beliefs, and started to read anarchist literature." Moro explained that every Saturday he went to Boston to get *Cronaca Sovversiva*, *Il Proletario*, and other radical papers. "That's all I was reading, it kept me going all week long," he recalled. From that moment, Moro worked closely with anarchist groups and served as the last secretary of the Sacco-Vanzetti Defense Committee.[19]

But the Italian American radical stage was not *just* a weapon in the class struggle; it also reflected the artistic needs of the *sovversivi*. In this sense, it tried to satisfy the demands of *both* art and politics, providing a major creative outlet for radical intellectuals as well as an important opportunity for political action. It also acquainted Italian Americans, many of whom had little formal schooling, with literary classics and important social issues and political ideas.

It was with this broad vision in mind that in 1918 Arturo Giovannitti launched the *sovversivi's* most ambitious theatrical venture, the *Teatro del Popolo*, a nonprofit dramatic society with its office located at 112 East 19th Street in New York City. Anticipating the contours of the American workers' theater movement of the 1930s and echoing the mission statements of other radical theaters of the time, the *Teatro del Popolo* intended to provide Italian Americans with an alternative to what it viewed as the banal and frivolous commercial stage. It was meant to be a "school, tribune, and forestage for the elevation of the mind . . . serving the cause of freedom and justice through the means of arts, and promoting critical thinking instead of just fun."[20]

The *Teatro del Popolo* aspired simultaneously to modernity, artistic experimentation, and political emancipation. Its founders recognized the theater's important social function as both a source of entertainment and a political and educational tool. They wanted to create a dramatic society that would invigorate the culture of Italian immigrants and simultaneously fashion a better world. Its mission, as Vincenzo Vacirca, one of the founders, explained, was to cultivate a specifically revolutionary aesthetic, to create an authentically "popular" theater, made by the people for the people, combining art and politics, education and entertainment, thought and action.[21]

The *Teatro del Popolo* presented its performances at the auditorium of the socialist People's House, a large hall that could accommodate 500 spectators. The program of its opening night, on January 26, 1918, included three short performances: a one-act Italian drama entitled *Liberazione* (Liberation), the reading of Oscar Wilde's dramatic story "The Happy Prince" narrated in Italian by Vincenzo Vacirca, and Robespierre's historic speech at the French National Assembly interpreted by Arturo Giovannitti. As in most other Italian American theatrical events, a choir and piano concert closed the evening. The *Teatro del Popolo* continued to operate for about a year, running weekly performances for the entire winter season of 1918. It is unclear why it came to an end, but one can easily guess that, as with many of the *sovversivi*'s educational projects, the financial cost could not be met on a long-term basis.[22]

The *Teatro del Popolo*'s repertoire did not differ from that of other Italian radical amateur companies. Most of the plays were Italian and European classics. Among the favorite Italian authors were Silvio Pellico (1789–1854), Paolo Giacometti (1816–82), Giovanni Verga (1840–1922), and Felice Cavallotti (1842–98). Translations of foreign plays by Alexandre Dumas, Victor Hugo, Émile Zola, and Henrik Ibsen were also regularly produced. But many other productions were written by the Italian American immigrants themselves. Radical publications contain dozens of titles by unknown authors that were staged throughout the country.[23]

Regrettably, these and many other radical scripts have been lost and there are scant, if any, records about their authors. Critical reviews are also rare, but occasionally newspapers presented synopses of forthcoming plays to stimulate readers' curiosity. *Il Proletario*, for example, devoted a whole page to *Luce e tenebre* (Light and darkness), written in 1907 by socialists Arturo Caroti and Gioacchino Artoni.[24] *Il Proletario* described the play as "absolutely new" because, instead of focusing on sentimental plots, such as passionate love stories or the misfortunes of the poor, it reflected the audiences' own experiences. The play put on a political debate between a priest and a socialist in view of governmental elections in a small town in Italy. The competition ended, quite predictably, with the triumph of the socialist speaker. With "remarkable arguments," he persuaded the audience, an honest priest, and even some policemen to join the cause of the oppressed, crushing the forces of "darkness" (religion) with the "light" of socialism. The play ended with the actors singing the "Hymn of the Workers" to the cheers of the audience, which quickly joined in.

Luce e tenebre was eventually performed on February 19, 1908, at the Turn Hall of Paterson, New Jersey. *Il Proletario* reported that the public filled the theater and applauded enthusiastically at the end of each of the three acts. In addition to the play's general idea, minor scenes were also commended for their rousing effect—for example, the newsboy selling copies of the anticlerical newspaper *L'Asino*; the begging woman who was driven out by the priest; and the old man who distributed free red flags to all the spectators in the last act.[25] Like the later, and more famous, Paterson Strike Pageant of 1913, when the strikers acted out their own struggle, *Luce e tenebre* employed techniques meant to promote a greater interaction between art and politics, and between the playwright and the audience. In fact, as we shall see, the *sovversivi* cultivated a close relationship with their audience, mediating between their political purposes and the audience's desire for entertainment.

This dialectical relationship between politics and leisure is also reflected in the *sovversivi*'s use of various popular nineteenth-century European and Italian art forms and styles, including melodramas, poetic dramas, romantic tragedies, "realistic" plays, and *commedie dell'arte*—professional improvised comedies based on intrigue plots, wit, mimes, and spirited wordplay. Indeed, the *sovversivi* were for the most part trying not so much to invent new genres as to reshape existing ones to serve the needs of the labor movement and the immigrant community. Melodrama was by far their favorite form despite its close association with mainstream and commercial theater. Its popularity, as scholars have pointed out, derived largely from its ability to appeal to the spectators' emotions through the use of polarized symbols of good and evil.[26] Adopting this dramatic weapon, the *sovversivi* idealized the hard life of workers over the corrupt, greedy, and lavish world of the middle class, presenting the socialist revolution as the ultimate, and inevitable, triumph of moral virtue over villainy. Like other melodramas, Italian radical plays were designed to impart a moral lesson; hence, they used dialogue and situations that Italian American workers could easily understand and characters with whom they could easily identify. Using conventional genres certainly limited, if not denied, the *sovversivi*'s claim of truly revolutionizing the theater, but it also allowed them to reach a broader audience.

With respect to the content, the stage echoed themes that reflected closely the main ideals of the *sovversivi*: their anti-clericalism, anti-nationalism, anti-militarism, and especially their utopianism and faith in the "Ideal." The subject matter was varied, ranging from the hardship of the immigrant experience to the working-class struggle and, later, anti-fascism. But the main focus was the same in all plays: to expose the problems engendered by industrial capitalism; educate Italian immigrant workers about working-class issues; and promote greater social and political awareness.

Entering this dramatic world allows us, among other things, to grasp the human side, the emotions, and the dedication of the *sovversivi*, revealing the many ways in which they used culture, literary traditions, and their Italian heritage to bring their political message to the immigrant masses. Their plays also offer revealing examples of the *sovversivi*'s conflicting views about class, gender, and ethnicity, denoting both a commitment to the working-class revolution and a connection to their homeland and culture. Indeed, while most of the plays were designed to awaken the workers, they also reflected the importance of traditional Italian values such as family, women's virtue, and honor. Women were occasionally given strong roles, as in the case of Gori's *Primo Maggio*, but were also inevitably depicted as the more gentle sex, who needed the protection of a stronger, virile revolutionary hero. They might have been brave and emancipated, but they also were frail and emotional, easily "offended" by physical labor and therefore still dependent upon men.

Religion was systematically attacked, yet plays were filled with Christian symbols and biblical language. On the one hand, the *sovversivi* may have deliberately employed these traditional aspects of popular culture in order to engage their audiences, as they did with the use of conventional literary forms. On the other hand, they might have been unable entirely to escape conventions despite their open criticism of them. Clearly, as the following plays suggest, family honor and respectability, masculinity, and Catholicism were issues to which the authors, consciously or not, attached much importance as markers of Italian ethnic identity.[27]

Riccardo Cordiferro's Plays

A case in point is the dramatic work of Riccardo Cordiferro, without doubt the most popular and prolific playwright of the early-twentieth-century Italian American community. Cordiferro was born Alessandro Sisca in 1875 at San Pietro in Guarano, in the southern region of Calabria. After completing elementary school in 1886, he was sent to attend the religious college of San Raffaele in Naples. His father planned for him to become a priest, but the boy soon began questioning religion and was expelled from the school after a year. He then continued to study on his own in Naples, revealing a talent for poetry and letters. Some of his early poems were published in literary weeklies and monthlies of the city under the pseudonym Riccardo Cordiferro (Iron-heart), taken from the novel *Ivanhoe* by Walter Scott and eventually replacing his real name.[28]

During these years, stirred by prominent Neapolitan radical intellectuals like Giovanni Bovio, Arturo Labriola, and Matteo Imbriani, Cordiferro began his conversion to radicalism. Like other youth of his generation, he embraced the libertarian values of post-*Risorgimento* Italy: the anti-statism, anti-clericalism, and free thinking. A firm believer in individual freedom, he was especially attracted to anarchist ideas. In his preface to a collection of poems published posthumously in 1967, he described himself as a bohemian, a free spirit and eccentric personality. On another occasion, he explained, "I have a rebellious mind and soul. I don't know the meaning of discipline, order, obedience. . . . I have no master, I don't serve anybody. I don't recognize the authority of any boss."[29]

Cordiferro migrated to the United States in 1892, apparently to avoid military service. He first lived in Pittsburgh, Pennsylvania, and then settled permanently in New York City, where together with his father, Francesco, and brother Marziale he founded *La Follia*, a widely read weekly that lasted until 1947 and featured, among other things, caricatures by the renowned tenor Enrico Caruso. Even though he never officially joined any political group, Cordiferro clearly opposed capitalism and embraced the *sovversivi*'s alternative culture. As the *New York Times* noted, he also was an avowed foe of Mussolini and the Roman Catholic Church, which he constantly attacked in his writings. His radical views won him the admiration and respect of the Italian immigrant workers, even as they earned him enemies among the prominent men of the Little Italies. Threats and persecutions against *La Follia* by the *prominenti* eventually forced Cordiferro to resign from the editorial board in 1909, although he continued to publish his pungent articles and poems.[30]

Cordiferro was an inexhaustible writer: He composed hundreds of poems, romances, and Neapolitan songs.[31] He also wrote two novels and more than thirty lectures, on subjects ranging from literature to history, humor, and working-class issues, that were presented at hundreds of gatherings and demonstrations.[32] But it was in the field of theater that Cordiferro's reputation had no match. His repertoire included twenty-three plays, among them social melodramas, monologues, and comedies.[33] Of the earliest ones—*Il genio incompreso* (The misunderstood genius, 1894), *Per la patria e per l'onore* (For the fatherland and for the honor, 1896), *Dio Dollaro* (God dollar, 1896), and *Il matrimonio in trappola* (The ensnared marriage, 1897)—there exist records only of their production dates, but for later plays scripts are available.

To a certain extent, Cordiferro's productions are not what we would call "proletarian" plays. They lack an explicit political content: They don't talk of strikes or revolutions but focus instead on the immigrant experience. Only one play, *La Rivale* (The rival, 1912), was openly propagandistic. Set against the background of the 1911 Italian war against Tripoli, it glamorized the worldview of a libertarian writer, probably modeled after Cordiferro himself, who consecrated his life entirely to socialism after his wife left him for another man.[34] Yet it would be a mistake to ignore Cordiferro's radicalism, for his art was essentially politically motivated. His texts grew out of a specific political struggle of which Cordiferro was an important producer—a struggle for the moral and political education of the Italian American workers and their emancipation from capitalist oppression.

His most successful play was *L'onore perduto* (The lost honor). Presented for the first time on February 20, 1901, at the Majestic Hall in Harlem, it was later staged hundreds of times by many other companies in and out of the city.[35] The plot was typical of revenge melodramas: full of passion, dark plotting, suspense, and strong emotionalism. It told the story of Alberto and Sofia, a married Neapolitan couple with a young daughter, who, lured by the American dream, migrate to New York. Here, thanks to a *compaesano*, Giuseppe Esposito, who works as a boss, Alberto finds a job in the office of a rich Italian banker on Mulberry Street. Soon, however, he is discharged for allegedly stealing $100. But Alberto is innocent. His deceitful friend Giuseppe has set up him up: He is in love with Sofia and will do anything to get her. Alberto is arrested and falls seriously ill in prison, leaving Sofia alone to fight poverty and growing debts. Giuseppe visits Sofia and promises to free her husband if she consents to sleep with him. Terrified at the thought of sacrificing her "honor," she first rejects him, but the fear of losing her beloved is stronger than her pride and she finally agrees. As promised, Alberto is set free and returns home. But Sofia can't live with her sin and decides to poison herself. Consumed by remorse and near death, she confesses to her husband and mother what she was forced to do for love. Beside himself with pain and anger, Alberto swears revenge over Sofia's dead body, and when Giuseppe arrives to congratulate him on his release, he stabs him. He is then also about to commit suicide when his little girl rushes onto the scene and implores him to live for her.[36]

The premiere of *L'onore perduto* was a great success: Antonio Maiori, the great tragedian of New York's Italian community, played Alberto, while Renata Brunorini, a famous Italian American actress of the early twentieth century, played the heroine. Before the play, a girl of about twelve recited several of Cordiferro's poems while Cordiferro himself seized the opportunity to state his philosophical faith in social anarchy.[37] On one occasion, however, Cordiferro sent the child back onstage to recite a religious hymn when he saw that the audience did not respond well to the anti-clerical overtones of his speech. As someone in the audience complained, "the crowd in the theatre was from the country and attached to the old, worn-out sentiments of humanity." The girl explained that the poem she was about to recite did not express Cordiferro's ideas but was written to please his wife, Lucia Fazio, who was very religious.[38] This incident reveals the fluid interactivity existing between the *sovversivi*'s stage and the audience. The spectators' reactions point out the powerful role of religion and the active role of the audience. But Cordiferro's action illustrates the *sovversivi*'s determination to use the stage as a social force to mold the opinion of the immigrant workers and, at the same time, amuse them.[39]

In 1905, Cordiferro wrote a sequel to *L'onore perduto*, entitled *Giuseppina Terranova ovvero l'onore vendicato* (Giuseppina Terranova or honor revenged). The play opened the following year in New York and was performed dozens of times by other companies. The script was also published as a book and translated into Sicilian dialect and into English.[40] Like *L'onore*, *Giuseppina Terranova* is essentially a revenge melodrama, a story of sexual abuse and vengeance. Both reflected the techniques and themes of sensational melodramas, including "the indulgence of strong emotionalism; moral polarization and schematization; extreme states of being, situations, actions; overt villainy, persecution of the good, and final reward of virtue."[41]

Though Cordiferro resorted to melodrama, his plays sketched vivid portraits of the difficult lives and problems of the Italian American community—from the *padrone* system and the oppressive working conditions to the painful experience of leaving Italy and adjusting to American society. Cordiferro's great popularity can indeed be attributed to the audience's familiarity with his plays' themes. All were only too aware of the abuses of opportunistic bosses and greedy landlords and the unequal distribution of wealth and power. They could easily indentify with the plays' characters and feel involved in the stories. As one reviewer of *L'onore* noted, "the greatest merit of the play is to expose, free from exaggerations, the relation of immigrants to American society as it really is." Cordiferro, wrote another critic, "has created a new form of drama which, from the sources of the myth enters the scenes of real life with all its vices, baseness, and all the injustices of modern society." It was, echoed *La Questione Sociale*, "a study of social truth on immigrant life."[42]

Cordiferro may have favored melodramatic themes and modes as their high passion and sentimentalism made performances more effective and appealing, allowing the audience to respond quickly to his social critique. He satirized society as it was found in the Italian quarter of New York, pointing out its main defects. He vilified the oppressor of the immigrant, be it the boss, the priest, or the capitalist, and made the Italian American worker the hero of his dramatic creations. Among his favorite targets were, of course, the Italian *prominenti*. Cordiferro, like the rest of the *sovversivi*, seized every opportunity to ridicule them. On stage he represented them with all their eccentricities, foibles, and mannerisms, exposing their ignorance, corruption, and arrogance.

In the comedy *Il paese dei cavalieri e dei commendatori* (The country of chevaliers and commanders), for example, he mocked the Italian government's practice of conferring honorific titles on prominent men of the Little Italies to spur patriotic sentiment and combat criticism against the Italian government.[43] The play tells the story of a Neapolitan immigrant who has become rich by contracting unskilled labor in New York. In view of his achievements, the Italian government decides to give him the title of *Commendatore*. Elated by the award, he begins to advance absurd claims over his maid and family. He explains, for example, that from now on he must be called *Commendatore* and not *Signore*. When the maid ironically asks him what she should call his wife, he proudly answers: "*Commendatoressa!*" "And your daughter?" inquires the maid. "*Commendatoressina!*" he replies, ignoring the jarring phonetics.[44]

Especially funny is the scene in which he proudly reads to his family a ludicrous speech he wrote for a banquet that will be given in his honor, imagining it to be profound. At the end of the reading, his friend, a poor artist of radical views, sarcastically tells him: "*Le mie condoglianze!*" (My condolences). Without even noticing the difference between *condoglianze* and *congratulazioni*—congratulations—he warmly thanks the friend.[45]

The boss's clumsiness, ingenuity, and ignorance are heightened by the scorn of the other characters, who seize every opportunity to laugh at his stupidity. Eventually, pressured by his family and his radical friend, he decides to give up the title of *Commendatore* for the sake of domestic peace. Finally, they are all happy and proud of him. As his daughter's fiancé emphatically tells the audience: "I will marry the daughter of a man who renounced the *commenda* to be proud, from now on, of his working-class background." Everybody answers: "Down with the chevaliers, down with the commanders!"[46]

Woven into the play is traditional Italian skepticism toward authority in general and the state in particular, which the peasants considered inherently oppressive and corrupted. By ridiculing the figure of the boss, Cordiferro defied the influence and power of the class of *prominenti* and offered Italian immigrants—isolated, despised, and exploited—a sense of working-class pride and dignity. His implicit message to the audience was that only through a sense of themselves as a group apart, as members of an oppressed class, could the workers deliver themselves from the slavery of the *padrone* system and capitalism.

Cordiferro's social criticism is particularly prominent in *Il pezzente* (The beggar), a monologue in verses that bristles with indignation at class inequality and oppression. First performed in 1895 at the Adler Theatre of New York by the actor Salvatore Melchiorri, it was later restaged hundreds of times by famous artists like Antonio Maiori and Giovanni De Rosalia throughout the United States, as well as in Italy, France, and South America.[47] Published as a book in 1896, it counted twenty editions and sold 60,000 copies.[48] The scene takes place in an empty prison cell, where the convict—"pale, poorly dressed and sorrowful"—transports the audience through the stages of his terrible crime: being poor and hungry. His monologue begins with a plea for mercy and ends with a powerful invective against social inequality and industrial capitalism. The beggar juxtaposes his misery with the luxurious lifestyle of the rich; and against disillusion and resignation, he invokes revolt and struggle. Despite its oversimplifications, Cordiferro's polarization of haves and have-nots pointed to the need for recognizing and confronting social inequality, so as to combat and change the social order. The subject, explained the anarchist Libero Tancredi for *Il Novatore*, was not new, but Cordiferro expressed particularly well the despair of victims of the most squalid and sordid misery.[49]

Cordiferro also used the dire conditions of the workers to attack religion. The protagonist of *Il pezzente* at one point cries out: "God! What an empty word! Oh what a folly! What a sad irony! What a lie! For he who dies of hunger and suffers the insult of the rich, there can be no God."[50] Similarly, in a dramatic scene from *L'onore perduto*, Sofia kneels to a picture of the Madonna and begins to pray. But suddenly she stops and with a gesture of defiance exclaims: "No, no, I don't want to pray to the Madonna any more; I don't want to invoke her because I am convinced that she is deaf to the cries of the suffering; that faith is deception; and that virtue is a lie."[51] Instead of openly attacking religion, Cordiferro presented to the audience the religious disillusionment of people who were victims of oppression or social inequality. As in the case of melodrama, this was in all likelihood a conscious strategy to allow a religious audience to respond to anti-religious propaganda. Using heightened dramatic utterances, Cordiferro enabled the spectators to sympathize with the characters and perhaps even identify with them, sharing their doubts and feelings.

Cordiferro's descriptions of the degradation of Italian immigrant life concealed a sharp critique of American materialism and individualism in defense of the Italian traditional family. This is particularly evident in one of his later dramas, *Mater dolorosa* (Grieving mother), which was originally written for the opera and presented at the Academy of Music of Brooklyn on January 16, 1926. Later converted into a play, it told the story of an Italian American mother whose daughter has become a prostitute, lured by the material promises of the American urban life.[52] In accordance with the sanctioned cultural values of the Italian traditional family, the daughter's sin is described as a terrible, unforgivable insult to the honor and good name of her family. Yet the daughter is also pictured, in the words of one of the characters, as "an innocent victim of the corrupted American environment."[53] It was the luxury and the pleasures of the American city that had seduced and corrupted the young woman. When the daughter decides finally to pay a visit to her mother, her Americanized appearance—her sumptuous dresses and jewelry, her makeup and perfume—is placed in stark contrast with the cherished image of the traditional, virtuous Italian woman. "You must be good," the mother tells her, "you must be humble, pious, as you were once. You must be worthy of me, your brother, and your poor dead father."[54]

But the young woman's repentance is not enough for her brother; she has dishonored him and he cannot forgive her. When he sees that she even had the nerve to bring her lover to their mother's house, he becomes enraged and puts her out. This is too much for their mother, who collapses on the floor and dies. The mother's dramatic death then becomes symbolic of the profound dislocation of the Italian American family—expressed especially in the form of generational conflict—and the erasure of traditional moral values under American materialism and consumer culture.

The negative effects of Americanization on Italian immigrant culture are also implied in *Il marito, la moglie e . . . Fofò* (The husband, the wife and . . . Fofò), a hilarious one-act comic skit about an Italian husband's exasperation over his wife's obsession with her dog, which he blames on the influence of American culture.[55] These plays are also interesting because they bring out the *sovversivi*'s ambivalence toward gender issues. Cordiferro urged women to educate themselves, to break away from religious values, to emancipate themselves. Yet, his plays—to borrow Paula Rabinowitz's words—"remained stuck in traditional renderings of femininity."[56] Women were acknowledged as important participants in the class struggle but were still depicted as subordinate to men and family, their roles still confined to the reproductive and domestic realms. Clearly, the issue of women's liberation receded in the face of the dominant gender distinctions and the belligerent masculinism of the labor movement of the time. Radical Italian men, in particular, seemed incapable of truly questioning male authority, even as they advocated gender equality.[57]

While constrained by contemporary gender prejudices, Cordiferro's plays also opened up the possibility for questioning and subverting traditional conventions. His remarkable success lay in the way he brought together familiar Italian themes and values with social criticism and political satire. We could say that his art represented a negotiation between the interests

of the audiences, which sought romantic, emotional, and spirited performances, and the *sovversivi*'s art, which was inextricably bound to promoting
social and political engagement. The result was a unique fusion of ethnicity,
class, and radical politics: On the one hand he interpreted the world through
Italian ancestral structures, which valorized traditional values such family,
honor, and conjugal fidelity; on the other, he filtered these themes through
the lenses of class and ethnicity to promote class and ethnic interests.

Arturo Giovannitti's Theatrical Production

Arturo Giovannitti's theatrical production also has a complex relation to the
sovversivi's radical culture. Giovannitti, as we will see in chapter 6, was one
of the most important leaders of the Italian American labor movement and a
revered revolutionary poet. But in addition to poems, he also experimented
with fiction and wrote seven plays: *La lanterna verde, Il disertore, Come era
nel principio, La sedia vuota, Il rivale di dio, The Alpha and the Omega,* and
Una donna onesta.

The first three were originally published in his literary review *Il Fuoco*
between 1914 and 1915. Drawing inspiration from World War I, they were
anti-militaristic plays meant to stir opposition to the conflict. Interestingly,
they do not offer any specific interpretation of the causes of the conflict.
They make no explicit charges against capitalism or imperialism. The focus
is rather on the effects of the war, on the trauma, the destruction, and pain it
inevitably causes—a pain that Giovannitti would eventually experience first-
hand when his younger brother Aristide was killed on the front on July 18,
1915, two months after Italy's entry into the war.

La lanterna verde (The green lantern) is a one-act drama about a signal-
man who dies trying to stop a military train on Easter's eve following a thun-
derstorm's destruction of a railway bridge. However, it is not his death at the
center of the story but his old mother's outcry against the insanity of war.
Having already lost two older sons in the war, she cannot bear the pain of yet
another loss and eventually kills herself.[58]

Giovannitti used the mother's pain to give a human face to the war and
convince the audience of its insanity. *Il disertore* (The deserter) further dramatizes these views. The play depicts a military trial against a soldier charged
with desertion. Found ten miles away from his camp, according to the military code he must be executed, for "he who denies his fatherland does not
deserve to see the sun again." One general, however, is convinced that the
soldier is just a poor man gone crazy, for "wars do not create only heroes

but also timorous, fearful men who at the sight of blood and death lose their minds." The jury eventually sentences the soldier to death to deter others from deserting. But after the execution the captain who fired the shot comes back to the camp visibly upset. When asked what happened and why he looks so disturbed, he stammers out: "That man . . . oh no . . . it is not possible . . . Oh God! He looked at the sky with his dark eyes and said: Father forgive them once again because they do not know what they are doing."[59] At this point, the curtains drop, leaving the audience wondering about the soldier's real identity.

Like the mother's suicide, the allegory of Christ's second coming can be seen as an artistic device to promote greater sensitivity about the brutality of war, by moving the audience to sympathize with its victims. This strategy becomes particularly evident in Giovannitti's third and most successful play, *Come era nel principio* or *Tenebre rosse* (As it was in the beginning or Red darkness). Written originally as a short story, it was later modified into a three-act drama and performed on October 10, 1916, at New York's People's Theatre with the actress Mimì Aguglia, a famous Sicilian star whose acting the *New York Times* described once as "powerful and astonishing," in the leading role. An instant success, a year later it was also performed once in English on Broadway.[60]

Set in an imaginary town of contemporary France, the play, in the words of Giovannitti's friend Vincenzo Vacirca, illustrates "the collective social drama, enormous and monstrous, of the war" and, we could add, the dehumanizing effect it has on people. The first act describes the German invasion of a small French village. This, as Vacirca points out, is probably the best, most convincing part of the play: One can feel the growing terror, anger, and pain of the French people forced to capitulate. The real drama, however, regards not the war itself but the collapse of the worldview of the protagonist, Maurizio—a famous poet who believes in socialism, internationalism, and nonviolence. When he is informed that the Germans have occupied the town, he begs his fellow citizens not to resist and not to respond to their violence. But in spite of his pacifism, during his absence his house is attacked and his wife, Bianca, and his maid are raped by two soldiers.[61]

As the second act unfolds, we find out that the incident has transformed the pacifist poet into a brute, and that, thirsty for blood and revenge, he has enlisted in the army. After four months, he loses his eyesight in a fight and returns home. But he is not the same man any longer; the war has awakened in him a primordial instinct. With growing tragic catharsis, the third and final act dramatizes the intense emotions and turbulent passions of Maurizio and his wife as they finally confront each other about what happened on the night of the German invasion. Just when they seem about to reconcile, Maurizio discovers that Bianca is pregnant with the baby of the German soldier and tries to kill her. They fight violently and eventually Bianca grabs a gun and shoots him.

In a sense, the play's message was pretty simple: The war brutalizes and corrupts. Echoing psychological and philosophical arguments of the time, Giovannitti insisted that the war laid bare "the gregarious instinct," the "herd impulse," and the "blind tribal instincts" of men. These views were especially influenced by Freud's theories on the power of instinct, desire, will, and dream and had great resonance among radical intellectuals debating the Great War, as evidenced above all in the anti-war essays by Randolph Bourne.[62]

But *Come era nel principio* is also inscribed with complex meanings about gender and masculinity. As the harsh sexual conflict, both verbal and physical, between Bianca and Maurizio exemplifies, the play could also be read as an expression of what Michael Denning has called the "gender unconscious." Discussing the early American proletarian avant-garde, Denning noted that it was pervaded by "masculinist metaphors of sexual conflict" and "sentimental maternalism." As Michael Topp has argued, sexism was a familiar part of the vocabulary of Italian radicals too. Positive images of revolution, for example, were often compared to women's purity. By contrast, references to "whores" or "fallen" women were used to describe the failures of the movement.[63]

Such masculine rhetoric also informed *Come era nel principio*. The play's language and imagery are deeply gendered. Violence, for example, is male, love female. Maurizio considers himself responsible for his wife's rape in that he failed to protect her. As he explained, "When the woman called her man for help, to protect her, defend her, save her, he wasn't there, he was powerless, without muscles, without the cudgel. He had spent his life feminizing an entire race of warriors with his naïve sentimentalities of peace and brotherly love." Enfeebled, he transforms himself into a brute to prove that he is still a man. Bianca, by contrast, is compassionate, patient, and submissive. She promises Maurizio that she will "suffer in silence . . . stifle any pride, and kill any rebellion."[64] She will do anything as long as he gives her love. The title itself, "as it was in the beginning," implied a return to traditional patriarchy. Yet, the play's ending, with Bianca eventually killing Maurizio, could also suggest a rebuff of masculinity and a vindication of the *sovversivi*'s underlying belief in equality and love. The whole text, indeed, is multilayered—

permeated by a strategic ambiguity with competing meanings and ideas that enabled different interpretations.

The only other plays of Giovannitti that have survived, *The Alpha and the Omega* and *Il rivale di Dio*, explore the circumstances that compel the poor to commit crimes. *The Alpha and the Omega*, presented in 1917 at Brooklyn's Prospect Hall, is a bold, experimental text in the form of an imaginary conversation between John D. Rockefeller and a burglar, caught by the millionaire in his home.[65] *Il rivale di Dio* (God's rival), published through installments in *Il Veltro* in 1924, also delves into the question of what constitutes evil. It tells the story of a doctor renowned all over the world for his ability to cure blindness and his generosity toward the poor, whom he treats for free. But we learn that in order to complete his doctoral studies and fulfill his dream of using medicine to help the poor, he had killed his landlord, a greedy and insensitive man, and stole his money. At first sight, the central theme seems to be the moral condemnation of modern society, but here, too, the real drama takes place in the mind of the doctor, who is haunted by his crime. The real question that Giovannitti tries to untangle is whether it is ever right to use immoral means to achieve moral ends.

A striking feature of Giovannitti's plays is the psychological depth of his characters. In this respect, his theatrical production went beyond the scope of most Italian American radical plays. In contrast to other dramatic productions that were confined to themes and problems of the ethnic community, his work reflected the influence of American and European avant-garde—especially Brecht, Ibsen, and Strindberg—which tried to overcome the formulaic conventions of the commercial theater and create new forms of art. Unlike the melodramatic plots with their predictable endings, Giovannitti's plays were essentially explorations of the multiple and contradictory aspects of human nature. Instead of one-dimensional heroes, described purely in terms of good versus evil, his characters had both negative and positive traits. At the core of his art lay in fact the question of human existence itself.

Alberico Molinari's I martiri di Chicago

A play closer to the acclaimed "proletarian" theater of the 1930s is Alberico Molinari's *I martiri di Chicago* (Chicago's martyrs). The son of a well-to-do landowning family in Cremona, near Milan, Alberico Molinari (1876–1948) became one of the most important figures of reformist socialism in the United States. His political activism began in Italy, while he was studying medicine at the University of Modena. By the age of twenty-four, he was an active and influential member of the Italian Socialist Party. A powerful orator, he carried on subversive propaganda among agricultural and industrial workers in his native region. As a result, in February 1902, just a few months after receiving his degree in medicine, he was arrested and eventually sentenced to three months in prison for "incitement to class hatred." The incarceration, however, never took place because Molinari, guessing a likely conviction, managed to leave Italy before the warrant was issued. Like other *sovversivi*, he migrated to the United States to escape political persecution.[66]

He first settled in New York City, where he began contributing to *Il Proletario*, but in 1905, following the arrival of his wife and daughter, he moved to Pennsylvania, establishing a medical practice in Philadelphia and the mining communities of Wilkes-Barre and Scranton. Because of his generosity and kindness, he soon won the respect and affection of local Italian immigrants, among whom he became known as "*il medico dei poveri*," the doctor of the poor.[67]

In addition to his medical practice, Molinari devoted much of his time and energy to political activism, conducting conferences, contributing to socialist publications, and helping to organize Italian workers. In 1907 he founded *L'Ascesa del Proletariato*, an important socialist publication that lasted until 1910. According to the Italian consul in Philadelphia, his socialist campaign was very influential and won many converts among the Italian immigrants who had settled in Pennsylvania. Frustrated, in 1909 the consul wrote to the Ministry of the Interior in Rome:

> It is because of his propaganda that many hard-working and good young men, who before his arrival did not care about anything but work, are today rebellious to all that is justice and law. At Wilkes-Barre, Old Forge, Plainsville and all places where Molinari goes there are now active anarchists and socialists—whereas, until a few years ago, there were only people full of reverence and love of the motherland.[68]

From 1911 to 1921, Molinari was an active member of the reformist Italian Socialist Federation, founded by Giuseppe Bertelli, and the editor of its official organ, *La Parola del Popolo*. Compelled by family reasons (his wife was homesick), in 1921 he left the United States and returned to Italy. After Mussolini's coming to power, he became involved in clandestine anti-fascist activities and in 1930 was arrested and sentenced to five years of confinement on the island of Sardinia.[69]

Besides editing and contributing to radical publications, Molinari published a book of aphorisms devoted to the moral education of the workers, a treatise on the theories of the Italian criminologist Cesare Lombroso, an historical account of the Haymarket affair, and two plays: a one act-drama entitled *La bandierina di Karl Marx* (Karl Marx's little flag) and the already mentioned *I martiri di Chicago*.[70]

Written in 1909, *I martiri di Chicago* is essentially an historical reconstruction of the famous incident in Chicago's Haymarket Square, where, on May 4, 1886, a bomb exploded, causing the injury of sixty-eight policemen and the arrest of eight German immigrant anarchists. Despite the lack of specific evidence against them, four were hanged, while a fifth killed himself in his cell. The other three were later pardoned.[71]

In dramatizing the event, the play used biographical material and followed closely the historical developments of the case. Its main goal was didactic: to educate the audience about the Haymarket tragedy and expose its injustice. The play, however, went beyond historical commemoration. For Italian immigrants, as well as other workers, the martyrdom of the Haymarket anarchists came to symbolize revolt, audacity, defiance, and integrity. The generating force behind the story was the belief in class solidarity and internationalism; its primary message was to encourage unionization by linking the heroic struggle of the Haymarket anarchists with the working-class struggle. While perhaps too celebratory and emphatic, the script was nevertheless compelling and moving.

The first act describes the tragic events that led to the arrests of the five German anarchists: August Spies, Michael Schwab, Adolph Fisher, Samuel Fielden, and George Engel. The scene takes place at the editorial office of the *Arbeiter Zeitung*, a German anarchist publication. A careful setting tries to re-create a distinctively revolutionary milieu. Some pictures of international heroes of the working-class movement, a red flag, and a banner with the slogan "Long live eight hours" hang on the walls. The act ends with the police breaking into the office of the *Arbeiter* and arresting all those present.

The second and third acts focus on two other victims of the Haymarket affair, Louis Lingg and Albert Parsons. A carpenter of anarchist ideas, Linng chose to kill himself in his cell by exploding a cartridge of dynamite in his mouth, rather than die by the hand of the authorities. Parsons, instead, successfully escaped the arrest but decided to turn himself in during the trial, in solidarity with his comrades. Linng's and Parsons' actions are glorified, represented by Molinari as ultimate acts of pure heroism. Through their examples, Molinari wanted to impart a lesson on the importance of class unity and self-respect.

The fourth and final act jumps to November 10, 1887, the day before the execution, and ends with the condemned men going to the scaffold and shouting: "Long live Socialism! Long live Anarchy!" This declamatory device, which became very popular in the agitprop productions of the 1930s (notably Odets' *Waiting for Lefty*), was clearly meant to involve and arouse the spectators.

One might wonder what motivated Molinari to write this play. Unlike anarchists and syndicalists, he believed that social transformation should be achieved through gradual reforms and education, not violent revolution. One possible explanation is that Molinari was outraged at the unfairness of the proceedings and believed that the men were executed not for the sake of justice but to disrupt the American revolutionary movement. Much like the later case of Sacco and Vanzetti, he saw the trial of the Haymarket anarchists as a travesty of justice and used it to expose the myth of America as a land of liberty. "Taken as a whole, the American people," wrote Molinari, "believe what the mainstream press wants them to believe. There is no country in the whole world like the United States, where the press has the power to mold the sentiments of public opinion. In no other country is the press so completely in the hands of the capitalist class as in the United States."[72]

Molinari wanted essentially to vindicate the Haymarket anarchists and give the audience a sense of the great ideals and dreams that moved them. As the lawyer for the Haymarket defendants explains to the audience in the play's concluding speech:

> They have been portrayed as blood-thirsty men but they were of peaceful and generous disposition, loved by all those who came to know their pure and altruistic spirit. It seemed natural to them to live for a sublime ideal and now it seems natural to them to die for it. They have been called anarchists, but by anarchy they meant an ideal society where order and justice are possible without oppression.[73]

The play offered many moments like this that called for high lyricism and passionate acting. The major strength lay exactly in the ardent dialogues of the characters; their words powerfully resonated with the idealism, courage, and fervor of the time. With its historical setting and characters, *I martiri di Chicago* was realist in form and highly predictable, but it fulfilled the idea of a good revolutionary play—strong, moving, and propagandistic. Like Gori's *Primo Maggio*, Molinari's play helped popularize the Haymarket tragedy among Italian immigrants, taking on, as Rudolph Vecoli has documented, almost a religious bent among Italian radicals in the United States with the martyrs of Chicago frequently portrayed as Christ-like figures.[74]

Ludovico Caminita and the Romance Plays

A dramatic genre used frequently in the Italian American radical plays was also the romance—the impossible love story between a man and woman belonging to different social classes, as narrated in *Orgoglio funesto* (Fatal pride), a drama in three acts published in installments in *Il Proletario* throughout 1937.[75] Gino, the son of a wealthy baron, is in love with Livia, the family's maid, with whom he grew up. But his parents insist that he needs a wife more appropriate to his social status and demand that he marry the daughter of a well-known marquis, a friend of theirs. Gino refuses to give in, preferring to face poverty than a marriage without love. Banished from his native house, he marries Livia, converts to socialism, and starts work as a typographer. But he soon falls ill and eventually dies. When the news of his death reaches his parents, his mother, consumed by remorse, commits suicide.

Using the techniques and narrative modes of naturalist novels in the style of Émile Zola or Gustave Flaubert, plays like *Orgoglio funesto* or, among others, Gori's *Gente Onesta* (Honest people) essentially provided a critique of the bourgeois world, exposing its immorality, corruption, and hypocrisy. Simply put, they were a mockery of middle-class respectability.

Sonata Elegiaca (Elegiac sonata) is another compelling example of this genre. Its author, Michele (alias Ludovico) Caminita, was born in Palermo, Sicily, in 1878 and came to the United States in 1902. An active socialist in Italy, he converted to anarchism after hearing a lecture by Pedro Esteve and by 1906 had become, according to American authorities, "one of the most dangerous Italian anarchists." In 1907 he began editing *La Questione Sociale*, and when a year later the American government banned it from the mails he launched *L'Era Nuova*, which was eventually also suppressed by federal authorities, in 1917. While integral to the Italian American anarchist community, Caminita also forged important connections to other anarchist groups, particularly Spanish and Jewish. From 1908 to World War I, he worked at the office of *Mother Earth,* the anarchist publication of Emma Goldman, and between 1917 and 1918 he contributed to *Blast,* the bi-weekly published by Alexander Berkman in San Francisco. He also interacted with Ricardo Flores Magon and other Mexican anarchists, giving lectures for the *Partido Liberal Mexicano* (which helped organize the Mexican revolution of 1910) and contributing drawings for its organ, *Regeneraciòn.*[76]

A draftsman by trade, Caminita was highly educated. He wrote and published several sociological books, a biography, a novel, and two plays.[77] He also composed cartoons, drawings, and posters—most notably the cover for the *Blast* issue of February 5, 1916, and an anti-militarist cartoon against Italy's invasion of Libya published by *Mother Earth* in September 1912, creating a stir among the Italian community of Paterson for its alleged anti-patriotism.[78]

American authorities believed the group of *L'Era Nuova* to be behind the 1919 bombing of Wall Street and considered Caminita, who had launched another anarchist paper, *La Jacquerie*, to be directly involved or to have knowledge of who was involved. He was arrested on February 14, 1920, and interned at Ellis Island, an experience he recounts in his autobiographical book *Nell'isola delle lacrime: Ellis Island* (The island of tears, 1924). Threatened with deportation and questioned by the police, he eventually cooperated with them, providing crucial information on anarchist groups. In 1922, he publicly recanted his anarchist beliefs in the *New York World*, for which he had begun to work.[79]

Sonata elegiaca was first presented at New York's Olympic Theatre on May 16, 1921, while Caminita awaited the decision of the American government on whether he would be deported to Italy. Organized in four acts, the plot revolved around the lives of Errico Parsons, an artist of working-class origins who had become rich writing commercial novels, and Lillian Owen, his daughter's piano teacher, who was active in the working-class movement. Errico is a cynical, disillusioned man, tired of the superficiality and frivolity of his environment, and is slowly overcome by the vitality and revolutionary fervor of Lillian. Pressured by her, he agrees to give a speech on behalf of the workers and soon finds himself immersed in her revolutionary struggle. He soon learns that the police want to arrest Lillian and tries, in vain, to convince her to leave the city. Eventually, policemen break into her apartment, find some dynamite in the closet, and arrest her. We learn, however, that Lillian is innocent—the dynamite had been placed there by order of the police captain, who in turn had been convinced to do so by Errico's wife. Worried that her husband's involvement with the workers could endanger their social reputation, she had promised the captain, in love with her, to give herself to him if he helped her. When Errico finds out the truth it is too late: Lillian has already died in prison.[80]

Contemporary critics and friends characterized *Sonata elegiaca* above all as a moral exposé of bourgeois hypocrisy and conventionalism. With pungent sarcasm, Caminita juxtaposed Errico's sophisticated but immoral world of manners and wit with Lillian's poor but earnest and caring environment. Considering the time and circumstances of its creation, *Sonata elegiaca* can also be seen as a reflection of the author's own experience in the aftermath of the Red Scare. The figure of Errico Parsons is in many ways clearly auto-biographical: Errico's political cynicism represents Caminita's own repudiation of anarchism while his torment echoes Caminita's likely inner struggle between his revolutionary past and his adjustment to bourgeois society.

Anti-Fascist Plays

As we have seen, by the mid-1920s the *sovversivi*'s main preoccupation became fighting Mussolini. That fascism was the new *raison d'être* of Italian American radicalism is amply reflected in the stage too. Many of the plays performed during the 1920s and 1930s were essentially anti-fascist plays—written by, among others, Vincenzo Vacirca, Virgilio Gozzoli, and Carlo Tresca.

"One of the most genuine and interesting figures of Italian socialism," Vacirca was born in Sicily. At thirteen he joined the local section of the Socialist Party and at sixteen was arrested and sentenced to twenty-six days in prison for organizing and leading a revolt of Sicilian peasants. Between 1902 and 1907 he conducted an intense campaign of propaganda, covering important positions for the Italian Socialist Party and directing important socialist newspapers such as *L'Azione Socialista* of Bari, *Parola Socialista* of Ravenna, and *Secolo Nuovo* of Venice.[81]

In 1908 he began his long journey as a political emigre, which brought him first to Brazil (1908), then to Argentina (1908–11), and finally to the United States, where he lived from 1913 to 1919 and then again from 1925 to 1946. His first six years in America were spent between New York and Chicago, organizing Italian American workers and editing socialist newspapers such as *Lotta di Classe*, *La Parola dei Socialisti*, and *Notizia Quotidiana*, which he founded in Boston.

An anti-militarist, he vehemently opposed Italy's entry into the Great War, and during one of his anti-war speeches in New Orleans, in 1915, he was shot by an unidentified group of Italian nationalists. In 1919, after twelve years of exile, he returned to Italy, where he was elected a member of the Chamber of Deputies for the Socialist Party. Sent to Russia by the party, he interviewed Lenin, Trotsky, and Kamenev and wrote a series of articles on the state of socialism in Russia for *Avanti!*, the official organ of the Italian Socialist Party. These articles were later published in the form of an important, but neglected, book, *Ciò che ho visto nella Russia Sovietica* (What I have seen in Soviet Russia).

Instead of the long-awaited socialist victory, in Italy he witnessed the rise of fascism. His opposition to Mussolini was so intense that the Blackshirts tried to kill him on several occasions. In 1925, after being sentenced to five years in prison for his campaign against the fascist government, he returned to the United States to escape imprisonment, distinguishing himself as one the most active anti-fascist organizers and orators. He conducted propaganda tours, directed the anti-fascist daily *Il Nuovo Mondo*, and founded his own newspapers: *L'Internazionale, Il Solco,* and *La Strada*.[82]

Local fascists in America threatened his life many times and in 1927 tried to kill him with an iron pipe in a New York City subway station. Luckily, he got away with only several stitches in his head. In the meantime, the fascist Italian government passed a law against the *fuorusciti* that deprived them of Italian citizenship and confiscated all their properties. The first of these decrees was issued against Vacirca, Carlo Tresca, and Pietro Allegra.[83]

In addition to intense journalistic and anti-fascist activity, Vacirca also wrote many political books, three social novels, and five plays.[84] *Madre* (Mother) is, unfortunately, the only play that has survived. Written in 1931, it was published in Chicago by the Italian Labor Publishing Bureau and presented for the first time on April 19, 1931, at the Civic Repertory Theatre in New York. The premiere had a full house and was received with great enthusiasm. As Arturo Di Pietro wrote for *Il Nuovo Mondo*, "The audience, which included the modest worker as well as the professional and the artist, did justice to this work. As we had predicted, it was a great success both for its subject and its literary and artistic value. Since the first dialogs, the drama got the attention of the audience, which followed it with intense agitation, bursting into warm and spontaneous applause, and calling enthusiastically author and actors at the end of each act."[85]

Madre was the dramatic story of a family torn apart by the advent of fascism. Giorgio, the first-born, is a good lawyer and a convinced anti-fascist. But his brother Leonardo, who is younger, impetuous, and arrogant, has been seduced by the rhetoric of fascism and joined the local Blackshirts. For him fascism represents modernity, vitality, Italy's redemption and future. Disgusted, Giorgio tries to dissuade him: "Don't you see Italy plunging into the abyss? Don't you see the torrents of hatred that you have stirred up? Don't you see your superiors, yesterday's thieves, getting rapidly rich at the expense of the country?"[86]

To the despair of their poor mother, who cannot comprehend how political ideology can be stronger than family ties, they grow more and more apart, each in the certainty of being right. In the meantime, as fascist repression against dissenters intensifies, Giorgio is forced to flee. He returns home after three years of exile in Paris to organize a revolt against the regime. For the first time, he finds his brother changed—he seems quieter, more humble, and more mature. After a short and moving reunion with his mother and fiancée, Giorgio again leaves the house to join other anti-fascists. When he comes back, terrible news awaits him: Leonardo, repented and ashamed of his support for Mussolini, has killed himself.[87]

The play's purpose was to illustrate not only the negative impact of fascism on the political life of the nation but also the devastating effect it had on the private lives of Italians. *Madre* exposed the brutal repression of freedom, the corruption of the regime, the violence used to dominate people, and the suffering of many, like Giorgio, forced to hide or live in exile. But, more important, like the anti-war plays it explored the disruption of human relationships in the face of terror, coercion, and force—the disintegration of the family, the repression of emotions, the loss of humanity itself. Leonardo's dramatic suicide was the most poignant allegory of this loss of human feeling and self-respect. But as the title suggests, it was the figure of the mother with her sorrow, her love, and abnegation who dominated the entire drama, awakening in the spectator a desire for justice and redemption.

Like other radical plays, *Madre* helped carry the *sovversivi*'s views and dreams outside of the narrow political circles and groups and into the larger community of Italian immigrant workers. As Ernesto Valentini put it, *Madre* was "a pure revolutionary act of useful and effective propaganda." Di Pietro for *Il Nuovo Mondo* said: "it was Vacirca's most important contribution to the anti-Fascist cause. It by itself could usefully substitute fifty speeches."[88] Clearly, the play drew its vitality and strength from the author's own personal experience of fascism and his vision of a more humane and just society. But like other plays discussed here, it also relied on ancestral values of Italian culture that could evoke immediate emotional involvement. Like Cordiferro, who used honor to denounce the exploitation of Italian immigrants at the hand of the boss, Vacirca resorted to family drama to redress the profound injustice caused by fascism.

Fascism was also the subject of two plays by the anarchist Virgilio Gozzoli: *Il Cancro* (The cancer) and *Il Ritorno* (The return), both of which re-created the terror of the fascist regime. A mechanic by trade, active organizer, newspaper editor and contributor, as well as a self-taught poet and playwright, Gozzoli represented in many ways the quintessence of the transnational *sovversivo*. Forced into exile in 1921, he lived in many different cities, including Paris, Luxembourg, Barcelona, and finally, from 1938 until the late fifties, New York, where he joined the editorial board of Tresca's *Il Martello* and later published his own paper, *Chanteclair* (1942–45).[89]

Tresca too ventured into playwriting, composing two anti-fascist plays: *L'attentato a Mussolini ovvero Il segreto di Pulcinella* (The attempt on Mussolini's life or Pulcinella's secret) and *Il vendicatore* (The avenger).[90] *L'attentato a Mussolini* was originally scheduled to open on Sunday, December 13, 1925, at New York City's Central Opera House. The actors were ready to go on stage in front of several thousand spectators when local authorities broke into the theater and stopped the performance for violating the "Blue Laws," which forbade entertainment on Sundays.[91] The Blue Laws, however, were just a pretext. As Nunzio Pernicone has explained, the real reason behind the closing of the show was the attempt of Italian fascist authorities to prevent "an injurious theatrical performance" and to silence Tresca, whom Mussolini's regime considered the "*deus ex machina* of anti-Fascism" in America. Having learned of his play, Italian consular officers had promptly informed the Department of Justice of Tresca's violation of the blue laws, compelling local authorities to intervene and close the performance.[92]

The subject of Tresca's play was indeed cause for embarrassment, if not worry, for fascist emissaries in the United States. Inspired by true events, the story unveiled a plan conceived by Mussolini's foremost followers, Roberto Farinacci and the renegade syndicalist Edmondo Rossoni, to infiltrate anti-fascist opponents and convince them to organize an attempt on Mussolini's life. The attack was to be promptly stopped and the attempt on Mussolini's life would become the pretext for carrying out a powerful repression.

L'attentato a Mussolini did not possess the poetic elegance and sophistication of other *sovversivi*'s works but excelled at satire and inventiveness. Using a plain language, at times characterized by coarse dialogue, it brought alive the bleakness and gross materialism of fascism. Tresca used the play to expose the illegal means used by the fascist regime to crush the opposition. The State Department's interference with the play's recital using such a lame excuse as the Blue Laws, which were regularly broken by millions New Yorkers, also indicated Mussolini's ties to both Italian consular offices and the U.S. government.

Ironically, the performance shutdown generated more curiosity about and sympathy toward the play. The people who went to see the performance at Bryant Hall on January 23, 1926, were so many that hundreds could not be accommodated. Taking place on a Saturday instead of a Sunday, the play was this time beyond the police's power to do anything about.[93]

The Italian American radical theater remained primarily a first-generation phenomenon. Unlike the Yiddish or the Finnish ethnic theaters, which were important agents of Americanization, the Italian American radical stage kept a strong bond to the homeland and Italian culture and events. The plays were written and performed in Italian. The settings, themes, characters, and audience were also unmistakably Italian. The cessation of large-scale immigration with the new quota laws of 1924 shrank Italian immigrant audiences and influence. Serving extremely poor communities, the *sovversivi*'s dramatic societies also lacked a stable or permanent support. Like that of the radical press, their survival depended on erratic subsidies from friends, parties, and subscriptions, and whatever profit came from the box office was always used to fund other radical activities.

These factors, combined with the advent of movies and radio, made the decline of the *sovversivi*'s theater inevitable. Radical groups continued to put on performances on special occasions throughout the 1930s and even after World War II, attracting a coterie of dedicated militants. But the days when hundreds of Italian workers attended plays on a weekly basis were long gone—and never came back.

During its existence, however, the Italian American radical theater produced an admirable stream of plays that included a great variety of genres, themes, and meanings. As this chapter has demonstrated, these productions played an important role in the Italian radical movement and in the lives of immigrant workers. They were an important means of educating audiences about labor issues, sustaining the movement, and supporting radical campaigns. The theater gave a dramatic form to ideas that were already propagandized through the press, speeches, and group meetings, amplifying and invigorating the *sovversivi*'s radical message. They taught important lessons about working-class solidarity and internationalism; they also gave voice to the dreams and aspirations of the immigrant workers; finally, they provided working men and women, particularly those who were illiterate, with an opportunity—sometime the only opportunity—to engage in the central issues of their time and to question existing structures of power.

Italian American
Literary Radicalism

> What intellectuals write for public consumption is more impor-
> tant than what movements they join or what petitions they sign.
> Richard Pells, *Radical Visions and American Dreams*

In addition to parties, newspapers, and theatrical groups, Italian immigrant radical politics also spawned a rich artistic and literary culture. The revolutionary syndicalist Arturo Giovannitti, for example, emerged as one of the most articulate radical voices of the early twentieth century, greatly admired not only by his co-nationals but by Americans as well. Progressive sculptor and illustrator Onorio Ruotolo became one of New York's most distinguished artists,[1] while communist Pietro Di Donato, whose *Christ in Concrete* was chosen as a Book-of-the-Month Club novel in 1939, has been recognized as one of the most effective "proletarian" writers.[2]

While we now know something of these artists, no attempt has been made to study the larger radical culture of which they were a part. Although a few literary scholars—Martino Marazzi, Fred L. Gardaphè, and Francesco Durante[3]—have recently brought attention to the radical writing of Italian Americans, particularly that which emerged from the Great Depression, the role of literature in the life of the *sovversivi* and the narratives, poems, and dramas they produced still remain, as Nunzio Pernicone has lamented, an untouched field.[4] Significantly, this indifference toward the radical tradition persists even though more and more scholars, including Giuseppe Prezzolini, the director of the Casa Italiana of Columbia University during the 1930s and 1940s, have recognized that the best Italian American writing came from the pens of political radicals.[5]

The reasons for the lack of interest in Italian American literary radicalism can be attributed in part to Anglo-Saxon disdain for things Italian as well as to objective difficulties inherent in the sources themselves because almost all the texts are in Italian. But this neglect is also a result of the marginal role that American and Italian American literary studies have traditionally given to radicalism. Although the cultural legacy of the U.S. Left is now under serious reconsideration[6]—especially regarding the 1930s—literary critics, with their emphasis on the aesthetic categories of "quality," "value," and "cultural achievement," have tended to treat literary radicalism as a subaltern phenomenon, dismissing it, often indiscriminately, as nothing but political propaganda and assuming that the official attitude of socialists, anarchists, and communists toward culture was a negative one.[7]

Contrary to general perception, the *sovversivi* held literary and artistic expression in very high regard. "Art," explained the communist-oriented paper *Alba Nuova*, "is the highest expression of the human mind," and "to disregard the importance of culture and education in the name of political activism is the equivalent of sowing without reaping."[8] Not only did the *sovversivi* recognize the central role of art and literature in human life, they also engaged in sophisticated discussions about the relation of art and revolution, in an effort to create an entirely new aesthetic culture to fit the needs of workers.[9] Nor were they indifferent to canons of beauty and style; as one anarchist, Carlo Prato, pointed out, "independently from the subject or the topic, the most important thing is the art of writing, the artist's ability to write well."[10]

Moreover, the *sovversivi*'s interest in and sensitiveness to literature and art are evident from the pages of their newspapers, which published in great abundance serialized novels, short dramas, poetry, and drawings. Many of these writings were the works of renowned international writers and revered Italian socialist novelists, such as Edmondo De Amicis or Leda Rafanelli Polli. But other stories were written by working-class men and women, who often used pseudonyms or did not even bother to sign their work.

The plots varied, but the themes were those typical of proletarian and socialist literature—that is, a literature written for the workers, about workers, and from a left-wing perspective: narratives of political oppression and injustice, working-class life, and revolution. The term "proletarian" in American literature is generally used to refer to the literary works produced by the 1930s generation of artists and intellectuals aligned with Marxist/Leninist ideology and the Communist Party.[11] As the following discussion will show, the literary writing of Italian immigrant radicals was proletarian long before the Depression era. True, the *sovversivi* never used the term "proletarian literature," but they did consciously align with the workers and were directly involved in the labor movements of their time. This allowed them to write from the "inside" and speak of a world with which the workers could identify. Moreover, like most proletarian literature, Italian immigrant radical stories and poems included agitators and workers as the main heroes and overt political propaganda as a constitutive part of the text. In this respect, Italian immigrant radical literature would probably fall into the category of agitprop production, or in other words directly political art, art of commitment, art with a message.[12] Behind the literary pieces we can always feel the writer's sense of responsibility and commitment to transform society. The tone is usually dramatic, the message rhetorical, the intent explicitly didactic.

While many would probably see in this overt political propaganda the major weakness of literary radicalism—along with a justification of its alleged inferiority—a close and serious reading of these texts can tell us much about the political and ideological base of the Italian immigrant radical culture.

The Novelettes

Until the 1930s, when the expansion of popular culture and secondary education made books more marketable, the central form of Italian immigrant radical literature was the short story, not the novel. The absence of novels also probably had to do with the *sovversivi*'s intense absorption in labor struggles and propaganda, which left little time for writing long books. Called *novelle* or *bozzetti*, these tales ranged in length from about 1,000 to 5,000 words and were published in newspapers and magazines, appearing, if they were too long for one issue, in serial form in two or three consecutive installments.[13]

Focusing on a single major incident and character, most of these stories were variations on the theme of class oppression and social inequality: explorations into how "the other half" lived, dramatizations of the world of labor and immigration, or social exposés of the evils of capitalist society. Their primary characters were working-class men and women, prostitutes, beggars, orphans, and hoboes. Using the same literary strategies and narrative modes as muckracking literature, these stories aimed at describing the bitter conditions brought by industrial capitalism, while at the same time giving expression to the struggle and aspirations of radical agitators. Realism, in this respect, was closely identified with social purpose.

Not surprisingly, immigrant life, with its degradation and hardship, was one of the most popular subjects of narration. The massive migration of poor Italians between 1890 and 1920 represented without doubt the starting point in the making of the Italian American literary consciousness. Like most new immigrants, Italians lived in horribly crowded and unsanitary slums and worked under brutal conditions for preposterously low pay.[14] Struck by the poor living conditions of their co-nationals, many felt compelled to voice the disillusionment with life in the New World. For example, in "Scenes from the Street," the author, a woman named Fanny Barberis Monticelli, re-creates the desperation of an immigrant woman who has no money to feed her children. A victim of capitalism, she is eventually arrested by a policeman for accepting a crust of bread from a kind passer-by.[15]

Another woman, Matilde Bertoluzzi, wrote a story about a young Italian boy "about ten years old, thin, pale, with big and intense eyes that revealed infinite sadness," who is forced to sell plaster figurines in the rich neighborhoods of New York City.[16] The poor life of the child is set against the background of the indifferent, superficial world of the well-to-do families. As Walter Rideout has pointed out, the device of juxtaposition was a standard technique in radical novels.[17] The contrast, in this case, served to uncover the miserable conditions of life of the immigrants; to arouse moral indignation, social criticism, and compassion; and, above all, to expose the faults of capitalism. The story ends with a cliché of socialist literature: the cry for revenge and promise of justice. Describing the death of the boy, who is knocked down by the carriage of a rich lady, the author emphatically declares: "The blood of one of the many martyrs of civilization has stamped on the clothes of the rich the curse of the unfortunates who demand justice—and will get it!"[18] This inclination to admonish and castigate is significant in that it connotes the degree to which the *sovversivi* believed in the imminent coming of the revolution and the inevitable overthrow of capitalism.

As these two stories exemplify, early Italian immigrant radical writing had its roots in the literature of protest, social realism, and naturalism that emerged in Europe at the end of the nineteenth century. Zola's novels seem in particular to have been a source of inspiration and a model for many stories. The *sovversivi*'s reading and admiration of Zola is evident by the widespread publication of his novels, famous citations, and critical reviews of his works. Like Zola, Italian immigrant radical writers paid great attention to the setting of the story and the milieu, providing specific names of streets and cities as well as detailed descriptions of the main characters. This literary pretense to objectivity and historical truth was often reinforced by the use of subtitles like "*storia dal vero*" (real story), meant to assure readers of the authenticity of the facts narrated. Italian immigrant radical stories came especially close to Zola in their attempt to illustrate the demoralizing effect of industrialization on human character and fate. For example, in "The Anarchist and the Prostitute," the author, a certain Ronchi, describes the condition of prostitution (the prostitute in the story is significantly named Nanà, as is one of Zola's most memorable characters) as a cause/effect of capitalist society.[19]

"Amate!" (You Must Love!), another story written by Matilde Bertoluzzi, illustrates a special theme of the *sovversivi*'s worldview and late-nineteenth-century socialist literature: that of universal love and brotherhood. Elena is a woman destroyed by the loss of her beloved son. She feels she no longer has a reason to live, until, with the help of a socialist friend, she realizes that she can and must love again. "Love! . . . Love! . . .," insists the friend, "Human beings were born to love infinitely, and the only law in our world should be love."[20] Expressions like this one, which dominate Italian immigrant radical prose, shed light on the *sovversivi*'s intense idealism and humanism. Italian socialists, and even more so the anarchists, believed that human nature is fundamentally good and that it is the environment that promotes hatred. Consequently, they assumed that after socialism replaced the harsh and unjust structure of capitalism, love would prevail.

The *sovversivi*'s belief in love, as the highest of all values, was consistent with their anti-militarism. Italian radicals had always been traditionally anti-militaristic and anti-nationalistic. The reasons for their opposition were ethical, cultural, and, of course, political. Like other rebels, they traced the origins of militarism to economic and material interests and considered it nothing more than an instrument of the established classes to oppress and suppress the working class.

As World War I broke out, dozens of anti-military stories were published in anarchist, socialist, and syndicalist papers along with plays and articles.[21] Most of these anecdotes mocked patriotic and nationalist propaganda and, through the dramatic experiences of fictional soldiers, mothers, and wives, showed the real side of war: the pain, destruction, and suffering caused by warfare. These stories attacked the rhetorical language of heroism (expressions such as "sacred duty," "holy war," "crusade for democracy"), challenging the construct of manhood in terms of physical strength, impassivity, and virility that the conservative press blatantly employed to encourage patriotism. Far from positive, these traits—insisted radical writers—incarnated the brutal, primitive, and irrational side of men, destroying the most important element of human character: dignity.

The comments of the anarchist poet Virgilia D'Andrea on the subject of the war are illuminating. When asked whether it was right for Italians to abandon the national fight of their "brothers" of Trento and Trieste, she answered: "And the men of the rest of world, aren't they equally our brothers? Those Italians who are forced to go abroad to work, don't they feel more at home among the textile workers, the farmers, the miners in Germany than among the arrogant and insolent prominent men in our country?"[22]

One of the most prolific and popular anti-war writers was Arturo Giovannitti. As we saw in the previous chapter, he wrote several anti-militarist plays. One of them, *Come era nel principio*, bore the same title as a short story he wrote earlier. But whereas the play is pervaded by a sense of horror and brutality, the story is a hymn to creation and life. It describes a mutilated soldier and a mourning woman who meet in a destroyed, empty village after the war is over. The man represents anguish, violence, death; the woman instead stands for hope, peace, and life. Significantly, Giovannitti chooses May 1 as the imaginary date of his story, denoting a symbolic new beginning. "Today," the woman explains, "the great mystery of life will occur again. . . . But this time the apple that I eat and you eat after me will be that of supreme knowledge, and all those who are born of me will not kill their brothers and will not earn their bread by the sweat of their brows." When the man asks the woman how they should name their first-born, whether *Amore* (Love) is the most appropriate name, she replies: "No, it will not be a man, it will be a woman and we'll name her *Giustizia* [Justice]."[23] (In Italian the noun *amore* is masculine whereas *giustizia* is feminine.)

The sanctity of life is the major theme of another short story written by Giovannitti, in 1914. Entitled *La vita è sacra*, it tells the story of a burglar who on Thanksgiving night enters a house in Flatbush, Brooklyn, and is shot by the owner. With sarcasm Giovannitti shows how the owner, an honest man, "respectful of the law and the church," decides to kill the thief even after he realizes he has not stolen anything. Giovannitti's social satire becomes even more evident when he describes the attitude of the police, who without even looking at the dead man congratulate the owner for his "excellent" job. Emphatically Giovannitti concluded: "Life is sacred!"[24]

Italian immigrant radical literature took also the narrative form of Christian parables or tales, using religious allegories, symbols, and metaphors to make political propaganda. Like the Gospel's religious parables, these radical stories imparted a moral lesson, using characters and actions that personified the qualities and meanings that the author wanted to be read beneath the story itself. In one instance, for example, the socialist agitator is compared to a madman—and implicitly to Christ. Unappreciated and mocked at first by his countrymen, he then becomes the spokesman for the commoners of his village.[25] Despite its exaggerated rhetoric and prophetic tone, this kind of writing powerfully reveals the religious texture of the *sovversivi*'s culture. Even though, as we saw in chapter 2, they overtly rejected religion, the Catholic culture in which they were raised still infiltrated their imagination, surfacing in the form of symbols, myths, and images. At the same time, however, the use of religious allegories may have well been a deliberate strategy to attract immigrants, especially women.

Another popular theme of Italian immigrant radical literature was the conversion of unorganized workers to socialism. Usually written in the first person, these stories traced the worker's ideological evolution, from the passive acceptance of the status quo to class awakening, and, eventually, the endorsement of socialist principles. For example, "The Night of a Worker" is at once a lament of the miserable life of workers and a utopian vision of a just society in which there are no oppressed, no poor, no slaves.[26]

Finally, Italian immigrant radical stories also took the form of direct dialogue among workers. This narrative mode was first popularized by Errico Malatesta in *Fra contadini* and *Al caffè* and became a very popular form of literary propaganda in all radical papers.[27] Using highly stereotypical and one-dimensional characters, the dialogues involved two or more persons, either men or women, and re-created real or plausible conversations among Italian immigrants. One of the speakers was a bigot, fatalist, skeptical of politics, and submissive; the other was instead rebellious, erudite, and aggressive. Using the question/answer format, the writer explained complex principles and theories of socialism and anarchism, such as the abolition of private property, the concept of class struggle, the importance of unions, or anti-clericalism, clarifying some of the most widespread misconceptions about radical ideologies.

—Is it really true—asks a young lady—that socialists want to share everything?
—Miss, you must be kidding me. . . .
—No, no for real! I heard it from a married man, a "*commendatore*," well educated, an economist!
—Then, Mister *Commendatore* must have made fun of you, he was in bad faith, or he is stupid. No, we, socialists do not want to share everything, first of all because a just distribution of goods would be impossible. Men would naturally want to be in competition, the strongest, smartest, and luckiest would prevail, individual conflicts would arise and slowly we would be in the same situation as today: rich on the one side, poor on the other. Instead, we want that the means of production, land and all that is used to produce, become collective property, the patrimony of all, not a few.[28]

Similarly, in a column under the title "Popular Propaganda," *La Questione Sociale* regularly featured a conversational serial between two fictional immigrants, Giacomo and Michele, with the obvious intent of educating its readers to the principles of anarchism.

> —Well *compare* Giacomo, I will let you come to my house because I have known you for the longest time but the fact that you belong to the anarchist sect does bother me; well—if you pardon my frankness—I believe you have lost your mind.
> —I am grateful—dear Michele—of the affection you have for me, but don't you see? You feel sorry for me because you don't know what is anarchy. Otherwise you'd be an anarchist too.
> —No, never. It's enough for me to know that anarchists don't want any master, religion, state, or motherland. They want to destroy society. You call that nothing?
> —No, my dear friend, anarchists do not aim at destroying society. What do we mean by society? An association of individuals who work for the commonwealth, because they know that other people's good is their good too. In other words, in a society everyone must work for the collective welfare if . . .
> —Excuse me; what does COLLECTIVE mean?
> —It means of EVERYBODY. Thus, all of us must work to improve the conditions of all if we want to improve our own. [. . .] Now, this should be the case, but it is not. Then how could you say that we want to destroy society when, considered in its real meaning, society does not even exist?
> —Slow down, *compare* Giacomo. Do not confound me. I, for society, mean all those things that govern us, that rule us, that make us live.
> —I see, you mean all institutions that constitute our actual social system.
> —Exactly. See you can speak like a literary man.
> —Well, the institutions, yes we do want to destroy them and we are right to do so. You'll see . . .[29]

Two things are striking about this type of literature: the vivacity of the language, informal and yet very precise and alive, and the literary artificiality of the conversations despite their pretense to realism. This peculiar literary form was probably a response to the problem of low education among Italian immigrants and peasants. It moved away from abstract theories and explained in simple words, in a language the workers could understand, the principles and goals of various radical ideologies, while deconstructing Italian immigrants' prejudices and bigotry.

This literary strategy was also used to educate Italian workers, especially women, to the principles of unionism and to combat the problem of "scabbism." For example, the labor paper *Il Lavoro* had a regular column called "*Cose piane tra vicine*" run by Nerina Gilioli Volonterio that employed the conversational format to encourage the unionization of women.[30] Drawing inspiration from genuine settings and characters, these dialogues used a "real" language, often characterized by ironic and satirical tones to accentuate the naïveté of immigrants.

Religious bigotry and provincialism were also regularly ridiculed. For example, Clara Vacirca Palumbo, wife of socialist deputy Vincenzo Vacirca, wrote a short story entitled "Il Miracolo" in which she described a mother's desperate attempt to marry off her three daughters.[31] To expedite her wish, she decided to go on a three-day pilgrimage to an ancient sanctuary of Our Lady of Sorrows to beg for a grace. Tired, but full of hope, she returned home only to find out that in her absence one of her daughters had become pregnant and her lover had deserted her for America.

Clara Vacirca was also the author of an anti-fascist serialized novel, *Cupido tra le camicie nere*, that narrated the pure and great love of two subversives against the adversities of fascism.[32] What is interesting about this novel is its use of literary conventions and themes typical of popular romance and melodrama in combination with the principles of engaged, committed art. One could say that despite her contempt for bourgeois society, Vacirca was unable to break completely free from the canons of bourgeois literature. However, as we discussed earlier, the use of melodrama was not necessarily passive; as in the case of the plays, the author may very well have consciously employed popular themes to attract more readers. The major goal was indeed to persuade the reader to convert to radicalism through the exemplary life of the hero or heroine.

Like the plays, the passionate love between a man and a woman from different social classes or different political beliefs was a common plot used in short stories to popularize radical ideas. In one of these stories, Pietro Zanelli is a well-educated Italian immigrant, libertarian, and anti-militarist. He belongs to a socialist circle and writes articles against the government, the priests, and the bourgeoisie for the party's newspaper. Unfortunately, he is in love with Marta, a beautiful girl from a wealthy, conservative family. It is the second year of World War I and Marta decides to participate in a military parade that will take place on Fifth Avenue to support the United States' entry into the conflict. Her action, however, inevitably provokes the disappointment and irritation of Pietro. Terribly sorry, she asks for his forgiveness and promises him she will never obstruct his political ideas. They eventually get married—she has to be content with civil marriage—and live happily ever after.[33]

The theme of love that is impossible because of political circumstances became particularly widespread in anti-fascist literature. A good example is a story published by "Maltempo" in 1927. Cesiria is a young peasant girl, living with her old father and her brother Attilio, an idler and bully, addicted to gambling and fraud, who joins the fascist squad of his town. When Cesiria falls in love with her neighbor Ambrogio, a serious young man who spends his free time reading libertarian books and studying social issues, Attilio confronts his sister with the intention of putting an end to their relationship. In contrast to the naïve female character of the previous story, Cesiria exhibits a strong personality and political consciousness of her own. Ready to die for her love, if necessary, she does not let her brother intimidate her and rages against him: "From idler to slacker the step was short: at last you became a disgusting criminal!"[34]

The examples discussed here are only a few among the many Italian immigrant literary voices lost in the pages of radical newspapers and periodicals. These voices took different forms and expressed a great variety of themes, ideologies, and messages that demand reassessment and more attention in both immigration and radical history. Some messages were obvious, other more subtle. Among the major topics in their writings we find a critique of capitalism, religion, and nationalism. While these themes are not entirely original, one is nevertheless struck by the abundance of the stories as well as the incredibly large number of ordinary men and women who ventured into literary writing.[35]

Poetry

Poetry was perhaps the richest, oldest, and most interesting expression of Italian immigrant literary radicalism. Poetry indeed has occupied a key role in the Italian literary tradition, assuming myriad forms—from the popular folk poetry of the *cantastorie* (storytellers), the classical epic of Dante, to Ada Negri e Pietro Gori's poetry of social revolt. For generations of immigrants, poetry represented a way to retain a link to their native land and assess their *italianità*. The success and persistence of dialectal poetry over the years exemplify perfectly the cultural and ethnic function of poetry among Italian immigrants.[36]

The importance of poems in the culture of the *sovversivi* becomes particularly evident in the pages of the radical press, which abound in verses, often embellished with drawings and occasionally published on the first page. Yet, with the single exception of Giovannitti's poetry, this important aspect of Italian American cultural identity has been completely, consciously or unconsciously, ignored—buried in the pages of equally forgotten newspapers of the Italian immigrant Left.

Like the prose, much of the radical poetic production is characterized by excessive sentimentalism and revolutionary rhetoric. Like other political and social verses, Italian immigrant radical poetry overdoes what it attempts, overstressing its intention and message. But the kind of thoughts and feelings expressed in socialist lyrics are, because of their political significance and educational nature, difficult to manifest without faults of tone. The overinsistence and rhetoric that sound so old-fashioned today were a deliberate, conscious artistic choice to stir and inspire the reader. In other words, when we judge these poems we must always remember that they were written with the intention not to amuse but to educate. In addition, we must always be aware of the literary taste and manners—the aesthetic ideologies—that rule in any given period.[37] The sense of what is good, true, and beautiful is not absolute but changes over time, reflecting the standards and tastes of the culture it attempts to convey. Radical poems should be examined within the cultural context in which they were written and in the social context of their intended audience and effect.[38]

As in the case of fiction and drama, Italian immigrant radical poetry bore the specific influence of Italian literary traditions and genres, especially the social-realistic tradition of the late nineteenth century; the classical-humanist tradition of Giacomo Leopardi, Ugo Foscolo, and Giovannni Pascoli; and the patriotic tradition of the post-*Risorgimento*, exemplified by Giosuè Carducci's anti-clerical, republican, and libertarian poetry. The most-admired poets were the so-called social poets or poets of social protest, notably Mario Rapisardi (1844–1912), Pietro Gori (1865–1911), and Ada Negri (1870–1945), the famous "poetess of revolt." Their poems were constantly reprinted in Italian immigrant radical newspapers and magazines, especially from the early twentieth century to the World War I years. Poems like Gori's "Primo Maggio" or Rapisardi's "Canto dei mietitori" were indeed published so often, and in so many different papers, that they could be considered official anthems of the *sovversivi*'s culture.[39]

But poetry in the *colonie italiane* was not exclusively imported from Italy. The Italian radical movement in the United States produced dozens of poets, some well educated and middle class in origin, others emerging from the ranks of the working class.[40] In addition to Giovannitti, whom I discuss in the next chapter, among the most productive and interesting poets were Simplicio Righi, Riccardo Cordiferro, Antonino Crivello, Bellalma Forzato-Spezia, Francesco Pitea, Virgilia D'Andrea, Efrem Bartoletti, and Francesco Greco. These men and women, however, never considered themselves professional poets or literary persons. Instead, they saw themselves as social rebels who experimented with poetry writing in their spare time, in addition to organizing the immigrants, founding newspapers, and participating in radical activities. Opposing the nineteenth-century concept of art for art's sake, they used poetry as a vehicle to advocate a solution to the social problems of their time.

Despite its obvious Italian influence, the *sovversivi*'s poetry was not a mere carbon copy of that of the "old country." Italian immigrant poets may have looked back at their motherland for literary models and themes, but they drew inspiration from their American experience. Their poetry grew out of real conditions and concrete realities of immigrant working-class life. It was, for example, the Lawrence strike of 1912 that inspired Giovannitti's best lyrics; it was the need for unionization that animated Crivello's verses; and it was the corruption of the world of the *prominenti* that heartened Cordiferro's bitter satire.

Most of these poets' names are today almost completely unknown to specialists in the field of Italian American studies and are generally absent from literary studies of both American and Italian American poetry and culture. With some exceptions, most of this poetic production appeared in the pages of radical papers and was never published in books. Yet, these men and women enjoyed a considerable popularity within Italian communities in the pre- and post–World War I eras and exerted a strong influence among their co-nationals.[41] While not always beautiful by today's literary standards, their poems often possess a high spiritualism and poetic force that naturally appealed to the Italian immigrant masses.

Simplicio Righi

A well-respected doctor, Simplicio Righi was one of the earliest militants in the Italian section of the Socialist Labor Party of New York. From 1901 to 1902 he directed the socialist newspaper *Il Proletario*, where he published most of his early poems under the female pseudonym Rosina Vieni.[42] He also edited a popular serialized column called "Alfabeto igienico del lavoratore" (Hygienic Alphabet of the Worker), which was published simultaneously in different papers and aimed at educating Italian immigrants to healthy norms of life and widespread problems like alcoholism, venereal diseases, and food poisoning.

Righi's poems are usually melodramatic and laconic but do not degenerate into mawkishness.[43] They celebrate the working class, voicing at the same time their sorrows and their aspirations. His middle-class background notwithstanding, Righi identified himself as far as possible with the Italian workers and was able to re-create successfully both the material and spiritual world of the immigrants. In one of his most convincing poems, published on the front page of *Il Prolerario* on May 1, 1902, Righi concedes that the world "today" has much injustice and oppression but also believes that "tomorrow" will bring redemption, freedom, and equality for all. In another poem he gives further voice to the theme of the workers' liberation and triumph, envisioning a future in which workers are no longer slaves, where science rules, and the only true deity is consciousness:

Non più catene ai polsi ed	No more chains around the
al pensiero.	wrists or the mind.
Maestra e donna ai popoli,	Science will be teacher and
la scienza;	mother of all peoples,
Unico nume, il vero,	Truth, the only god:
E, duce, la coscienza.[44]	And conscience the chief of all.

It is not difficult to see in Righi's poetry the influence of the realistic school of the late nineteenth century with its emphasis on the social question—the increasing attention to the social, economic, and environmental problems brought by industrialization. Frequent also is the evocation of Jesus, the redeemer of humankind, with his revolutionary message of brotherhood and equality.[45]

The image of Christ as a militant figure, appearing now as an agitator, now as revolutionary, now as persecuted, was by no means restricted to the *sovversivi*'s poetry. Donald Winters in his important study of the spiritualism of the Wobblies has convincingly documented the "religious texture of the IWW message," pointing out interesting parallels between the themes of political martyrdom and Christian images of sacrifice and persecution.[46] A comparison between Jesus and the revolutionary appeared frequently in the *sovversivi*'s literature, revealing a dialectic relationship between Italian socialism and Christianity. Despite their proclaimed atheism, the *sovversivi* borrowed from Christianity not only its prophetic tone and biblical language but also the values of solidarity, brotherhood, compassion, and universal love with which it is imbued.

Righi's humble, compassionate language and sensitivity, which significantly is reflected in his choice of a female pseudonym, won him the reputation of "*poeta gentile*," gentle poet. Yet, in the mid-1920s he became a fascist sympathizer, contributing regularly to the literary magazine *Il Carroccio*, edited by Agostino De Biasi, the founder of the first fascist organization in the United States.[47] Righi's ideological journey from socialism to fascism was, however, not unique: Mussolini himself had been an active and prominent socialist leader until World War I, and so had been, as discussed earlier, other renegades like Edmondo Rossoni, Aldo Tarabella, and Libero Tancredi.

Antonino Crivello

If Righi classifies as the idealistic bard of Italian immigrant workers in the United States, Antonino Crivello (1888–1969) stands out as their practical prophet. Born in Palermo, Sicily, he emigrated to the United States at the age of fifteen and became one of the most active and important union organizers of tailors and dressmakers in New York.[48] He also was one of the founders of *Circolo Libertario Pensiero ed Azione* and a member of many labor and anti-fascist groups. He was a man of culture whose education did not pass unnoticed by the Italian consulate, which in its files pointed out that he spoke and wrote Italian very well.[49]

A convinced and active socialist, Crivello had a political creed that was, as he himself put it, "Labor Solidarity." "It was a joy," he wrote to his union comrades, "to inspire you with faith in the Union, and to teach you that in Union there is strength. Please make sure that our work has not been in vain, and that you shall proceed with our International and its leadership from victory to victory, towards the highest peak of social justice, progress and civilization."[50] Crivello's poetry is the quintessence of his unionist faith. Poems such as "Fratello, ascolta!" "Speed up," "Insanity," "Lottiamo!" "La Parola," and "Dressmakers, Avanti!" are all calls to action.[51] Written in the form of folk ballads, generally in end rhyme, they attest to his passionate crusade for unionism, solidarity, and working-class rights. Addressing Italian immigrants in Italian, English, and often Sicilian dialect, he urged them "to awaken," to leave their "hovel," their "indolence" and to finally rebel against those who exploit and oppress them.[52] "Salvation," he insisted, "can only be in the unity of those who suffer and are enslaved," and only "in joined struggle can workers win freedom and put an end to injustice."[53]

While Crivello's purpose of developing class consciousness is even too obvious, the impact of his lyrics in unionizing Italian immigrants is less apparent. As in the case of American syndicalist poets such as Joe Hill and Ralph Chaplin, Crivello's words contributed undoubtedly to popularizing working-class unity and organization among Italian immigrants. Crivello's leadership and influence are also evident from the letters of the Italian consulate to the Ministry of the Interior, in which he is described as an active socialist and "relentless" anti-fascist. In 1934, for example, Consul Grossardi deemed it necessary to send the Prefect of Rome a copy of a poem Crivello wrote in memory of Antonio Fierro, killed by fascists on July 14, 1933, in Astoria, Queens, assuring him that he was being carefully monitored.[54]

As we have seen, anti-militarism was one of the central components of the *sovversivi*'s *Weltanschauung*. This fervent anti-militarist tradition found in Crivello one of its best representatives. Set against the background of World War II, his "*Guerra!*" illustrates the anti-militarist soul of the *sovversivi*. Published as a pamphlet and sold at 5 cents a copy, this long and ambitious poem (218 lines) was dedicated to "every man who in good faith approves the present war, believing it to be a war of vindication." In it, Crivello exposed the hypocrisy, infamy, and ruthlessness of the war. Condemning the media's attempt to picture it as a crusade for democracy and freedom, he argued that the real motive of the conflict was the same as always: "the sordid greed of the great and powerful."[55] "Let us not be fooled," he declared in a speech to a union meeting; "we entered the war to save the world for democracy, but instead we saved the world for dictators. Today let us spread good propaganda which cries for peace."[56]

Crivello's poetic muse was not limited to political themes. In addition to working-class verses, he wrote sonnets dedicated to family life, his native land, and love. In one of them, "'*Sta notti puru cusi!*" (This night, too, you sew), he re-evoked the grief he felt as an immigrant boy, watching his mother sewing all night to make a living, while his father was unemployed. Written in Sicilian, the lyric powerfully dramatizes the great loneliness and desperation behind the immigrant experience, as exemplified by these lines:

Senza pani è l'America,	How can America be
matruzza?	without bread, mother?
Tutti papà truvò li porti chiùsi!	Father found all doors shut!
Puru iddu 'un dormi! Sentu	He also can't sleep! I can
chi singhiùzza[57]	hear him sobbing . . .

Like the political movement, Italian radical poetry was male dominated. However, as we have already seen, women were not absent from either politics or literature. Turning the pages of the radical newspapers, one can find several female names. These names attest to the fact that women were contributors to and subscribers of radical newspapers; active members of social, political, and feminist clubs; as well as authors of political articles, short stories, and poems.[58] Unfortunately, records about these names are often scant, and it is therefore impossible to reconstruct their owners' biographies. Two important exceptions are the socialist-syndicalist Bellalma Forzato-Spezia (1877–?) and the anarchist Virgilia D'Andrea (1888–1933).

Bellalma Forzato-Spezia

Bellalma Forzato-Spezia was born in Mirandola, a small village in the province of Modena, in northern Italy, on January 1, 1877. She emigrated with her husband to America a few years after the death of her parents in 1891, settling in West Hoboken, New Jersey.[59] There, at 416 Spring Street, she opened a bookstore that became renowned for its large selection of booklets of socialist propaganda and social novels. It remains unclear whether she was already active in Italy or whether she embraced revolutionary ideas after her arrival in America. Practically nothing, except for his last name, Forzato, is known of her husband. In any case, by 1907 she had joined the *Federazione Socialista Italiana*, and her name became associated with that of important revolutionary socialists and syndicalists of the time, such as Edmondo Rossoni, Giacinto Menotti Serrati, Camillo Cianfarra, and Dino Rondani. She gave dozens of lectures to socialist and anarchist gatherings and regularly wrote poetry and articles for Italian-language radical newspapers. Police records indicate that she was well known within the Italian radical community of the early twentieth century in the United States. Categorized as "subversive," she was carefully monitored by consular officers, and all information about her activities was systematically forwarded to the Ministry of the Interior in Rome.[60]

Like other radicals, Forzato-Spezia emphasized education and knowledge as a pre-condition of revolutionary organizing and emancipation. Consequently, most of her writings were meant to educate, inform, and awaken immigrants. A strong supporter of Ferrer's Modern School, in 1911 she published a pamphlet entitled *Per le nuove generazioni* in which she attacked traditional teaching and advocated a rational, secular, and libertarian education. Conventional schools, she wrote, instead of enlightening and elevating the minds of future generations, had become "the most powerful instrument of domination and enslavement": a means for the bourgeois state "to fabricate docile citizens, respectful of laws, authorities, and pre-established orders." True education, she insisted, should free children "from the shackles of dogmatic education" and create a revolutionary milieu fit for preparing "a new generation of conscientious, free, and innovative men." Her educational plan included, among other things, "the demolition of religious, patriotic, militaristic, and capitalist dogmas" as well as the promotion of a "compassionate rationalism" conducive to fighting all social injustices and creating a better future.[61]

In addition to publishing articles and pamphlets, between 1907 and 1915 Forzato-Spezia also wrote poetry, most of which appeared in *Il Proletario*. Her poetry clearly reveals the influence of her classical and humanistic education, exhibiting a careful attention to the form and the metrics, technical precision, balance, and emotional restraint. In contrast to typical working-class or socialist poetry, which is generally very accessible, Forzato-Spezia's poetic language is carefully chosen, studied, and affected. Most of her poems are long and elaborate, filled with panegyrics, allegories, and metaphors.

As in her other writings, the importance of knowledge and education to emancipate the workers is also the major theme of her poems. With aggressiveness, she urges the masses, especially women, to fight the prejudices and ignorance that keep them enslaved and follow the road of "Reason."[62] In the poem "O donna, vieni!" she especially defies religious faith—"the eternal despot"—insisting repeatedly that the rhetoric of resignation, inherent in the Christian discourse of Salvation, is one of the most powerful means of controlling the masses and justifying class inequality.[63] Only after the workers have freed themselves from the yokes of religion, bigotry, and ignorance:

Sorgerà non remota	It will rise not distant
un'aurora sanguigna,	a bloody dawn,
e allor la scalza plebe,	and by then, the barefoot populace,
Niobe non più serva	no longer servant
a una schiatta proterva,	to an insolent race,
svincolerà rombando,	will free itself roaring
sull'espugnata vetta,	on the stormed top,
a volo la vendetta	revenge will take off
e correran gli abissi	and from the abysses of the air
dell'aria i gridi a flutti:	will come running the screams in billows:
"salute o Terra, alfine	blessed thee oh Earth, at last
equa madre per tutti!"[64]	just mother to all!

Often, her criticism betrayed a bourgeois contempt for Italian immigrant workers (or plebeians, as she called them), who with their coarseness helped ruin the good name of Italy. For example, in "L'emigrato italiano in America" (The Italian immigrant in America) she describes Italian immigrants as "squat, lazy, and slack," complaining that because of them:

> *La regina un dì del mondo, ora è fatta avventuriera,*
> Once the queen of the world, she has now become an adventurer
> *Olè! La sordida e pezzente, abbruttita e abbietta Italia!*
> The sordid and imploring, ugly and abject Italy!
> *Mai nutrirono le Pampas dei selvaggi più vil schiera:*
> Never did the Pampas feed savages of a more cowardly kind:
> *non son forse i nostri cani di meno ignobil schiatta?*
> Aren't perhaps our dogs of a less ignominious stock?
> *Basta, basta, troppo è già!*[65]
> Enough, enough, this is already too much.

Forzato-Spezia's wounded nationalist pride would emerge openly with the outbreak of World War I, when she joined the group of syndicalists led by Edmondo Rossoni in support of Italy's intervention. In 1915 she founded *L'Italia Nostra*, a fiercely nationalist paper, along with Rossoni and Onorio Ruotolo. Her last articles of a feminist/socialist nature appeared in *Il Lavoro*, the organ of the Amalgamated Clothing Workers of America, in 1917. After the war she retreated from political activism and ceased to write for radical newspapers, and following the death of her husband in 1926, she returned to Italy, settling with her son in Rome and working as a translator. In 1936 she was officially registered in the Fascist Party, openly in favor of the regime, and her dossier was consequently removed from the police files.[66]

Virgilia D'Andrea

While Forzato-Spezia returned to Italy to cheer fascism, new radicals were flooding the United States to escape Mussolini's regime and persecution. Among them was the anarchist poetess Virgilia D'Andrea. Born in Sulmona, Abruzzo, also Tresca's birthplace, in 1880, she came from Paris to the United States in 1928 and settled in Brooklyn, along with her lover Armando Borghi, a well-known anarchist and anti-fascist (fig. 5.1). Italian authorities described her as a short, petite woman with dark eyes and dark short hair, of "fine intelligence, culture, and education" but also "a violent type, of inconstant character and reprehensible moral behavior."[67] Her alleged immorality resulted from her contempt of social conventions and her belief in free love. In reality, as some of her autobiographical writings reveal, she was a very

Figure 5.1
Anarchist poetess Virgilia D'Andrea (1880–1932), who fled fascist Italy with her lover, Armando Borghi, in 1922, taking refuge in Germany and France and eventually landing in New York in 1928, where she lived until her premature death from cancer. She was a beloved figure of the movement, known for her poetry and oratorical skills.

sensitive and idealistic woman "with the head full of dreams, fantasies and tears."[68]

At a very young age she tragically lost her entire family and was forced to go to a boarding school run by nuns to become a teacher. Her only consolation there was reading: "I devoured," she recalls in one of her stories, "hundreds and hundreds of books; the poetry of Rapisardi, Leopardi and especially Negri were [sic] my favorite."[69] Inspired by these readings, she gradually converted to anarchism, becoming, in the words of Italian authorities, a "dangerous propagandist and organizer of radical activities, which she disguised under the cover of anti-Fascism."[70]

When she arrived in America she was already well known among the Italian immigrants as both a poet and an anarchist and revered by many. She conducted lecture tours in Florida, Louisiana, Pennsylvania, Illinois, and Massachusetts that, as the newspapers of the time reported, were always well attended, with people filling the conference rooms to their capacity.

D'Andrea's popularity, however, was due to her poetic eloquence as much as to her political activism. In 1922 she published her first book of poetry, *Tormento* (Torment), with an introduction by the Italian anarchist theorist par excellence, Errico Malatesta. The book sold 8,000 copies and was issued a second edition in 1929 while she was in exile in France. Italian authorities promptly impounded the book on the ground that it "excited the spirits," and denounced her for inciting rebellion. Her verses, noted the questor, are "imbued with a feline bile against Italy; they are verses carefully composed to instigate lawbreaking, to incite class hatred, and to vilify the army."[71]

Tormento consists of nineteen poems in rhyme, many of which were originally published in *L'Avanti!*, the official organ of the Italian Socialist Party. The cover pictured a winged woman in the act of freeing herself from her chained wrists, symbolizing bourgeois power. As the title of the collection suggests, these poems recount the poet's personal anguish, grief, and anger for the political defeats of the Left that followed World War I. Most of her poems were written in the aftermath of the so-called *biennio rosso* (1919–20), a time characterized by widespread social protests, strikes, and upheavals in Italy, when many believed that the Bolshevik revolution would naturally extend to the Italian nation and the rest of Europe and socialism would finally triumph. Instead, to the disbelief of leftists, Italy gave birth to the world's first fascist regime while Germany established a Nazi party. In the years following Mussolini's seizure of power in 1922, the Left in Italy was artfully silenced, its publications were banned, and its prominent leaders were either arrested or forced into exile.

Even in such a climate of terror, D'Andrea refused to give up her anarchist dream: Her verses speak to the unredeemed and nonaffiliated on the fringes, providing at the same time a radical critique of the movement and a visionary aspiration. As Malatesta explained to readers, in her book "you will especially find the faith that does not die with defeat—the firm conviction and the sure hope."[72] This unshakeable devotion to the "Ideal" is perhaps best represented in these verses, written while she was held in prison in 1920:

No, non son vinta.	No, I am not defeated.
Vibra, in me, più forte,	Despite this sad cell,
	the ardent faith
L'ardente fede ne l'angusta cella,	lives in me, stronger,
E frange i ferri e batte le ritorte,	And the dream wave that
	scourges my heart
L'onda del sogno, che il mio	transcends the bars and
cor flagella	defeats all barriers

Contrary to most Italian American radical poetry, which tended primarily to talk of general social and political conditions rather than individual experiences, D'Andrea's poems fused the personal and the political. Themes of revolutionary change and social inequality intermix with her inner feelings, while pessimism about her political time is softened by the awareness of the power of love and the beauty of life. In this respect her verses display perhaps the influence of Leopardi's romanticism more than Rapisardi's or Negri's social protest. This subjectivity is particularly evident in her second book, *Torce nella notte* (Torches in the night), published by her comrades in 1933 after her premature death from breast cancer. A combination of prose and poetry, autobiography and history, remembrances and political commentaries, the book consists of sixteen stories, of which seven are tributes to the memory of anarchist martyrs and leaders— the "torches in the night" to which the title implicitly refers. The book's cover depicts a naked female figure, handcuffed, in the act of hurtling toward an imaginary abyss, her eyes closed in silent despair, symbolizing perhaps the fall of anarchism. But if D'Andrea recognizes the decline of the anarchist movement, the anarchist ideal still remains her main source of inspiration:

Per una grande Idea;	For a great Ideal
Di lotta in lotta, di prigione	From struggle to struggle,
in prigione;	from prison to prison
Discacciata dalla patria, attraverso	Banned from my country, across
le vie del mondo,	the streets of the world,
senza mai la tua casa,	without ever a home,
il tuo nido di rifugio,	a nest
senza mai un sicuro domani;	without ever a certain tomorrow;
In piedi, dove finisce	Standing up, where injustice
l'ingiustizia e	ends and
dove passa la sventura;	bad luck passes by;
In piedi come oggi, tra i feriti,	Standing today, among the
i caduti e	wounded, the dead
gli scampati d'una più feroce	and those eascaped to a
tragedia;	fiercer tragedy;
Verso una visione d'umanità e	Towards a vision of humanity
di giustizia;	and justice;
Verso l'ostinato sogno di pace	Towards the stubborn dream
e di amore;	of peace and love;
Sotto le flagellanti burrasche della vita;	Under the scourging storms of life;
E sempre a bandiera spiegata.	And always with flying colors.

Even though her free-love union with Borghi clearly defied gendered norms, D'Andrea did not specifically address women's problems in her writings. Unlike Forzato-Spezia or other radical feminists like Maria Roda, she did not denounce sexism and she did not issue specific calls for female liberation. Instead she formulated a broader class-based analysis and internationalist vision that aimed at the liberation of all oppressed people.

Riccardo Cordiferro

While most Italian immigrant poets chose formal, classical verses, others used satirical, popular tones to advocate social change. Among them, Riccardo Cordiferro was certainly the most popular.[73] A prolific playwright, journalist, and lecturer, he also wrote hundreds of verses, touching on different subjects and genres. Like other *sovversivi*, Cordiferro had no literary pretense or ambition. He considered poetry "the interpreter of human aspirations and passions" but looked down on "lyrics that have nothing to say and are written only for the so-called aesthetes and intellectuals."[74] Despite his classical formation, his poems reflected the themes and motifs of popular culture, and, despite the affectation of the rhymes, the language he used is always frank, simple, even rough at times. This explains Cordiferro's wide popularity among Italian immigrants, even though, aesthetically speaking, his poetry is probably the poorest amongst the *sovversivi*'s. As in the case of his plays, he sang of a world that Italian immigrants could identify with and understand—parodying the bigotry and provincialism of the Little Italies; unmasking the opportunism, hypocrisy, and corruption of the *prominenti* and the priests; and at the same time indicting American society, with its exasperating individualism and harsh materialism. Whereas Giovannitti or D'Andrea seduced the workers with their eloquence, Cordiferro reached them with his humor and sarcasm, and, after making them laugh, he left them thinking.

With a few exceptions, Cordiferro's poetic production rests above all in the pages of *La Follia*, the popular weekly newspaper he co-founded in New York in 1893 with his father and brother. Although the paper cannot be defined as radical, at least not by the *sovversivi*'s standards, Cordiferro wrote in it fierce articles and poems of social criticism that often got him into trouble with local authorities. He published two volumes of poetry, *Singhiozzi e Sogghigni* (Sobs and smirks, 1910) and *Il Poema dell'Amore* (The poem of love, 1928).[75] A third volume, *Poesie scelte* (Selected poems), appeared posthumously in Italy in 1967.[76] In addition to poems, he also wrote as many as forty-nine musical romances that were performed by famous lyric tenors of the time.[77]

His earliest and most radical poems appeared in the anarchist newspaper *La Questione Sociale* between 1894 and 1898.[78] Poetry here becomes a means of protest against tyrannies and injustices, an angry cry against the inhumane conditions of the immigrant workers, a hymn to revolution and revolt against social inequality and working-class oppression. Sarcasm dominates the lyrics, becoming a weapon with which to attack, expose, and provoke, as for example in this tercet: "*Dovremmo chiamarci padroni di tutto / ma abbiamo soltanto nell'anima il lutto . . . / siam stanchi, siam stanchi perdio di servir.*"[79] (We should own everything / but we have in our soul only mourning / we are tired, for goodness' sake, we are tired of serving.)

Anti-clericalism is another important theme of Cordiferro's poetry. In "Osanna a Satana," which echoes Carducci's "A Satana," Cordiferro opposes the Christian theory of God's existence with an atheistic and materialistic conception of life. His religious critique flows into "satanism": He curses God, responsible for so much misery, and celebrates Satan, symbol of freedom and knowledge.

Francesco Pitea

Political satire is also the cultural form used by Francesco Pitea (1894–1981), a mill worker of Paterson, New Jersey. Born in Gallico Superiore, a small village in the southern province of Reggio Calabria, Pitea left Italy for America in 1913, joining two of his brothers who had emigrated before him. He worked as a coal miner in West Virginia, then moved to Brooklyn, and finally settled in a town near Paterson called Dundee Lake (today's Elmwood Park), where he worked, along with his wife, as a mill machine operator for most of his life. In addition to being active in the labor movement as member of the ILGWU, he was a convinced anti-fascist and anti-war militant.[80]

His ideas and involvement in the Italian immigrant Left led to his arrest in 1920; he avoided deportation only through the intervention of his comrades.[81] Most important, he was one of the founders and the director of the anti-fascist weekly newspaper *La Scopa*, published in Paterson for three years (1925–28). It was here, assuming the pseudonym of Libero Arsenio, that Pitea wrote most of his invectives against Mussolini and his fascist supporters in America. His poems appeared under a column called "*Serenata*" (Serenade), accompanied by a little drawing of a man with a guitar. As the word "serenade" suggests, Pitea intended his verses more as songs than poems. However, unlike a wooer, instead of praising the object of his songs, he launched long denunciations against the abuses of fascist policy.

His poetry drew inspiration from the historical developments of fascism and aimed at revealing to the increasing number of immigrants who, driven by nationalist pride, had embraced fascism, the real nature of Mussolini's ideology. With impudent, pungent, and biting irony he ridiculed fascism and Mussolini, comparing fascist groups to "The League of Cudgels,"

King Vittorio Emanuele to "a dull, ridiculous king," and Mussolini to an "impostor," a "coward," an "opportunist," "a false Caesar" who was ruining Italy.[82] Even harsher were the words against fascist *prominenti* in America, such as Vincenzo Giordano of *Il Bollettino della Sera* and Carlo Barsotti of *Il Progresso Italo Americano*, who were nothing more than *"patriottardi / Ben pronti ai ricatti, / Vil, falsi e bugiardi"*[83] (jingoists / always ready to blackmail / vile, false and deceitful), and *"volta gabbana / che stanno a campare / con qualche puttana"* (weathercocks / who live their lives / with whores).[84]

Like Cordiferro's verses, Pitea's poems cannot be appreciated unless they are seen in their historical context. In the mid-1920s fascism was forging a large consensus among Italian American, as well as American, public opinion. To counter fascist propaganda without running the risk of being prosecuted became almost impossible. What better cultural way, then, to expose the incongruity that existed between the appearance of fascism and its real nature than satire? After all, satire by definition involves the act of "ridiculing folly, vice, stupidity—the whole range of human foibles and frailties—in individuals and institutions."[85] Pitea's poetry was tailored to do exactly that: to present the paradoxes of fascism while providing a radical critique of the *prominenti*, and it did so in a language fit for the workers. Anti-fascist satirical poetry was a significant force in articulating anti-fascist sentiments and spurring sympathies toward liberalism and democracy.

Italian immigrant literary radicalism was not limited to the works discussed here. In fact, it would have been easy to pile up further evidence. The communist Vittorio Vidali published several poems under the pseudonym of Enea Sormenti during his short but active sojourn in the United States. Efrem Bartoletti, a self-educated miner from Umbria who came to the United States in 1909, wrote regularly poems for *L'Avvenire* and *Il Proletario*, publishing several volumes of poetry. Francesco Greco, a carpenter from Calabria, was one of the best-known poets in the Calabrian dialect. His poems appeared in various radical papers, and a collection of his best poetry, *L'Anima allo Specchio*, was published in 1964. Giuseppe Zappulla, an anti-fascist emigre and the editor of various literary magazines, was also the acclaimed author of several stories and poems. Finally, Nino Caradonna, a journalist and writer, published more than ten volumes of poetry, some of which have been translated into various languages. Dozens of examples of other literary writings that touch upon various aspects of Italian immigrant radical culture can be found in radical papers.[86]

Limitations of space, however, have made it necessary to limit the discussion to the most representative material, focusing on those themes and issues that appeared most commonly. Certainly, not all the prose or the poetry analyzed in this chapter is "great" literature. Yet, considered as a whole, this body of radical work remains important for several reasons. First, their wide production and popularity suggest that while illiteracy was widespread among Italian immigrants, its rate was considerably lower among the radicals. Radical literary production also shows that literature flourished and grew along with radical ideas, challenging the assumption that Italian immigrants were indifferent to politics and education. In fact, within the Italian immigrant communities no one was as educated as the *sovversivi*, many of whom reached a degree of intellectual sophistication far beyond the average level of working-class education.[87]

Literary radicalism also brought alive the sense of radical possibility that shaped the immigrant experience of first- and second-generation Italian Americans. Set against the background of international as well as internal political events, these poems and novelettes supplied hundreds of Italian immigrants with their first understanding of the meaning and possible achievements of socialism. To paraphrase what Donald Winters has written about the IWW poets, these kinds of proletarian songs and writings provided the rootless Italian workers with a vision and faith greater than that of any other political movement.[88]

Ultimately, the importance of Italian immigrant literary radicalism lies exactly in what is usually considered the major limitation of radical literature: the overt political message and social criticism it conveys. For all their faults of tone and exaggerations, the poems and stories discussed here captured all the key elements of Italian immigrant radical culture. In them we find the clearest expression of the spirit that moved the *sovversivi*—their commitment to the workers, their devotion to the ideas of equality and freedom, their hatred of privilege and arrogance, their desire for a counterculture different from that of the middle class. This vision was rooted in the core values of the European Left—liberty, justice, and equality—and had as its ultimate goal the overthrow of capitalism. What the *sovversivi* hoped for, however, was not only a new political world but also a new cultural world in which literature and art would help change the way people thought and acted.

Arturo Giovannitti

Poet and Prophet of Labor

Thursday, December 31, 1959, was a sad New Year's Eve for the Italian American community: Arturo Giovannitti, one of their greatest crusaders and beloved leaders, had passed away. The *New York Times*, among other newspapers, recalled him as a key figure of the "idealistic radicalism that shaped the immigrant Italian labor movement in the United States":

> Until the end of World War II, when his health failed, he wrote and spoke extensively in the struggle to establish organized labor. At various times he was a close associate of Max Eastman, Norman Thomas, David Dubinsky and many others. At fiery labor rallies of the Nineteen Twenties and Thirties, Mr. Giovannitti was in great demand as a speaker. A colorful figure, with a Van Dyke beard, a Lord Byron collar and flowing tie, he addressed Italian and English-speaking audiences with an equally flowery fluency.[1]

The *Times*'s obituary, however, failed to acknowledge Giovannitti's literary standing, particularly his poetic eloquence that, as the thousands of workers who packed the auditorium at his memorial attested, inspired many a young radical.[2] Giovannitti, in the words of the American socialist Norman Thomas, "brought to the labor movement the gifts not only of an orator but of a poet of passion and power." "These gifts," he continued, "are of extraordinary value; no great movement can live by bread alone. It requires that feeling for humanity, that passion for justice, that outrage against wrong, that faith in brotherhood which the young Giovannitti exemplified and expressed so nobly."[3]

The remembrances and tributes published by his friends and many common workers clearly indicate that Giovannitti was considered a hero, a symbol of the socialist struggle on behalf of the poor and oppressed. His fame rested principally upon the Lawrence strike of 1912, when, along with Joseph

Figure 6.1
Revolutionary poet Arturo Giovannitti (right) with Joe Ettor (center) and Joseph
Caruso (left) at the 1912 Lawrence trial. Library of Congress Prints and Photograph
Division.

Ettor, an Italian American Wobbly organizer, he risked capital punishment
on the fabricated charges of inciting violence and being an accessory to murder (fig. 6.1). He almost certainly would have never attained the status of a
hero without the publicity he accrued from the Lawrence case. But it was
his poetic talent that enlivened his legend and thrust upon him the role of
"prophet" of the workers. As Joseph Salerno, vice president of the Amalgamated Clothing Workers of America (ACWA), noted, he "above all was an artist. . . . He used his pen as a weapon for the emancipation of the working class
and the passion of his voice to free mankind from the scourge of poverty and
war. . . . He was an electrifier of multitudes. He was one of the greatest orators
of his time. He was the poet of labor."[4]

Giovannitti's dedication to the cause of workers and his commitment
to social justice are plainly reflected in his literary work. He wrote articles,
plays, and especially poems throughout his life, even when, in the 1950s, he
was paralyzed and bedridden. Much of his poetry appeared in the pages of
Italian American labor newspapers and the American radical magazines *The
Masses* (1911–17) and *The Liberator* (1918–24), but his best work was also pur-

sued by prestigious reviews such as *The Survey, Atlantic Monthly, Current Opinion*, and *Current Literature*.[5] Five collections of his poetry, three in Italian and two in English, have also been published, although none is complete. The earliest one, *Arrows in the Gale*, published in 1914 with an introduction by the famed radical socialist Helen Keller, contained verses that were at the time described as some "of the greatest poems ever produced in the English language."[6]

Yet today, just fifty years after his death, the legendary "Poet of the Workers" has been almost completely forgotten: His memory, like much of Italian American radicalism, has been erased by Americanization and social mobility, his verse exiled to a few old anthologies of radical poetry.[7] True, labor historians have long recognized Giovannitti's central role in the Lawrence strike, and his name does usually appear in the indexes of social and labor histories.[8] But Giovannitti is completely absent from traditional critical studies of both American and Italian American cultural radicalism, despite the fact that many contemporary literary critics, radical and nonradical alike, considered him one of America's finest poets.[9] Daniel Aaron, in his pioneering work on American literary radicalism, was one of the few cultural scholars to at least acknowledge Giovannitti, calling him "the *Liberator*'s bard of revolution" and citing him along with the other radicals of Greenwich Village as a model "of the intellectual doer who combined imaginative with practical pursuits, art with the life of action." But only Donald Winters has actually discussed Giovannitti within the larger context of the IWW poetry.[10]

More recently, as part of a more general attempt to recover "the lost world of Italian American radicalism," a few scholars of Italian Americana have offered insightful commentaries on Giovannitti's poetry. Still, with the exception of a biography by Renato Lalli and a recent collection of poems edited by Martino Marazzi, both in Italian, remarkably little has been done to rescue the most popular Italian American poet from complete oblivion.[11]

This chapter offers a re-reading of Giovannitti in his dual capacity—as a radical leader and as a poet. It is an attempt to bridge the political and "lyrical" sides of Giovannitti and re-situate his poems in the broad cultural context of the early American labor movement. As Mark Starr, a worker from New York, aptly put it, Giovannitti gave "eloquent voice" to the radical message of revolutionary unionism and more particularly to the struggle of Italian American workers against "the inhumanity of the robber barons and the gross materialism of the reigning industrial system."[12] He became a symbol, in the words of *The Survey* magazine, of the "polyglot internationalism of the industrial workers"—the vision of a united humanity, not only for the working class but for all people.[13] His poetry, in particular, is a tangible testimonial of the times and places in which he lived and the ideals for which he and the *sovversivi* fought. As Nunzio Pernicone has written, it represents a "paradigm of the *sovversivi*'s literature of social protest and revolt, and a reflection of the confluence of culture and politics amidst the clash between American capitalism and the Italian immigrant working class."[14]

Yet, as Wallace P. Sillanpoa noted in 1987, critics have tended to split Giovannitti's "poetic animus" between lyrics that express his emotions and inner sentiments and those that recount his ideas and political commitment. Such dichotomy, he lamented, has led to a "florilegium of Giovannitti's verse, based on isolated lines determined by *a priori* criteria as to what constitutes poetic authenticity."[15] Echoing Sillanpoa's argument, I maintain that Giovannitti's poetry blurs traditional distinctions between art and propaganda. His idealism, lyricism, and intense melancholia were never separated from his deeds, and his poetry was never exclusively expressive of his personal inner world. In fact, his political views formed not only the background of but also the impetus for his poetry.

From Protestant Minister to Revolutionary Socialist

Arturo Massimo Giovannitti was born on January 7, 1884, in Ripabottoni, "a God-forsaken village" of about 4,000 inhabitants in the region of Molise, southern Italy. Its history, notes Giovannitti's biographer Renato Lalli, was the same as that of other southern villages: "a long history of earthquakes, epidemics, and misery." Even after Italy achieved unification, living conditions in Ripabottoni remained dreadful. Its people, lamented Giovannitti in 1911, "have remained through the last forty years the same people of old, mostly addicted to agriculture, stock raising, and other labors that are strictly confined to the surface land."[16] Artisans constituted only a tiny minority of the population. Professionals were almost nonexistent. Giovannitti's was actually one of the few well-to-do families of the village. They were not wealthy, but they lived more comfortably than the average people in the South. A cultured and liberal man, his father, Domenico Giovannitti, was a pharmacist; his mother, Adelaide Giannina Levante, belonged to a well-known bourgeois family in Larino, a nearby town. Giovannitti was the first-born of three sons—the middle brother, Giuseppe, became a pharmacist like his father; the youngest, Aristide, a lawyer. Both were killed in World War I.[17]

As a child Giovanniti was described as being reserved and serious, interested more in books than games. His neighbors in Ripabottoni recalled him spending hours inside his father's library reading, especially history books. In keeping with his bourgeois status, after completing primary schooling Giovannitti went to study in the regional capital, Campobasso, at the prestigious *liceo classico* Mario Pagano, the most ancient and, for many years the only, secondary school in Molise specializing in classical studies. Established originally in 1816 by the Bourbon King Ferdinand I, after Italy's unification the school was elevated to a lyceum and renamed for Mario Pagano, a Jacobin martyr of the Neapolitan revolution of 1799. In the late 1890s, the school became famous for its emphasis on the classical and humanist tradition, and especially for its attempt to promote a new national culture in post-*Risorgimento* Italy. It was here that Giovannitti first demonstrated his literary talent, winning a poetic contest among the youth.[18]

It is impossible to ascertain how much the school influenced the young Giovannitti, but there is no doubt that the anti-clericalism, the republicanism, and the libertarian ideas that circulated at the time had a lasting effect on him. In his autobiographical poem "Psicoanalisi minima," for instance, he cites Giosuè Carducci, the bard of Italian unification, who fiercely attacked the residues of the feudal and clerical past, as one of his favorite poets and the Italian revolutionary Giuseppe Garibaldi and the French Jacobin Jean-Paul Marat, symbols of the struggle against authoritarianism, as his favorite heroes.[19] The school's imprint is particularly evident in Giovannitti's poetry, which picked up the styles and themes of popular nineteenth-century Italian poets he studied at the Mario Pagano. Besides Carducci's classicism, he was inspired in particular by Giacomo Leopardi's romanticism and the social poetry of Lorenzo Stecchetti, Felice Cavallotti, and Mario Rapisardi.

There is no evidence that Giovannitti was involved or interested in politics while he lived in Italy. Lalli tells of a protest he organized in front of the mayor's house that caused some uproar among the town's richest men. But he concludes that despite a rebellious nature and a manifest sense of social justice, Giovannitti had not yet embraced any particular political ideology. Unlike other *sovversivi*, it was not political persecution that drove him at the age of seventeen to leave the security of home, family, and position for America. As he told the jury of Salem after his arrest during the 1912 Lawrence strike, neither was it hunger. Rather, it was his desire to "visit the world" and the belief that America was a "better and a freer land" than his own. A restless and inquisitive youth, he found the isolation and provincialism of his rural village suffocating. "I come from a country that for thousands of years has been oppressed by the old aristocracy . . . and is still oppressed by the present monarchy," he explained to the jury.[20] Feeling utterly frustrated and demoralized, at the age of fourteen, police reported, he tried to kill himself with a gun. It was this frustration, this revulsion against the wreckage of the past, that must have impelled him to leave.[21]

However, according to his son, Len—so named after Lenin, the Russian revolutionary hero—there might have been another, more dramatic, explanation for his father's migration. Not long before he died, Giovannitti allegedly revealed to his son a scar under his chin, confessing that he had been wounded by a sword in a duel over a question of honor while a student in Italy. He emerged victorious, perhaps killing his opponent, and as a result, wrote Len, he had to leave Italy and his family because duels were prohibited by law, and punishments were severe in cases of bloodshed.[22]

Whatever the real reason for his departure, Giovannitti left Italy in 1901 and never returned. Few facts are known about his early years in America. His life did not become a matter of public interest until after the Lawrence strike of 1912. Even then, the information provided by journalists and commentators of the time are very general and frequently imprecise. Giovannitti himself rarely discussed his private life, and he never explained his political choices and decisions.

Upon arriving in North America he landed first in Canada, where he lived for three years, probably working as a railroad laborer and coal miner and, at the same time, studying English and French in Montreal. Like other immigrants', his initial experience in the New World was one of deep disillusionment. Instead of the equality, opportunity, and freedom he had envisioned, he crashed into the hard realities of industrial capitalism. What he saw, commented the critic Louis Untermeyer, "was the whiplash and legal trickery, the few ruling the many, the misery and exploitation of the helpless."[23]

During this period Giovannitti became interested in the work of the Protestant church and, thinking of entering the ministry, began to attend a Presbyterian theological school at McGill University in Montreal. Why and how he became interested in theology is another of the mysteries of his life. Mario De Ciampis has suggested he came under the influence of Alfredo Taglialatela, an Italian Protestant minister mostly famous for debating Mussolini in 1904, who attracted a small following in the regions of Abruzzo and Molise. According to Len Giovannitti, however, his father's decision to study religion rested mostly on material considerations: He wanted to continue his education, and the theological school at McGill provided him with free education. Had he chosen a different field of study he would have had to pay tuition.[24] Even though Len's hypothesis is not to be excluded, Protestantism did have a genuine appeal for Giovannitti, complementing well his personality—his messianic disposition, his sensitivity, and his kindness. As he once explained, "I was not exactly a minister, but a sort of missionary. I preached to the people on Sundays and taught them during the week."[25]

In 1904, after receiving a call to take charge of a Presbyterian mission in Brooklyn, Giovannitti moved to New York and enrolled in the Union Theological Seminary at Columbia University. About a year later he was sent to Pittsburgh or a nearby town to lead another Protestant mission among Italian immigrants until "socialism came to impersonate religion in his life and led him through the vanishing stages of unbelief into atheism." Though Giovannitti might have been influenced by the radical ideas circulating in Italy, the major catalyst of his conversion to socialism was the raw spectacle of poverty and exploitation he saw in America. Giovannitti had experienced such abuse first-hand: "He wielded a pick in the coal mines of Canada," wrote his friend Justus Ebert, "and he has slept and starved in winter, on the benches of the parks in the city of New York." Giovannitti's resentment intensified after a visit he made to the coal mines of Pennsylvania as a Presbyterian pastor. It was there that "he seems to have come, for the first time, into close contact with the socialists and to have espoused their cause." He was influenced in particular by Carlo Tresca, who lectured regularly in the mining and mill towns around Pittsburgh. The two naturally bonded, starting what became a lifelong friendship.[26]

Around 1906 Giovannitti returned to New York, then as now the cultural and financial capital of the nation. These early years in the great "Cosmopolis"—as Giovannitti would call New York—were the turning point of his political and literary career. The 1910s were years of unprecedented political struggle in America, when for the first time socialism reached millions of people and working-class struggles shook the country. They were also years of great artistic and literary ferment. People spoke of a "little Renaissance," a "joyous season," and "confident years": It was "America's coming-of-age." There was, as Max Eastman, the editor of *The Masses*, recalled, "a sense of universal revolt and regeneration of the just-before-dawn of a new day in American art and literature as well as in politics." New York's Greenwich Village, with its streets filled with bars and cafés and populated by people of all nationalities, became the natural home of this emerging political and cultural radicalism.[27]

In this free and exuberant ambiance Giovannitti found the excitement and stimulation he had longed for. He fell so completely under the spell of New York City that he would call it home for the rest of his life.[28] His relationship with his adopted city, however, was, and remained, one of love and hate. New

York's exuberance, modernity, and multiculturalism clearly seduced him, as one can garner from the following verses of his poem "O Labor of America: Heartbeat of Mankind:"

> If this is not the fullness of your glory, O American Labor,
>   there is your New York, Cosmopolis of Mankind,
>   Whose towers you raised to mock the hurricanes
>   and to shame and debase the clouds,
>   Whose harbor shallows the nations, whose people,
>   myriad-tongued, absorb and reshape and amalgam
>   all creeds, all races in one humanity.[29]

But New York was for Giovannitti also the "Grey City of Hunger and Toil," the city of "Common Men who work and eat and breed," the "Ferocious City" by the "sick and voracious breath." Needless to say, it was this New York that inspired his pen and tortured his soul:

> I shall sing of your slums where you bleed,
> Your machines, iron claws of your greed,
> And your jails, viscid coils of your mind,
> The light of your eyes that dazzles the sun
> And turns your midnights into moons,
> The street where you buy and resell
> Each day the whole world and mankind,
> Your foundations that reach down to hell
> And the glory of your nameless dead,
> And the bitterness of your bread,
> And the sword that shall hallow your hand,
> And the dawn that shall garland your head![30]

Upon his arrival in New York, Giovannitti began working as a bookkeeper while immersing himself in the Italian immigrant radical milieu. By 1907 he had become an active member of "La Lotta Club" (The Struggle Club) and joined the lower Manhattan section of the Italian Socialist Federation (FSI). Its secretary, Raimondo Fazio, and other members of the FSI considered atheism a condition of membership and initially objected to Giovannitti's admission.[31] Distrust toward Giovannitti became even greater after he delivered a religious talk to the uptown branch of the YMCA, an incident that provided the material for "The Blind Men," one of his few English poems written before his Lawrence arrest. Evidently, however, it was not long before Giovannitti "dropped God out of his program" and converted unconditionally to syndicalism and revolutionary action.[32] But, as Renato Lalli and other scholars have pointed out, there are distinct elements of continuity between Giovannitti's activity as a pastor and as a labor agitator: In both cases he saw himself as a sort of missionary, a prophet of the poor and the oppressed. He Christianized socialism, making the struggle to overthrow capitalism congruent with the "pure" Christian values of love, brotherhood, and social equality; Jesus himself became a revolutionary not unlike the working-class rebels and martyrs of his own time. As in the case of other *sovversivi*, Giovannitti's socialism was fundamentally shaped by ethical concerns and assumed a special dimension of idealism and spirituality.

This religious imprint is particularly evident in his poetry. Scriptural allusions, biblical prophecies, and parallels between the workers' oppression and Jesus' own suffering surfaced repeatedly in his poems, as in the *sovversivi*'s literature in general.[33] It was a vision deeply rooted in a humanistic and spiritual conception of life, as articulated in his poem "Credo"—perhaps Giovannitti's clearest profession of faith. In it Giovannitti proclaims his belief in "the beauty and grandeur of life"; in "Love, the only one who defies, engages and hurls back, even if it does not conquer, the great Enemy"; in "Science," "Liberty," "Justice," and finally god:

> . . . I believe in Thee also, Oh Lord, whoever Thou art,
> Wherever Thou art, whatever Thy name,
>   Oh Love, Oh Truth, Oh Father and Mother of all, not only because
> Thou seest above and beyond my mortal eyes, but because
> I also need in my pride and pain to bend and
> kneel before a Supreme Pity that will illumine, even if it
> does not explain to me, the terrible mystery of Life.[34]

Ironically, it was the study of theology that turned him into an atheist, out of his conviction that "the church strangled the mind." "It was the Bible," explained Giovannitti to his son, "that made me a poet *and* a revolutionary. I enjoyed the lies and was thrilled with the poetry. I became a blasphemer, thanks to the church. . . . I wanted to tell the masses of the downtrodden that God was not their salvation. They were their own salvation—not singularly, selfishly, but together, united."[35]

The teachings of Marx became eventually his new Bible and the workers' struggle his *raison d'être*. By 1909, he had joined the editorial staff of *Il Pro-*

letario and two years later at the FSI annual Congress was appointed director of the newspaper and general secretary of the federation, a position that
exemplified his growing importance in the movement. The Consul General
of Italy in New York did not fail to notice Giovannitti's rise among the *sovversivi*. In a report to the Minister of the Interior, he underscored Giovannitti's intense journalistic and propagandistic activities, bringing attention to
his "violent words against the Italian government and its institutions" as well
as his opposition to Italy's 1911 invasion of Libya. In another letter, the consul
alerted the Italian minister that under Giovannitti's directorship, *Il Proletario*
had become the voice and defender of "the most advanced syndicalist, revolutionary, and anarchist theories."[36]

By then, Giovannitti had indeed become a fierce advocate of revolutionary syndicalism, opposed to militarism, reformist socialism, and electoral
politics. Although not officially a member, he nurtured particularly strong
ties to the IWW, urging Italian immigrants to embrace industrial unionism
as the only way to achieve their own liberation. Under his leadership, wrote
Michael Topp, the FSI became a "transnational organization in its strictest
sense," striving to shape the politics of both Italy and the United States.[37]
Contrary to other *sovversivi* who remained confined to the world of Little
Italy, Giovannitti established strong personal and political relationships with
American radical leaders and bohemians. He spoke Italian, English, and
French fluently. His language skills, coupled with his education and charm,
helped him transcend ethnic barriers, effectively strengthening the connections of Italian radicals with the American Left. He became a regular guest
at Mabel Dodge's famous salon at 23 Fifth Avenue, where socialists, anarchists, syndicalists, feminists, radical artists, and intellectual bohemians met
every Wednesday evening to talk about poetry, philosophy, sex, and revolution. He also wrote in English for *The Masses*, which Giovannitti eloquently
described as "the recording of the Revolution in the making . . . a blazing
torch running madly through the night to set afire the powder magazines
of the world."[38] He grew especially close to socialist artists and intellectuals
such as Helen Keller, John Macy, and Lewis Mumford and bohemian rebels like Max Eastman, Floyd Dell, Art Young, and John Reed—the American
"romantic revolutionary," subject of the movie *Reds* and best known for his
first-hand account of the Russian Revolution, for whom Giovannitti wrote
the epitaph on his tomb in the Kremlin.[39] This group of dissidents appeared
to some as just "strolling players" and "overgrown children" who wanted to
live "vibrantly and indecorously."[40] But, as Christine Stansell has observed,
they also "injected into the politics of the Left a new cultural dimension, as

well as psychological identification between working-class and middle-class people, that lent tremendous flexibility and originality to the popular politics of the era."[41]

Giovannitti was simultaneously a product and a producer of such a new culture; he was an important, albeit hitherto unrecognized, figure of what John Diggins has termed the "Lyrical Left."[42] Like New York's young rebels, he was a cultural modernist who sought to "break down the dualism between contemplative life and active life" in an attempt to fuse politics and art.[43] As he nostalgically recalled in the early 1950s: "We were all bohemians then, writers and artists, coming together for an evening to read to one another or display our paintings to keep our hopes up and to warm our talents."[44]

From 1910 until the late 1920s he was at the forefront of both the Italian immigrant and the American Left. A volcano of energy, he participated in everything that had to do with the cause of workers, seeking every opportunity to discuss political and philosophical matters. Traveling extensively to spread the message of revolutionary syndicalism, he distinguished himself as one of the Wobblies' most powerful and eloquent orators.

Immersing himself in the political and cultural radicalism of New York, Giovannitti fed his own appetite for art by writing verses. The first one, "Il vecchio del mare," appeared in *Il Proletario* on May 1, 1908. Written in quatrain stanzas rhyming alternately, it was a long ode to the sea expressing Giovannitti's faith in internationalism—the hope that like the ocean that "disdains borders and barriers," the earth too could be "free, open to all."[45] In another early poem published that year, "Al colubro nero," also written in quatrains in alternate rhyme, Giovannitti offered an unequivocal repudiation of his previous religious beliefs. The "black snake" is the priest by the "cold scales" and the "foul belly, engorged of others' hunger"—the "yellow," "toothless," "obscene," and "infamous" priest. The poem trembles with rage and passion. Looking back at his youth when he contemplated the ministry, Giovannitti admits to having been foolishly seduced by the Christian message of love but makes clear that he is now moving "to new dawns and new struggles." Defiant, he declares to the priest:

> . . . *De la notte esosa*
> *come te venne un uom da i foschi lidi*
> *Ed a me plebe ignara dolorosa*
> *Gridò come tu gridi*
> *Gridò amore, silenzio e sofferenza,*
> *e io che lo ascoltai e lo nutrii*

ne la mia stolta e pavida credenza
amai, tacqui, e soffrii—
Ma quando il suo pensier che or più non gabba
Se non per te, conobbi e il cor suo tristo,
prete ricorda: io liberai Barabba
e crocifissi Cristo.[46]

Giovannitti's conversion to socialism is also attested by two poems he wrote in 1909 in memory of two "saints" of the revolution: the French anarchist Luise Michel (1830–1905) and the Russian socialist Maria Spiridonova (1884–1941), both persecuted and imprisoned for many years for their heroic struggles on behalf of liberty and social justice.[47]

Other poems of this early phase of Giovannitti's poetic production include "Morte di fame," "La leggenda di Caino," "Il canto della scure," and, most notably, "Samnite Cradle Song" and "Son of the Abyss." The last two stand out as prime examples of Giovannitti's "moral" socialism—his indictment of social inequality and his faith in a "beautiful tomorrow." Characterized by disquieting rhythms and tones that are simultaneously desperate and heartening, they resemble litanies of peasant cultural traditions.

"Samnite Cradle Song" evoked the terrible living conditions of the *contadini* in his native land, Molise—their toil, hunger, despair, and resentment against a government deaf to their suffering. "So rendering is the new art of this poem," wrote a critic for the *New Review*, "that one sees all the misery of the world rise up and stalk before one; everybody that has ever been bereaved, shattered, hurt unto death, is included, is remembered."[48] It was written in the form of a lullaby that a poor mother sings to the baby in her arms at the end of her long day, but unlike lullabies, Giovannitti's song was "meant to awaken, and not put to sleep":

Hush-a-by, lullaby, listen! Don't sleep!
Lullaby, hush-a-by, mark well my word!
Thou shall grow big. Don't tremble. Don't fail! . . .
And if thou livest with sweat and with woe,
Grow like a man, not a saint, not a knave;
Do not be good, but be strong and be brave,
With the fangs of a wolf and the faith of a dog.
Die not the death of a soldier or slave,
Like thy grandfather who died in a bog,
Like thy poor father who rots in the rain.

But for this womb that has born thee in pain,
For these dry breasts thou has tortured so long,
For the despair of my life, my lost hope,
And for this song of the dawn that I sing
Die like a man by the ax or the rope
Spit of their God and stab our good king.[49]

As Nunzio Pernicone has noted, "Son of the Abyss," while evoking similar themes of social protest, was the first poem in which Giovannitti gave
voice to the plight of Italian immigrants in America. The poem was inspired
by the coal miners' strike of 1910–11 in Westmoreland, Pennsylvania, which
involved more than 10,000 mineworkers. After the Slavs, Italians constituted
the largest contingent of the strike and were described by contemporary
observers as "the staunchest and most resolute group engaged in the battle."
Though Giovannitti did not personally participate in the strike, he followed
the reports of the FSI members who hurried there to help the strikers and,
as director of *Il Proletario*, received a stream of letters from the striking
workers.[50]

Like "Samnite Cradle Song," "Son of the Abyss" begins with a lament—the
cry of the miners "buried" beneath the coal—and ends with a prophecy of
vengeance and redemption. The young "son of the abyss" will not "dream of
life in a tomb" like his father, nor will he bow his "proud fair-haired head."
Nourished with "a bitter drink of sweat and tears" and "lit by the flames of
steel," he will join "the priests of the greater ideal" who "slowly wear down
and undo the foundations of many a crumbling temple," eliciting at last "the
final avalanche that will shallow all."[51]

Giovannitti's revolutionary exhortations emerged not only in his poetry
but also in his articles and lectures. Between 1911 and 1912 he gave dozens
of talks on topics such as "The Class Struggle," "Capital and Work," "Science
and Religion," and "Government and Church." More important, during this
period he filled *Il Proletario* with articles on revolutionary theories, serial-
izing most notably *Sabotage*, a celebrated syndicalist pamphlet written by
Emile Pouget that he translated from French into Italian, and then into English for Charles H. Kerr, the socialist publishing house of Chicago.

Syndicalism, direct action, and sabotage, wrote Giovannitti, "have been
purposely denaturalized and twisted by the capitalist press in order to terrify
and mystify a gullible public." Far from the discrediting images of violence
and chaos it has taken on in the popular mind, sabotage, explained Giovannitti, is simply "the chloroforming of the organism of production, the 'knock-

out drops' to put to sleep and out of harm's way the ogres of steel and fire that watch and multiply the treasures of King Capital." Giovannitti distinguished between two main forms of sabotage: first as "a relaxation of work"—"going slow" and "taking it easy"—in order to limit the production and profits of the boss when wages and conditions are not satisfactory; then as "a mischievous tampering with machinery" in order to make impossible the work of scabs, thus securing the complete stoppage of work during a strike. Responding to the doubts and accusations of reformist socialists, Giovannitti argued that sabotage was both morally justifiable and necessary. Sabotage was not meant to be a "spiteful revenge" but an "expedient of war to obtain redress." It represented, he concluded, "the most formidable weapon of economic warfare, which will eventually open to the workers the great iron gate of capitalist exploitation and lead them out of the house of bondage into the free land of the future."[52]

Clearly, by 1912, when the strike was called in the Lawrence mills of Massachusetts, Giovannitti was a "full-fledged radical," part of every major political and social movement of New York's vigorous leftist community. His room on West 28th Street became a "nightly meeting place" for intellectuals of various nationalities, who engaged in passionate discussions of religion, art, literature, and politics. But it was his leadership in the memorable "crusade for bread and roses" strike and his near-martyrdom that threw Giovannitti into the national limelight and established him as a folk hero of the radical labor movement.[53] Recalling the Haymarket anarchists' case of 1886, when he was arrested he became an instant cause célèbre, winning international support and widespread press coverage. The articles published during and after the trial leave no doubt about Giovannitti's popularity and fame: "Of all the men in this country thrown up into public view by the seething, bubbling social discontent of the Twentieth Century, none is more interesting than Arturo Giovannitti," wrote *Current Opinion*. He had, continued the magazine, "the soul of a great poet, the fervor of a prophet, and added to these, the courage and power of initiative that mark the man of action and the organizer of great crusades."[54]

Lawrence

Coming at a time of labor unrest and industrial turmoil, the Lawrence strike became the most publicized and extraordinary working-class protest of the time. This was not because it was numerically large or because the strikers won, but because thousands of unskilled, uneducated immigrant workers of many different nationalities were able to transcend ethnic barriers and fight side by side against American manufacturers. "It was more than a union," recalled Elizabeth Gurley Flynn; "it was a crusade for bread and roses." Within a few weeks of its inception on January 11, 1912, the protest drew remarkable national publicity, acquainting the American people with the unskilled workers' deplorable living conditions and spreading the philosophy of radical unionism.[55]

The issue of the strike was a wage cut resulting from the reduction of the working week from fifty-six to fifty-four hours, but the loss of pay was only the last straw for the workers. The average weekly income was $8.00 to $9.00 for men, but women and unskilled workers, who represented the overwhelming majority of the labor force, received well below the norm, making only $6.00 a week and often as little as $4.00. People lived amassed in filthy, infested, overpriced tenements; children's mortality rate was one of the highest in the nation (17 percent); tuberculosis, pneumonia, and other respiratory diseases resulting from poor ventilation in the mills ravaged adult workers. Whole families, including pregnant women and children, worked in the mills to eke out a bare existence. As one exasperated worker put it: "Better to starve fighting than to starve working!"[56]

Led by the Italians, who constituted the largest ethnic group in Lawrence, about 14,000 workers eventually deserted their machinery, and after a few days the mills were completely empty. The strike went on for nearly three months, until March 14, when mill owners and state governments finally capitulated and granted the workers' demands—a 5 to 20 percent wage increase, increased compensation for overtime, reforms in the premium or bonus system, and no action against the workers who had participated in the strike.[57]

Advocating the abolition of the wage system and the need for social revolution, the IWW was the largest labor organization in Lawrence, counting about 1,300 members, and took on the difficult task of organizing the strikers. Arturo Giovannitti, along with Joseph Ettor, supplied the crucial leadership that made it possible.

Born of Italian immigrant parents in Brooklyn, New York, Ettor was "a man of unlimited physical vitality, a wonderful capacity for leadership, and a pronounced Socialist." Educated by his father to radicalism, he had been a Wobbly agitator and organizer since 1906. Unlike Giovannitti, he was of working-class origin and had only a grammar school education. Nonetheless, Ettor was fluent in English, Italian, Polish, and Yiddish and distinguished himself with his personal magnetism and eloquence. He arrived in

Lawrence on January 13, at the request of Angelo Rocco, head of the IWW's Italian section in Lawrence. A contemporary writer described Ettor as "a short, stocky Italian with a well shaped head, crowned with a thick shock of hair upon which a small hat sets rather jauntily." He used to wear "a flannel shirt and a large bow for a tie," his clothes "typically Italian in cut." He had dark brown eyes and flowing black hair; a kindly, boyish face "which lights up with humor and then sobers with scorn"; and a strong, resonant voice. By no means handsome, Ettor had yet "a touch of the artistic bohemian. Looking [like] anything but a wage worker, he nevertheless magnetized laboring groups."[58]

Arturo Giovannitti, in contrast, was tall, slender, and handsome. With straight brown hair and intense blue eyes, typically wearing Byronic collars and flowing cravats, he had the air of an aristocrat. As the historian Melvyn Dubofsky observed, he "played the mature intellectual to Ettor's boyish radical; where Ettor impressed audiences with his childish enthusiasm, Giovannitti did it with a romantic, mystical intensity."[59] But for all their physical differences, Ettor and Giovannitti were bound together by their faith in revolutionary syndicalism and the construction of a cooperative commonwealth through social revolution. Throwing themselves enthusiastically into the conflict, in short time, under their aggressive leadership, the unorganized revolt grew into an industrial union strike. Ettor developed a plan for a strike committee composed of fifty-six delegates representing twenty-seven different languages, urging a complete tie-up of all the mills. This committee organized mass picket squads to keep nonstrikers out of the mills and held meetings and parades with music and songs to encourage unity and solidarity among workers. Giovannitti, who arrived in Lawrence on January 20 at Ettor's request, assumed the work of relief for the strikers' families. Particularly useful was his connection with the Italian Socialist Federation, which by then had officially endorsed the program and objectives of the IWW. He corresponded with the FSI's secretary, soliciting contributions and arranging meetings to help the strikers in every way possible.[60]

A powerful, incisive speaker, he also played a crucial role in inspiring and unifying the strikers, especially the Italians, who constituted, because of their large numbers and militancy, the backbone of the strike. On January 21, a day after his arrival in Lawrence, he gave a moving speech about the importance of class consciousness and self-reliance, so that the workers could realize their power and strength:

Capitalism is the same in the Fatherland as it is here. . . . You are considered nothing but machines. Human machines in the old countries, human machines in this country. . . . Nobody has any interest in your conditions. If any effort is made to improve your conditions and raise you to the dignity of manhood and womanhood[,] that must come from yourselves alone; you can have no hope in no one but yourselves. It is only by your own power, your own determined will, your own solidarity, that you can rise to better things.[61]

Giovannitti invested a tremendous amount of energy to fighting ignorance and teaching Italian immigrant workers that their salvation depended on themselves. In so doing, he gave them what they needed most: a sense of dignity and self-respect, as well as hope for a brighter future. His inspirational power became particularly evident when, a few days later, before thousands of workers gathered on the Lawrence Common, he recited a poem that subsequently became known as the "Sermon on the Common." Written during the early days of the Lawrence strike, this poem/address is a paraphrase of Christ's "Sermon on the Mount." But unlike Jesus' message of passive perseverance, Giovannitti's sermon was a cry for revolutionary action. After listing the new "beatitudes" of the apostles and the warriors of labor, he launched a fierce attack on the dominant churches for having taught people to "be humble, resigned, patient, submissive, lowly and prone even as a beast of burden." Then, echoing the prophetic voice of Jesus, he announced to the workers that a "new evangel shall be proclaimed unto you" that would purify their souls:

> Therefore I say unto you, Banish fear from your
>   hearts, dispel the mists of ignorance from
>   your minds, arm your yearning with your
>   strength, your vision with your will, and
>   open your eyes and behold.
> Do not moan, do not submit, do not kneel, do
>   not pray, do not wait.
> Think, dare, do, rebel, fight - ARISE!"[62]

Walter Weyl, who was present at the meeting, was considerably impressed by the effect of Giovannitti's words on the masses of immigrant workers. Describing the thousands of men and women who gathered on the Common, he commented in the stereotypical language of the period:

I saw in this plain of upturned white faces that mask of infinite patient resignation, which is so tragic a mark of the peasant face in Eastern and Southern Europe. I saw also a new obscure enthusiasm, a new halting self-confidence breaking through the mists of apathy. The souls behind these white faces were beginning to stir. The minds behind these white faces were beginning to think.[63]

Giovannitti and Ettor's activity in Lawrence was cut short by their arrest on January 30. The day before, one of the largest demonstrations of the strike had taken place: Following clashes between the police and the strikers, one officer was stabbed and a young Italian woman, Anna LoPizzo, was killed. The following day the police charged a striker who was on the picket line, Joseph Caruso, with the murder and arrested Ettor and Giovannitti as accessories on the ground that "they did feloniously and maliciously move, procure, aid, counsel, and command" the homicide, even though the witnesses maintained that LoPizzo had been shot by an agent provocateur. The government charged that the bullet had been intended for Patrolman Oscar Benoit but missed him and killed LoPizzo instead.[64] The charge was preposterous: None of the three men was near the scene of the incident, and, as it turned out, Caruso did not even know Giovannitti and Ettor. Clearly, the arrests were aimed at putting the leaders of the strike out of action, in the hope of disrupting the protest. Surprisingly, they had a decidedly contrary effect: "First, they increased the number of the strikers. . . . Second, the purpose was so evident, as to create sympathy for the strike."[65]

A defense committee, including among others Elizabeth Gurley Flynn, Bill Haywood, and Carlo Tresca, was formed to mobilize public opinion and raise money for the defendants' legal expenses. Radical and liberal newspapers across the country expressed their outrage at the American judicial system, while the entire Italian American press, even that controlled by the *prominenti*, came out strongly in support of their co-nationals. Demonstrations in support of the three prisoners were held all over the world. Giovannitti's father turned for help to the president of the Italian Socialist Party while his fellow citizens in Ripabottoni issued a call of solidarity, collecting signatures for a petition to be sent concurrently to U.S. President William Howard Taft, the governor of Massachusetts, and the district attorney. Several Italian cities nominated Giovannitti as a candidate for Parliament; and Swedish labor unions even threatened to boycott American goods if the men were not released.[66]

The prolonged delay of the trial added fuel to workers' resentment against the state. "To-day the people of the United States are demanding the doors of the jail to be open," reported the *New York World*, "or they will close the doors of every mill in the United States and nail up every railroad in the country." Despite Ettor and Giovannitti's opposition to the idea of a general strike, 12,000 people left the Lawrence mills and marched toward the jailhouse demanding immediate freedom. The three prisoners, however, had been secretly moved out of the Essex County Jail at 4:00 A.M. the day before and taken to Salem, Massachusetts, home of the 1692 infamous witchcraft trials, which resulted in the execution of nineteen people.[67]

The threat of a general strike apparently worked: The following day, after ten months of imprisonment, the defendants' trial finally opened. After a fifty-eight-day hearing, on November 26 the jury found Ettor, Giovannitti, and Caruso innocent of all charges. Near the close of the trial, instead of their counsel's closing statement, Giovannitti and Ettor made their own final addresses to the jury. According to James Heaton, who wrote a detailed account of the trial, their statements proved to be the greatest strength of the defense. Addressing the jury in perfect English, Giovannitti spoke for twenty minutes, holding his listeners spellbound.[68] In a voice vibrant with passion, he first apologized for his emotional state and his limited knowledge of "your wonderful language." Demonstrating a thorough knowledge of American history and an exceptional understanding of the psychology of the American jury, he first invoked the great American traditions and ideals—the Revolution, the abolition of slavery, the Constitution—and went on to express respect for American laws and institutions.[69] His greatest merit, however, was to glorify his cause, emphasizing the ethical reasons and moral ideals that prompted Ettor and him to go to Lawrence:

> . . . One side alone of our story has been told here. . . . Only the method and only the tactics. But what about, I say, the ethical part of this question? What about the human and humane parts of our ideas? What about the grand condition of tomorrow as we see it . . . , where at last there will not be any more slaves, any more masters, but just one great family of friends and brothers. It may be, gentlemen of the jury, that you don't believe in that. It might be that we are dreamers; it may be that we are fanatics, Mr. District Attorney. We are fanatics. But yet so was a fanatic Socrates. . . . And so was a fanatic the Saviour Jesus Christ. . . . And so were all the philosophers and all the dreamers and all the scholars of the middle ages who

preferred to be buried alive by one of these very same churches which you reproach me now of having said that no one of our membership should belong to. . . .

A long hush followed Giovannitti's conclusion, broken only by the sobs of his listeners. "In twenty years of reporting," commented a journalist for *Current Opinion* afterward, "I have never heard the equal of that speech."[70]

Ultimately, the three men were freed because of the weakness of the case against them: The man who fired the shot was not identified, and the claim that Ettor and Giovannitti had incited the violence was impossible to prove.[71] But in part, the acquittal was also a result of the enormous solidarity that workers and radical leaders had built in support of the prisoners and, consequently, of the fear of what the workers' and leaders' response might have been had they been convicted.

Arrows in the Gale

During the ten long months of forced idleness and isolation in jail awaiting trial, Giovannitti transformed his cell into a study room, feeding his mind with the masterpieces of great writers. Almost as soon as he was imprisoned, he expressed a desire to read literature, philosophy, and history and was granted access to the warden's library. He read poetry in particular with "insatiate eagerness," dipping deeply into Shakespeare, Carlyle, and Balzac and finding in Shelley and Byron "the heady wine which his rebellious nature craved."[72]

The jail experience marked Giovannitti's best literary phase. Though he had already written verses for various Italian-language newspapers before his arrest, it was during his imprisonment that he produced his finest and most impassioned poems. "The Walker," which many consider Giovannitti's best poem, was first published in the *Atlantic Monthly* and soon appeared in all the main literary periodicals of the time and was translated into all major languages, including Chinese, Japanese, and even Esperanto.[73] In about 150 lines Giovannitti expressed "as it has never been expressed in English" the psychological torture of the prisoner locked within the bare confines of his cell.[74] The poem begins as follows:

> I HEAR footsteps over my head all night.
> They come and they go. Again they come and
>   they go all night.

They come one eternity in four paces and they
　　go one eternity in four paces, and between the
　　coming and the going there is Silence and
　　the Night and the Infinite.
For infinite are the nine feet of a prison cell, and
　　endless is the march of him who walks between
　　the yellow brick wall and the red iron
　　gate, thinking things that cannot be chained
　　and cannot be locked, but that wander far
　　away in the sunlit world, each in a wild
　　pilgrimage after a destined goal.[75]

Several contemporary critics compared Giovannitti's poem to Oscar Wilde's "Ballad of Reading Gaol" (1897) about the despair of a prisoner sentenced to death, some regarding it as "more real, more subjective, and yet at least as impassioned."[76] In it Giovannitti, like Wilde, conveys the terror, anguish, and obsession of the prisoner for "a small brass key that turns just half around and throws open the red iron gate." But whereas Wilde's ballad is pervaded by gloom and the death that awaits the prisoner, "The Walker," in the words of Joseph Tusiani, an Italian American poet and literary critic who became a close friend of Giovannitti in his last years of life, "is a hymn to life, a paean to the sanctity of the dynamic energy of life which prison only interrupts but can never halt."[77]

But "The Walker" goes even beyond that. "It is more than a poem," wrote *Current Opinion*. "It is a great human document." As Louis Untermeyer commented, "it is a poetic epitome of a creed, a movement that is both political and religious."[78] "The Walker" transcends the inner emotions of Giovannitti, the prisoner, and gives voice to the thoughts of Giovannitti, the revolutionary prophet. The result: a synthesis of lyrical beauty and political purpose. The psychological torment is in fact fused with the indictment of society— "the monstrous cabala that can make the apostle and the murderer, the poet and the procurer, think of the same gate, the same key and the same exit on the different sunlit highways of life"—and the supreme faith in a common humanity. And it is this hopeful thought that finally gives the prisoner comfort and rescues him from total despair:

Stop, rest, sleep, my brother, for the dawn is well
　　nigh and it is not the key alone that can throw
　　open the gate.[79]

Another acclaimed poem inspired by his jail experience was "The Cage," which, like "The Walker," also appeared originally in the *Atlantic Monthly*. It was written one evening, in response to Bill Haywood's request that he write something about "Sixteenth Century courts trying to solve Twentieth Century problems." It describes three men sitting in a green iron cage, where Giovannitti, Ettor, and Caruso themselves were held during the trial, symbolic of the injustice of capitalist society. Giovannitti powerfully re-creates the coldness and deadness of the jail: "Senility, dullness and dissolution were all around the green iron cage, and nothing was new and young and alive in the great room, except the three men."

In net contrast to the mournful silence of the jail and the old judges who preside over them, the three prisoners represent the exuberant youth and hopeful future. While outside the prison "the terrible whirl of life" moves on, the three men contemplate the injustice of the present law that keeps them in prison and wonder: "what subtle and malignant power could be in the metal of this cage that is so mad to imprison us?" In response, the metallic soul of the cage speaks to them, pleading for a return to the bygone joy of labor:

> O Man, bring me back into the old smithy,
> purify me again with the holy fire of the forge,
> lay me again on the mother breast of the
> anvil, beat me again with the old honest hammer
> —O Man, remould me with thy wonderful
> hands into an instrument of thy toil,
> Remake of me the sword of thy justice,
> Remake me of the tripod of thy worship,
> Remake of me the sickle for thy grain,
> Remake of me the oven for thy bread,
> And the andirons for thy peaceful hearth,
>   O Man!
> And the trestles for the bed of thy love,
>   O Man!
> And the frame of the joyous lyre, O Man![80]

Here, according to a contemporary critic for *The Survey*, "is Giovannitti's message of freedom at its noblest."[81] "The Cage" is indeed at once a powerful attack on authority, law, and tradition and a glorification of Giovannitti's new gospel of labor. "We are not prepared to debate the question whether Syndicalism has a soul, but if it has, 'The Cage' gives a picture of it," commented *Atlantic Monthly*. The reviewer clearly did not sympathize with the content of the poem, finding it "harshly materialistic" and warning that "a rebel wrote it." Yet, it recognized its spiritual character and admitted that "to the very poor, bread, bed, and sunshine may suggest something very different than materialism."[82]

"The Cage" and "The Walker" were re-published in 1914 along with twenty-two other poems in a volume entitled *Arrows in the Gale*, which remains the best of Giovannitti's collections of poetry. At times Giovannitti used formal verse and end rhyme, but his best poems were written in blank free verses with a predominance of pentameters. As many critics have pointed out, his style comes especially close to the free rhythmic mode of Walt Whitman. Giovannitti resembles Whitman not only in form but also in his vigor, energy, and exuberance. However, Joseph Tusiani suggests that it was the lesser-known American poet Edward Markham, author of "The Man with the Hoe," more than Whitman who influenced the young Italian. Characterized by traditional metrics, Markham's poetry, explains Tusiani, helped Giovannitti to combine the classical and humanistic formation of the *liceo* Mario Pagano with the new revolutionary verve of the early twentieth century.[83]

Regardless of the style, however, the dominant theme of all of Giovannitti's poems is that of class conflict and the faith in a better tomorrow. As *The Survey* put it: "In the poems of Giovannitti we are forced to recognize the first American poems in a world-wide outpouring of the working class verse that is giving literary expression to that revolt against our present day institutions, industrial and political, which has expressed itself in action in the last three years in the mass strikes all over Europe."[84] Similarly, in her introduction to *Arrows in the Gale*, Helen Keller presented Giovannitti as "a poet of revolt against the cruelty, the poverty, the ignorance which too many of us accept in blind content." Giovannitti, continued Keller, provides the reader with a poetry that is "the spiritualization of a lofty dream that he seeks to realize—the establishment of love and brotherhood and social justice for every man and woman upon the earth."[85] This sublime conception of the world never deserted him; it is at the center of all his poems: his battle cries, his invectives against organized religions, as well as his more lyrical and dispassionate verses.

Because of its revolutionary content, Giovannitti's poetry has raised the question of the relationship between art and propaganda. Is his poetry—asked Untermeyer—cramped and distorted by the message? Does the political nature of politically inspired art affect the quality of the art? Apparently to most literary critics, the answer is yes. Giovannitti's inability to detach himself from the labor cause represented, according to them, his main limitation as a poet. For example, Florence Converse, a contemporary critic for *The Survey*, argued that, with a few exceptions, Giovannitti remains the poet of emotion rather than of thought, a lyrist rather than a dramatist or a narrative poet. In most of his poems, continues the critic, he fails because of his irresistible tendency to declaim and to accuse.[86]

Similarly, for Joseph Tusiani, the reputation of "poet of the workers" that Giovannitti gained through the Lawrence strike and the publication of *Arrows in the Gale* marked the limitation and the death of his poetic talent. Tusiani believes that because of the responsibility Giovannitti felt to remain faithful to his role as spokesman of the laborer, he suppressed any other sentiment and produced monotonous lyrics that found in labor both their point of departure and their point of arrival. Tusiani recognizes Giovannitti's poetic talent: His fervor, eloquence, and sensitivity, Tusiani explains, can be sensed even in his most mediocre verses. Yet, concludes Tusiani, his poetic message is often too explicit, too manifest, too often characterized by rhetorical expressions and demagoguery.[87]

Joseph Zappulla, a contemporary poet and friend of Giovannitti, seems to concur with Tusiani. Writing a review of *Quando canta il gallo*, Zappulla separates Giovannitti, the poet/apostle, from the lyrical poet—singer of the nature, spectator of the world's beauty, forgetful at last of the social struggles, tyrannies, injustices, and human evil. His preference and praise are unmistakably for the latter. He admits that it is difficult to separate what is "pure poetry" from the propagandistic poetry, for love, charity, piety, enthusiasm, vehemence, and desire of good inevitably merge. He also understands that Giovannitti was essentially born as a social poet, from and for the struggle. Yet, he concludes that "the best of Giovannitti"—what, to those who love and understand poetry, makes him a poet in the modern sense of the word, without adjectives that indicate his tendencies—can be found in his idyllic poems.[88]

Such criticism has two major limits: First, it is based on a vague, preconceived notion of "authenticity" or "pure art" that is never clearly defined. Second, and more important, it fails to grasp the most significant and compelling part of Giovannitti's poetry: its idealistic spirit. As Charles Ashleigh wrote for the *Little Review*, "There is something that flames through these poems that abashes one who would content himself with a sterile commentary on the versification."[89] That spirit—the utopian vision of the world—which is the spark of all of Giovannitti's poetry, is what makes it poetry. Class struggle, social injustice, economic inequality, bourgeois hypocrisy and self-interest—all these are matters of great concern for Giovannitti, inspiring him to write something meaningful.[90] This, however, is not to say that Giovannitti's poetry should be reduced to political propaganda. Rather, we should acknowledge that there exists perhaps an inherent tension within radical culture between art and politics, and that one cannot be judged apart from the other. The idealism and rhetorical tones that characterize and, according to some, undermine Giovannitti's poetry cannot be separated from the vision burning within him. "His hopes," wrote Jacob Panken, a judge and active socialist of the 1920s, "were his beliefs. His dreams were real to him . . . that life could be good, that the world can be beautiful, that the future is full of promise of a world in which fear, conflict and suffering will disappear; that was his religion."[91] If Giovannitti's later art became poorer, as Tusiani lamented, it was not because of his inability to detach himself from the cause of labor but exactly for the opposite reason, because he lost his revolutionary enthusiasm. The disillusionment with the Russian Revolution, the rise of fascism in Italy, and the execution of Sacco and Vanzetti were terrible blows to Giovannitti's political ideas. Believing in the triumph of justice and equality became harder and harder, if not impossible. As a result, his inspiration ran dry once he became disaffected with the revolutionary dream.

Giovannitti's poetry was always the direct expression of his political experiences and aspirations, and not of some literary caprice. As his friend Carmelo Zito commented in the preface to *Quando canta il gallo*, his poems were written "with the disclosure of the street in mind, and not the hush of the drawing room."[92] Like other contemporary IWW and radical poets—such as Joe Hill, Ralph Chaplin, and Charles Ashleigh—he rejected the art-for-art's-sake function of literature and used poetry as a means of advocating political and social change. Giovannitti removed himself from the "ivory towers" of intellect and "took on another role: the poet as prophetic rebel."[93] In doing so, he accomplished a tremendous task—the awakening of the workers to a realization of their power and their dignity.

What made Giovannitti exceptional was not simply his poetic talent but his great eloquence and proficiency in his acquired language. An expert eye could probably notice occasional shortcomings in Giovannitti's English poems, but his command of English is impressive. And this raises another issue. There is no doubt that the workers were Giovannitti's intended audience. Yet, whether in English or Italian, his poems do not speak the tongue of the laborer. In a way, this was a natural result of Giovannitti's formal education—the study of the classics at the lyceum of Campobasso, the study of the Bible in the theological schools, and the self-study of nineteenth-century American literature. But it also reflected the difficult struggle of his generation of radicals to forge a truly "revolutionary" means of expression to suit the "revolutionary" inspiration of the content.

We will never know how many workers read or understood Giovannitti's verses, but Giovannitti's great reputation among the workers suggests that they nonetheless found his poetry moving and powerful. This tendency to glorification was in part "a spontaneous expression of the pride which the workers felt for the incipient literature of their own class."[94] But it also reflected the inspirational character that Giovannitti embodied so proudly.[95] Giovannitti saw himself as the apostle of the poor, the spokesman of the oppressed; and the workers could spontaneously identify with him and his poems, for he spoke of their hopes, their struggles, and their dreams. As he wrote in the preface of *Parole e Sangue*, "the author does not possess anything of his own, not even his scarce talent, if it weren't for the working people."[96]

After Lawrence

After the Lawrence strike, Giovannitti, acclaimed as both a great poet and a labor leader, went on to seize his moment of literary and political fame. On January 24, 1913, he started an intense *giro di propaganda* (propaganda tour) that took him from New Haven and other towns in Connecticut to Massachusetts, Rhode Island, Vermont, and then Pittsburgh and Chicago.[97] In the spring of 1913, the memory of prison still fresh in his mind, he returned to Massachusetts to help lead the strike of the Draper foundry plant workers in Hopedale, which lasted about thirteen weeks and resulted, as did the Lawrence strike, in the death of one Italian, Emilio Bacchiocchi, shot by police while picketing. Giovannitti was leading a crowd of 400 men and women from Milford to Hopedale on May 3 when a large squad of officers blocked their way. "Giovannitti and other strike leaders were allowed to pass," reported the Milford history bulletin, "only to be arrested on their arrival in front of the Draper works." Although found guilty in District Court and fined $10, Giovannitti appealed the sentence, and the charge against him was eventually dropped.[98]

From Hopedale he went to Paterson, New Jersey, where another historic working-class struggle—the strike of the silk workers—was unfolding. Together with Tresca, Flynn, and Haywood, Giovannitti once again helped galvanize the strikers through speeches, meetings, and marches. When John Reed and Mabel Dodge proposed organizing a public pageant to publicize the strike and raise money for the strikers, Giovannitti enthusiastically agreed to help, becoming a member of the executive committee that planned the event. The pageant opened on June 7 in Madison Square Garden in New York. While a sensation from an artistic point of view, the pageant failed to generate money for the workers, and the strike eventually ended in their defeat.[99]

As Michael Topp has pointed out, the loss in Paterson profoundly shook the workers' confidence in the IWW and their tactics. Giovannitti's faith began to fade too. In June 1914, at the annual Congress of the FSI, he stepped down as director of *Il Proletario*, citing personal reasons. Mario De Ciampis speculated that he was probably tired and wanted more time for his literary endeavors.[100] Three months later he launched together with Onorio Ruotolo, the founder of the Da Vinci Art School, the illustrated bimonthly magazine *Il Fuoco*. Echoing *The Masses*'s experimental and modern stamp, by the third issue *Il Fuoco* had reached a circulation of 10,000 copies. Its success, however, was soon undermined by the outbreak of World War I. At first the magazine took an anti-militaristic stance, but when Italy entered the conflict the ideological differences between Giovannitti and Ruotolo, who favored intervention, became irreconcilable. In the June 15, 1915, issue Giovannitti announced his resignation, explaining to readers that "after this brief journalistic vacation, he was ready to resume his role as a militant in the struggle for social change."[101]

A stern anti-militarist, Giovannitti fought fiercely against Italy's and then America's entry into World War I, speaking at anti-war meetings and writing for anti-military newspapers, including his own *Vita*, which he founded in 1916 after leaving *Il Fuoco*. As we saw in chapter 4, the war also inspired him to write some of his best plays and stories, as well as poems such as "One against the World," "The Day of War," and "The Pacifist." As a result of his anti-war activity, on September 29, 1917, he was arrested on charges of seditious conspiracy as part of a federal roundup that led to the indictment of 168 radicals, mostly IWW members. He managed, however, to escape conviction by pursuing an independent legal strategy together with Tresca and Flynn, who were also among the arrested. Arguing that the strategy of a collective trial advocated by Bill Haywood was tantamount to political suicide, Flynn, Tresca, and Giovannitti won a severance motion of their case from that of the other Wobblies and, as a result, were never tried.[102]

During these difficult times of repression and disillusionment, Giovannitti's revolutionary dreams were revived by the outbreak of the Russian Revolution. Like other radicals of the time, he was thrilled by the news of the overthrow of the czar and the hope that the Soviet experiment could be the beginning of a new world. He attended conferences, meetings, and all kinds of activities in favor of the Soviet comrades. He composed new poems celebrating the triumph of the revolution and "the great day to come."[103] He even named his son, born in 1920, after Lenin. Giovannitti's voice, wrote De Ciampis, "roared" in all principal communist gatherings of New York, prompting the Italian consul to notify Italian authorities that he "had joined the Bolshevik movement." Actually, Giovannitti was never a member of the Communist Party, though he associated with the members of the communist-led Federation of Italian Workers of America, writing frequently for their organs, *Alba Nuova, Il Lavoratore*, and *Il Lavoro*.[104]

His flirtation with communism, however, did not last long. As Massimo Salvadori has noted, Giovannitti's socialism was at the heart a "libertarian socialism" based on the idea that the abolition of capitalism must occur within the respect of individual liberties and democracy to have positive effects. By the mid-1920s, his revolutionary faith began to wane and his political ideas shifted more and more toward reformist socialism. But even after his disillusionment with communism, Giovannitti did not become an anti-Soviet, keeping good relationships with his communist friends, particularly Anthony Capraro, with whom he maintained a close correspondence until his death. He refused to publicly condemn the Soviet Union, which, if only symbolically, represented to him still an alternative to capitalism and an emblem of his prophetic dream:

> To rise and stand up together,
> To rise and stand up together against nature and destiny,
> To rise and stand up together in one holy fraternity,
> To rise and conquer the earth
> With labor and love and mirth
> One race, one tongue, one birth
> One dream of eternity.[105]

In this sense he was unique among the *sovversivi* in that he was able to transcend the sectarian divisions that plagued the Italian American radical movement, moving easily through the entire spectrum of the Italian American, and American, Left, to the point that socialists, communists, syndicalists, and anarchists, wrote his friend Rosario Dramis, all claimed Giovannitti as one of their own.[106] Only Carlo Tresca among the *sovversivi* was able to enjoy comparable respect and support.

In the early 1920s Giovannitti participated actively in the campaign to save Sacco and Vanzetti and to fight Mussolini and fascism. He served as secretary of the Anti-Fascist Alliance of North America, founded the anti-fascist newspaper *Il Veltro*, and wrote for *Il Nuovo Mondo*, serving briefly as its editor from 1928 to 1930. He was especially in great demand as an orator at anti-fascist meetings, distinguishing himself on various occasions.[107]

On September 14, 1930, he moved to Hollywood, where he was offered a job as a translator for the Metro-Goldwyn-Mayer (MGM) studio, which was then starting an Italian production. He was probably planning to stay there a long time, for his friends had organized a farewell banquet in his honor at John's Spaghetti House before his departure. However, according to information provided by the Italian consul in Los Angeles, MGM fired Giovannitti in June 1931 under fascist pressure via the influential Giannini family, which had founded Bank of America and controlled the banking industry in California. While in Los Angeles Giovannitti wrote a motion picture, but the film was never produced for lack of funds. Discouraged and perhaps perturbed by the superficiality and commercialism of Hollywood life, he returned to New York penniless on January 10, 1932. To help him out financially, the ACWA created the "Italian Labor Education Bureau" and made Giovannitti its secretary, a post he held until 1940, although he never had a real function there. At this point, his political activities began to recede more and more into the organized labor establishment and its leaders.[108]

Information about Giovannitti's private life remains, like that of other *sovversivi*, somewhat elusive. He was apparently married twice: first to a German woman who left him a daughter, Vera, and then to a Russian Jew, Carrie (Carolina) Zaikaner, a garment worker he met during a union meeting. Giovannitti dedicated *Arrows in the Gale* to her. They had two children: a daughter, Roma, in 1913, and Lenin in 1920. Each of the children's names—Vera (truthful), Roma (Rome), and Lenin—offers hints of Giovannitti's romanticism and idealism: his faith in knowledge, his confidence in the revolution, and his nostalgic attachment to Italy.

The glamorous public image of Giovannitti—compassionate, sensitive, unselfish, completely devoted to the cause of the oppressed—contrasts stridently with the spiteful memories of his son, Len, who, following in his father's footsteps, became a writer. In Len's autobiography instead of the magnificent revolutionary hero adored by Italian workers and friends we find a verbally abusive and chauvinist husband, a distant and intimidating father, and a hopeless alcoholic besmirched by his own drinking. The relationship between Giovannitti and Zaikaner was indeed filled with tensions; they were poor and struggled to support their children. They fought frequently and she periodically walked out on him, but—remembered Vera—he would court and win her back each time with beautiful flowers and romantic letters. In 1939, after twenty-five years of bitter quarrels due especially to Giovannitti's increasing problems with alcohol, Zaikaner finally left him. He then lived for a short period with another woman, Margherita Di Maggio, but, as he jokingly confessed to his friend Vincenzo De Lalla, his lovers were at least a dozen.[109]

A complex, contradictory, and multifaceted personality—it is not easy to come to grips with Giovannitti the man. "He could be cruel and arrogant and yet tender and thoughtful," recalled his daughter Vera. He seems to have grown more and more intolerable after he returned from Hollywood, when, as he lamented to his friends, he began to suffer from rheumatism and to drink heavily. By then he was clearly disillusioned with the revolution and considered himself a failure as both a poet and a man. As Zaikaner explained to Len, "your father's a tortured soul."[110]

Giovannitti's health began to decline dramatically after World War II, and by the early 1950s his rheumatism deteriorated into paralysis of the legs. He lived the last ten years of his life in great poverty and solitude, first at George-town, Connecticut, and then on Pelham Parkway in the Bronx. Deserted by his family, he was assisted by an old friend, Florence Rauh, a Greenwich Village socialist feminist who had been particularly active in the movement for women's suffrage and birth control during the early twentieth century.[111] The poet Joseph Tusiani could not conceal his disappointment on his first visit to "the legendary poet of labor" in 1950. He had envisioned him "as the tall, handsome, fiery fighter of Lawrence," but, he wrote, "there he lay, half-paralyzed, immobile—the ghost of his own past." "Had it not been for something commanding in his voice and, most especially, in his eyes," he continued, "I would have failed to link that conspicuous mound of flesh to the battling angel of my prenatal days."[112]

Giovannitti's anguish emerges with particular vividness in a letter he wrote to his friend Vincenzo De Lalla in 1951:

Physically, I am not well; spiritually I live in mortal anguish; and for all the rest I stagger blindly on the edge of the abyss. My "influential" friends of the wealthy and fat labor movement, which I have served with devotion, sorrow, and anxiety, have completely abandoned me, to the point that with only $15–20 a week they could save the little dignity that I have left.[113]

Despite his physical suffering, Giovannitti continued to play an important role in the history of the Italian American Left as an orator of labor and as an anti-fascist. The Italian consul still deemed Giovannitti a "dangerous *sovversivo*" in the 1940s.[114] Giovannitti also kept on writing poetry and contributing to radical papers. But he left the best of his political energy and art behind in the revolutionary syndicalism of Lawrence. His myth was sustained by the workers as long as he lived, but by the late 1920s he had already become merely a shadow of what he had once been. The 1910s were the grandest years of Giovannitti's life. Unfortunately, he never approached them again. As his son sadly commented, "Somewhere, somehow, along the line of his life, the fire in him rapidly burned down."[115]

Figure 7.1
"The Pro-Fascist press in support of the club." Il *Nuovo Mondo*, November 22, 1925. This cartoon exposed the ignominious role of the mainstream Italian American press in raising funds for the Italian fascist state. The figure with the megaphone urges immigrants to "help the treasury of the fatherland" while the caption below the cartoon alerts readers that "Every cent given for the Italian debt is an aid to Mussolini's dictatorship."

7

Allegories of Anti-Fascism

The Radical Cartoons of Fort Velona

On November 22, 1925, the anti-fascist daily Il *Nuovo Mondo* published a striking cartoon on its front page (fig. 7.1). It caricatured the Italian dictator Benito Mussolini in his typical pose: standing erect with arms by his side, his lips sticking out in a serious, almost frowning, expression, and a defiant, threatening-looking gaze. Emblazoned on his hat are all the terrible effects of the fascist regime: persecution, destruction, working-class slavery, Blackshirt violence, militia, unemployment, and debt. Next to Il Duce stands a figure with a megaphone representing the Italian-language mainstream press—the most important vehicle of fascist propaganda in the United States. The cartoon's title, "The pro-Fascist press in support of the cudgel," commented on the ignominious connection between influential Italian Americans and fascism, while the caption below, "Every cent given for the Italian debt is an aid to Mussolini's dictatorship!" alerted readers that any money donated to the fascist regime would be turned into weapons against them.

The artist, Fortunato Velona, was an Italian immigrant socialist and labor organizer of working-class origins who, like other *sovversivi*, fought passionately and relentlessly against fascism. His dramatic cartoons poking fun at Mussolini and his corrupt regime filled the pages of Italian American radical papers from the early 1920s through the end of World War II and were frequently reproduced into gigantic posters that were used at anti-fascist protests and rallies. Their humor, impertinence, and insight still catch the eye; yet, despite their abundance and quality Velona's illustrations remain completely unknown to American and Italian American audiences.[1] The historian Cécile Whiting in her study of anti-fascism in American art does not mention Velona at all, let alone Italian American contributions to the subject. In fact she argues that American artistic responses to fascism were almost nonexistent until Hitler came to power in the mid-1930s.[2]

187

This chapter is an attempt to correct this view and bring Velona's artwork to wider scholarly attention. While the American Left did not react against fascism until the formation of the Popular Front in 1935, Italian American radicals, as we saw earlier, mobilized as soon as the fascists began to organize. Not only did they establish political organizations and papers through which they launched innumerable anti-fascist activities such as demonstrations, parades, and lectures, but they also used a variety of cultural forms to awaken the Italian American, and American, public to the brutal reality of fascist rule. Anti-fascist politics inspired, for example, many poems, such as Giovannitti's "To Mussolini," "Italia Speaks," and "Battle Hymn of the New Italy"; Antonino Crivello's "Ad Antonio Fierro" (written in memory of the young Italian killed by the Khaki Shirts in 1933) and "Giustizia"; and Francesco Pitea's poetic invectives. During the 1920s and 1930s fascism also increasingly became the foremost subject of dramatic performances and novels discussed earlier, like Vincenzo Vacirca's *Madre*, Carlo Tresca's *L'attentato a Mussolini*, Virgilio Gozzoli's Il *cancro*, and Clara Vacirca's *Cupido tra le camicie nere*.

But with the rapid ascendency of Mussolini, the privileged art form in the Italian American crusade against fascism became the cartoon. In many respects, cartoons were more effective than other cultural media. Because of their immediacy, dynamism, and directness, they allowed for a broader audience and a more direct message than other artistic or cultural forms. As Randall Harrison has put it, the cartoon is "communication to the quick. It is fast; it grabs the reader on the run. And it is penetrating; it can tickle the funny bone or hurt to the quick."[3]

It is impossible to assess how many people saw Velona's cartoons and how they responded. The fact that they appeared in Italian-language radical papers certainly limited their readership and influence. Yet, Velona's illustrations should be considered in the vanguard of "American" anti-fascist visual representations as they pre-dated them by more than a decade, anticipating the contours of the anti-fascist social-realist art of the Popular Front. The themes and style of Velona's cartoons were the same attributes that Whiting found in the anti-fascist illustrations of *The New Masses*, *The Daily Worker*, and *Leftward* in the mid-1930s by artists like Willam Gropper, Jacob Burck, and Art Young. Like their drawings, Velona's cartoons were politically engaged, didactic, and propagandistic. They also largely covered the same anti-fascist themes—repression, terror, corruption, and war. This resemblance suggests that artistic responses to anti-fascism developed along with political activism and political consciousness. Art and politics mutually reinforced each other: Growing awareness of the threat of fascism stimulated artistic expression, while art served as the means through which ideological strategies against fascism were articulated.

Figure 7.2
Artist Fort Velona
(1893–1965) in New
York City in the 1940s.
A socialist and labor
organizer, Velona
became best known
for his anti-fascist
cartoons, which were
reproduced widely
in the Italian-
language radical press.
Photograph courtesy
of Velona's grandson,
Steve Fanti.

Early Life

Fortunato Velona or Fort, as he became known in America, was born on January 18, 1893, in the town of Bova Superiore near the Calabrian city of Reggio Calabria, located on the toe of the Italian peninsula and founded by Greek settlers in the eighth century BCE. He was the second of four children born to Domenico Velona and Severina Marino. The Velonas owned a little farm producing grapes, olives, and silkworms—the main staples of the Calabrian economy at the time. The land represented the only source of income for the entire family.[4]

Inspired by the propaganda of local socialist leaders, when he was little more than a boy Velona joined the Italian Socialist Party and the Chamber of Labor of Reggio Calabria (fig. 7.2). Through these organizations he met many "noble comrades" who served as his "teachers and brothers," instilling in his conscience "the flame of the ideal and the repugnance for all forms of social injustice."[5] The root of his radicalism was the wretchedness of life in the South. Of humble birth, Velona experienced first-hand the financial straits of rural life, the exploitation of the peasants by the *signori*, and the widespread corruption of governmental authorities. His socialism, like that of many other *sovversivi*, grew to a large extent out of a moral desire to correct those wrongs and create a better and more just world.

Velona's exposure to socialist ideas came also from the reading of *La Luce*, the organ of the Socialist Federation of Calabria. "I recall," he later wrote, "the struggles against the local bosses carried on by this paper, which was quite widespread and feared by the dominant classes, especially the clergy which seized every opportunity to admonish the faithful not to read it." He also referred to another influential newspaper, *Germinal*, published in the nearby Sicilian city of Messina, which conducted a virulent campaign against Italy's invasion of Libya and the conservative government of Prime Minister Giovanni Giolitti, despite the fierce censorship against the radical press that existed at that time.[6] Out of this Calabrian radical milieu emerged many leaders who would later play an important role in the Italian American radical movement—for example, the lawyer Carmelo Zito, who became the editor of *Corriere del Popolo* of San Francisco; Emilio Grandinetti, a major organizer of the garment workers in Chicago; and the poet Francesco Greco.

Hoping for a better life than he had in his native town, Velona left Italy in 1912, at the age of nineteen, following the outbreak of a terrible cholera epidemic in the South that caused further impoverishment and unemployment. Italy, recalled Velona years later, "was continuously perturbed by popular agitations against the rising cost of living and the fierce governmental surveillance of subversive forces. . . . Emigration seemed the best way to resolve the severe crisis and avoid a popular uprising."[7]

He reached the United States through Canada, settling originally in Rochester, New York, where he worked as a dressmaker for the Stein Block Clothing Company. There he became a member of the local branch of the reformist wing of the Italian Socialist Federation and with Girolamo Valenti, Gioacchino Artoni, and Giacomo Battistoni strove to spread socialism and organize his co-national workers. A few years later, in 1916, he married Angelina Patemì, also originally from Calabria, and moved to New York City, where he joined the Amalgamated Clothing Workers of America, distinguishing himself as one of the most important organizers of Italian Local 63.[8]

In December 1921 Velona decided to return to Italy with his wife and two children. However, what was supposed to be a permanent homecoming turned into just a temporary visit. A few months after his arrival, the postmaster of Bova informed Velona's father that a warrant for his son's arrest had been issued. The reason for the arrest warrant remains unknown, but one can speculate that his labor activism in America had been monitored by Italian authorities as in the case of other *sovversivi*. Hastily, Velona decided to return to the United States, leaving his children and wife behind in hope perhaps of returning soon to Italy. The rapid rise of fascism, however, changed his plans yet again and, reunited with his family, he remained in America for the rest of his life.[9]

Back in New York, he began working as a tailor, a trade he had probably learned from an uncle in Calabria. At the same time, he immersed himself in the anti-fascist struggle, becoming one of the most outspoken opponents in America of Mussolini's regime. On April 15, 1933, together with his best friend, Girolamo Valenti, he spoke in front of a crowd of 30,000 people who had gathered in Union Square to protest international fascism.[10] Valenti spoke in English, exposing the crimes of fascists and warning about the rise of Nazism while Velona addressed the crowd in Italian, speaking of the resistance of workers in Italy and calling for a united front.[11]

In the same year, on July 14 he took part in the punitive expedition against the American fascist Khaki Shirts, in Astoria, Queens. Fearing a possible rise of fascism among Americans, the *sovversivi* published a last-minute appeal in their press: "ANTI-FASCIST MOBILIZATION: This evening all at the Columbus Hall at Astoria against the Khaki Shirts." The plea was a call to arms. Anti-fascists of various tendencies showed up in Astoria, from Brooklyn, the Bronx, Manhattan, Staten Island, and New Jersey. Clashes between the two factions erupted after the leader of the Khaki Shirts, Art J. Smith, ordered the fascist salute; amidst the fights a young anti-fascist, Antonio Fierro, was killed and another Italian anti-fascist, Athos Terzani, was arrested, brought to trial, and eventually acquitted a year later.[12] According to police reports, Velona was one of the leaders of the protest. Along with Fierro and Terzani he had infiltrated the meeting, and when Smith ordered the fascist salute, he is said to have cried: "Down with Mussolini!" provoking the violent reaction of the Khaki Shirts. Velona was severely wounded by several blackjack blows on the head and hospitalized. Although he recovered quickly from the immediate injury, he suffered terrible migraines thereafter.[13]

Like the rest of the *sovversivi*, Velona tied fascism to capitalism, seeing it as the ultimate expression of a reactionary system that protected the interests of the bourgeoisie. But his socialist politics combined anti-fascism with a relentless anti-communism. As he explained in an unpublished essay entitled "La piovra bolscevica" (The Bolshevik octopus), "when applied to the ethical, political, economic, and social fields the communist system is in obvious contrast with the real, pure, and sane democracy." Democracy for Velona rested on freedom, and freedom was irreconcilable with the austerity and absolutism of the Bolshevik state. Like other socialists, he had initially hailed the Russian Revolution as a harbinger of the imminent rise of a new world founded upon working-class unity and brotherhood. But the Soviet Union, which had promised to free the Russian proletariat completely from oppression, had itself become an oppressive regime: "Russian workers," commented Velona, "have passed from the economic slavery of capitalism to the political slavery of the communist dictatorship."[14]

Velona's principal contribution to anti-fascism, however, was neither his oratory nor his political theorizing but rather his artwork. Even the fascist regime took its influence seriously. Because of his "disrespectful" caricatures of Il Duce and the fascist hierarchy, he secured himself a file in the Central Political Records Office of the Italian Interior Ministry and was barred from entering Italy.[15] By lampooning Mussolini and the fascist movement, Velona's imagery added new strength to the *sovversivi*'s struggle, reinforcing their anti-fascist politics and values and adding a touch of humor to an intensely tragic aspect of Italian and Italian American history.

The Cartoons

Political cartoons had a long tradition of humorous dissent in Europe and had been commonly used in Italy to satirize society and politicize the masses. The term "cartoon" itself comes from "*cartone*," the Italian and French word for paper, and referred to a preliminary sketch of a work of art done on paper. Italy boasted a particularly rich tradition in the art of caricature, which was invented by two Italian brothers, Annibale and Agostino Carracci, in the late sixteenth century. In fact, the term "caricature" derives from their *ritrattini carichi* (loaded portraits), which satirized famous personages and ordinary individuals of their era.[16]

For a long time, the art of caricature remained the almost exclusive preserve of the Italians. However, by the eighteenth century, both the term and its practice had extended to all of Europe, evolving into what would later be called cartoon: "a form no longer devoted simply to cataloguing external human idiosyncrasies, but one with an enlarged field of vision encompassing the whole political, social and cultural scene—indeed the human condition itself."[17] The subject of the cartoonists was now life in its entirety and particularly those aspects or events of society they felt compelled to criticize or mock. Thus, in the course of the nineteenth century, the cartoon became a powerful weapon of social protest and one of the most effective visual arts of political persuasion. Humor and illustrated magazines flourished all over Europe and America, attaining, by the beginning of the twentieth century, an extraordinary surge in their number, quality, and popularity.[18] In Italy, the most impressive political cartoons in the early twentieth century appeared in the pages of the anti-clerical newspaper *L'Asino* (1892–1918) and the socialist daily *Avanti!* (1896–1926), by talented cartoonists such as Gabriele Galantara (art name "Rata Langa," 1865–1937), Giuseppe Scalarini ("Rini," 1873–1948), and Albano Corneli ("Caponeo," 1890–1965), all three uncompromising critics of capitalism, clericalism, and later fascism.[19]

In America the art of cartooning was firmly established by the eighteenth century (carried on most effectively by Benjamin Franklin), but it became a mass medium only in the late nineteenth century with the publication of illustrated magazines such as *Puck, Judge*, and *Life*.[20] The phenomenal growth of cartooning in the late nineteenth and then the twentieth century can be traced in large measure to the explosive growth of the publishing industry and its increasing emphasis on entertainment to attract the mass audiences. Meanwhile, newer printing techniques and technological developments that came into use in the late nineteenth century reduced dramatically the costs of graphic reproduction, making illustrations simpler, faster, and of a better quality.[21] As society became more modern, more urban, and more dominated by mass consumption, cartoons and visual images in general began to serve another purpose besides that of a cultural and political one: to attract readership.[22]

As we saw in chapter 2, many Italian American radical newspapers inserted in their pages logos and illustrations to complement and embellish their articles. Their immediate use, however, was not only graphic but also propagandistic and didactic. Sometime the drawings and captions were funny, but they always tried to make a social, political, or moral point, reflecting the editors' commitment to educating or converting readers. Many of these cartoons were taken from existing Italian and American radical publications. The artists' names were often omitted and the English captions, if any, were replaced with Italian translations. However, the bulk of anti-fascist cartoons, which appeared regularly in Italian American radical papers from the mid-1920s through World War II, came from the pencil of Velona.[23]

It is unclear where and when Velona learned to draw. He might have briefly frequented an art school in Rome before coming to America, but in all likelihood his art was a natural gift. His son recalled his drawing on the dining room table of their apartment at 230 Second Avenue, on Manhattan's Lower East Side, whenever he had some free time. If the cartoons were too large to fit on the dining table, he would then work on the floor.[24]

Whether he drew cartoons before the 1920s also remains unknown, for virtually all his art dates to the period after the rise of fascism. Most of the illustrations appeared in the pages of *Il Nuovo Mondo*, *La Stampa Libera*, *Il Martello*, and *Il Proletario*. Their purpose is self-evident: Like other radical artists, Velona used the cartoons as a tool of political propaganda to inform, reform, and make a point. He sought, to use Rebecca Zurier's words, to give his drawings "an easily recognizable meaning," or to make them into "constructive cartoons," conveying a critique of fascism in its most direct and simple way that even the least sophisticated audiences could understand. In this respect most of his cartoons speak for themselves.[25] Stylistically, they are also remarkably consistent: They are in black and white, characterized by heavy lines with brief titles or inscriptions.

Yet, while the message of Velona's cartoons might be obvious, their content reveals a broad range of meanings and themes, providing us with a unique insight into the anti-fascist politics of the *sovversivi*. Velona's art stands as a powerful emblem of the anti-fascist culture of the Italian American Left during the 1920s and 1930s as well as the American Popular Front. His cartoons restated four recurring themes of anti-fascism: Mussolini's repression and dictatorship, fascist demagoguery, corruption, and imperialism. First, we find the attacks on Mussolini and his fascist experiment. News coverage of Il Duce, Velona warned in his cartoons, was deliberately misrepresented; behind the glaring image of "the savior" of Italy lay in reality just an opportunist and murderer who ruled through terror and racketeering. Second, fascism was depicted as a terrible delusion—a façade of autocracy that needed to be unmasked. Third, like other attacks by the *sovversivi*, Velona's cartoons also went beyond Mussolini and his movement to expose the complex power structure that supported him—the Catholic Church, business, and diplomats. Finally, like other radicals, Velona considered fascism the most extreme expression of capitalism and imperialism and urged workers to unite and take action against it. In the end it was war, not working-class revolution, that brought an end to fascism, but the lesson of Velona and the *sovversivi* helped educate Italian immigrants and the American Left to the real dangers that fascism and Nazism posed to world democracy, presaging the spirit of the Popular Front.

Il Duce's "Other" Face

Throughout the 1920s, most mainstream publications, including American newspapers, presented glorifying portraits and celebratory photographs of Mussolini, the "redeemer" of Italy, to their readers. For twenty years Italians lived surrounded by Mussolini's image, his portrait hanging in every classroom, every public building, and many private homes. Official images of Mussolini were reproduced everywhere throughout Italy and the Little Italies: in statues, films, illustrated newspapers (most notably the *Domenica del Corriere* and *Illustrazione Italiana*), postcards, and stamps. Most of the pictures showed him in static and solitary poses wearing the fascist black shirt or a military uniform, surrounded by nationalist, fascist, or sacred symbols. Others adopted the style and iconography of imperial Rome, portraying him as a great Roman *condottiero*, such as Julius Caesar or Augustus, a comparison that Mussolini himself cultivated and encouraged through the use of Latin inscriptions such as DUX (leader) and REX (king).[26]

This grandiose image was simultaneously softened by other depictions of him as "modern-day leader" or "average man," fond of children and nature, sympathetic to the poor, and interested in music, sports, and arts. These pictures were clearly construed to manufacture a celebrity, to make of Mussolini a popular hero of muscle, mind, and heart—a living symbol of the presumed regeneration, vigor, and greatness of fascist Italy. They powerfully enforced dominant views of him as a forceful leader—courageous, resolute, and virile—and strongly contributed to the creation of Mussolini's cult. Indeed, as John P. Diggins has suggested, this multifaceted imagery of heroic character was crucial in promoting respect and even admiration for the Italian leader nationally as well as abroad.[27]

Velona exposed, of course, a far more sinister, darker, and brutal side of Il Duce. Through bold brushstrokes he subverted the glamorous image of Mussolini, transforming him from "the redeemer" into "the tyrant"—a villain, betrayer, and liar. In official images, Mussolini's physical characteristics—his massive jaw, his baldness, his prominent forehead and chest beating—were used to emphasize his virility, youth, and intellect. Velona exploited those traits to assert instead his menacing disposition. His squared jaw becomes even more firm, his prominent forehead grows deliberately disproportionate with respect to the rest of the face, his body instead is greatly diminished. Particular emphasis is given to facial features: the eyes, mouth, and eyebrows. As if his mean grimaces were not enough, Velona used punching utterances—such as "Obey without arguing," "Only one brain, that of Il

Duce," and "Italy has only one head . . . that of Fascism"—to highlight Mussolini's authoritarianism and absolutism (fig. 7.3).

Sometimes the physical distortion is such that Mussolini assumes monstrous forms, as in a drawing published on the front page of the August 2, 1924, issue of *Il Proletario*, in which he is transformed into an ugly pig sowing death and destruction. Another cartoon that appeared in *Il Solco* depicts him as a wild and ferocious gorilla with evil eyes and a huge, open mouth ready to devour his victims, symbolized by a skull below his feet pierced by the sword of fascism. While exposing Il Duce's brutality, Velona made also a point of attacking his presumed heroism by noting in the narrative text that he was "very fierce with defenseless men, but at the view of the enemy's weapon his cowardliness surpasses his ferocity" (fig. 7.4).

But like all great caricatures, no matter how deformed, Velona's cartoons always capture Mussolini's personality—his egocentrism, bravado, and arrogance. It is almost as if the reader is watching him through a magnifying glass through which his image, although distorted, can still be clearly recog-

Figure 7.3
Il Proletario, April 1, 1930. This cartoon epitomized Mussolini's authoritarianism. The plaque at Mussolini's neck reads, "Obey without arguing." The captions at the side of Mussolini's head are also suggestive of the brutal nature of his dictatorship; they read, "Italy has only one head . . . that of Fascism" and "Only one brain . . . that of the Duce."

Il "GORILLA" ITALICO!

Alcuni audaci esploratori, inoltrandosi nella famosa foresta del Littorio, tra altre bestie selvaggie, hanno scoperto questo nuovo tipo di gorilla. Esso è ferocissimo specie contro gli uomini inermi. Ma alla vista d'un'arma nemica è d'una vigliaccheria che supera la sua ferocia.

Figure 7.4
"The Italian gorilla," *Il Solco*, September 1927. This cartoon exposed Mussolini's brutality by comparing him to a savage gorilla. The following narrative text accompanied the cartoon: "Some brave explorers, venturing in the famous Fascist forest, discovered among various savage beasts, this new type of gorilla. He is extremely fierce, especially with unarmed men. But at the view of the enemy's weapon he is of a cowardice that surpasses his ferocity."

nized. Velona especially enjoyed ridiculing Il Duce's foibles and megalomania. He largely exploited Mussolini's own self-comparisons to military heroes such as Napoleon and Caesar, depicting him in humorous pompous poses and militaristic clothes in combination with whips, swords, and cudgels.

Velona's and the *sovversivi*'s disgust for Mussolini was all the more intense because he had once been one of them. He had started his political career as a socialist fighting for the workers, and ended as a champion of reaction. He had once despised the church, capitalism, and the king, and now banqueted with them. For the *sovversivi*, who held ideological coherence and moral integrity as the highest of all qualities, he was a renegade and traitor—a "Judas Iscariot" driven simply by a thirst for power and success. Hence, in denunciatory articles and, even more, through satire they constantly exposed Mussolini's opportunistic changes of attitude toward his past enemies—the clergy, the king, and big business.

His religious "conversion" was in particular the subject of many jokes and ironic commentaries in the Italian American radical press. For example, one unsigned cartoon in *La Scopa* entitled "Il Duce's metamorphosis" presented two scenes: In the first, "when Mussolini was red," the premier is contemptuously spitting on Jesus' cross; in the second, he is respectfully praying.[28] In another vignette by Albano Corneli featured in *Il Nuovo Mondo* a perplexed Mussolini is contemplating a religious picture at an exhibition. His companion tells him, "That man behind Jesus is Judas, your Excellency." Mussolini replies, "How weird! He has a strange resemblance to me!"[29]

The young Mussolini, indeed, was not only a socialist but also a declared atheist and author of a viciously anti-clerical novel, *The Cardinal's Mistress* (1909). The son of a republican and anti-clerical, he was not baptized at birth and, in keeping with the socialist tradition, had a secular civil wedding instead of a religious one. His anti-clericalism had actually achieved legendary fame in 1904 after he confronted the evangelical minister Alfredo Taglialatela in a debate on "Man and Divinity" at the People House of Lausanne, Switzerland, where he was living in exile. Carlo Tresca, who coincidentally was in Lausanne for a few days in that period before he departed for America, was told by some comrades who attended the debate that at one point Mussolini placed his watch on the table in front the crowd and dared God to strike him dead within five minutes, concluding that if he failed to do so, he did not exist. Curious, Tresca asked to meet this impetuous comrade. But after spending a night "arguing and gesticulating" with the future dictator, he concluded, quite prophetically, that he was just an opportunist and a poseur.[30]

Indeed, once he rose to power, Mussolini acted quickly to foster good relations with the Church, granting political appointments to Catholics, exempting the clergy from taxation, introducing mandatory religious instruction in the schools, and, above all, fiercely denouncing communism. To gain credibility, he had his children baptized in 1923, and he too underwent formal baptism in 1927. In 1926, he also had a religious wedding ceremony to legitimize his civil union in the eyes of the Church. Perhaps more important, Mussolini effectively incorporated religious faith and values into his fascist doctrine, drawing on sacred rituals and describing to a large extent his political activity—as the *sovversivi* also did—as an act of faith.[31]

"The curses of Italy are three: pope, dux, and king"

Mussolini's decision to settle relations with the Vatican became emblematic of another important theme of the *sovversivi*'s anti-fascist crusade: the collusion between the fascist regime, the Church, and the monarchy. As Carlo Fama, an eminent Italian American anti-fascist physician, explained, Mussolini's rise to power was "made possible first by the opportunism of the Monarchy, but most important by an agreement between Mussolini and the Roman Catholic Church."[32] Indeed, fearful of communism and almost equally distrustful of the liberal government, the Vatican welcomed fascism even before Mussolini officially took power, singing the praises of the "moral regeneration" brought by fascism and hailing its leader as a man, in the words of Pope Pius XI, "sent by Providence" to rescue his country from the Bolshevik malaise. The veneration of Mussolini by the Church reached its peak with the Concordat and Lateran Accords of 1929, which put an end to the dispute between the Italian state and the papacy—the so-called Roman question that resulted from the annexation of the Papal States during the struggle for unification. The agreement created the independent state of Vatican City in Rome, paid the Church a large sum for the loss of the annexed territories, and regulated the religious affairs of the country, declaring de facto Catholicism Italy's official religion. The Concordat represented a major setback from the lay character that the Italian state had inherited from the *Risorgimento*, but for Mussolini it meant a crucial step toward cementing his regime and enhancing its prestige among Catholics both domestically and abroad, particularly in the United States.[33]

Mussolini adopted a similar appeasing strategy with the monarchy. Although he was a republican at heart and resented the idea of sharing power, he went along with King Vittorio Emanuele III because he recognized the popularity and influence he still exerted on both the conservative elites and the armed forces. But although constitutionally he remained the head of the state throughout the fascist dictatorship, the king had to accept various infringements on the monarchy's traditional power and was considered by many just a puppet of Il Duce.[34]

Velona made the triple alliance of fascism, the papacy, and the monarchy one of his favorite subjects of satire. In one of his best caricatures, he simply portrayed Mussolini, Pope Pius XI, and King Vittorio Emanuele III standing next to each other (fig. 7.5). The vignette's concise title, "The curses of Italy are three: the pope, Il Duce, and the king," could not have been more fitting. It powerfully exposed Mussolini's characteristic tendency to temporize and compromise with

D'ITALIA LE PIAGHE SONO TRE PAPA·DUCE·RE /

VELONA

Figure 7.5
"The curses of Italy are three: Pope, Duce, and King." Fort Velona Papers, IHRC2786, Immigration History Research Center, University of Minnesota.

powerful groups to consolidate his power, while simultaneously it accused the Church and the monarchy of providing support for the fascist regime, implying that without their consent fascism could not have come to power.

Velona made it clear that of the three men it is Mussolini who has the reins of power, while the king and the pope are just his followers. As in other, similar cartoons, he emphasizes their passivity and subordination by making them physically smaller than Mussolini, who clearly presides over them. Velona exploited in particular the notoriously short stature of the king, who stood at just over five feet, to stress his feebleness and diminish his power.

Propaganda in the Little Italies

As John P. Diggins and other scholars have documented, Mussolini and fascism generated enormous consensus in the United States, not only among Italian immigrants but also among Anglo-Saxon Americans. Their popularity was to a great extent the product of the press. Influential publications such as the *Saturday Evening Post*, the *New York Times*, and *Time*—which featured Mussolini eight times on its cover between 1923 and 1943—wrote approvingly of fascism and the "wonders" its leader was doing for Italy. Lavish accolades of Mussolini and his government reverberated also across Washington, Wall Street, and other prominent constituencies of American society. To most American admirers, fascism was simply the best answer to anarchy and radicalism, but to others Il Duce and his fascist experiment were truly a marvel worthy of support and even emulation.[35]

Paralleling fascist sympathies in Anglo-Saxon America was the triumph of fascism in the Italian immigrant communities. The "fascistization" of the Little Italies derived, as we will discuss soon, first and foremost from a pervasive and subtle nationalist campaign promoted by fascist emissaries. Indeed, Mussolini's emphasis on "Old World" traditional values, captured by the slogan *"La religione, la patria e la famiglia"* (religion, fatherland, and family), successfully played upon immigrants' nostalgic nationalism and fears of family and community disintegration resulting from Americanization. As the historian Fraser Ottanelli has pointed out, the main strength of fascist propaganda in the United States was its ability to associate love of Italy with support for Mussolini, making it appear, by implication, that any form of opposition to fascism was un-Italian, even unpatriotic.[36]

But if fascist propaganda "provided the fertilizer," American society "planted the seed." For decades Italians in the United States had been denigrated, stigmatized, and marginalized. A number of post–World War I events—Italy's "Mutilated Victory," President Woodrow Wilson's dismissive treatment of Italy, as well as the rise of American nativism, exemplified by the resurgence of the Ku Klux Klan and the discriminatory immigration laws of 1921–24—further isolated Italian Americans, predisposing them to embrace "a heightened ethnic consciousness, which easily evolved into philo-Fascism."[37] This interpretation is supported by the contrasting experiences of Italian immigrants in other countries. Comparative studies show that fascism did not attract Italians everywhere in the world. In nations where Italians were not generally discriminated against, such as in France, Belgium, and Argentina, they tended to side with the Left and became anti-fascists.[38]

American anti-radical policies and repression also contributed to throw Italian immigrants into the clutches of fascism. The psychological impact of the Red Scare and the execution of Sacco and Vanzetti on the minds of Italian Americans has yet to be studied. While their case helped radicalize some workers—like sixteen-year-old Pietro di Donato, who joined the Communist Party on August 3, 1927, after police attacked demonstrators in New York

City's Union Square—the climate of terror created by anti-radical hysteria undoubtedly encouraged Italians to distance themselves from "un-American" radical values and to embrace conservatism. Unlike radicalism, fascism with its emphasis on "order, discipline, and work" appeared to be very much within the mainstream of American conservative values and was therefore generally tolerated. As Mussolini increasingly gained international prestige, Italian Americans, wrote Diggins, "could not help but to look on with a new sense of pride and self-respect."[39]

The power base of Mussolini's Italian American "empire" was the institutional infrastructure of the immigrant community. The press, consulate, schools, clubs, radio programs, and social and cultural organizations—all succumbed to the influence of Mussolini's regime, becoming de facto transmission belts of fascist propaganda. The press in particular provided Mussolini with an enormous source of support. Almost 90 percent of the Italian-language newspapers published in the United States—basically all except the radical papers—were philo-fascist or overtly fascist. The two most influential organs were *Il Progresso Italo-Americano* of New York, owned by Generoso Pope, the millionaire president of the Colonial Sand & Cement Company, and *L'Italia* of San Francisco, published by Ettore Patrizi. Other important newspapers included *Il Corriere d'America* and *Il Bolletino della Sera*, both published in New York and also owned by Pope; *L'Opinione* of Philadelphia; *L'Italia* of Chicago; and *La Voce del Popolo Italiano* of Cleveland.[40]

Mussolini found an especially powerful ally in the class of Italian American *prominenti* who controlled the power structure of the *colonie italiane*, including the press. Traditionally conservative, nationalistic, and anti-labor, they did not hesitate to side with Mussolini, even though only a few of them—most notably Luigi Barzini, Agostino de Biasi, and Giovanni Di Silvestro—belonged to actual fascist organizations. Fascism in their eyes represented patriotism and nationalism against the "anti-Italian" forces of socialism, communism, and anarchism; as such, it served well their economic and political interests. Working in unison with the American political world on the one hand, and Mussolini's emissaries on the other, they used fascism to advance their own self-interests and to promote sentiments and values designed to create consensus and marginalize their radical adversaries.[41]

As we have seen, the *sovversivi* had long attacked the *prominenti*, but after the rise of fascism their accusations and insults became even more fierce and more frequent. Velona unequivocally pictured them as political opportunists with no integrity and turncoats ready to sell themselves to the best buyer. One caricature, for instance, shows "Gigetto" (Luigi Barzini), the director of

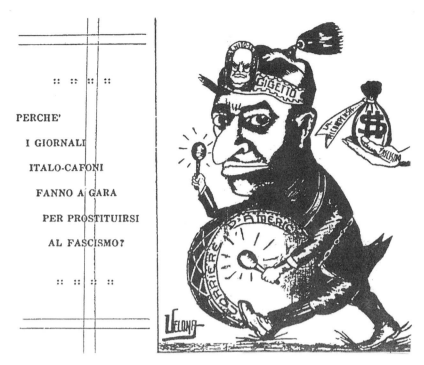

PERCHE'

I GIORNALI

ITALO-CAFONI

FANNO A GARA

PER PROSTITUIRSI

AL FASCISMO?

Figure 7.6
"Why do Italian-boorish newspapers vie to prostitute themselves to Fascism?" *Il Proletario*, June 25, 1927.

Corriere d'America, drumming up support for fascism through his newspaper (fig. 7.6).

The question "Why do Italian-boorish [*cafoni*] newspapers vie to prostitute themselves to Fascism?" accompanied the cartoon. The reader did not need much time to figure out the answer: The little bag of dollars tendered by the fascist hand was the obvious recompense for their propaganda.

In another biting caricature, Velona pictured Barzini pushing an unwilling donkey toward a big bowl from which an ugly animal, resembling a dog, is already avidly munching. The donkey represented the "affectionate readers" of *Corriere d'America* while the other animal symbolized fascism. The platform on which the dog is standing carried the title "Il Grido della Trippa" (The cry of the tripe), clearly a satirical paraphrase of *Il Grido della Stirpe*, the arch-fascist paper published in New York by Domenico Trombetta.[42] Through these satirical vignettes Velona powerfully exposed the influence that prominent men like Barzini and Pope exerted over the Italian immigrant masses through their mainstream newspapers. At the same time, by comparing them to ugly animals, he unveiled the base and wicked nature of fascism.

As in Italy, fascism in America also received considerable support from the Catholic Church. Priests were notoriously effusive in their praise of Mussolini and his regime, and consistently used their parishes and parochial schools to spread fascist propaganda. As the anti-fascist paper *Il Mondo* denounced in 1941: "if any one should assume the task of gathering together all the utterances of American cardinals and bishops concerning Mussolini . . . from the beginning of Fascism to the death of Pius XI, we should have the most impressive and astounding anthology of Fascist glorification made in any country outside Italy."[43]

But perhaps the most effective agents in promoting respect and loyalty for Il Duce were the official consuls and ambassadors. Consular officials had long served as informants for Italian authorities on subversive activities, labor organizations, and radical leaders abroad. But in the mid-1920s, after Mussolini issued a series of "exceptional decrees" that established the basis of the fascist dictatorship, the definition of "subversive" was broadened to include all opponents of the regime. Anyone who was identified as anti-fascist underwent regular harassment, intimidation, and persecution. Italian radicals who illegally entered the United States were promptly reported at the immigration offices for deportation, and anti-fascist leaders were constantly denounced to the local authorities on libel charges or on the grounds that they had engaged in radical activities. Several of them had their Italian citizenship or titles of studies revoked. When legal action proved inefficient, consuls turned to other measures, such as reprisals against friends and relatives in Italy, confiscation of property, and personal threats.[44]

In order to assert greater control in the Italian communities in the United States, Mussolini created a secret office called *Ufficio Riservato* that operated through the Consulate General of New York in 1926. As Fraser Ottanelli has observed, by the end of the 1930s consular authorities had collected information on more than 6,000 Italian Americans "affiliated to subversive parties considered dangerous to public order and security." Mussolini also expanded the role of consuls and ambassadors, providing them with greater financial resources to disseminate fascist sentiments, to suppress dissent, and, as the cartoon entitled "Fascist Diplomacy" alleged, to nurture economic ties with the United States (fig. 7.7).

UNCLE SAM: *Mio caro, you "persona grata , but business is business! Ii non paghi non mangi.*
SUA ECCELLENZA: *L'Italia à ricostruita... Siamo pronti a pagar !...*
PANTALONE: *Uncle Sam, per l'onor d'Italia non tartela dir grossa. Le tasche mie son vuote, ho sol...la pelle ed ossa!...*

Figure 7.7
"Fascist diplomacy." *Il Martello*, March 21, 1926. Uncle Sam reminds the Italian fascist ambassador that even though he is *"persona grata*, business is business: he who does not pay does not eat." The ambassador replies, "Italy has been rebuilt: We are ready to pay." And Pantalone, representing the average Italian, adds: "Uncle Sam, for Italy's honor, don't be fooled. My pockets are empty, all I have is skin and bone."

Fascism's True Face

For most Italian immigrants who supported Mussolini, fascism was simply the party of "*la religione, la patria e la famiglia*," the embodiment of Old World traditions of discipline, honor, and morality. Velona's depictions of fascism, often represented by allegories of death or grotesque monsters, were intended to awaken Italian Americans to the reality of Mussolini's rule and show them that, far from the respectable and idyllic image that the regime tried to export, fascism was a totalitarian and oppressive system based on violence. One cartoon conveyed this message particularly well: It showed a crowd of cheerful Blackshirts in their fascist uniforms hoisting Il Duce on a pedestal formed with their swords. As in most of his caricatures of Mussolini, Velona emphasized the dictator's fierce look and menacing expression. The labels emblazoned upon each medal on Mussolini's chest and on the Blackshirts' daggers bear the names of famous anti-fascist martyrs, such as Giacomo Matteotti, Michele Schirru, and Giovanni Amendola. The sense of terror is also captured by other details—for example, the placard with the fascist motto "Il Duce is always right," the gallows reserved for the anti-fascists that appear in the background, or, more vividly, the bent woman chained to the wrist of Mussolini, symbolizing the defeat of democratic Italy. Everything in the vignette pointed out the obvious: that Mussolini held power through violence and terror (fig. 7.8).

Often in his representations of fascism Velona used the typical insignias of the Blackshirts: skulls, spiral puttees, crossbones, and the *manganello*, the short club they used to beat their enemies. But while the fascists used them as a glorification of combat, Velona reversed their symbolism to express horror and doom for the future of Italy and the world at large. The grim mood of Velona's imagery was not unjustified. The early Blackshirts were violent and nationalist fanatics—war veterans, military officers, revolutionary interventionists, and exuberant students. They organized fascist cells (*fasci di combattimento*) that terrorized Italy throughout the 1920s, raiding houses, destroying properties, beating socialists and their sympathizers, often forcing them to drink castor oil, and, in some cases, killing them.[45]

Constantly evoked by the *sovversivi*, the victims of fascism surfaced repeatedly in Velona's cartoons. One drawing, published in the front page of *Il Martello* on May Day 1925, a few months following Mussolini's historic speech in which he formally declared the dictatorship, exploited their death, urging workers to fight back. It shows the ghost of Giacomo Matteotti, the socialist deputy kidnapped and killed by the fascists on June 10, 1924, coming back to life to avenge his murder as well as those of his comrades, whose names—Lavagnini, Di Vagno, Piccinini, Oldani—appear on the crosses of a cemetery in the background.

To highlight the repressive and brutal nature of fascism, Velona compared it to terrible monsters whipping the resigned masses, or a hideous force crushing Italian freedom and democracy. He used in particular the image of freedom "crucified" as a brutal allegory of fascist despotism. The cartoon entitled "The Calvary," for example, exposed Mussolini's repression of civil liberties by showing a woman representing liberty gagged and tied on a cross, while another woman representing Italy is witnessing indifferently or powerlessly the martyrdom that is unfolding in front of her eyes (fig. 7.9).

An interesting variation from the gloom that pervaded Velona's anti-fascist cartoons was the use of humor to show the disastrous effects of fascism

Figure 7.8
Fort Velona Papers, IHRC2786, Immigration History Research Center, University of
Minnesota.

Figure 7.9
"The calvary." *Libertas*, August 21, 1927. The caption in the left corner reads, "Fascism brought to an end all civil liberties of Italy."

on the Italian nation. Immigrants were told day after day that Mussolini had transformed the poor nation they had left behind into a country "where there was no unemployment, where everybody had baths in their home, and the trains ran on time." Italy, thanks to fascism, had finally become "rich, prosperous, respected and feared."[46] Again, Velona used his artwork to expose the falsehoods of such propaganda and counter the popular impression that Mussolini had saved Italy and restored it to its ancient greatness. In one image entitled "In the regime of Mussoland" Italy is transformed into a nation of small prison cells, from which come a variety of complaints and desperate calls for help such as "I am hungry!" "I need air!" "Poor Italy!" "We want jobs!" and "Enough is enough!" In this image Mussolini seems to have lost his usual confidence and sternness. Visibly nervous and frustrated, for the first time he seems actually to pay attention to what the king has to say (fig. 7.10).

A similar cartoon entitled "Italian prosperity" shows a clueless Mussolini confronting a mountain of rock-hard problems, including inflation, war debt, unemployment, and political opposition (fig. 7.11). As in the previous illustration, Mussolini presides not over the regeneration of Italy but over collapse and disaster. Challenging the official rhetoric that all was well in fascist Italy, Velona showed that the government under Mussolini had actually created more problems than it had solved.

Velona's mockery of fascism's "marvelous" achievements is particularly evident in the cartoon entitled "Ten years of Fascist promises" (fig. 7.12). It pictures an ordinary Italian carrying on his back four men: Mussolini, J. P. Morgan, the king, and the pope. Each is ordering the poor man to keep going, promising him glory, riches, power, and heaven. But as the vignette sarcastically alleges, at the end of the day all the man has gained is more taxes. The image mocked not only the personal ties between fascism, business, monarchy, and the Vatican but also the naïveté of the Italian people, fooled by the blare of Mussolini's propaganda. Through the use of satire,

Figure 7.10
"In the Mussoland regime." *Il Proletario*, June 18, 1927.

Figure 7.11
"Italian prosperity." Fort Velona Papers, IHRC2786, Immigration History Research Center, University of Minnesota.

Velona sought again and again to undermine widespread sympathy for Mussolini, reminding Italian immigrants that beneath its demagogical veil fascism was nothing but a capitalist conspiracy set up to protect the interest of the bourgeoisie and to crush the working class.

Business and Labor

Like the rest of the *sovversivi*, Velona considered fascism a generic malady of capitalism and imperialism, and his cartoons frequently alluded to the economic connections between fascism and corporate interests abroad. Mussolini's initial success in stabilizing the Italian economy and in removing the specter of communism and bolshevism favored in effect economic relations with the United States. As early as May 1923, a newly formed American concern named The Italian Power Company invested in Italy a capital of $2 million. Similarly, many important banks and big corporations, such as the Hallgarten Bank, the National City Bank, and the Blair and Rollins companies, made conspicuous investments in Italy throughout the 1920s. More significantly, in 1925 J. P. Morgan granted Italy a loan of more than $50 million.[47]

Figure 7.12

"Ten years of Fascist promises." The pope says, "We will touch heaven"; the king says, "Go forward, we will reach the empire"; J. P. Morgan says, "To us: there, we will find an immense treasure"; Mussolini says, "Come on, Pantalone, forward, to the top of the world"; and finally the poor Pantalone, whose shirt is covered by the word "taxes," ironically comments: "At last we will tumble!" Fort Velona Papers, IHRC2786, Immigration History Research Center, University of Minnesota.

Figure 7.13
"Sacco and Vanzetti." *Il Proletario*, April 30, 1927.

One of the most powerful and explicit statements of the shady financial ties between Mussolini and American bankers appeared on the cover page of *Il Solco* in July 1927. Using traditional anti-capitalist images of corpulent industrialists with money bags, the author, Albano Corneli, depicted a huge J. P. Morgan and an unusually tiny, submissive Mussolini offering his favors to the big magnate. "Master," read the caption, "what can I do for you today?"

Velona's artwork expressed the connection between fascism and capitalism with particular vigor in his illustrations of Sacco and Vanzetti. Like the rest of the *sovversivi*, he saw significant parallels between the execution of the two Italian anarchists and the persecutions of anti-fascists: All were victims of the capitalist system. Even though Velona recognized that there were obvious differences between the American government and the fascist regime, his cartoons seemed to suggest there was little variation in the way Italy and the United States handled the opponents of capitalism. The hand that is about to grind Sacco and Vanzetti in 1927 (fig. 7.13) resembles strongly the hideous force of fascism devouring Italy. Similarly, the cartoon depicting the crucifixion of Sacco and Vanzetti symbolizes the death of freedom, a recurrent theme, as we have seen, in Velona's imagery of fascism (fig. 7.14).

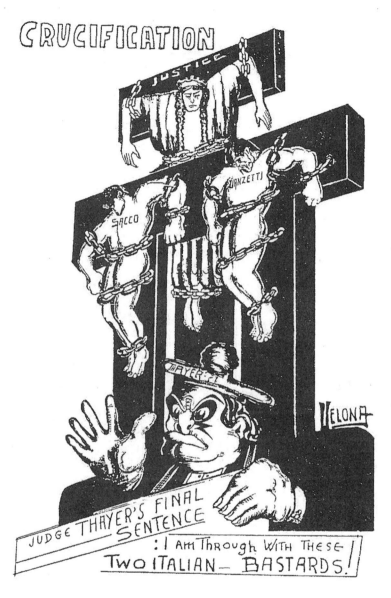

Figure 7.14

"Crucification." Fort Velona Papers, IHRC2786, Immigration History Research Center, University of Minnesota.

Figure 7.15
Cover of the magazine *Prometeo*. Fort Velona Papers, IHRC2786, Immigration History
Research Center, University of Minnesota.

As in the case of the anti-fascist struggle, Velona's cartoons of Sacco and Vanzetti also suggested that only the massive mobilization of the workers could crush the capitalist forces that had made possible the incarceration of two innocent anarchists and the triumph of Mussolini (fig. 7.15). The theme of social revolution is always in the background. Indeed, Velona and the sovversivi wished not only to defeat fascism but also to restructure society according to socialist principles. Thus, they connected the fight against fascism to the defense of workers' rights.

In these images, it is interesting to note that when the masses are depicted in relation to fascism they appear as an anonymous and demoralized crowd, the passive victims of wrongs that will be addressed by others. But when the masses are depicted in relation to the Left or labor, they become fully alive and determined. This sharp contrast served to stress the class consciousness of the leftist workers and the Left's continuing hope that the people united could overthrow fascism as well as capitalism. But it also betrayed the bias of the sovversivi, and radicals in general, toward the people who did not align with the Left, dismissing them as puppets, having no will of their own. As Gaetano Salvemini has observed, perhaps the biggest mistake of the sovversivi's was their failure to take into account the peculiar conditions under which fascism developed. By reducing fascism to simply sheer capitalist reaction, they largely underestimated the broad nationalistic, religious, and cultural appeals of fascism to Italian immigrants, with disastrous consequences for their anti-fascist campaign.

Imperialism and War

The link between fascism, capitalism, and imperialism that the sovversivi had exposed since the rise of Mussolini was made manifest on October 3, 1935, when Italian troops invaded Ethiopia, at the time the only African nation still independent of colonial rule. The war ended less than a year later, on May 5, 1936, with the formal annexation of Ethiopia to the Italian kingdom.[48]

For the sovversivi, the Ethiopian war was the ultimate evidence of the imperialist and expansionist nature of fascism. Because capitalism strives naturally toward conquest and expansion, and because fascism was only the latest disguise of capitalism, war, they concluded, was inevitable. As Carlo Tresca noted, war was inherent to fascism and essential to the survival of the regime. Fascism, he wrote, is "violence erected into a system," requiring 'war for its own sake' as a self-sustaining mechanism."[49]

However, for many Italian immigrants blinded by the nationalistic campaign run by Italian American agencies financed by the fascist regime, the conquest of Ethiopia represented the coronation of Mussolini's promise of a "Greater Italy" and the proving ground for the Italian race. Tens of thousands of Italian Americans participated into pro-war rallies in New York, Chicago, Philadelphia, and Boston where gold and monies were collected to fund the military enterprise. Following the example of Queen Elena, who gave up her wedding ring for the military campaign, Italian American women donated en masse their wedding rings and other jewelry to their homeland, receiving by the Italian government replacement iron wedding rings that were in turn blessed by parish priests during symbolic remarriage ceremonies organized throughout the Italian American communities. Donations continued throughout the war, culminating in a Madison Square Garden meeting at which Generoso Pope presented the Italian consul with a check for $100,000, while his newspaper *Il Progresso Italo-Americano* bragged that it had collected $700,000 for the Italian Red Cross. Outside the Garden, a large contingent of anti-fascists was beaten by the police to prevent them from disrupting the meeting.[50]

While the majority of Italian Americans embraced Mussolini's imperialistic venture, his ruthless aggression toward Ethiopia also made more and more Americans aware of the "ugly side" of fascism that the *sovversivi* had forcefully exposed for thirteen years. Once again, Velona's cartoons provided a powerful commentary on the enfolding debate. A few months before Mussolini invaded Ethiopia, *Il Martello* published a Velona cartoon entitled "Fascist civilization" that anticipated the events to come (fig. 7.16). It showed Mussolini ordering a soldier of the militia to get ready for war. "The moment of trial is close," blasted Il Duce. "LOOK OUT! For the glory of the EMPIRE you must bring to my feet another slave: ETHIOPIA!" The other slave was of course Italy, which is represented in the vignette as a chained corpse. By using words such as "slave" and "empire," Velona made the connection between fascism and imperialism crystal clear: Italy's thrust into Africa was the culmination of fascism's primary impulse toward conquest. The "rape of Ethiopia" was Mussolini's first step toward the creation of an international fascist empire.

As the war progressed, the negative portrayal of Mussolini as a conqueror became more forceful. In a later cartoon, Il Duce's face is transformed into a military ship, an unmistakable symbol of Mussolini's expansionist designs (fig. 7.17). The image not only captured the imperialist drive of Mussolini but also emphasized the serious threat that fascism posed to world peace and security, a point that was emphasized by the minuscule League of the Nations, incapable of stopping him.

Figure 7.16

"Fascist civilization." *Il Martello*, August 17, 1935. Mussolini commands the soldier, "Be aware: for the glory of the empire you must conquer and bring to my feet another slave: Ethiopia." The other slave, Italy, lies on the floor with a banner displaying its main problems: "taxes, debts, hunger, espionage, mafia, unemployment, hatred, exile, confinement, prison, and death."

Figure 7.17
"The Face of Capitalism." Fort Velona Papers, IHRC2786, Immigration History Research
Center, University of Minnesota.

Meanwhile, diplomatic relations between Italy and the United States began to deteriorate, and Mussolini's popularity in America irreparably dropped. American journalists were now publishing strong anti-fascist editorials, and unflattering cartoons of Il Duce appeared more frequently in the American press. At last, the *sovversivi* were no longer alone in the fight against fascism. Once awakened, the American Left would respond with a visual and political rhetoric already mapped by the *sovversivi*.

It must have been with this sense of satisfaction that Velona drew the cartoon that appeared in *Il Proletario* a few days before the end of the Ethiopian war (fig. 7.18).[51] It showed Mussolini "the quack" at the pillory, his tongue

Figure 7.18
"The quack at the pillory." *Il Proletario*, May 1, 1936.

brutally nailed to the stand as a punishment for his lies. The word "imperialism" is printed on his club, while the nail piercing his tongue symbolizes world opinion. His tongue displays the label "war speeches," but its clear phallic resemblance also lampooned Mussolini's vaunted virility. The whole image was construed to suggest that Mussolini was finally near the end of his rope.

Indeed, by the time Il Duce signed the anti-Semitic laws in 1938, the decline of his reputation in America had become almost complete. Although some Italian Americans remained loyal to the fascist regime even during World War II, most *prominenti*, including Generoso Pope, and the Catholic priests began quickly to distance themselves from Mussolini once he announced the Pact of Steel with Hitler, fearing American repercussions.

The *sovversivi's* persistent and long struggle eventually paid off. By December 10, 1941, after Italy declared war against the United States, their exposés, attacks, and accusations began to attract the attention of the American press and authorities. New radical papers published by the *fuorusciti* like *Il Mondo* and *Nazioni Unite*, the organ of the Mazzini Society, founded in 1940, contributed to educating the American public about fascist activities in the United States and discussing the future of Italy. Many of their articles were republished in major American publications, successfully acquainting the American public with Italian events.

As for Italian Americans, when the war compelled them to choose between Italy and the United States, they did not hesitate to assert their American loyalty. The *prominenti* hastily returned their medals and decorations to the fascist government, burning their membership cards and publicly severing all ties with Mussolini. Similarly, hundreds of thousands of Italian Americans who had first hailed Il Duce now participated in huge rallies to declare their opposition to fascism and reaffirm their devotion to democracy. Finally, they too conceded what the *sovversivi* had maintained all along: that Mussolini was the real betrayer of the Italian nation, and that true love of Italy would mean unrelenting opposition to the fascist regime.[52]

Conclusion

For fifty years, from 1890 to 1940, Italian radicals in the United States created and sustained a small but vigorous movement that sought simultaneously to elevate the moral and social conditions of their co-nationals and promote a more just, equal, and democratic society. As we saw in the first chapter, the movement as a whole was sharply divided among anarchists, socialists, syndicalists, and communists. Not only was the movement fragmented, but members within each faction constantly argued with one another. Although a few radical leaders like Arturo Giovannitti and Carlo Tresca managed to transcend these ideological divisions and forge broader alliances, the *sovversivi* were never really able to achieve unity. Rather than channel their militancy toward political ends, they wasted valuable energy and time fighting over theoretical issues and the "correct" method of struggle. In doing so, they succumbed to the kind of ideological rigidity that sabotaged other leftist movements, hindering them from effectively challenging the hegemony of bourgeois culture.[1]

But this ideological fragmentation coexisted with a broader and distinctive culture rooted in communal ethical values and political ideas centered on universalism, solidarity, social justice, and equality. As I have argued, this shared culture was a rich and vital dimension of the *sovversivi*'s radical movement that acquired almost a religious and millenarian quality. In stark opposition to middle-class values of competition, materialism, and individualism, the *sovversivi* provided an alternative social vision that fired the hopes and dreams of thousands of oppressed workers.

Throughout the book I have documented the importance of the *sovversivi*'s faith in the "Beautiful Ideal" by discussing the various forms through which it was expressed. While political groups constituted the base of the movement, a constellation of subsidiary institutions and cultural forms provided the main source of support, education, and inspiration. Newspapers represented the central communication link and means of propaganda; lectures and informal schools helped elucidate complex political concepts promoting education and working-class consciousness; dramatic performances, picnics, and dances created and sustained a rich social life for the movement's members while providing the main source of fundraising. Finally, poetry, literature, and art amplified and invigorated the radical dream while also offering radical intellectuals and artists opportunities to express creatively their feelings and aspirations.

Literary and social clubs, theater groups, people's universities, cultural events, and artistic and literary expressions were all important social formations that allowed the movement's members and sympathizers to be part of a distinctive community of rebels. While it is impossible to quantify precisely their participation in these events, there is evidence that cultural programs were able to reach out and influence Italian workers beyond the confines of the workplace. Many of the cultural initiatives organized by the *sovversivi*, particularly theatrical performances and dances, drew wider audiences than union or party meetings. Conversion to radicalism and recruitment of new members often took place through this informal cultural network rather than in the more overtly political ways. Perhaps more important, informal social and cultural life helped keep alive the dream behind the movement, giving radical politics continuous support and plausibility.

Looking at Italian American radicalism through the lens of culture allows us to better grasp the idealism and missionary zeal that inspired and moved early-twentieth-century radical leaders and supporters. It shows that besides political change, the *sovversivi* also aspired to fashion a "revolutionary" culture—in literature, in art, and on the stage—that could change the way people saw the world and how they lived. Many of their noble dreams remain unfulfilled—social inequality, economic insecurity, and class, ethnic, and racial oppression have hardly been settled. But the story of the *sovversivi* still has much to teach historians of immigration and radicalism.

As other scholars have argued, the recovery of the "lost world of Italian American radicalism" demonstrates that the responses of Italian immigrants to the New World were neither uniformly passive nor acquiescent. The *sovversivi* were a visible and important presence, a "vital minority" that played important roles as ethnic leaders in their communities and within the larger labor movement.[2] Their vital presence powerfully challenges Edward Banfield's stereotypical views of southern Italians as amoral and apolitical familists. In fact, the *sovversivi* contributed in important ways to establishing a radical tradition in the United States, playing a central role in the working-class struggles of the early twentieth century and the anti-fascist movement of the 1920s through the 1940s. The cultural institutions, plays, poems, and art forms discussed in this book provide compelling evidence of the richness of this tradition.

The study of Italian immigrant radical culture also underscores the complex attitudes of leftists toward class, gender, race, and ethnicity. This book has provided many examples of how the *sovversivi*'s radical politics were informed by personal, cultural, and political ties to Italy. As I discussed in my analysis of plays, newspapers, and literature, family and gender values (particularly those of honor and respectability) Christianity, and Italian events and developments profoundly affected the *sovversivi*'s ethnic and class identities. In some cases their *italianità* served as a catalyst to class consciousness and mobilization, but in other cases it conflicted with their internationalist claims. Similarly, while in theory the *sovversivi* supported women's equality and liberation, they overlooked women's activism and often behaved tyrannically at home.

Perhaps more important, the *sovversivi*'s story suggests that politics and culture are interlocking parts of the same whole. Radicalism cannot be understood merely as a component of the social structure or defined simply in relation to the means of production. As cultural historians, such as Robin Kelley, Alan Wald, Michael Denning, and Salvatore Salerno, among others, have suggested, radical politics must rather be seen in terms of reciprocal interactions between cultural values and political ideologies. So far, too little effort has been made to document the social and cultural impact of the Italian immigrant Left or study the intellectuals and artists who helped shape and sustain the radical movement. Although many of the sources that could have provided us with a sense of the lively culture of Italian immigrant radicals have been lost, the remaining cultural artifacts discussed in this book clearly indicate the importance of art and culture in the *sovversivi*'s world. Cultural institutions and literary forms became a critical way for Italian radical leaders to express their class politics and inspire the rank-and-file, creating a language and symbolism that made radicalism meaningful within the context of the Italian immigrant experience.

My analysis, in other words, suggests that radicalism was shaped not only in response to economic and social conditions but also in relation to the larger culture that Italians brought with them when they migrated. Their political ideas, social experiences, and cultural traditions all influenced their response to labor conditions in America. At the same time, the American environment redefined those ideas, transforming, and eventually erasing, Italian radicalism.

Indeed, the victory against fascism represented the last struggle of the Italian immigrant Left. Italian American radicalism pretty much vanished after World War II. Two anarchist papers—Aldino Felicani's *Controcorrente* and *L'Adunata dei Refrattari*, the successor to Luigi Galleani's *Cronaca Sovversiva*—actually survived until 1967 and 1971 respectively. The socialist *La Parola del Popolo* and the ILGWU's *La Giustizia* also lasted well into the 1980s, but all other Italian radical papers ceased publication between 1940 and 1950.

Italian American unions, once the core of radical activities, eventually receded into the organized labor establishment, becoming mere appendages to the mainstream conservative American labor movement. The whole generation of the *sovversivi* also began to die out after the 1940s: Carlo Tresca was mysteriously murdered in 1943, Arturo Giovannitti died in 1959, and Fort Velona died in 1965. Others like Girolamo Valenti, Vittorio Vidali, and Alberico Molinari left the United States altogether and returned to Italy, while newly arrived radicals such anarchist Armando Borghi or communist Michele Salerno were deported under the political repression of the McCarthy era that followed World War II.

A few incorrigibles and some of their children, mostly anarchists, continued to sustain the subculture created decades earlier by their comrades. As the oral interviews collected by Paul Avrich attest, they still went to plays, picnics, and lectures; they still read and contributed to radical newspapers published in Italy and the United States, holding on to their "Beautiful Ideal" for their entire lives.[3] But as Nunzio Pernicone has sadly commented, these gestures "could not turn back the biological clock. The Italian American Left failed to reproduce itself," and with its demise "a unique breed of dreamers and rebels also passed into extinction.[4]

Notes

INTRODUCTION

1. John Bruce McPherson, *The Lawrence Strike of 1912* (Boston: Rockwell and Churchill Press, 1912), 8. Collection Development Department, Harvard University.

2. For example Philip Foner, *The Industrial Workers of the World, 1905–1917* (New York: International Publishers, 1965); Melvyn Dubofsky, *We Shall Be All: A History of the IWW* (Chicago: Quadrangle Books, 1969); Edwin Fenton, *Immigrants and Unions, A Case Study: Italians and American Labor, 1870–1920* (New York: Arno Press, 1975); Salvatore Salerno, *Red November, Black November: Culture and Community in the Industrial Workers of the World* (Albany: State University of New York Press, 1989).

3. The most recent monographs include Philip V. Cannistraro and Gerald Meyer, eds., *The Lost World of Italian American Radicalism* (Westport, Conn.: Praeger, 2003); Donna R. Gabaccia and Fraser M. Ottanelli, eds., *Italian Workers of the World: Labor Migration and the Formation of Multiethnic States* (Urbana: University of Illinois Press, 2001); Donna Gabaccia and Franca Iacovetta, eds., *Women, Gender and Transnational Lives* (Toronto: University of Toronto Press, 2002); and Michael M. Topp, *Those Without a Country: The Political History of Italian American Syndicalists* (Minneapolis: University of Minnesota Press, 2001).

4. For a discussion of the meaning of "culture" see Raymond Williams, *Keywords* (New York: Oxford University Press, 1976), 87–93; *Problems in Materialism and Culture* (London: Verso, 1980); and *Culture and Society, 1780–1950* (New York: Columbia University Press, 1958).

5. Robin D.G. Kelley, *Yo' Mama's Disfunktional! Fighting the Culture Wars in Urban America* (Boston: Beacon Press, 1997), 8.

6. See for example Paul Buhle, "Jews and American Communism: The Cultural Question," *Radical History Review*, 23 (Spring 1980): 9–33; Irving Howe, *World of Our Fathers* (1976; repr., New York: New York University Press, 2005); Robin D.G. Kelley, *Race Rebels: Culture, Politics and the Black Working Class* (New York: Free Press, 1994); Peter Kivisto, *Immigrant Socialists in the United States: The Case of Finns and the Left* (Madison, N.J.: Fairleigh Dickinson University Press, 1984); and Carl Ross, *The Finn Factor in American Labor, Culture and Society* (New York Mills, Minn.: Parta Printers, 1977).

7. Antonio Gramsci, *Quaderni del carcere*, 6 Vols. (1949; repr., Turin: Editori Riuniti, 1996). In English see Quintin Hoare and Geoffrey Nowell Smith, ed. and trans., *Selections from the Prison Notebooks* (New York: International Publishers, 1999), especially "Problems of Philosophy and History" and "Problems of Marxism." For a critical study

of Gramsci's major ideas, see James Joll, *Antonio Gramsci* (New York: Penguin Modern Masters, 1977).

8. For example Paul Avrich, *Sacco and Vanzetti: The Anarchist Background* (Princeton, N.J.: Princeton University Press, 1991); Dorothy Gallagher, *All the Right Enemies: The Life and Murder of Carlo Tresca* (New Brunswick, N.J.: Rutgers University Press, 1998); Nunzio Pernicone, *Carlo Tresca: Portrait of a Rebel* (New York: Palgrave, 2005); and Gerald Meyer, *Vito Marcantonio: Radical Politician, 1902–1954* (Albany: State University of New York Press, 1989).

9. On the role and forms of ethnic leadership, see John Higham, ed., *Ethnic Leadership in America* (Baltimore: Johns Hopkins University Press, 1979), especially his introductory chapter, "The Forms of Ethnic Leadership."

10. For recent examples of studies on Italian immigrant women and radicalism see above all Gabaccia and Iacovetta, eds., *Women, Gender and Transnational Lives* and Jennifer Guglielmo, *Living the Revolution: Italian Women's Resistance and Radicalism in New York City, 1880–1945* (Chapel Hill: University of North Carolina Press, 2010).

CHAPTER 1

1. Rudolph Vecoli, "The Italian Immigrants in the United States Labor Movement from 1890 to 1929," in Bruno Bezza, ed., *Gli italiani fuori d'Italia: gli immigrati italiani nei movimenti operai dei paesi d'adozione, 1880–1940* (Milan: F. Angeli, 1983), 259. The term "new immigration" refers to the migration of Slavs, Italians, and eastern European Jews, which added to the old one formed by British, Irish, Germans, and Scandinavians. On Italian emigration see Gianfausto Rosoli, ed., *Un secolo di emigrazione italiana: 1876–1976* (Rome: Centro Studi Emigrazione, 1978); John and Beatrice MacDonald, "Italy's Rural Social Structure and Emigration," *Occidente* 12 (1956): 437–57; "Chain Migration, Ethnic Neighborhood Formation and Social Networks," *Milbank Memorial Fund Quarterly* 42 (January 1964): 82–91; Andreina De Clementi, *Di qua e di là dell'oceano. Emigrazione e mercati nel Meridione, 1860–1930* (Rome: Carocci, 1999); and Piero Bevilacqua, Andreina De Clementi, and Emilio Franzina, eds., *Storia dell'emigrazione italiana. Partenze* (Rome: Donzelli, 2001).

2. Rudolph Vecoli, "Italian American Workers, 1880–1920: *Padrone* Slaves or Primitive Rebels?" in Silvano M. Tomasi, ed., *Perspectives in Italian Immigration and Ethnicity* (New York: Center for Migration Studies, 1977), 25. See also Thomas Kessner, *The Golden Door: Italian and Jewish Immigrant Mobility in New York City, 1880–1915* (New York: Oxford University Press, 1977), "Table 1: Occupational experiences of Italian, Jewish, and all immigrants arriving in the United States, 1899–1910," 33–34. For a social profile of the *contadini* see Rudolph Vecoli, "*Contadini* in Chicago: A Critique of *The Uprooted*," *Journal of American History* (December 1964): 404–17.

3. Vecoli, "The Italian Immigrants in the United States Labor Movement," 262.

4. Matthew Frye Jacobson, *Whiteness of a Different Color: European Immigrants and the Alchemy of Race* (Cambridge, Mass.: Harvard University Press, 1998), 57.

5. There is copious literature on "whiteness." See especially Theodore Allen, *The Invention of the White Race*, 2 vols. (London: Verso, 1994 and 1997); Thomas A. Guglielmo, *White on Arrival: Italians, Race, Color, and Power in Chicago, 1890–1945* (New York: Oxford University Press, 2003); Jennifer Guglielmo and Salvatore Salerno, eds., *Are Italians*

White? How Race Is Made in America (New York: Routledge, 2003); Noel Ignatiev, *How the Irish Became White* (New York: Routledge, 1995); Jacobson, *Whiteness of a Different Color*; David Roediger, *The Wages of Whiteness: Race and the Making of the American Working Class* (London: Verso, 1991), and *Towards the Abolition of Whiteness: Essays on Race, Politics and Working Class History* (London: Verso, 1994); and Alexander Saxton, *The Rise and Fall of the White Republic: Class Politics and Mass Culture in Nineteenth Century America* (London: Verso, 1990).

6. Guglielmo, *White on Arrival*.

7. "The New Orleans Affair," unsigned, *New York Times*, March 16, 1891, 4. Cited also in Jerre Mangione and Ben Morreale, *La Storia: Five Centuries of the Italian American Experience* (New York: HarperCollins, 1993), 211; and Jacobson, *Whiteness of a Different Color*, 56. See also Salvatore LaGumina, ed., *Wop! A Documentary History of Anti-Italian Discrimination in the United States* (San Francisco: Straight Arrow, 1973); and John Higham, *Strangers in the Land: Patterns of American Nativism, 1860-1925* (New Brunswick, N.J.: Rutgers University Press, 1992, first edition 1955), 65–66, 90–92, 160–61.

8. See Rudolph Vecoli, "Pane e giustizia," *La Parola del Popolo* (September/October 1976), 57, and "The Italian Immigrants in the United States Labor Movement," 264–65; Donna Gabaccia, *Militants and Migrants: Rural Sicilians Become American Workers* (New Brunswick, N.J.: Rutgers University Press, 1989), 6–7; Bruno Cartosio, "Gli emigrati italiani e l'Industrial Workers of the World," in Bezza, ed., *Gli italiani fuori d'Italia*, 371. For a more detailed study of nativism within the AFL see Robert Asher, "Union Nativism and the Immigrant Response," *Labor History* 23 (1982): 325–48.

9. Samuel L. Baily, "The Adjustment of Italian Immigrants in Buenos Aires and New York, 1870–1914," *American Historical Review* 88, 2 (April 1983): 281–305, and *Immigrants in the Land of Promise: Italians in Buenos Aires and New York City* (Ithaca, N.Y.: Cornell University Press, 1999). See also essays by Angelo Trento, Mirta Zaida Lobato, and Carina Frid De Silberstein in Donna Gabaccia and Fraser Ottanelli, eds., *Italian Workers of the World: Labor Migration and the Formation of Multiethnic States* (Urbana: University of Illinois Press, 2001).

10. Banfield, *The Moral Basis of a Backward Society* (New York: Macmillan, 1958). See also Richard Gambino, *Blood of My Blood: The Dilemma of Italian Americans* (New York: Guernica, 1996, first edition 1974); Humbert S. Nelli, *From Immigrants to Ethnics: The Italian Americans* (Oxford: Oxford University Press, 1983); and the works of the early labor historians affiliated with the "Wisconsin School," particularly John R. Commons, ed., *A Documentary History of American Industrial Society. Vols. 1–10* (Cleveland, Ohio: The Arthur H. Clark Co., 1910); John Commons et al., *History of Labor in the United States. Vols. 1–4* (New York: Macmillan, 1918–35); John Laslett, *Labor and the Left: A Study of Socialist and Radical Influences in the American Labor Movement, 1881–1924* (New York: Basic Books, 1971); and Gerald Rosenblum, *Immigrant Workers: Their Impact on American Labor Radicalism* (New York: Basic Books, 1973).

11. Vecoli, "The Italian Immigrants in the United States Labor Movement," 260.

12. Donna Gabaccia, *From Sicily to Elizabeth Street* (Albany: State University of New York Press), 4–9. See also Jane Schneider and Peter Schneider, *Culture and Political Economy in Western Sicily* (New York: Academic Press, 1976); Carol White, *Patrons and Partisans: A Study of Politics in Two Southern Italian Comuni* (New York: Cambridge University Press, 1980); Giuseppe Carlo Marino, *Movimento contadino e blocco agrario nella*

Sicilia Giolittiana (Palermo: S. F. Flaccovio, 1979); Sidney Sonnino, *I contadini in Sicilia,* vol. 2 of Lepoldo Franchetti and Sidney Sonnino, *La Sicilia nel 1876* (Florence, 1877), 19–23, 316–17, 427–42, 457–59; and Francesco Nitti, *Scritti sulla questione meridionale. Vol. 4: Inchiesta sulle condizioni dei contadini in Basilicata e in Calabria* (Bari, 1968), 320–30.

13. Nunzio Pernicone, ed., *The Autobiography of Carlo Tresca* (New York: The John D. Calandra Italian American Institute, 2003), 85.

14. Clementi, "La grande emigrazione," in Bevilacqua, Clementi, and Franzina, eds., *Storia dell'emigrazione italiana,* 189. (The translation from the Italian is mine.) For a revisionist interpretation of the rural South, see above all Franco Cassano, *Il pensiero meridiano* (Rome: Laterza, 1997); Mario Alcaro, *Sull'identità meridionale: Forme di una cultura meridionale* (Turin: Bollati Boringhieri, 1999); and Bevilacqua, "Società rurale ed emigrazione," in Bevilacqua, Clementi, and Franzina, eds., *Storia dell'emigrazione italiana.*

15. E. J. Hobsbawm, *Primitive Rebels: Studies in Archaic Forms of Social Movements in the 19th and 20th Centuries* (New York: W. W. Norton, 1959). See also Fernand Braudel, *The Mediterranean and the Mediterranean World in the Age of Philip II, Vol. 2* (New York: HarperCollins, 1977).

16. Humbert Gualtieri, *The Labor Movement in Italy* (New York: S. F. Vanni, 1946), 71–79; and Gabaccia, *Militants and Migrants,* 7.

17. *Statistica del Regno d'Italia. Istruzione pubblica per Comuni. Anno scolastico 1862–1863* (Modena, 1864) and *Censimento al 10 Giugno* (Roma, 1911), cited in Gualtieri, *The Labor Movement in Italy,* 10–11. See also Edward R. Tannenbaum, "Education," in Edward Tannenbaum and Emiliana Noether, eds., *Modern Italy: A Topical History Since 1861* (New York: New York University Press, 1974), 231–53; and John Briggs, *An Italian Passage: Immigrants to Three American Cities* (New Haven, Conn.: Yale University Press, 1978), chapter 3, "Schooling in Southern Italy."

18. For a short overview of Mazzini's ideas see Giuseppe Mazzini, *The Duties of Man and Other Essays* (London: J. M. Dent and Sons, 1907).

19. Gualtieri, *The Labor Movement in Italy,* 137; Alexander De Grand, *The Italian Left in the Twentieth Century: A History of the Socialist and Communist Parties* (Bloomington: Indiana University Press, 1989), 6; Gabaccia, *Militants and Migrants,* 30–35; and Briggs, *An Italian Passage,* chapter 2, "Workers' Mutual Benefit Societies in Southern Italy."

20. Nunzio Pernicone, "The Italian Labor Movement," in Tannenbaum and Noether, eds., *Modern Italy,* 198–201.

21. See Nunzio Pernicone, *Italian Anarchism, 1864–1892* (Princeton, N.J.: Princeton University Press, 1993), 11–32; and Pier Carlo Masini, *Storia degli anarchici italiani da Bakunin a Malatesta* (Milan: Rizzoli Editori, 1969). On anarchism in Andalusia see Temma Kaplan, *Anarchists of Andalusia, 1868–1903* (Princeton, N.J.: Princeton University Press, 1977); and Hobsbawm, *Primitive Rebels,* chapter 5. Hobsbawm, however, incorrectly maintains that rural Italy was little affected by Bakunin's ideas.

22. Gualtieri, *The Labor Movement in Italy,* 160.

23. Bruno Cartosio, "Sicilian Radicals in Two Worlds," in Marianne Debouzy, ed., *In the Shadow of the Statue of Liberty: Immigrants, Workers and Citizens in the American Republic, 1880–1920* (Urbana: University of Illinois Press, 1992), 120; and John Alcorn, "Sophisticated Liberals," in Spencer M. Di Scala, ed., *Italian Socialism: Between Politics and History* (Amherst: University of Massachusetts Press, 1996), 41. For a detailed history of the Sicilian *Fasci* see "I Fasci Siciliani" special issue of *Movimento Operaio* 6 (Novem-

ber–December 1954): 801–1111; Francesco Romano, *Storia dei Fasci Siciliani* (Bari: Laterza, 1959); and Francesco Renda, *I Fasci Siciliani, 1892–94* (Turin: Einaudi, 1977).

24. Gualtieri, *The Labor Movement in Italy*, 190.

25. Vecoli, "The Italian Immigrants in the United States Labor Movement," 261; Cartosio, "Sicilian Radicals in Two Worlds," 130; and Denis Mack Smith, *Modern Italy: A Political History* (Ann Arbor: University of Michigan Press, 1997, first edition 1959), 157. See also Theda Skocpol, "What Makes Peasants Revolutionary?" in Robert Weller and Scott Guggenheim, eds., *Power and Protest in the Countryside: Studies of Rural Unrest in Asia, Europe, and Latin America* (Durham, N.C.: Duke University Press, 1983), 157–78.

26. Randolph Bourne was the first to use the term "transnationalism" in opposition to "Americanization," suggesting the inclusion of immigrants' distinctive cultures into American values and traditions. "Toward a Trans-national America," *Atlantic Monthly* (July 1916). For transnational studies of Italian immigrant radicalism see Cartosio, *Sicilian Radicals in Two Worlds*; Gabaccia, *Militants and Migrants;* Gabaccia and Ottanelli, eds., *Italian Workers of the World*; Ernesto Ragionieri, "Italiani all'estero ed emigrazione di lavoratori italiani: un tema di storia del movimento operaio," *Belfagor* 17 (November 1962); 641–69; Bruno Ramirez, "Immigration, Ethnicity, and Political Militance: Patterns of Radicalism in the Italian American Left, 1880–1930," in Valeria Gennaro Lerna, ed., *From Melting Pot to Multiculturalism: The Evolution of Ethnic Relations in the United States and Canada* (Rome: Bulzoni Editore, 1990), 115–41; and Michael Topp, *Those Without a Country: The Political Cultural of Italian American Syndicalists* (Minneapolis: University of Minnesota Press, 2001), and "The Transnationalism of the Italian American Left: The Lawrence Strike of 1912 and the Italian Chamber of Labor of New York City," *Journal of American Ethnic History* 17, 1 (Fall 1997): 39–64.

27. Cited in Virginia Yans-McLaughlin, *Family and Community: Italian Immigrants in Buffalo, 1880–1930* (1971; repr., Urbana: University of Illinois Press, 1982), 89–90. The letter was published in *La Fiaccola*, a socialist newspaper published in Buffalo, on November 20, 1909.

28. Bartolomeo Vanzetti, *The Story of a Proletarian Life* (The Sacco-Vanzetti Defense Committee, Boston, 1923), 18–20. Cited also in Vecoli, "The American Republic Viewed by the Italian Left," 20; and Paul Avrich, *Sacco and Vanzetti: The Anarchist Background* (Princeton, N.J.: Princeton University Press, 1996), 27.

29. Rudolph Vecoli, "Negli Stati Uniti," in Bevilacqua, De Clementi, and Franzina, eds., *Storia dell'emigrazione italiana*, 55–56; and Kessner, *The Golden Door*, 14–17.

30. For a historical interpretation of the May events see Louise Tilly, "*I Fatti di Maggio*: The Working Class of Milan and the Rebellion of 1898," in R. J. Bezucha, ed., *Modern European Social History* (Lexington, Mass.: D. C. Heath, 1972), 124–58.

31. On Italian political migration during the *Risorgimento* see Donna Gabaccia, "Class, Exile, and Nationalism at Home and Abroad: The Italian Risorgimento," in Gabaccia and Ottanelli, eds., *Italian Workers of the World*, 21–40. On the arrival and activities of these early Italian anarchists in America see Manet Immota Fides, "Italian Anarchism in the United States," unpublished manuscript, International Institute of Social History (IISH), Amsterdam; Avrich, *Sacco and Vanzetti*, 46–48; Michael Topp, "The Italian American Left: Transnationalism and the Quest for Unity," in Paul Buhle and Dan Georgakas, eds., *Immigrant Left in the United States* (Albany: State University of New York Press, 1996), 123–24, and *Those Without a Country*, 28–31.

32. For further biographical information on Merlino see Gianpietro Berti, *Francesco Saverio Merlino: Dall'anarchismo socialista al socialismo liberale, 1856–1930* (Milan: Franco Angeli, 1993).

33. See "Gori Pietro," in Franco Andreucci and Tommaso Detti, eds., *Il movimento operaio italiano. Dizionario biografico, 1853–1943*, 6 vols. (Rome: Editori Riuniti, 1979), 522–31.

34. For more information see Ugo Fedeli, *Giuseppe Ciancabilla* (Cesena: Edizioni Antistato, 1965).

35. Emma Goldman, *Living My Life*, Vol. 1 (New York: Dover Publications, 1977), 404. Biographical works on Malatesta include Luigi Fabbri, *Malatesta: L'uomo e il pensiero* (Naples: Edizioni RL, 1951); and Armando Borghi, *Errico Malatesta: 60 anni di lotte anarchiche: storia, critica, ricordi* (Milan: s.n. 1947). For a critical discussion see also Pernicone, *Italian Anarchism*, 68–71, 87–88, 210–213, 225–26.

36. On Galleani see Rudolph Vecoli, "Galleani Luigi," in Mary Jo Buhle, Paul Buhle, and Dan Georgakas, eds., *Encyclopedia of the American Left* (Urbana: University of Illinois Press, 1992), 251–53; M. Nejorotti, "Galleani L.," in Andreucci and Detti, *Il movimento operaio italiano. Dizionario biografico*, Vol. II, 418–24; and Nunzio Pernicone, "Luigi Galleani and Italian Anarchist Terrorism in the United States," *Studi Emigrazione* 30, 111 (September 1993), 469–88. For a full biography see Ugo Fedeli, *Luigi Galleani. Quarant'anni di lotte rivoluzionarie* (Cesena: Edizioni L'Antistato, 1956).

37. Mario De Ciampis, "Storia del movimento socialista rivoluzionario italiano," *La Parola del Popolo* (December 1958–January 1959), 136. See also Vecoli, "The Italian Immigrants in the United States Labor Movement," 272–73; and Elisabetta Vezzosi, *Il socialismo indifferente: immigrati italiani e il partito socialista negli Stati Uniti* (Rome: Edizioni Lavoro, 1991), 23–30.

38. Vecoli, "The American Republic Viewed by the Italian Left," in Debouzy, ed., *In the Shadow of the Statue of Liberty*, 27; and De Ciampis, "Storia del movimento socialista rivoluzionario italiano," 137.

39. Pernicone, *Italian Anarchism*, 21; and Topp, "The Italian American Left," 121. For a general history of Italian socialism see Alexander De Grand, *The Italian Left in the Twentieth Century: A History of the Socialist and Communist Parties* (Bloomington: Indiana University Press, 1989).

40. Nunzio Pernicone, "Italian Immigrant Radicalism in New York," in Philip V. Cannistraro, ed., *The Italians of New York: Five Centuries of Struggle and Achievement* (New York: The John D. Calandra Italian American Institute, 1999), 78; and Paul Avrich, *Anarchist Voices: An Oral History of Anarchism in America*, abridged edition (Princeton, N.J.: Princeton University Press), 172.

41. This "sojourner mentality" was reflected in the composition of the Italian immigration, which consisted initially almost exclusively of working-age males. See Vecoli, "The Italian Immigrants in the United States Labor Movement," 260; Kessner, *The Golden Door*, 30–31; and Gabaccia, *Militants and Migrants*, 155–63. On the return migrations to Italy see Francesco Paolo Cerase, "L'onda di ritorno: i rimpatri," in Bevilacqua, De Clementi, and Franzina, eds., *Storia dell'emigrazione italiana*, 113–26; Betty Boyd Caroli, *Italian Repatriation from the United States* (New York: Center for Migration Studies, 1973); and Dino Cinel, *The National Integration of Italian Return Migration* (1991; repr., Cambridge: Cambridge University Press, 2002). On voting among Italian Americans see Stefano

Luconi, "La partecipazione politica in America del Nord," in Bevilacqua, De Clementi, and Franzina, eds., *Storia dell'imigrazione italiana*, 489–510.

42. Pernicone, "Italian Immigrant Radicalism in New York City," 78.

43. Information about these groups and their activities can be found in anarchist newspapers.

44. Paul Avrich, *Anarchist Voices: An Oral History of Anarchism in America* (1995; repr., Oakland, Calif.: AK Press, 2005), 111 and 154; Manet Immota Fides, "Italian Anarchism in the United States," 5. For a study of the group *Diritto all'Esistenza* see Salvatore Salerno, "No God No Master" in Philip V. Cannistraro and Gerald J. Meyer, *The Lost World of Italian American Radicalism* (Westport, Conn.: Praeger, 2003). Nunzio Pernicone concluded that the group *Diritto all'Esistenza* counted 85 to 100 members and its newspaper, *La Questione Sociale*, had a circulation of 1,000. See his *Carlo Tresca: Portrait of a Rebel* (New York: Palgrave, 2005), 64.

45. Pernicone, "Italian Immigrant Radicalism in New York," 78; Avrich, *Sacco and Vanzetti*, 52–53, and *Anarchist Voices*, 4–5.

46. "The Social Question," English Supplement to *La Questione Sociale*, August 30, 1901; and "Agli amici e compagni," July 15, 1895, 1.

47. Salerno, "No God, No Master," 174.

48. Pernicone, "Luigi Galleani and Italian Anarchist Terrorism in the United States," 470–75.

49. Manet Immota Fides, "Italian Anarchism in the United States," 5.

50. Avrich, *Anarchist Voices*, 174; "Continuando," *Il Novatore*, October 15, 1910, 2; Camillo Signorini, "Il mio individualismo," *Il Novatore*, November 30, 1910, 56.

51. "Dopo sei mesi" and "Continuando," *Il Novatore*, April 1, 1911, 1, and October 15, 1910, 3.

52. Pernicone, *Carlo Tresca*, 251; Avrich, *Anarchist Voices*, 174; and Raffaele Schiavina, "Brevi note autobiografiche," *L'Internazionale*, January–February 1988.

53. See Topp, *Those Without a Country*, 27–34. On Giacinto Menotti Serrati see Maria Susanna Garroni, "Serrati negli Stati Uniti: Giornalista, socialista e organizzatore degli emigrati italiani," *Movimento operaio e socialista* 7, 3 (1984): 321–44.

54. James Weinstein, *Ambiguous Legacy: The Left in American Politics* (New York: New Viewpoints, 1975), 6.

55. For a detailed history of the FSI see De Ciampis, "Storia del movimento socialista rivoluzionario italiano"; and Topp, *Those Without a Country*, chapter 1.

56. Bruno Cartosio, "Gli emigrati italiani e l'Industrial Workers of the World," 359–95; see also Salerno, "No God No Master."

57. Topp, *Those Without a Country*, 35–36; Pernicone, *Carlo Tresca*, 28–31; and Salvatore Salerno, *Red November, Black November: Culture and Community in the Industrial Workers of the World* (Albany: State University of New York Press, 1989).

58. Pernicone, "Italian Immigrant Radicalism in New York," 79, and *Carlo Tresca*, 21–31.

59. Giuseppe Bertelli, "Cenni Biografici," Casellario Politico Centrale (CPC), busta 554, Archivio Centrale dello Stato (ACS), Rome. For a discussion of Bertelli see Vezzosi, *Il socialismo indifferente*, 39–41, 80–83, 110–13, and "Radical Ethnic Brokers: Immigrant Socialist Leaders in the United States between Ethnic Community and the Larger Society," in Gabaccia and Ottanelli, eds., *Italian Workers of the World*, 124–25.

60. Topp, *Those Without a Country*, 41 and 44.

61. Vezzosi, *Il socialismo indifferente*; De Ciampis, "Storia del movimento socialista rivoluzionario italiano," 146–47 and 154–56.

62. See for example Paul Buhle, "Italian-American Radicals in Rhode Island," *Radical Historical Review* 17 (Spring 1978); Melvyn Dubofsky, *We Shall Be All: A History of the IWW* (Chicago: Quadrangle Books, 1969), 228–58; Edwin Fenton, *Immigrants and Unions, A Case Study: Italians and American Labor, 1870–1920* (New York: Arno Press, 1975), 320–66; Philip Foner, *The Industrial Workers of the World, 1905–1917* (New York: International Publishers, 1965), 306–50; Calvin Winslow, "Italian Workers on the Waterfront: The New York Harbor Strikes of 1907 and 1919"; and Paola Sensi Isolani, "Italian Radicals and Union Activists in San Francisco," both in Cannistraro and Meyer, eds., *The Lost World of Italian American Radicalism.*

63. Topp, "The Lawrence Strike: The Possibilities and Limitations of Italian American Syndicalist Transnationalism," in Gabaccia and Ottanelli, eds., *Italian Workers of the World*, 143, and *Those Without a Country*, 88–93, 111–15; Pernicone, *Carlo Tresca*, 54; and Elizabeth Gurley Flynn, *The Rebel Girl* (New York: International Publishers, 1994, first published in 1955), 135–38.

64. For a history of Local 89 see Serafino Romualdi, "Storia della locale 89," Fifteenth Anniversary pamphlet, 1934. In Antonino Crivello Papers, IHRC479, Box 1, Immigration History Research Center, University of Minnesota. For a general history of garment workers see Louis Levine, *The Women's Garment Workers* (New York: B. W. Huebsch, 1924); and Charles Zappia, "Unionism and Italian American Workers," in Cannistraro and Meyer, eds., *The Lost World*, 189–90.

65. Steve Fraser, "*Landslayyt* and *Paesani*: Ethnic Conflict and Cooperation in the Amalgamated Clothing Workers of America," in Dirk Hoerder, ed., *"Struggle a Hard Battle": Essays on Working Class Immigrants* (DeKalb: Northern Illinois University Press, 1986), 291–92.

66. Colomba M. Furio, "The Cultural Background of the Italian Immigrant Woman and Its Impact on Her Unionization in the New York City Garment Industry, 1880–1919," in Pozzetta, *Pane e Lavoro*, 89.

67. See Carol Lynn McKibben, *Beyond Cannery Row: Sicilian Women, Immigration, and Community in Monterey, California, 1915–99* (Urbana: University of Illinois Press, 2006); Diane C. Vecchio, *Merchants, Midwives and Laboring Women: Italian Migrants in Urban America* (Urbana: University of Illinois Press, 2006); and Jennifer Guglielmo, *Living the Revolution: Italian Women's Resistance and Radicalism in New York City, 1880–1945* (Chapel Hill: University of North Carolina Press, 2010).

68. Colomba M. Furio, "Immigrant Women and Industry: A Case Study, Italian Immigrant Women and the Garment Industry, 1880–1950" (unpublished dissertation, New York University, 1979), 188; Jean Vincenza Scarpaci, "Angela Bambace and the International Ladies' Garment Workers' Union," in Pozzetta, *Pane e Lavoro*, 99–118; Topp, *Those Without a Country*, 119–22, 193–98; and Jennifer Guglielmo, "*Donne Ribelli*: Recovering the History of Italian Women's Radicalism in the United States," in Cannistraro and Meyer, eds., *The Lost World of Italian American Radicalism*, 122–23.

69. For a full discussion of the chambers of labor see Topp, *Those Without a Country*, 234–44.

70. See Zappia, "Unionism and the Italian-American Worker," chapter 3, and "From Working-Class Radicalism to Cold War Anti-Communism."

71. Cannistraro and Meyer's "Introduction" to *The Lost World of Italian American Radicalism*, 19.

72. Topp, *Those Without a Country*, 135–73. Among those who moved from radicalism to fascism were, for example, Edmondo Rossoni, Aldo Tarabella, and Bellalma Forzato-Spezia. See also anarchists Domenico Trombetta and Libero Tancredi, and socialists Giovanni di Silvestro and Simplicio Righi.

73. On the interventionist debate and its effect on Italian American radicalism see Marcella Bencivenni, "A Magazine of Arts and Struggle: The Experience of *Il Fuoco*," *Italian American Review* 8, 1 (Spring/Summer 2001): 75–80; and Pernicone, *Carlo Tresca*, 86–87.

74. Avrich, *Sacco and Vanzetti*, 93–94. For further information on governmental repression during the Red Scare see William Preston, *Aliens and Dissenters: Federal Suppression of Radicals, 1903–1933* (New York: Harper, 1963); and Robert Justin Goldstein, *Political Repression in Modern America: 1870 to the Present* (Cambridge, Mass.: Schenkman Publishing, 1978), chapter 5.

75. For example Giovanni Baldazzi, Duilio Mari, Luigi Parenti, and Angelo Faggi. See De Ciampis, "Italiani d'America," in *La Parola del Popolo* (September–October 1976): 85; and Constantine Panunzio, *The Deportation Cases of 1919–1920* (New York: Federal Council of Churches of Christ, 1921).

76. Avrich, *Sacco and Vanzetti*, 94–101, 122–36; Pernicone, "Luigi Galleani and Italian Anarchist Terrorism in the United States," 469–89, and *Carlo Tresca*, 96–97, 114–21.

77. The Sacco and Vanzetti case, no doubt the best-known event associated with Italian American radicalism, has generated a huge body of scholarship. For recent examples see John Davis, *Sacco and Vanzetti: Rebel Lives* (New York: Ocean Press, 2004); Michael Topp, *The Sacco and Vanzetti Case: A Brief History with Documents* (New York: Bedford/St. Martin's, 2004); Jerome H. Delamater and Mary Anne Trasciatti, eds., *Representing Sacco and Vanzetti* (New York: Palgrave, 2005); and Bruce Watson, *Sacco and Vanzetti: The Men, the Murders and the Judgment of Mankind* (New York: Viking, 2007).

78. Vecoli, "Italian Immigrants in the United States Labor Movement," 302.

79. *Alba Nuova*, October/November 1921, 4.

80. Cannistraro, *Blackshirts in Little Italy: Italian Americans and Fascism, 1922–1929* (West Lafayette, Ind.: Bordighera, 1999), 14, 59, 112–13; and "Per una storia dei fasci negli Stati Uniti," *Storia Contemporanea*, 6 (December 1995): 1061–145. See also Domenico Fabiano, "I fasci italiani all'estero," in Bezza, *Gli italiani fuori d'Italia*.

81. Vecoli, "The Making and Un-Making of the Italian American Working Class," in Cannistraro and Meyer, *The Lost World of Italian American Radicalism*, 54; and Pernicone, *Carlo Tresca*, 127–34. On fascist propaganda in the Little Italies see Gaetano Salvemini, *Italian Fascist Activities in the United States*, edited with an introduction by Philip V. Cannistraro (New York: Center for Migration Studies, 1977), Part II: "Fascist Transmission Belts"; Daria Bicocchi Frezza, "Propaganda fascista e comunità italiane in USA: la Casa Italiana della Columbia University," *Studi Storici* (October/November 1970): 661–97; John P. Diggins, *Mussolini and Fascism: The View from America* (Princeton, N.J.: Princeton University Press, 1972), chapter 5; and Charles Fama, "Fascist Propaganda in the United States," in Girolamo Valenti Papers, Box 2, folder "Miscellaneous," Tamiment Library, New York University (a shorter version of this article appeared in *La Parola del Popolo*, December 1958–January 1959), 91–92.

82. Salvemini, *Italian Fascist Activities in the United States*, 244–45. On the reasons for the fascist appeal among Italian Americans see also Constantine Panunzio, "Italian Americans, Fascism and the War," *Yale Review* 31 (Summer 1942); Philip V. Cannistraro, "Fascism and Italian Americans," in Silvio M. Tomasi, ed., *Perspectives in Italian Immigration and Ethnicity* (New York: Center for Migration Studies, 1977); Vincent M. Lombardi, "Italian American Workers and the Response to Fascism," in Pozzetta, *Pane e Lavoro*, 141–57; and the studies produced by anti-fascist emigres: Massimo Salvadori, *Resistenza e azione. Ricordi di un liberale* (1951); Carlo Sforza, "The Italians and America," in his *The Real Italians* (1942); Vanni B. Montana, *Amarostico. Testimonianze euro-americane* (1975); and Luigi Sturzo, *La mia battaglia da New York* (1949).

83. "Mussolinianism" referred to the cult of Mussolini the man, rather than fascism. Diggins, *Mussolini and America*, 68.

84. Vecoli, "The Italian Immigrants in the United States Labor Movement," 305; and Salvemini, *Italian Fascist Activities in the United States*, 244. For information on Italian American anti-fascism see Pernicone, *Carlo Tresca*, chapters 11–19; John P. Diggins, "The Italo-American Anti-Fascist Opposition," *Journal of American History* (December 1967): 579–98 and chapter 6 of his *Mussolini and Fascism*; Charles F. Denzell, *Mussolini's Enemies: the Italian Anti-Fascist Resistance* (Princeton, N.J.: Princeton University Press, 1961); Fraser Ottanelli, "Italian American Antifascism" in Gabaccia and Ottanelli, eds., *Italian Workers of the World*, 178–95; Philip V. Cannistraro, "Luigi Antonini and the Italian Anti-Fascist Movement in the United States, 1940–1943," *Journal of American Ethnic History* (Fall 1985): 21–37; Topp, *Those Without a Country*, 244–55; Madeline Goodman, "The Evolution of Ethnicity: Fascism and Antifascism in the Italian American Community, 1914–1945 (unpublished Ph.D. dissertation, Carnegie-Mellon University, 1993); and Vecoli, "The Making and Un-Making of the Italian Working Class." See also the memoirs of anti-fascist exiles listed in note 83.

85. Vecoli, "The Italian Immigrants in the United States Labor Movement," 304.

86. Charles F. Delzell, "The Italian Anti-Fascist Emigration, 1922–1943," *Journal of Central European Affairs* 12 (April 1952): 20–55; Max Salvadori, "Antifascisti italiani negli Stati Uniti," in *Atti del I Congresso internazionale di storia Americana: Italia e Stati Uniti dall'indipendenza ad oggi* (Genoa: Bastagi, 1978), 269–80. On Salvemini see Charles L. Killinger, *Gaetano Salvemini: A Biography* (Westport, Conn.: Praeger, 2002).

87. Pernicone, *Carlo Tresca*, 135–37.

88. Pernicone, "Italian Immigrant Radicalism in New York," 86; and Diggins, *Mussolini and Fascism*, 112–13.

89. For an account of the Matteotti affair see Christopher Seton-Watson, *Italy from Liberalism to Fascism, 1870–1925* (New York: Barnes & Noble, 1967). For the reactions to the Matteotti case in the United States, see *Il Nuovo Mondo*, November 21 and December 10, 1925; Pellegrino Nazzaro, "Fascist and Anti-Fascist Reaction in the United States to the Matteotti Murder," in Francesco Cordasco, ed., *Studies in Italian American Social History* (Totowa, N.J.: Rowman & Littlefield, 1975), 50–65; and Pernicone, *Carlo Tresca*, 163–65.

90. Pernicone, "Italian Immigrant Radicalism in New York," 86, and *Carlo Tresca*, 175–81.

91. On the Greco–Carillo case see Nunzio Pernicone, "Murder under the 'El': The Greco-Carillo Case," *The Italian American Review* 6, 2 (Autumn 1997/Winter 1998): 20–44, and *Carlo Tresca*, 186–94. On the Terzani case see Diggins, *Mussolini and Fascism*, 131–33;

Pernicone, *Carlo Tresca*, 206–8; and John Herling and Morris Shapiro, *The Terzani Case* (pamphlet, New York, 1934).

92. Pernicone, *Carlo Tresca*, 137.

93. Ibid., 195.

94. Fraser Ottanelli, "'If Fascism Comes to America We Will Push It Back into the Ocean': Italian American Antifascism in the 1920s and 1930s," in Gabaccia and Ottanelli, eds., *Italian Workers of the World*, 186–87.

95. Gerald Meyer, "Italian Americans and the American Communist Party," in Cannistraro and Meyer, eds. *The Lost World of Italian American Radicalism*, 206–7.

96. Nunzio Pernicone, "Introduction to A Special Issue of the Italian American Press," *The Italian American Review*, 8, 1 (Spring/Summer 2001): 1–6; and Gerald Meyer, "*L'Unità del Popolo*," 127–28.

97. See Zappia, "From Working-Class Radicalism to Cold War Anti-Communism," in Cannistraro and Meyer, eds., *The Lost World of Italian American Radicalism*.

98. See above all Lizabeth Cohen, *Making a New Deal: Industrial Workers in Chicago, 1919–1939* (Cambridge: Cambridge University Press, 1990).

99. Vecoli, "The Making and Un-Making of the Italian American Working Class," in Cannistraro and Meyer, eds., *The Lost World of Italian American Radicalism*, 52.

100. Michael Denning, *The Cultural Front: The Laboring of American Culture in the Twentieth Century* (London and New York: Verso, 1996).

101. For a discussion of Italian American radical writers in the 1930s see Fred Gardaphè, "Follow the Red Brick Road: Recovering Radical Traditions of Italian American Writers," in Cannistraro and Meyer, eds., *The Lost World of Italian American Radicalism*, 265–72. See also Simon Gerson, *Pete: The Story of Peter V. Cacchione, New York's First Communist Councilman* (New York: International Publishers, 1976); and Gerald Meyer, *Vito Marcantonio, Radical Politician, 1902–1954* (Albany: State University of New York Press, 1989).

CHAPTER 2

1. John Higham, ed., *Ethnic Leadership in America* (Baltimore: Johns Hopkins University Press, 1978), 1, 8. See also Victor R. Greene, *American Immigrant Leaders, 1800–1910: Marginality and Identity* (Baltimore: Johns Hopkins University Press, 1987).

2. The origin of the word "*prominente*" is still obscure. The fact that it was used as a noun, even though syntactically speaking it is an adjective, suggests that it was a distinctive Italian Americanism. The word first appeared in the written language before World War I and became popular in the 1920s. Cf. Philip V. Cannistraro, "The Duce and the Prominenti: Fascism and the Crisis of Italian American Leadership," *Altreitalie* (July–December 2005): 79.

3. I am borrowing the term "programmatic" from Nathan Irvin Huggins, "Afro-Americans," in Higham, ed., *Ethnic Leadership in America*, 93. For an example of positive leadership see Nathan Glazer, "The Jews," in ibid., 19–35.

4. Gaetano Salvemini, *Italian Fascist Activities in the United States*, edited with an introduction by Philip V. Cannistraro (New York: Center for Migration Studies, 1977), 7-8.

5. See "La colonia italiana di New York," *Il Grido degli Oppressi*, June 5, 1892, 2; "The Padrone System in the United States," *New York Times*, May 23, 1897; and the study written by M. Van Etten in 1892 for the *New York Herald* and republished in 1903 in *Il Proletario*,

cited in Mario De Ciampis, "Italiani in America," *La Parola del Popolo* (September–October 1976): 73–77. For a scholarly study see Luciano Iorizzo and Francesco Cordasco, *Italian Immigration and the Impact of the Padrone System* (New York: Arno Press, 1980).

6. Rudolph Vecoli, "The Italian Americans," *La Parola del Popolo*, The USA Bicentennial–The Italian Contribution (September–October 1976): 49; Gerald Meyer, "Italian Harlem: Portrait of a Community"; and Peter D'Agostino, "The Religious Life of Italians in New York City," both in Philip V. Cannistraro, ed., *The Italians of New York* (New York: The John D. Calandra Italian American Intitute, 1999); and Lydio Tomasi, *Piety and Power: The Role of Italian Parishes in the New York Metropolitan Area* (Staten Island, N.Y.: Center for Migration Studies, 1975). For a more detailed study of Italian religious practices see Robert A. Orsi, *The Madonna of 115th Street: Faith and Community in Italian Harlem, 1880–1950* (New Haven, Conn.: Yale University Press, 1985).

7. Gunnar Myrdal, *An American Dilemma: The Negro Problem and Modern Democracy* (New York: Transaction Publishers, 1996, first edition 1944); Vezzosi, "Radical Ethnic Brokers: Immigrant Socialist Leaders in the United States Between Ethnic Community and the Larger Society," in Donna Gabaccia and Fraser Ottanelli, eds., *Italian Workers of the World* (Urbana: University of Illinois Press, 2001), 121–38; Rudolph Vecoli, "The Italian Immigrants in the United States Labor Movement, 1880–1929," in Bruno Bezza, ed., *Gli italiani fuori d'Italia* (Milan: Franco Angeli, 1983), 275.

8. Quintin Hoare and Geoffrey Nowell Smith, ed. and trans., *Selections from the Prison Notebooks* (New York: International Publishers, 1971), 5, 9–10.

9. Nunzio Pernicone, *Carlo Tresca: Portrait of a Rebel* (New York: Palgrave, 2005), 22.

10. The collection is held at the Archivio di Stato in Rome. Cited in Fraser M. Ottanelli, "Fascist Informant and Italian-American Labor Leader: The Paradox of Vanni Buscemi Montana," *The Italian American Review* 7, 1 (Spring–Summer 1999): 104–6.

11. Nunzio Pernicone, "Italian Immigrant Radicalism in New York," in Cannistraro, ed., *The Italians of New York*, 89.

12. Donna Gabaccia, "Neither Padrone Slaves nor Primitive Rebels: Sicilians on Two Continents," in Dirk Hoerder, ed., *"Struggle a Hard Battle": Essays on Working Class Immigrants* (DeKalb: Northern Illinois University Press, 1986), 105; Vecoli, "The Italian Immigrants in the United States Labor Movement," 278; Pernicone, "Italian Immigrant Radicalism in New York," 81.

13. Nunzio Pernicone, ed., *The Autobiography of Carlo Tresca* (New York: The John D. Calandra Italian American Institute, 2003), 43.

14. Cf. Sally M. Miller, *The Radical Immigrant* (New York: Twayne Publishers, 1974), 164–65.

15. This was the case for example of Vincenzo and Clara Vacirca, Nino Capraro and Maria Bambace, Maria Roda and Pedro Esteve, Ersilia Grandi and Giuseppe Ciancabilla, and Virgilia D'Andrea and Armando Borghi.

16. Michael Topp, *Those Without a Country: The Political Culture of Italian American Syndicalists* (Minneapolis: University of Minnesota Press, 2001), 48–51; Pernicone, *Carlo Tresca*, 16–18, 71–84.

17. Vanzetti, *The Story of a Proletarian Life* (Boston: Sacco-Vanzetti Defense Committee, 1923), 18.

18. Arturo Meunier, "Omaggio a Gioacchino Artoni," *La Parola del Popolo* (December 1958–January1959), 58. See also Giacomo Battistoni, "Ricordando I settant'anni di Gioacchino Artoni," *La Stampa Libera*, August 16, 1936.

19. Vecoli, "The Italian Immigrants in the United States Labor Movement," 278. See also Irving Howe, *World of Our Fathers* (1976; repr., New York: New York University Press, 2005), 244–49.

20. Richard Jules Oestreicher, *Solidarity and Fragmentation: Working People and Class Consciousness in Detroit, 1875–1900* (Urbana: University of Illinois Press, 1989).

21. Paul Buhle, "Anarchism and American Labor," *International Labor and Working Class History* 23 (Spring 1983): 21–34. See also James H. Billington, *Fire in the Eyes of Men: Origins of the Revolutionary Faith* (New York: Basic Books, 1980).

22. Arturo Giovannitti, "Utopia," in *Arrows in the Gale* (Riverside, Conn.: Hillacre Bookhouse, 1914), 56.

23. Paul Avrich, *Anarchist Voices: An Oral History of Anarchism in America* (1995; repr., Edinburgh: AK Press, 2005), 150.

24. E. J. Hobsbawm, *Primitive Rebels* (New York: W. W. Norton, 1959), 82; and Gerald Sorin, *The Prophetic Minority: American Jewish Immigrant Radicals, 1890–1920* (Bloomington: Indiana University Press, 1985).

25. Oral interview with Luigi Nardella, Cranston, R.I., 1977. Archives of the American Left, Tamiment Library, New York University.

26. Hobsbawm, *Primitive Rebels*, 100–1.

27. Pernicone, ed., *The Autobiography of Carlo Tresca*, 23.

28. See Paul Arpaia, "Constructing a National Identity from a Created Literary Past: Giosuè Carducci and the Development of a National Literature," *Journal of Modern Italian Studies* 7, 2 (August 2002): 192–214.

29. On immigrant anti-clericalism see Rudolph Vecoli, "Prelates and Peasants," *Journal of Social History* 2 (Spring 1969): 217–68.

30. Pernicone, ed., *The Autobiography of Carlo Tresca*, 167–69.

31. Donna Gabaccia and Franca Iacovetta, eds., *Women, Gender and Transnational Lives: Italian Workers of the World* (Toronto: University of Toronto Press, 2002); Jennifer M. Guglielmo, "Negotiating Gender, Race and Coalition: Italian Women and Working-Class Politics in New York City, 1880–1945" (Ph.D. dissertation, University of Minnesota, 2003), "Italian American Women's Political Activism in New York City, 1890s–1940s," in Cannistraro, ed., *The Italians of New York*, 103–13, "*Donne Ribelli*: Recovering the History of Italian Women's Radicalism in the United States," in Philip V. Cannistraro and Gerald Meyer, eds., *The Lost World of Italian American Radicalism* (Westport, Conn.: Praeger, 2003), 113–42, and "Italian Women's Proletarian Feminism in New York City's Garment Trades, 1890s–1940s," in Gabaccia and Iacovetta, eds., *Women, Gender and Transnational Lives*, 247–98.

32. Paul Avrich, *Sacco and Vanzetti: The Anarchist Background* (Princeton, N.J.: Princeton University Press, 1991), 104-118; "Travel Advisory: Political Sculpture Alfresco in Upstate New York," *New York Times*, May 9, 1993.

33. See *La Questione Sociale*, January 4 and 11, 1902, 3 and 4. On the history of these groups see Guglielmo, "Negotiating Gender, Race and Coalition," chapter 3, 132–40; and Waldron Merithew, "Anarchist Motherhood: Toward the Making of a Revolutionary Proletariat in Illinois Coal Towns," in Gabaccia and Iacovetta, eds., *Women, Gender and Transnational Lives*, 217–46.

34. "Italians in Buenos Aires's Anarchist Movement: Gender Ideology and Women's Participation, 1890–1910," in Gabaccia and Iacovetta, eds., *Women, Gender and Transnational Lives*," 195.

35. Avrich, *Sacco and Vanzetti*, 107–21, 215–16; and *Anarchist Voices*, 134–35.

36. Maria Roda, "Che cosa vogliono gli anarchici," *Il Grido degli Oppressi*, December 30, 1893, 2. (The translation from the Italian is mine.)

37. Cesare Balzarini Roda, CPC, busta 4367; Maria Balzarini Roda, CPC, busta 4368; Goldman, *Living My Life*, I, 150–51. For a profile of Maria Roda see also Guglielmo's "*Donne Ribelli*," 116–17.

38. See Rudolph Vecoli, "Anthony Capraro and the Lawrence Strike of 1919," in Pozzetta, ed., *Pane e Lavoro*, 3–27.

39. Angela Bambace Papers, IHRC279, Box 1, Folder 6, Immigration History Research Center, University of Minnesota.

40. See Paul Buhle, "Italian American Radicals in Rhode Island, 1905–1930," *Radical History Review* 17 (Spring 1978): 121–51; George W. Carey, "'The Vessel, the Deed, and the Idea: Anarchists in Paterson, 1895–1908," *Antipode* 10/11 (1979): 46–58; Gary Mormino and George Pozzetta, *The Immigrant World of Ybor City: Italians and Their Latin Neighbors in Tampa, 1885–1995* (Gainesville: University Press of Florida, 1998); Gianna S. Panofsky, "A View of Two Major Centers of Italian Anarchism in the United States: Spring Valley and Chicago, Illinois," in Domenic Candeloro, ed., *Italian Ethnics: Their Languages, Literature and Lives* (Chicago: Proceedings of the 20th Annual Conference of the AIHA, 1987), 271–96; Paola Sensi Isolani, "Italian Radicals and Union Activists in San Francisco," in Cannistraro and Meyer, eds., *The Lost World of Italian American Radicalism*, 189–204; Mari Tomasi, "The Italian Story in Vermont," *Vermont History* 28, 1 (January 1960): 73–87.

41. Pernicone, "Carlo Tresca's Il Martello," *Italian American Review* 8, 1 (Spring/Summer 2001): 7–56, *Carlo Tresca*, 103, and "Italian Immigrants Radicalism in New York City," 85–86; Vanni Montana, *Amarostico: Testimonianze euro-americane* (Livorno, Italy: U. Bastogi Editore, 1975), 101 and 110; Avrich, *Sacco and Vanzetti*, 99. Many Italian American radical papers published ads of John's Restaurant; see for example *Il Lavoratore*, December 25, 1926, 4.

42. See Judah J. Shapiro, *The Friendly Society: A History of the Workmen's Circle* (New York: Media Judaica, 1970); Steve Fraser, *Labor Will Rule: Sidney Hillman and the Rise of American Labor* (Ithaca, N.Y.: Cornell University Press, 1993), 221–26; Howe, *World of Our Fathers*, 244–49; and Bruce C. Nelson, *Beyond the Martyrs: A Social History of Chicago's Anarchists, 1870–1900* (New Brunswick, N.J.: Rutgers University Press, 1988), 103–13.

43. "Circolo di cultura moderna," *Il Grido della Folla*, May 20, 1916, 4.

44. "Mario Rapisardi Literary Society," *Alba Nuova*, September 1921, 3.

45. On the function of socialist and anarchist club life see Nelson, *Beyond the Martyrs*, 103–13.

46. For most lectures little remains save the titles and the advertisements in radical newspapers. But a few were published in pamphlets and have survived. See for example Ludovico Caminita, *Che cosa e' la religione* (Tipografia Editrice G. Di Sciullo, 1906) or Pietro Gori, *Scienza e Religione* (Roma: F. Serantoni Editore, 1905).

47. "Bomb Sleuth Lived with Anarchists," *New York Times*, March 3, 1915, 6.

48. Avrich, *Anarchist Voices*, 73.

49. Cited in Mormino and Pozzetta, *The Immigrant World of Ybor City*, 145.

50. Ibid., 144.

51. A list of the books offered by these "red bookstores" was published on the last page of radical newspapers.

52. Mormino and Pozzetta, *The Immigrant World of Ybor City*, 104, 117.

53. Pernicone, *Carlo Tresca*, 26–27.

54. *La Questione Sociale*, September 15, 1895, 1; *Il Lavoro*, March 24, 1917.

55. Avrich, *Anarchist Voices*, 120.

56. Cited in Pernicone, *Carlo Tresca*, 87–88.

57. Avrich, *Anarchist Voices*, 117–19.

58. Ibid., 111.

59. Cited in Pernicone, *Carlo Tresca*, 27. See also Pernicone, ed., *The Autobiography of Carlo Tresca*, 84–85.

60. Cited in Cannistraro and Meyer, eds., *The Lost World of Italian American Radicalism*, 13. See also Vecoli, "The Italian Immigrants in the United States Labor Movement," 276–77.

61. For a history of the *Università Popolare* see Maria Grazia Rosada, *Le Università popolari in Italia, 1900–1918* (Roma: Editori Riuniti, 1975).

62. Ibid., 40–41.

63. See Avrich, *Sacco and Vanzetti*, 56, and *Anarchist Voices*, 107–12; Pernicone, *Carlo Tresca*, 36; Pernicone, ed., *The Autobiography of Carlo Tresca*, 90.

64. "Appunti locali," *La Questione Sociale*, February 28, 1903, 4.

65. *Il Lavoro*, January 12, 1918, 2, and January 26, 1918, 1.

66. Paul Avrich, *The Modern School Movement* (Princeton, N.J.: Princeton University Press, 1980); and Emma Goldman, *Living My Life* (Dover Publications), 456–58, 475.

67. Vecoli, "The Italian Immigrants in the United States Labor Movement," 277.

68. "Memorandum for Mr. Fairfield Osborne, Director of the National Youth Administration," Onorio Ruotolo Papers, IHRC232, Box 2, Folder 10, Immigration History Research Center, University of Minnesota. See also Lucio Ruotolo, "Onorio Ruotolo and the Leonardo Da Vinci Art School," *Italian American Review* (Winter 2000): 1–20.

69. Nelson, *Beyond the Martyrs*, 103. See also Oestreicher, *Solidarity and Fragmentation*.

70. Dieter Dowe, "The Workingmen's Choral Movement in Germany before the First World War," *Journal of Contemporary History* 13, 2 (April 1978): 269–96; cited in Nelson, *Beyond the Martyrs*, 130.

71. Richard Brazier, "The Story of the I.W.W.'s Little Red Songbook," in Archie Green, David Roediger, Franklin Rosemont, and Salvatore Salerno, eds., *The Big Red Songbook* (Chicago: Charles H. Kerr Publishing Company, 2007), 375.

72. Bartolomeo Vanzetti, *The Story of a Proletarian Life* (Boston: Sacco-Vanzetti Defense Committee, 1923), 12.

73. Avrich, *Anarchist Voices*, 155.

74. *Il Grido degli Oppressi*, November 30, 1894; see also the report in the September 29, 1894, issue and *La Questione Sociale*, August 15, 1895, and February 11, 1899.

75. Avrich, *Anarchist Voices*, 180.

76. "To the American People," *La Questione Sociale*, November 17, 1900, December 8, 1900, and February 14, 1901.

77. Nelson, *Beyond the Martyrs*, 135.

78. Avrich, *Sacco and Vanzetti*, 56.

79. Eric Hobsbawm, "Mass Producing Traditions: Europe, 1870–1914," in Hobsbawm and Terence Ranger, eds., *The Invention of Tradition* (1983; repr., Cambridge: Cambridge University Press, 2006, first published 1983), 283–86.

80. There is a rich literature on May Day. See among others Rudolph Vecoli, "Primo Maggio: May Day Observances Among Italian Immigrant Workers, 1890–1920," *Labor's Heritage* (Spring 1996): 29–41.

81. Vecoli, "Primo Maggio," 32–35.

82. "The Red Flag and a Riot" and "Police Seize Red Flags," *New York Times*, September 3, 1895, 1, and May 2, 1909, 2.

83. Carlo Tresca, "Vieni, o Maggio," *Il Proletario*, May 1, 1906.

84. Numero Speciale dedicato al Primo Maggio," *La Questione Sociale*, May 1, 1904, 1.

85. L. M. Bottazzi, "Fra il passato e l'avvenire," *La Lotta*, May 1, 1909, 1.

86. "Festa o lotta," *La Questione Sociale*, May 1, 1904, 3.

87. Cited in Vecoli, "Primo Maggio," 33.

88. *Alba Nuova*, May 1, 1922, 8. Other multiethnic May Days were organized also in Paterson, Spring Valley, Barre, and San Francisco. Cf. Vecoli, "Primo Maggio," 32.

89. See for example *Cronaca Sovversiva*, May 19, 1906; *L'Era Nuova*, May 14, 1910; *Il Proletario*, May 7, 1905.

90. Vecoli, "Primo Maggio," 37.

91. Vecoli, "The Italian Immigrants in the United States Labor Movement," 277.

CHAPTER 3

1. "Ai compagni d'Italia," *L'Anarchico*, February 1, 1888, 1. Only two issues of *L'Anarchico*, which was published monthly until June 1888, have survived. They are available in microfilms at the Immigration History Research Center, University of Minnesota.

2. Germans published 240 radical papers, Jews 207, Italians 189. Taken together German, Jewish, and Italian radical newspapers account for about 50 percent of the entire ethnic radical press in the United States. See Dirk Hoerder, *The Immigrant Labor Press in America*, 3 vols. (New York: Greenwood Press, 1987), I, 30. For a full list of Italian radical papers and their location see Vol. 3.

3. Bruce C. Nelson, *Beyond the Martyrs* (New Brunswick, N.J.: Rutgers University Press, 1988), 103. For the role of the press in the history of the American Left see Joseph R. Conlin, ed., *The American Radical Press*, 2 vols. (Westport, Conn.: Greenwood Press, 1974); Elliott Shore, Ken Fones-Wolf, and James P. Danky, eds., *The German-American Radical Press* (Urbana: University of Illinois Press, 1992); and Hoerder, *The Immigrant Labor Press in America*.

4. Pernicone, "Italian Immigrant Radicalism in New York," 83.

5. Hundreds of dollars were collected for the defense of persecuted revolutionaries, Italian and non-Italian alike, such as Joseph Ettor and Arturo Giovannitti in 1912, Tom Mooney in 1916, and Sacco and Vanzetti in the 1920s. The communist paper *Alba Nuova* collected more than $500 for the Friends of Soviet Russia in 1922 and more than $600 a year later for victims of fascism. See "Friends of Soviet Russia. Rendiconto generale," June 1, 1922, 4, and "Fundraising for the Victims of Fascism," February 10, 1923, 4.

6. "Mario Rapisardi Literary Society," *Alba Nuova*, September 1921, 3.

7. For an example of the journalistic diatribes among the *sovversivi* see Nunzio Pernicone, "War among the Italian Anarchists: The Galleanisti's Campaign against Carlo Tresca," in Cannistraro and Meyer, eds., *The Lost World of Italian American Radicalism* (Westport, Conn.: Praeger, 2003), 77–98.

8. "Reminiscences of Aldino Felicani," Columbia Oral History Collection, Columbia University. Cited in George Pozzetta, "The Italian Immigrant Press of New York City," *American Immigration and Ethnicity Series*, vol. 5, 248.

9. Pozzetta, "The Italian Immigrant Press of New York City," 249; and Hoerder, *The Immigrant Labor Press in America*, 4.

10. Robert E. Park, *The Immigrant Press and Its Control* (New York: Harper, 1922), 360; cited in Bruno Cartosio, "Italian Workers and Their Press in the United States, 1900–1920," in Christiane Harzig and Dirk Hoerder, *The Press of Labor Migrants in Europe and North America* (Bremen: Publications of the Labor Newspaper Preservation Project, 1985), 425.

11. Nunzio Pernicone, "Introduction" to the Special Issue on the Italian American Radical Press, *Italian American Review*, 8, 1 (Spring/Summer 2001): 2.

12. "Importante," *La Questione Sociale*, June 30, 1897, 3.

13. Mario De Ciampis, "Storia del movimento rivoluzionatio socialista italiano," *La Parola del Popolo* (December 1958–January 1959): 142.

14. Cartosio, "Italian Workers and Their Press in the United States," 425.

15. Pernicone, "Introduction" to the Special Issue on the Italian American Radical Press, 2.

16. Cited in Cartosio, "Italian Workers and Their Press in the United States," 435.

17. Nunzio Pernicone, *Carlo Tresca: Portrait of a Rebel* (New York: Palgrave, 2005), 104.

18. *Cronaca Sovversiva*, for example, changed its name into *L'Anarchia*, then *Il Diritto*, and finally *Il Refrattario* between 1918 and 1919. Similarly, *Il Proletario* relocated to Chicago in 1916 and was renamed *La Difesa*, then *Il Nuovo Proletario*, until, finally, in 1920, it resumed its original title. See also *La Questione Sociale*, which became *L'Era Nuova* in 1908 after being suppressed by federal authorities; the anarchist *Il Pensiero* (1938–39), organ of the Camillo Berneri Group, which became *Il Ribelle* in 1939; and the communist *Alba Nuova* (1921–24), which led the way to *Il Lavoratore* (1924–31).

19. For a detailed history of *Il Proletario* see De Ciampis, "Storia del movimento socialista rivoluzionario italiano," 136–63, and "Nel cinquantennio del giornale," *Il Proletario*, May 1946, 3.

20. Cited in Pernicone, "Carlo Tresca's *Il Martello*," *Italian American Review*, 8,1 (Spring/Summer 2001): 28.

21. Hoerder, *The Immigrant Labor Press*, III, 6–10.

22. *La Plebe* was founded in Philadelphia in 1907 and in July 1909 was transferred to Steubenville, Ohio, and renamed *L'Avvenire*. In 1910 Tresca relocated *L'Avvenire* to New Kensington, Pennsylvania, and in 1912 transferred it once more to New York, where he had moved. *L'Avvenire* was eventually suppressed by American authorities in 1917. At the end of 1917 Tresca purchased *Il Martello* from Luigi Preziosi and made it his forte for twenty-six years. See Pernicone, "Carlo Tresca's *Il Martello*."

23. First published in Barre, Vermont, from 1903 to 1912, *Cronaca Sovversiva* relocated to Lynn, Massachusetts, where it continued to be published until Galleani's deportation to Italy in June 1919. With a circulation of some 5,000, it exerted a powerful influence over a substantial segment of Italian immigrant workers. After Galleani's departure, in 1921, his foremost disciples founded a new publication in New York, *L'Adunata dei Refrattari*, that continued to propagate Galleani's beliefs until 1971. See Nunzio Pernicone, "Luigi Galleani and Italian Anarchist Terrorism in the United States," *Studi Emigrazione/Etudes*

Migrations, XXX, n. 111, 1993, 469–88; and Rudolph Vecoli, "Luigi Galleani," in Mari Jo Buhle, Paul Buhle, and Dan Georgakas, eds., *Encyclopedia of the American Left* (Urbana: University of Illinois Press, 1992), 251–53.

24. See for example Giuseppe Ciancabilla's anarchist *L'Aurora* published in Chicago and San Francisco between 1899 and 1902, Giovanni Gallina's progressive *La Sentinella* (Hoboken, N.J., 1903–7), Libero Tancredi's (alias Massimo Rocca) anarchist *Il Novatore* (New York, 1910–11), Aldino Felicani's *Controcorrente* (Boston, 1938–67), Antonio Capraro's communist *Utopia* (Rochester, N.Y., 1927–28), and Vincenzo Vacirca's anti-fascist *Il Solco* (1927–28) and *La Strada* (1937–38), both published in New York.

25. Pozzetta, "The Italian Immigrant Press," 243.

26. Ambrogio Donini, "L'Unità del popolo e lo stato operaio," in Antonio Varsori, ed., *L'antifascismo italiano negli Stati Uniti durante la seconda guerra mondiale* (Rome: Achivio Trimestrale, 1984), 340. Cited in Gerald Meyer, "*L'Unità del Popolo*: The Voice of Italian American Communism, 1939–51," *Italian American Review*, 8,1 (Spring/Summer 2001): 128.

27. "Per Alba Nuova," *Alba Nuova*, August 18, 1923, 1.

28. Cannistraro and Meyer, "Italian American Radicalism: An Interpretative History," in Cannistraro and Meyer, eds., *The Lost World of Italian American Radicalism*, 13.

29. George Pozzetta and Gary Mormino, *The Immigrant World of Ybor City: Italians and Their Latin Neighbors in Tampa, Florida, 1885–1985* (Urbana: University of Illinois Press, 1987).

30. Rebecca Zurier, *Art for The Masses (1911–1917): A Radical Magazine and Its Graphics* (New Haven, Conn.: Yale University Art Gallery, 1985).

31. *La Questione Sociale*, July 24, 1915, 2.

32. *The Divine Comedy of Dante Alighieri. Inferno*, trans. Allen Mandelbaum (New York: Bantam Books, 1982), Canto I, lines 100–5.

33. In introducing the paper the editors did not explain the meaning of *Il Veltro* but simply said it referred to Dante's prophecy, symbol of all aspirations of freedom. They assumed that the readers would be familiar with Dante's lyrics. *Il Veltro*, August 15, 1924, 12.

34. Riccardo Cordiferro (pen name of Alessandro Sisca), "La conquista del libro," conference held at the Settlement of All Nations, New York, December 2, 1920. Alessandro Sisca Papers, IHRC2408, Box 1, folder 1 and Box 8, Immigration History Research Center, University of Minnesota.

35. "Pel giornale quotidiano," *Il Proletario*, December 6, 1902, 1.

36. The paper was published until 1919. See Hoerder, *The Immigrant Labor Press*, Vol. 3, 97–98.

37. "La colonia italiana di New York," *Il Grido degli Oppressi*, June 5, 1892, 2–3; see also in the same newspaper "Schiavi italiani negli Stati Uniti," June 30, 1892, 1–2.

38. Letter by B. Fratoddi, *Il Proletario*, August 12, 1906; cited in De Ciampis, "Italiani in America," *La Parola del Popolo* (September–October 1976): 77.

39. "Alla colonia italiana," *Il Grido Degli Oppressi*, June 5, 1892, 1. See also "La colonia italiana," *Il Proletario*, February 3, 1900, 2.

40. Cited in Pernicone, *Carlo Tresca*, 24.

41. "Contro le camorre consolari," *Il Proletario*, September 24, 1905. See also Pernicone, *Carlo Tresca*, 24–25.

42. Among other articles see especially "I consoli italiani," *Il Proletario* June 30, 1899, 2; Raimondo Fazio, "A cosa serve il consolato di New York" and "Limitiamo le funzioni consolari," *Il Fuoco*, November 1 and 15, 1914, 15–16.

43. See above all "Contro i camorristi del Progresso," *Il Proletario*, September 6, 1902, 1; and "La bile di un asino al soldo di Barsotti," November 20, 1904.

44. *Il Progresso Italo-Americano* was established in 1889 by Carlo Barsotti, a wealthy New York contractor–labor agent. It quickly became the most influential Italian daily newspaper in the United States with an estimated circulation of 118,580 by 1918. *Il Corriere* was established in 1909 and had a circulation of about 50,000. See George E. Pozzetta, "The Italian Immigrant Press of New York City: The Early Years, 1880–1915," 240–55, and *N. W. Ayer & Son's Newspaper Annual and Directory* (Philadelphia: Ayer & Son, 1918). For information on Generoso Pope see Philip V. Cannistraro, "Generoso Pope and the Rise of Italian American Politics, 1925–1936," in Lydio Tomasi, ed., *Italian Americans: New Perspectives in Italian Immigration and Ethnicity* (Staten Island, N.Y.: Center for Migration Studies, 1985), 264–88; and Pernicone, *Carlo Tresca*, 218.

45. "I prominenti," *Il Grido della Folla*, June 15, 1916, 4.

46. See the articles under the title "Il gionalismo coloniale: boicottiamo I giornali italiani!" published on June 28, July 3, July 12, July 26, and August 26, 1902.

47. G. M. Parrasio (pen name for Giacinto Menotti Serrati), "Ai compagni ed ai simpatizzanti!" *Il Proletario*, August 23, 1902, Supplement n. 34.

48. See for example the exposés against Dr. Collins published in *Il Proletario*, January 20, 1900, 2; and May 19, 1900, 2.

49. Pozzetta, "The Italian Immigrant Press," 243.

50. See "Lega di resistenza anticlericale," *La Questione Sociale*, February 3, 1906, 1; and Arturo Salucci, "Anticlericalismo," *Il Proletario*, November 16, 1901, 2.

51. "Perchè noi combattiamo la religione," *Il Grido degli Oppressi*, August 4, 1892, 3–4.

52. "Il Perchè," *Il Proletario*, December 25, 1903, 1.

53. For example "A voi donne religiose," *Avanti*, November 23, 1904, 2.

54. See above all the following articles in the December 25, 1903, special issue of *Il Proletario*: "L'essenza della religione," "I misteri," and "Natale e Primo Maggio"; and "Dio" and "La dannosità della religione," both in *La Questione Sociale*, November 15, 1896, 1, and June 16, 1900, 2.

55. "Contradittorio Tresca—Rev. Petrarca," *Il Proletario*, July 16, 1905, 1.

56. See Giorgio Candeloro, ed., *L'Asino è il popolo: utile, paziente, bastonato* di Podrecca e Galantara (1892/1925) (Milan: Feltrinelli, 1970).

57. Cited in Mormino and Pozzetta, *The Immigrant World of Ybor City*, 215. For other examples of anti-clericalism among Italian immigrants see Rudolph Vecoli, "Prelates and Peasants: Italian Immigrants and the Catholic Church," *Journal of Social History* 2 (Spring 1969): 217–68.

58. See Rudolph Vecoli, "The American Republic Viewed by the Italian Left," in Marianne Debouzy, ed., *In the Shadow of the Statue of Liberty* (Urbana: University of Illinois Press, 1992), 33.

59. *L'Asino*, May 16, 1909, 2.

60. Pernicone, *Carlo Tresca*, 45.

61. See for example "La festa della Madonna del Carmine," *Il Proletario*, July 20, 1901, 1; Giovanni Gianchino, "Tripoli e la Sicilia," *Il Proletario*, January 15, 1912.

62. On Italian American religious practices see Robert A. Orsi, *The Madonna of 115th Street: Faith and Community in Italian Harlem, 1880–1950* (New Haven, Conn.: Yale University Press, 1985).

63. Gaetano Mirtillo, "Lettera aperta a Nostra Signora del Carmine," *Il Proletario*, July 1, 1903, 3–4.

64. "Scuola laica e religione," *La Fiaccola*, July 30, 1910; cited in Virginia Yans-McLaughlin, *Family and Community: Italian Immigrants in Buffalo, 1880–1930* (Urbana: University of Illinois Press, 1982, first published 1977), 226–27.

65. *L'Asino*, vignettes entitled "Padre e marito spirituale," January 8, 1905, 7, and "Comunione di pensiero," June 18, 1905, 6.

66. See Pernicone, *Carlo Tresca*, 36–37. Sabato's misconduct is also reported in *L'Asino* in the September 24, 1905, issue, 6.

67. Pernicone, *Carlo Tresca*, 36; and Cannistraro and Meyer, "Italian American Radicalism: An Interpretative History," 10.

68. "Cristo e i Preti," *Il Proletario*, September 11, 1904, 2.

69. See for example "Il XX Settembre," *La Questione Sociale*, 15 September 1895, 15 September 1897, 15 September 1898.

70. Elisee Reclus, "La Patria," *La Questione Sociale*, May 16, 1903, 1. For similar arguments see also in *Il Proletario*, Fortunato Vezzoli, "I senza patria," May 11, 1912; and Giovanni Di Gregorio, "Patriottismo," May 3, 1913, both discussed in Michael Topp, *Those Without a Country: The Political Culture of Italian American Syndicalists* (Minneapolis: University of Minnesota Press, 2001), 80–82.

71. Cannistraro and Meyer, "Italian American Radicalism: An Interpretative History."

72. "Le cause piscologiche della guerra europea," *Il Fuoco*, November 15, 1914, 8.

73. Maffei, "Alla rivolta," *Il Grido della Folla*, May 20, 1916, 1.

74. Vecoli, "The American Republic Viewed by the Italian Left," 33–34; and Salerno, "*I Delitti della Razza Bianca*: Italian Anarchists' Racial Discourse as Crime," in Jennifer Gugliemo and Salvatore Salerno, eds., *Are Italians White?* (New York: Routledge, 2003), 111–23.

75. "Chi fu Cristoforo Colombo," *Il Grido degli Oppressi*, June 30, 1892, 1. See also "I delitti della razza bianca" and Razze superiori: imparate!" both in *L'Era Nuova*, February 20, 1909, 1, and February 27, 1915.

76. See *Il Proletario*, "Civiltà di cannibali" (January 25, 1901, 1) on the lynching of Fred Alexander in Leavenworth, Kansas; and "Un linciaggio" (November 24, 1900, 1) on the burning alive of Preston Porter in Colorado. See also "L'americana," in *La Questione Sociale*, August 2, 1902, 3, on the lynching of William Ody *in Clayton,* Missouri. For general indictment of lynching see Luigi Galleani, "La legge del taglione," *Cronaca Sovversiva*, September 25, 1915; and *Guardia Rossa*, April 1920, 18, 20, and 21.

77. Ludovico Caminita, "Odio di razza?" *La Questione Sociale*, May 19, 1906, 2.

78. "E' una vergogna," *La Questione Sociale*, November 25, 1899, 2.

79. "Non lotta di razza, ma di classe," *Il Proletario*, June 4, 1909, 1.

80. *Those Without a Country*, 65–74; and "It Is Providential that There Are Foreigners Here: Whiteness and Masculinity in the Making of Italian American Syndicalist Identity," in Guglielmo and Salerno, eds., *Are Italian White?*, 98–110.

81. Gino Bardi, "Siamo Ariani?" cited in Gerald Meyer, "*L'Unità del Popolo*," 135.

82. See for example Alba, "Alle mie compagne," and "Due metodi," *Il Grido degli Oppressi*, December 9, 1893, 2, and December 30, 1893, 1. Among the many articles in *La Questione Sociale*, see above all Maria Barbieri, "Ribelliamoci!" November 18, 1905; Virgilia Buongiorno, "Alle compagne lavoratrici," October 15, 1895, 4; Evening (Pietro Raveggi), "La donna dell'avvenire," 1–2; Alba, "Eguali diritti," October 15, 1901; and Susanna Carruette, "La donna del domani," November 6, 1901, 2.

83. Maria Roda, "Alle operaie," *La Questione Sociale*, September 15, 1897, 4.

84. Alba, "Alle mie compagne."

85. Buongiorno, "Alle compagne lavoratrici."

86. Titì, "Alle mie sorelle proletarie," *La Questione Sociale*, June 23, 1906, 1. She contributed regularly between June 9 and August 25, 1906.

87. *L'Aurora*, August 24, 1901, 1. For a similar argument see also Alba Genisio, *La Questione Sociale*, March 7, 1908, and Ines Oddone Bidelli, "La donna," *Il Lavoro*, April 21, 1917, 2.

88. See Elizabeth Helsinger, ed., *Woman Question: Society and Literature in Britain and America, 1837–1883* (Manchester: Manchester University Press, 1987); and Kathryn Kish Sklar, *Florence Kelley and the Nation's Work: The Rise of Women's Political Culture, 1830–1900* (New Haven, Conn.: Yale University Press, 1997).

89. Judith Jeffrey Howard, "The Civil Code of 1865 and the Origins of the Feminist Movement in Italy," in Betty Boyd Caroli, Robert F. Harney, and Lydio F. Thomasi, eds., *The Italian Immigrant Woman in North America* (Toronto: The Multicultural History Society of Ontario, 1977), 14–20.

90. Ibid.

91. Emilia Gentili Zappi, *If Eight Hours Seem Too Few: Mobilization of the Women Workers in the Italian Rice Fields* (Albany: State University of New York Press, 1991), 71–75.

92. Buongiorno, "Alle compagne lavoratrici."Among Anna Maria Mozzoni's articles see "Alle figlie del popolo," *La Questione Sociale*, July 15, 1895, 3–4.

93. Isabel Bass, "La pagina della donna nuova," *Il Fuoco*, March 31, 1915, 7, and April 15, 1915, 12. Bellalma Forzato-Spezia, "Nel mondo femminile," March 10, 1917, 2; Ines Bidelli, "La donna," April 21, 1917, 2; R. Rende, "Sul femminismo," January 19, 2–3, all in *Il Lavoro*.

94. Bellalma Forzato-Spezia, "Alle madri proletarie," and "Emancipiamoci!" *L'Operaia*, September 13, 1913, 7, and January 10, 1914, 6.

95. "La donna nella legislazione moderna," *L'Operaia*, December 11, 1913, 4.

96. "La donna nel presente: assetto sociale," *Il Proletario*, June 16, 1907, 1.

97. *L'Aurora*, December 22, 1900, 2; cited in Caroline Waldron Merithew, "Anarchist Motherhood: Toward the Making of a Revolutionary Proletariat in Illinois Coal Towns," in Donna Gabaccia and Franca Iacovetta, eds., *Women, Gender and Transnational Lives: Italian Workers of the World* (Toronto: University of Toronto Press, 2002), 217–18.

98. *La Questione Sociale*, "Aiutiamoci a vicenda!" September 20, 1902, 3. See also "I gruppi femminili di propaganda," November 23, 1901, 1; letter by Angela Marietti to *L'Aurora*, August 10, 1901, 1, and letter signed "Una donna che pensa" (A thinking woman) to *L'Aurora*, January 12, 1901, 3.

99. *L'Aurora*, December 22, 1900, 2 (the translation is mine); cited also in Merithew, "Anarchist Motherhood," 218.

100. A. Guabello, "Alle donne," *La Questione Sociale*, February 18, 1899, 1.

101. "La donna e la famiglia," *Il Grido degli Oppressi*, October 10, 1892, 2.

102. Arturo Giovannitti, "Ai margini del grande sciopero: alcune riflessioni malinconiche," *Il Lavoro*, March 13, 1919; cited in Bènèdicte Deschamps, "*Il Lavoro* (1915–1932)," *Italian American Review*, 8, 1 (Spring/Summer 2001): 95; and Topp, *Those Without a Country*, 212.

103. A. Ferretti, "La donna: come era, com'è e come sarà," *La Questione Sociale*, October 29, 1896, 2; and "I Diritti della Donna," *Il Proletario*, March 3, 1907, 1. See also "Come vorrebbero la donna," *L'Operaia*, April 11, 1914, and "La donna e il problema dell'amore," *La Lotta*, January, 9, 1909, 3.

104. Titì, "Alle mie sorelle proletarie" and "Alle donne: Emancipiamoci!" *La Questione Sociale*, July 7, 1906, 3.

105. Jennifer Guglielmo, "Negotiating Gender, Race and Coalition: Italian Women and Working-Class Politics in New York City, 1880–1945" (Ph.D. dissertation, University of Minnesota, 2003), 129. See also her recent book *Living the Revolution: Italian Women's Resistance and Radicalism in New York City, 1880–1945* (Chapel Hill: University of North Carolina Press, 2010).

106. Topp, *Those Without a Country*, 119; and Ardis Cameron, *Radicals of the Worst Sort: Laboring Women in Lawrence, Massachusetts, 1860–1912* (Urbana: University of Illinois Press, 1995).

107. Jean Scarpaci, "Angela Bambace and the International Ladies' Garment Workers' Union: The Search for an Elusive Activist," 104–10., in George Pozzetta, ed., *Pane e Lavoro: The Italian American Working Class* (Toronto: Proceedings of the American Italian Historical Association, 1980), 99–118.

108. See Len Giovannitti, *The Nature of the Beast* (New York: Random House, 1977).

109. Elizabeth Gurley Flynn, *The Rebel Girl* (New York: International Publishers, 1955), 333–34; and Pernicone, *Carlo Tresca*, 39, 238–40, and 244–45.

110. Deschamps, "*Il Lavoro* (1915–1932)," 85–120. See also McLaughlin's discussion of *La Fiaccola*, the socialist paper of Buffalo, in her *Family and Community*, 229–40.

111. The figures come from the U.S. Bureau of Labor; cited in Jennifer Guglielmo, "Proletarian Feminism in New York City Garment Trades," in Gabaccia and Jacovetta, *Women, Gender and Transnational Lives*, 253.

112. Deschamps, "*Il Lavoro* (1915–1932)," 96.

113. Isabel Bass, "Il femminismo," *Il Fuoco*, March 31, 1914, 7.

114. See for example Raimondo Fazio, "La donna, il suffragismo e l'organizzazione industriale," *Il Proletario*, April 5, 1912; cited in Topp, *Those Without a Country*, 120.

115. "Le donne nel partito," *Alba Nuova*, February 16, 1924, 3.

116. Rossi-Doria's views were reprinted even in *La Questione Sociale*. See for example "Madre ed Operaia? Le leggi protettive del lavoro muliebre," *La Questione Sociale*, May 3, 1902, 1.

117. Sally Miller, "Socialism and Women," in John H. Lassett and Seymour M. Lipset, eds., *Failure of a Dream, Essays in the History of American Socialism* (Berkeley: University of California Press, 1984), 307; cited in Deschamps, "*Il Lavoro*," 96. See also Yans-Mclaughlin, *Family and Community*, 235–40.

118. "Alle Madri," *La Questione Sociale*, June 30, 1892, 3, and "La donna nuova," *L'Operaia*, October 4, 1913, 7.

119. Elisabetta Vezzosi, "Immigrate italiane e socialismo negli Stati Uniti agli inizio del Novecento," *Il Veltro: Rivista della civiltà italiana*, January–April 1990, 163, also cited in Deschamps, "*Il Lavoro*," 96.

120. Bellalma Forzato-Spezia, *La donna nel presente e l'educazione dell'infanzia* (West Hoboken, N.J.: s.n. 1913), 22; Waldron Merithew, "Anarchist Motherhood," 217–46.

121. "Alle Madri," *La Questione Sociale*, October 7, 1901, 2–3.

122. See for example "Alle Madri," *La Questione Sociale*, June 30, 1897, 3; Ersilia Grandi, "La mssione materna," *L'Aurora*, October 13, 1900, 2, and August 24, 1901, 1; Angela Marietti, letter published in *L'Aurora*, August 10, 1901, 1; Severino Cerutti, "La donna e il problema dell'amore," *La Lotta*, January 9, 1909, 3.

123. Linda K. Kerber, *Women of the Republic: Intellect and Ideology in Revolutionary America* (New York: W. W. Norton, 1980), 11.

124. Waldron Merithew, "Anarchist Motherhood," 222.

125. Checa, "Della donna," *Il Lavoro*, December 25, 1920; cited in Deschamps, "*Il Lavoro*," 96.

126. Sora Maria, "Per la donna: fra moglie e marito," *Il Nuovo Mondo*, November 17, 1925, 2.

127. Yans-McLaughlin, *Family and Community*, 218–59.

128. Among them were Laura di Guglielmo, Anna Fama, Maria and Angela Bambace, Lina Manetta, Angelna Limanti, Maria Prestianni, Anna Squillante, and Millie Terreno. See Furio, "The Cultural Background of the Italian Immigrant Woman," in Pozzetta, ed., *Pane e Lavoro*, 95–96.

129. Cf. Pernicone, "Carlo Tresca's *Il Martello*," 27.

130. Hoerder, *The Immigrant Labor Press in North America*, 90.

131. "I nostri propositi," unsigned, and John Di Gregorio, "To all Labor: Greetings" (English in the original), *Il Nuovo Mondo*, November 16, 1925, 1 and 3. See also John P. Diggins, *Mussolini and Fascism: The View from America* (Princeton, N.J.: Princeton University Press, 1972), 113.

132. Diggins, *Mussolini and Fascism*, 113; and Pernicone, "Italian Immigrant Radicalism in New York City," 83. The expression "citadel of Italian American anti-Fascism" is used by Montana in his *Amarostico*, 98–100. Besides *Il Nuovo Mondo*, East 10th Street housed the offices of *Il Lavoratore* and *Il Martello*.

133. Pernicone, "Italian Immigrant Radicalism in New York City," 86.

134. *Il Nuovo Mondo*, editorial, December 2, 1925, 1.

135. Pernicone, *Carlo Tresca*, 174.

136. On the relation of the Order of Sons of Italy to fascism see Gaetano Salvemini, *Fascist Activities in the United States*, edited and with an introduction by Philip V. Cannistraro (New York: Center for Migration Studies, 1977), 91–105.

137. Before *La Stampa Libera* Valenti edited also *La Domenica* (1912) and *La Parola Proletaria* (which became *La Fiaccola* and then *Avanti!*) in Rochester between 1917 and 1923. After *La Stampa Libera* he published *La Parola del Popolo* in New York from 1939 to 1946. For general biographical information see Rudolph Vecoli, "Valenti Girolamo," in Franco Andreucci and Tommaso Detti, eds., *Il movimento operaio italiano. Dizionario biografico*, vol. 6 (Rome: Editori Riuniti, 1975–1979), 171–74; Fort Velona, "Girolamo Valenti," *La Parola del Popolo*, April/May 1958, 5–6; "Giorolamo Valenti Is Dead," *New York Herald Tribune*, February 22, 1958; and "Valenti, 65, Dies; Foe of Fascism," *New York Times*,

February 22, 1958. For insights into his personality and political formation see Tommaso Toselli, "Girolamo Valenti: una vita per la libertà" and "Appunti di orientamento per la comprensione della figura di Girolamo Valenti," unpublished articles, Girolamo Valenti Papers, Box 2, folder "Notes on Valenti," Tamiment Library, New York University. On Valenti's political activism see his files in the collection of the Casellario Politico Centrale, Archivio Centrale dello Stato, Rome.

138. See for example "Italian Fascist Propaganda in the United States," *Look*, December 17, 1940; "Generoso Pope's Fascist Record," *La Parola*, May 24, 1941; and "Mussolini's Anti-Semitism Shall not Divide Us," *Jewish People's Voice*, October 1938, 1–2.

139. See for example *La Difesa* (1923–24), *Controcorrente* (1938–67), *Nazioni Unite* (1942–46), *Il Mondo* (1938–45), *Il Solco* (1927–28), and *La Strada* (1937–38).

140. For a detailed history of *Nazioni Unite* see Charles Killinger, "*Nazioni Unite* and the Anti-Fascist Exiles in New York City, 1940–1946," *The Italian American Review* 8, 1 (Spring/Summer 2001): 157–95.

CHAPTER 4

1. Pietro Gori, *Primo Maggio: bozzetto drammatico in un atto* (Barre, Vt.: Salvatore Pallavicini Editore, 1896), 9–10, 17, reprinted in volume XIII of Gori's collected *Opere*, edited by P. Binazzi, 12 vols. (Spezia, Italy: Cromo-tipo La Sociale, 1911–12). All the translations from the Italian are mine. For more information on Gori see chapter 1, p. 000.

2. Bartolomeo Vanzetti translated the poem into English shortly before his own execution. Published in Robert D'Attilio, "Primo Maggio: Haymarket as Seen by Italian Anarchists in America," in David Roediger, ed., *Haymarket Scrapbook* (Chicago: Charles H. Kerr, 1986), 229–30.

3. *Senza patria* (Buenos Aires: Librería Sociológica, 1899), reprinted in Pietro Gori, *Scritti scelti*, 2 vols. (Cesena: Edizioni L'Antistato, 1968), II, 342, 343, 361. Other popular plays by Gori were *Proximus tuus: bozzetto sociale in un atto*, con prefazione di L. Marenco (Milano: Demarchi, 1898); *Ideale: bozzetto poetico: atto unico con prologo*, prefazione di M. Pilo (Chieti: C. Di Sciullo, 1902); and *Gente onesta: scene della vita borghese in tre atti* (Roma/Firenze: Serantoni, 1905).

4. Michael Denning, *The Cultural Front: The Laboring of American Culture in the Twentieth Century* (London and New York: Verso, 1997), 366; and Irving Howe, *World of Our Fathers* (1976; repr., New York: New York University Press, 2005), 494. The importance of dramatic groups in the culture of the Italian anarchists is briefly noted by Avrich in *Sacco and Vanzetti: The Anarchist Background* (Princeton, N.J.: Princeton University Press, 1991), 55.

5. *La Follia*, February 3, 1907, 7.

6. For information on these groups see for example *La Questione Sociale*, May 6, 1899, 3; *La Follia*, March 2, 1907, 7; *Il Lavoro*, February 9, 1918; *Alba Nuova*, January 26, 1924, 4; Paul Avrich, *Sacco and Vanzetti: The Anarchist Background* (Princeton, N.J.: Princeton University Press, 1996), 55.

7. See *Il Grido degli Oppressi*, August 4, 1892, 4.

8. Paul Avrich, *Anarchist Voices: An Oral History of Anarchism in America* (1995; repr., Edinburgh: AK Press, 2005), 180, 140. Other references to the theater can be found at pages 97, 98, 107, 109, 111, 113, 136, 138, 143, and 155.

9. See Colette A. Hyman, *Workers' Theatre and the American Labor Movement* (Philadelphia: Temple University Press, 1997); David Lifson, *The Yiddish Theatre in America* (New York: Thomas Yoseloff, 1965); Edna Nahshon, *Yiddish Proletarian Theatre: The Art and Politics of the Artef, 1925–1940* (Westport, Conn.: Greenwood Press, 1998); Howe, *World of Our Fathers*, chapter 14; and Maxine Schwartz Seller, ed., *Ethnic Theatre in the United States* (Westport, Conn.: Greenwood Press, 1983). See also Emelise Aleandri, *Images of America: The Italian American Immigrant Theatre in New York* (Charleston, UK: Arcadia, 1999) and her doctoral dissertation "The Italian American Theatre, 1900–1905" (The City University of New York, 1983).

10. See for example Martino Marazzi and Ann Goldstein, *Voices of Italian America: A History of Early Italian American Literature with a Critical Anthology* (Madison, N.J.: Fairleigh Dickinson University Press, 2004).

11. Howe, *World of Our Fathers*, 464.

12. *La Questione Sociale*, Letter from Paterson, May 6, 1899, 3.

13. Lawrence W. Levine, *Highbrow/Lowbrow: The Emergence of Cultural Hierarchy in America* (1988; repr., Cambridge, Mass.: Harvard University Press, 1997), 194; Jerre Mangione and Ben Morreale, *La Storia* (New York: HarperCollins, 1992), 309.

14. See Avrich, *Sacco and Vanzetti*, 55; and *Anarchist Voices*, 97–98, 107, 109, 111, 113, 136, 138, 140, 143, 155, 180; and Jennifer Guglielmo, *Living the Revolution: Italian Women's Resistance and Radicalism in New York City, 1880–1945* (Chapel Hill: University of North Carolina Press, 2010), 172.

15. Guglielmo, *Living the Revolution*, 172–73; Nena Becchetti, *La figlia dell'anarchico. Dramma sociale in tre atti* (Jessup, Pa.: Gruppo Autonomo, 1920), Immigration History Research Center (hereafter IHRC), Andersen Library, University of Minnesota.

16. Cf. Seller, "Introduction" to *Ethnic Theatre in the United States*, 3–17.

17. Hyman, *Workers' Theatre and the American Labor Movement*, 2. See also Robert Leach, *Revolutionary Theatre* (London: Routledge, 1994); Malcolm Goldstein, *Political Stage* (Oxford: Oxford University Press, 1974); Augusto Boal, *Theatre of the Oppressed* (New York: Theatre Communications Group, 1993); Gerald Rabkin, *Drama and Commitment: Politics in the American Theatre in the Thirties* (Bloomington: Indiana University Press, 1964); Eugene Van Erven, *Radical People's Theatre* (Bloomington: Indiana University Press, 1988).

18. The scholarship on cultural production offers important insights for understanding the role of the audience and cultural reception. Key works include Hyman, *Staging Strikes*, chapter 3; Warren Susman, *Culture as History: The Transformation of American Society in the Twentieth Century* (New York: Pantheon, 1984); Raymond Williams, *Drama in Performance* (New York: Basic Books, 1969); Marvin Carlson, "Theatre Audiences and the Reading of Performance," in Thomas Postlewait and Bruce A. McConachie, eds., *Interpreting the Theatrical Past: Essays in the Historiography of Performance* (Iowa City: University of Iowa Press, 1989), 82–97; and Ira A. Levine, *Left-Wing Dramatic Theory in the American Theatre* (Ann Arbor: UMI Research Press, 1985).

19. Avrich, *Anarchist Voices*, 113.

20. "Teatro del Popolo," *Il Lavoro*, January 12, 1918, 4.

21. Vincenzo Vacirca, "Il Teatro del Popolo," *Il Lavoro*, January 19, 1918, 5.

22. "Il Teatro del Popolo: Prima rappresentazione," *Il Lavoro*, January 26, 1918, 6.

23. *La leva militare* (1903) by Pier Luigi Grazioli, *Tripoli* (1914) by Matteo Siragusa, *Ali tarpate* (1917) by Ulisse Barberi, *Povera gente* (1921) by Franco Liberati, and *Nemmeno in cielo* (1924) by Federico Polidori are a few examples.

24. *Il Proletario*, December 25, 1907.

25. "Rappresentazione di *Luci e Tenebre*," *Il Proletario*, February 25, 1908, 3.

26. See Hayman, *Staging Strikes*, 109–21; Peter Brooks, *The Melodramatic Imagination* (New Haven, Conn.: Yale University Press, 1976); Northrop Frye, *Anatomy of Criticism* (Princeton, N.J.: Princeton University Press, 1957); and Frank Rahill, *The World of Melodrama* (University Park: Penn State University Press, 1967).

27. On this issue see Anna Maria Martellone, "The Formation of an Italian American Identity through Popular Theater," in Werner Sollors, ed., *Multilingual America: Transnationalism, Ethnicity, and the Languages of American Literature* (New York: New York University Press, 1998), 240–45.

28. "Riccardo Cordiferro's Biography," Alessandro Sisca Papers, IHRC2408, Box 1, Folder 1, IHRC. See also Emelise Aleandri's biographical entry in Salvatore John LaGumina, *The Italian Immigrant Experience* (New York: Routledge, 1999), 146–48.

29. Riccardo Cordiferro, *Poesie Scelte* (Campobasso, Italy: Edizioni Pungolo Verde, 1967), 6; and Joseph Pantaleone, "Riccardo Cordiferro: Anima Libera—Cuore Sincero—Poeta e Scrittore Geniale," *La Sentinella*, March 15, 1930, in Sisca Papers, Box 12, Folder 112, IHRC.

30. "Riccardo Cordiferro's Biography," Sisca Papers, IHRC2408, Box 1, Folder 1, IHRC. See also "Alessandro Sisca," *New York Times*, August 27, 1940, 21.

31. Despite his enormous literary production and his immense popularity within the Italian American community, Cordiferro has received little or no attention by scholars of Italian Americana. Emelise Aleandri is the only scholar who has written about Cordiferro, but her work does not go beyond the informative level. See Aleandri, "Riccardo Cordiferro," in Richard N. Juliani and Philip V. Cannistraro, eds., *Italian Americans: The Search for a Usable Past* (Philadelphia: Proceedings of the Annual Conference of the American Italian Historical Association, 1986), 165–80. Cordiferro is also briefly discussed by Martino Marazzi in his *Misteri di Little Italy. Storie e testi della lettaratura italoamericana* (Milan: Franco Angeli, 2001), 85–86, and *Voices of Italian America*, 192–95.

32. Most of the lectures were of a literary nature, focusing on important Italian figures such as Dante, Giosuè Carducci, Edmondo De Amicis, Gabriele D'Annunzio, and Mario Rapisardi, or topics like "The Mission of Journalism," "The Conquest of the Book," and "On Defense of Dialectal Literature." Other lectures dealt instead with historical subjects such as September 20—the national festival commemorating the liberation of Rome during the struggle for unification—Christopher Columbus, Giuseppe Garibaldi, Italian immigration, and the history of Calabria. See Riccardo Cordiferro's "Conferenze," Sisca Papers, Box 1, Folder 1, IHRC2408 IHRC2408.

33. For a full list of his plays see the section of his bibliography entitled "Teatro." Sisca Papers, Box 1, Folder 1, IHRC.

34. Sisca Papers, Box 7, Folder 58, IHRC.

35. The last performance took place on October 26, 1933, at the Park Palace in New York. Cf. *L'onore Perduto* in Cordiferro's Bibliography, Sisca Papers, Box 1, Folder 1, IHRC.

36. "L'onore perduto. Dramma in quattro atti," by Riccardo Cordiferro, unpublished manuscript, Sisca Papers, Box 6, Folder 48, IHRC.

37. "An Italian Play," newspaper clippings, Sisca Papers, IHRC2408, Box 12, Folder 100, IHRC.

38. Ibid. English in the original.

39. It should be noted that while the audience's irritation with Cordiferro's anti-religious remarks was perhaps natural at the beginning of the twentieth century, when radicalism was still embryonic, it was probably less common in radical performances of later periods, as by the mid-1910s, the audiences of the plays sponsored by the *sovversivi* were more sympathetic politically.

40. "Giuseppina Terranova," Cordiferro's Bibliography, Sisca Papers, IHRC2408, Box 1, Folder 1, IHRC.

41. Brooks, *The Melodramatic Imagination*, 12.

42. "*L'Onore perduto* alla Verdi Hall," *Voce del Popolo* of Philadelphia, date unknown; *L'Operaio di New York*, Anno III, 15, both in Sisca Papers, IHRC2408, "Newspaper clippings," Box 12, Folder 100, IHRC.

43. "Il paese dei cavalieri e commendatori. Commedia napoletana in tre atti," unpublished manuscript, Sisca Papers, IHRC2408, Box 10, Folder 80, IHRC.

44. *Commendatoressa* is the Italian feminine for *commendatore*, while *Commendatoressina* is the feminine diminutive. Ibid., Act I, 14.

45. Ibid., Act I, 34–35.

46. Ibid., Act III, 28.

47. *Il pezzente* (New York: La Follia, 1896), in Sisca Papers, Box 7, Folder 50, IHRC.

48. "Il pezzente," *La Follia*, July 29, 1923. In Sisca Papers, "Tagliandi," Folder 115, IHRC.

49. *Il Novatore*, January 1911.

50. *Il Pezzente*, 7.

51. "L'onore perduto," Act IV, 31.

52. *Mater Dolorosa. Dramma in un atto* (Brooklyn, N.Y.: Union Press Co., 1936), in Sisca Papers, IHRC2408, Box 6, Folder 46, IHRC.

53. Ibid., 10.

54. Ibid., 15.

55. "Il marito, la moglie e . . . Fofò" (1938), Sisca Papers, IHRC2408, Box 6, Folder 45, IHRC.

56. Paula Rabinowitz, *Labor and Desire: Women's Revolutionary Fiction in Depression America* (Chapel Hill: University of North Carolina Press, 1991), 83.

57. For a discussion of women's images in the labor movement see Elizabeth Faue, *Community of Suffering and Struggle: Women, Men and the Labor Movement in Minneapolis, 1915–1945* (Chapel Hill: University of North Carolina Press, 1991); and Barbara Melosh, *Engendering Culture: Manhood and Womanhood in New Deal Public Art and Theater* (Washington, D.C.: Smithsonian Institution Press, 1991). On masculinity and Italian American radicals see Michael Topp, *Those Without a Country: The Political Culture of Italian American Syndicalists* (Minneapolis: University of Minnesota Press, 2001), chapter 4.

58. *Il Fuoco*, November 1, 1914, 14–16. The play was presented in Detroit in 1937. Cf. Nick Di Gaetano, "Death Takes Toiler's Champion," in "Omaggio ad Arturio Giovannitti," special issue, *La Parola del Popolo* (February/March 1960): 21.

59. *Il Fuoco*, May 31, 1915, 7–11.

60. *Come era nel principio ovvero tenebre rosse. Dramma in tre atti* (Brooklyn, N.Y.: I.W.W. Italian Publishing Bureau, 1918). The shorter story version appeared in *Il Fuoco*, April 15, 1915, 6–7. An ad for the play appeared in the *New York Times*, "What News on the Rialto?" October 15, 1916, 7. For the *New York Times*'s comments on Mimì Auguglia see "Sicilian Players at the Broadway," November 28, 1908, 7.

61. "Tenebre Rosse," *Il Lavoro*, July 27, 1918, 4.

62. See Randolph Bourne, *War and the Intellectuals: Collected Essays, 1915–1919* (New York: Harper & Row, 1964); and Max Eastman, "The Religion of Patriotism," *The Masses*, 9 (July 1917): 8–12.

63. Denning, *The Cultural Front*, 136–37; Topp, *Those Without a Country*, 157–73.

64. *Come era nel principio*, 118, 123, 124. The translation from the Italian is mine.

65. A copy of "'The Alpha and the Omega" is available in the Arturo Giovannitti Papers, IHRC775, Italian Miscellaneous Manuscript Collection, Folder 5, IHRC. It was presented together with "La sedia vuota" on December 3, 1917, at Prospect Hall in Brooklyn. The script of *La sedia vuota* was published in the May 1918 issue of *La Guardia Rossa*.

66. Alberico Molinari, "Cenni biografici," Casellario Politico Centrale (hereafter CPC), Busta 3335, Archivio Centrale dello Stato (ACS), Rome. Biographical information on Molinari can also be found in Tommaso Toselli, "Omaggio ad Alberico Molinari," *La Parola del Popolo* (December 1958–January 1959), 51; and Rudolph Vecoli, "Molinari Alberico," in *Movimento operaio italiano*, 507–9. See also Vezzosi, *Il socialismo indifferente*, 149–51, and "Radical Ethnic Brokers," 126.

67. Toselli, "Omaggio ad Alberico Molinari," 51.

68. Ministero dell'Interno, April 13, 1909. Alberico Molinari, Busta 3335, CPC, ACS, Rome.

69. Vecoli, "Molinari Alberico," 507–9.

70. *Discorsi Brevi* (1919), *Le teorie di Cesare Lombroso spiegate agli operai* (1920), *I Martiri di Chicago. Episodio storico ai primi arbori del movimento rivoluzionario presente* (1916). About the play *La bandierina di Karl Marx* there is no further information. A script of *I Martiri di Chicago* can be found in Alberico Molinari Papers, IHRC1617, Miscellaneous Italian Manuscript Collection, IHRC.

71. For further information of the Haymarket case see Paul Avrich, *The Haymarket Tragedy* (Princeton, N.J.: Princeton University Press, 1984); David Roediger, "Haymarket Incident," in Mary Jo Buhle, Paul Buhle, and Dan Georgakas, eds., *Encyclopedia of the American Left* (Urbana: University of Illinois Press, 1992), 295–97; and Roediger and Rosemont, eds., *Haymarket Scrapbook*.

72. Molinari, *I Martiri di Chicago, Episodio Storico ai primi albori del movimento rivoluzionario presente* (Chicago: Italian Labor Publishing Co., 1916), 74.

73. "I martiri di Chicago," Act IV, 16.

74. See Rudolph Vecoli, "The American Republic Viewed by the Italian Left," in Marianne Debouzy, ed., *In the Shadow of the Statue of Liberty* (Urbana: University of Illinois Press, 1992), 25.

75. Practically nothing is known about Antonio Ciccarelli, the author of this play, except that he was a professor of law at the University of Naples who wrote a famous pamphlet, *Per l'abolizione della pena pecuniaria* (Florence: Tipografia Cooperativa, 1898), which is available at Harvard University.

76. For biographical information on Caminita see Maurizio Antonioli, Giampietro Berti, Santo Fedele, and Pasquale Iuso, eds., *Dizionario biografico degli anarchici italiani* (Pisa: BFS Edizioni, 2003), 298–99; and Salvatore Salerno, "No God, No Master: Italian Anarchists and the Industrial Workers of the World," in Cannistraro and Meyer, eds., *The Lost World of Italian American Radicalism*, 174–75; and "*I Delitti della Razza Bianca*: Italian Anarchists' Racial Discourse as Crime," in Jennifer Guglielmo and Salvatore Salerno, eds., *Are Italians White?* (New York: Routledge, 2003), 118–20.

77. *Che cos'è la religione* (1906), *Free Country* (1910), *I delinquenti* (1910), *Augusto Crovelli* (1927), *L'idea che cammina* (1905), and *Sonata elegiaca* (1920).

78. For a brief analysis of Caminita's art see Allan Antliff, *Anarchist Modernism: Arts, Politics and the First American Avant-Garde* (Chicago: University of Chicago Press, 2001), 194–95.

79. For information on Caminita I am thankful to the late Paul Avrich, who generously shared his research with me. On Caminita's arrests and cooperation with the FBI see his *Sacco and Vanzetti*, 181.

80. *Sonata Elegiaca* (Paterson, N.J.: A. Fontanella, 1921). A copy is available at the New York Public Library.

81. "Personalità dei nostri tempi: Vicenzo Vacirca," *La Parola del Popolo*, 50th Anniversary (December 1958–January 1959), 279.

82. See Hoerder, *The Labor Press in North America* (New York: Greenwood Press, 1987), Vol. 3.

83. Biographical information on Vincenzo Vacirca can be found in "Personalità dei nostri tempi: Vicenzo Vacirca," and G. Miccichè, "Vacirca Vincenzo," in *Movimento operaio italiano*, 160–63.

84. His historical works include *Gli Italiani nella provincia di Mendoza* (1911), which discussed the conditions of Italian immigrants in Argentina; *L'Italia e la guerra* (1915); *La Russia in fiamme* (1919); *Ciò che ho visto nella Russia Sovietica* (1921); *La monarchia e il fascismo* (1925); *La crisi americana* (1940); and *La storia di un cadavere: biografia di Mussolini* (1942). His novels were *L'apostata* (1906), *Disertore* (1908), and *Il Rogo* (1928). Among his plays we find *Madre* (1931), *La Ragnatela* (?), *Tra le nuvole* (?), *Reginetta* (?), and *La scala del diavolo* (?).

85. Arturo Di Pietro, "La prima di *Madre*," in the published edition of *Madre* (Chicago: Italian Labor Publishing Co., 1931).

86. *Madre*, 33–34.

87. Ibid., 93.

88. Ernesto Valentini, "Preface to *Madre*"; and Di Pietro, "La prima di *Madre*."

89. For a biography of Gozzoli see Carlo Tresca, "Virgilio Gozzoli," *Il Martello*, October 17, 1938; and Michele Pandolfo, "Virgilio Gozzoli: un'anarchico italiano a New York," (Ph.D. dissertation, Università Statale di Milano). Among Gozzoli's theatrical works are *Il Mattaccio*, *I due macigni*, *Vanni Fucci*, *Mara*, *La moglie senz'anello*, and the anti-fascist *Il Cancro e il Ritorno*. Among his newspapers are *Iconoclasta*, *Tempra*, and *Fede*.

90. The play was published by Tresca's house Il Martello and sold for 25 cents. I am thankful to Professor Pernicone, who has lent me the booklet.

91. See *Il Nuovo Mondo*, December 14, 1925, 3.

92. Nunzio Pernicone, *Carlo Tresca: Portrait of a Rebel* (New York: Palgrave, 2005), 135, 167.

93. Ibid., 169.

CHAPTER 5

1. Among Ruotolo's most important works are a bust of Theodore Dreiser, life masks of Helen Keller and Ann Sullivan Macy (National Portrait Gallery); a bust of Lenin; "Statue of Black Woman (Stanford's Cantor Center for Visual Arts); a bust of Caruso (Metropolitan Opera, Lincoln Center); and the Woodrow Wilson Memorial (University of Virginia).

2. See for example Michael Denning, *The Cultural Front* (London and New York: Verso, 1998).

3. See Martino Marazzi, *Misteri di Little Italy: Storie e testi della letteratura italo-americana* (Milan: Franco Angeli, 2001), and *Voices of Italian America: A History of Early Italian American Literature with a Critical Anthology* (Madison, N.J.: Fairleigh Dickinson University Press, 2004); Francesco Durante, *Italoamericana. Storia e letteratura degli italiani negli Stati Uniti, 1776–1880* (Milan: Mondadori, 2001); Fred L. Gardaphè, "Left Out: Three Italian American Writers of the 1930s," in Bill Mullen and Sherry Lee Linkon, eds., *Radical Revisions: Rereading 1930s Culture* (Urbana: University of Illinois Press, 1996), 60–77, and "Follow the Red Brick Road: Recovering Traditions of Italian/American Writers," in Philip V. Cannistraro and Gerald Meyer, eds., *The Lost World of Italian American Radicalism: Ideas, Politics, and Labor* (Westport, Conn.: Praeger, 2003).

4. Nunzio Pernicone, "Arturo Giovannitti's 'Son of the Abyss' and the Westmoreland Strike of 1910–1911," *Italian Americana*, XVII, 2 (Summer 1999), 178. See also Donna Gabaccia and Franca Iacovetta, "Introduction" to *Women, Gender, and Transnational Lives: Italian Workers of the World* (Toronto: University of Toronto Press, 2002), 23.

5. See for example Kenneth Ciongoli and Jay Parini, eds., *Beyond the Godfather: Italian American Writers on the Real Italian American Experience* (Hanover, N.H.: University Press of New England, 1997); and Giuseppe Prezzolini, *I trapiantati* (Milan: Longanesi, 1963).

6. In addition to classics such as Walter B. Rideout's *The Radical Novel in the United States, 1900–1954* (1965), Daniel Aaron's *Writers on the Left* (1961), and James B. Gilbert, *Writers and Partisans* (1968), the new scholarship of American radical culture includes the works of Alan Wald (1987, 1992), Cary Nelson (1989), Paula Rabinowitz (1991), James Bloom (1992), Barbara Foley (1993), Paul Buhle (1995, 2006), and Michael Denning (1998).

7. For this argument see especially Alan M. Wald, "Introduction to Daniel Aaron," *Writers on the Left* (New York: Columbia University Press, 1992, first edition 1961).

8. Salvato Rossi, "L'arte e la rivoluzione," *Alba Nuova*, May 1, 1922, 2; "La cultura proletaria," *Alba Nuova*, September 1, 1923, 2.

9. See for example the article "Il socialismo e l'arte," *Il Proletario*, February 17 and 24, 1907, 3–4, and the literary magazine *Il fuoco* (1914–15).

10. Carlo Prato, "L'arte di scrivere," *Il Novatore*, March 16, 1911, 87.

11. Discussions about the definition of "proletarian" art and literature dominate literary studies of the 1930s. For a good overview of the scholarship see Barbara Foley, *Radical Representations: Politics and Form in U.S. Proletarian Fiction, 1929–1941* (Durham, N.C., and London: Duke University Press, 1993), especially chapter 3.

12. "Agitprop" is a portmanteau of "agitation" and "propaganda." See Denning, *The Cultural Front*, 57.

13. Significantly, as a modern genre, the novelette originated in the fourteenth century in Italy with Giovanni Boccaccio's *Decameron*, a collection of one hundred short stories.

14. For a first-hand documentary study of early immigrant life see especially Jacob A. Riis, *How the Other Half Lives* (New York: Dover Publications, Inc., 1971, first edition 1890).

15. Fanny Barberis-Monticelli, "Scene della strada," *La Lotta*, February 20, 1909, 1.

16. Matilde Bertoluzzi, "Il piccolo emigrato," *Il Proletario*, September 16, 1899, 2.

17. Walter B. Rideout, *The Radical Novel in the United States, 1900–1954* (Cambridge, Mass.: Harvard University Press, 1965, first edition 1956), 16.

18. Bertoluzzi, "Il piccolo emigrato."

19. A. Ronchi, "L'anarchico e la prostituta," *La Questione Sociale*, March 24, 1906, 3–4.

20. Matilde Bertoluzzi, "Amate!" *Il Proletario*, November 25, 1899.

21. See for example Evening, "Una fucilazione," *La Questione Sociale*, November 19, 1898, 2–3; E. Perrella, "Ricordi," *Avanti*, July 23, 1904, 3; Duvicu (Ludovico Caminita), "La guerra," *La Questione Sociale*, June 2, 1906, 3; Titì, "Bozzetto militare," *La Questione Sociale*, January 26, 1907, 3; Arturo Giovannitti, "Come era nel principio," *Il Fuoco*, April 15, 1915, 6–7, "Il disertore," *Il Fuoco*, May 31, 1915, and "La lanterna verde," *Il Fuoco*, November 1, 1914 (originally published with the title " La Cantoniera" in *Il Proletario*, September 17–October 15, 1909), "Una voce nella tormenta," *Lotta di classe*, May 3, 1918; Oronzina Tanzarella, "L'epidemia," *Lotta di classe*, March 31, 1916, 3.

22. Virgilia D'Andrea, *Torce nella notte* (New York, 1933), 31.

23. Arturo Giovannitti, "Come era nel principio," *Il Fuoco*, April 15, 1915, 7.

24. Arturo Giovannitti, "La vita e' sacra," *Il Fuoco*, December 1, 1914, 11

25. "Il matto," *Il Proletario*, May 1, 1902, 5–6. See also "I doveri dei ricchi," *Il Proletario*, October 28, 1899, 2–3.

26. G.,"La notte di un operaio," *Avanti*, December 31, 1904, 2; "Quello che dice un contadino," *Il Grido degli Oppressi*, June 14, 1893, 3; Senofonte Entrata, "Atto di fede del contadino," *Avanti*, October 4, 1904, 4.

27. See for example "Dialogo tra mastro Onofrio e mastro Cola," *Il Grido degli Oppressi*, October 24, 1892, 2–3; " Tra padre e figlio," *Il Grido degli Oppressi*, March 18, 1893, 2–3; "Quattro chiacchiere," *Il Proletario*, October 7, 1899, 2–3; Il villano, "Cristiani e socialisti," *Il Proletario*, October 21, 1899, 2–3; "La proprieta," *Il Proletario*, November 4, 1899, 2; Paola Lombroso, "Il socialismo in salotto," *Il Proletario*, July 7, 1900, 2; "Il diritto del padrone," *Il Proletario*, August 16, 1900, 2–3; "L'alcool è veleno," *La Questione Sociale*, November 8, 1914, 3.

28. Carlo Monticelli, "Il diritto di proprietà," *Il Proletario*, July 28, 1900, 2–3.

29. Sereno, "Propaganda popolare," *La Questione Sociale*, December 15 and December 22, 1906, 2.

30. See for example Nerina Gilioli Volenterio, "Cose piane tra vicine," *Il Lavoro*, August 25, 1917, 3, and October 27, 1917, 2.

31. "Il Miracolo," *Il Solco*, February 27, 1927, 39–41.

32. Published by La Strada Publishing Co., New York, 1938.

33. G. Procopio, "La Vendetta di Marta," *Lotta di Classe*, June 2–June 16, 1916.

34. Maltempo, "La verità: novella," *Libertas*, August 1927, 9–10.

35. "I monitori," unsigned, *La Questione Sociale*, July 24, 1906, 3; A. Alberti, "Barattin," *Lotta di Classe*, July 28, 1916, 3; Manfredi Bacciel, "Il suicidio di sua eccellenza," *Avanti*, June 25, 1904, 3; Adamo Zecchi, "Nobile cuore!" *Il Proletario*, August 2, 1902, 2–3.

36. On the dialectal poetry see for example Vincenzo Ancona, *Malidittu la lingua/ Damned Language*, edited by Anna L. Chairetakis and Joseph Sciorra, translated by Gaetano Cipolla (Toronto: Legas, 1990); and Herman W. Haller, *The Other Italy: The Literary Canon in Dialect* (Toronto: University of Toronto Press, 1999).

37. I. A. Richards, *Practical Criticism* (London: Routledge & Kegan Paul, 1987, first published 1927), 208.

38. Wallace Sillanpoa, "The Poetry and Poetics of Arturo Giovannitti," in Jerome Krase and William Egelman, eds., *The Melting Pot and Beyond: Italian Americans in the Year 2000* (Proceedings of the AIHA, 1987), 183.

39. Along with Rapisardi, Gori, and Negri, many other Italian poets of social protest, such as Felice Cavalloti (1842–98), Domenico Milelli (1841–1905), Lorenzo Stecchetti (alias Olindo Guerrini, 1845–1916), and Corrado Corradino (1852–1923), filled the pages of radical papers. See Pier Carlo Masini, *Poeti della rivolta, da Carducci a Lucini* (Milan: Rizzoli, 1978).

40. Pernicone, "Arturo Giovanniti's 'Son of Abyss,' and the Westmoreland Strike of 1910–1911," 179.

41. Ibid.

42. See Mario De Ciampis, "Storia del movimento rivoluzionario socialista," *La Parola del Popolo* (December 1958–January 1959): 136, 141.

43. Righi's poetry is briefly mentioned in Marazzi, *I misteri di Little Italy*, 91.

44. "Domani . . .," *Il Proletario*, June 9, 1900, 1. All translations of the poems are mine, unless otherwise noted. They are literal translations, therefore in their English version lose much of their poetic strength.

45. See for example "Piangi, Gesu," *Il Proletario*, December 25, 1904, 1.

46. Donald Winters, *The Soul of the Wobblies* (Westport, Conn.: Greenwood Press, 1985).

47. Cf. Marazzi, *I Misteri di Little Italy*, 91.

48. In 1917 he was hired as the Italian representative in the Education Ministry of Local 25 (ILGWU). He then became district manager of Local 25 in Brooklyn and treasurer of the Dressmakers' Joint Board. In the 1930s, Crivello was manager of Local 144 of Newark, New Jersey, a position he held for twenty-three years, until blindness forced him to retire. Antonino Crivello Papers, "Biographical sketch," Immigration History Research Center (hereafter IHRC), University of Minnesota.

49. Letter of Italian Consulate to the Ministry of the Interior, April 2, 1914. Antonino Crivello (hereafter CPC), busta 1540, Archivio Centrale dello Stato (ACS), Rome. Organized by the Italian police, the CPC files document the activities of Italian radicals in Italy and abroad.

50. "Letter of resignation to the ILGWU," Antonino Crivello Papers, IHRC479, May 24,1956, Box 1, IHRC.

51. Antonino Crivello Papers, IHRC479, Box 2, folders "Poesie II" and "Poesie III, " IHRC.

52. The original verses read: "Se uomo sei, esci dal tuo abituro, / da la tua ignavia, dal tuo viver duro . . . / De la tua croce un'arma fa', un martello, /E i dritti tuoi rivendica, fratello." (From "Fratello, ascolta!")

53. In the original poems: "La salvezza per tutti è una sola: /l'union di chi soffre e protesta, / di chi sgobba. L'alata parola / tutti appella e combatter l'infesta / vil genia che opprime il Lavor." (From "La parola.") and "Vincerem lottando uniti, / sfruttatori e parassiti, / vincerem la libertà. / Non vogliam essere oppressi. / L'ingiustizia al mondo cessi / Liberiam l'umanità!" (From "Lottiamo!").

54. Letter from Consul Grossardi to the Prefect of Palermo, April 10, 1934. Antonino Crivello, CPC, busta 1540, ACS.

55. Guerra . . .! (Bronx, N.Y, 1939), Crivello Papers, IHRC479, Box 1, IHRC. In another anti-war poem, "Ho bisogno di pace" (I need peace), he voiced his torment and sorrow for humankind and, with disarming candor, cried: Perchè far la guerra ci dobbiamo quando/ sta ne la pace il bene? / Perchè aggredirci, con piacere nefando, / e a vicenda forgiarci le catene? (Why must we make war when / Goodness is in peace? / Why attack each other, with nefarious pleasure, / And forge our chains with one another?).

56. Antonino Crivello Papers, IHRC479, Box 1, folder "Speeches," IHRC.

57. Published in *Biblioteca del Convivio*, vol. 10, Filippo Fichera, ed. (Milan: Editrice Convivio Letterario, s.n.), 30. In addition to the above-cited poem, the collection includes seven more poems by Crivello. In Antonino Crivello Papers, IHRC479, Box 1, folder "Poems," IHRC.

58. Among the names that I was unable to identify are for example Teresa Ballerini, Poem: "Ai Diatribi," *La Questione Sociale*, October 15, 1896, 2; Antonietta Bonelli, Poem: "I Pellagrosi," *Il Proletario*, December 7, 1901, 2; Elena Lavagnini, Poem: "Natale?" *Il Proletario*, December 25, 1904, 1; Hada Peretti, Poem: "La vita," *Avanti*, November 23, 1904, 2; Susanna Carruette, "La donna del domani," *La Questione Sociale*, November 6, 1901, 2; Virgilia Buongiorno, "Alle compagne lavoratrici," *La Questione Sociale*, October 15, 1895, 4; Matilde Bortoluzzi, "Sfruttamento e seduzione" *Il Proletario*, November 4, 1899, 1; Rosetta, "L'opinione di una donna sulle donne," *La Lotta*, March 27, 1909, 3; Argia Sbolenfi, Poem: "Le elezioni," *La Lotta*, March 27, 1909, 3; Ines Oddone Bidelli, "La donna," *Il Lavoro*, April 21, 1917, 2; Oronzina Tanzarella, Racconto: "L'epidemia," *Lotta di Classe*, March 31, 1916, 3.

59. Bellalma Forzato-Spezia, Biographical file, CPC, busta 4908, ACS.

60. The Consulate to the Ministry of the Interior, October 31, 1913. Bellalma Forzato-Spezia, CPC, busta 4908, ACS.

61. Bellalma Forzato-Spezia, "Per le nuove generazioni" (New York: Nicoletti Bros. Press, 1911), 12, 22, 27, 29. All translations from the Italian are mine.

62. See for example "S'accendeva l'aurora!" *Il Proletario*, February 20, 1915, 1.

63. "O donna, vieni!" *Il Proletario*, March 11, 1911, 1–2.

64. "Quel giorno," *Il Proletario*, May 1, 1908, 3.

65. Published in *Il Proletario*, May 1, 1907, 2. Other poems by Bellalma Forzato-Spezia include "Al Salto del Niagara," *Il Proletario*, December 25, 1907; "Maggiolata nuova," *Il Proletario*, May 1, 1909, 1; "Cavallo in fuga," *Il Proletario*, February 11, 1910; "Il Naviglio," *Il Proletario*, May 1, 1910, 6; "Bimbi mutilati," and "Il canto dei secoli," both in *L'Italia Nostra*, January 22, 1916.

66. Bellalma Forzato-Spezia, Police headquarters, March 2, 1939, CPC, busta 4908, ACS.

67. Virgilia D'Andrea, "Biographical sketch," CPC, busta 1607, ACS. See also Franca Iacovetta and Robert Ventresca, "Virgilia D'Andrea: The Politics of Protest and the Poetry of Exile," in Gabaccia and Iacovetta, eds., *Women, Gender and Transnational Lives*, 299–326.

68. Virgilia D'Andrea, *Torce nella notte* (New York: 1933), 10.

69. Ibid., 58.

70. Letter from the Italian Consulate, March 9, 1929, CPC, busta 3033, ACS.

71. Questura di Milano, February 27, 1923, CPC, busta 1607, ACS.

72. Errico Malatesta, "Introduction" to Virgilia D'Andrea, *Tormento* (Paris: La fraternelle, 1929, first edition 1922), 2.

73. For a brief discussion of Cordiferro's poetry see also Marazzi, *I Misteri di Little Italy*, 85–87.

74. See Cordiferro's own introduction to his *Poesie scelte*, Guido Massarelli, ed. (Campobasso, Italy: Edizioni Pungolo Verde, 1967).

75. His poems are deposited at the IHRC, University of Minnesota.

76. Riccardo Cordiferro, *Poesie scelte*.

77. See the detailed bibliographical records written by Cordiferro himself, Sisca Papers, IHRC2408, Box 1, Folder 1, IHRC.

78. See for example "Brindisi di Sangue," June 8, 1894, 3; "Ad un pezzente," April 30, 1896, 3; "Ideale," June 15, 1896, 3; "Osanna a Satana," July 15 and August 15, 1896, 3; "Anno novo," January 15, 1897, 4; and "Ai vili," September 15, 1898, all published in *La Questione Sociale*.

79. "Brindisi di sangue."

80. Francesco Pitea has never received any scholarly attention. Thanks to Rudolph Vecoli, who interviewed Pitea in August 1965 and collected his poetry and papers, it is now possible to study his life and work. For biographical information see the biographical sketch written by his son Joseph. Francesco Pitea Papers, IHRC2085, Miscellaneous Italian Manuscript Collection, IHRC.

81. Reported in *La Parola del Popolo* (December 1958–January 1959): 287.

82. "Il Duce si lagna al conte Thaon di Revel," *La Scopa*, July 24, 1925, 4; "Sempre con lui," *La Scopa*, September 24, 1927, 4; and "E la battaglia continua," *La Scopa*, July 16, 1927, 4.

83. "Giordano e le truffe," *La Scopa*, October 16, 1925, 4.

84. "Il Duce si lagna al Conte Thaon di Revel"; in addition to the above-cited poems see also in *La Scopa* "A tutti i prominenti fascisti di America," May 14, 1927, 4; "E' nato il futuro imperatore," October 8, 1927, 4; "Morte agli imbelli," December 3, 1927, 4. Another poem, "La giustizia," was published in the single issue *Libertas*, August 1927, 14.

85. Kathleen Morner and Ralph Rausch, eds., *NTC's Dictionary of Literary Terms* (Chicago: NTC Publishing Group, 1991).

86. By Vittorio Vidali see in *Alba Nuova* "Il Minatore," February 16, 1924, 3; "Donna," March 1, 1924, 3; "Il Lavoratore," March 29, 1924, 3; and "Malgrado tutto," March 22, 1924, 3. Efrem Bartoletti, *Nel sogno d'oltretomba: cantico libero* (Scranton, Pa.: 1931) and *Riflessioni poetiche* (Milan: Gastaldi Editore, 1955). Giuseppe Zappulla, *Vette e abissi. Liriche e poemi* (New York: V. Vecchioni Printing, 1936).

87. Nunzio Pernicone, "Arturo Giovannitti's 'Son of the Abyss' and the Westmoreland Strike of 1910–1911," 79.

88. Winters, *The Soul of the Wobblies*, 131.

CHAPTER 6

1. "Arturo Giovannitti Dies at 75; Poet, Long-Time Labor Leader," *New York Times*, January 1, 1960, 19.

2. The memorial service took place under the auspices of the Italian American Labor Council on January 5, 1960, in the large auditorium of the Amalgamated Clothing Workers of America, at 111 East 15th Street in New York City. Information on the ceremony can be found in "I funerali" in "Omaggio a Arturo Giovannitti," special issue, *La Parola del Popolo* (February/March 1960): 6–8.

3. Norman Thomas, in "Omaggio a Arturo Giovannitti," 4.

4. Joseph Salerno, in "Omaggio a Arturo Giovannitti," 18.

5. See for example "The Cage," *Atlantic Monthly*, June 1913, 751–55, also published in *Current Opinion*, July 1913, 56–57; "Songs of a Revolutionary," *Current Opinion*, July 1914, 54; "The Walker," *Current Literature*, November 1912, 593; "Malebolge, A Glimpse of Mulberry Street," *Current Opinion*, December 1915, 430–31; "Revolution," *The Survey*, June 24, 1916, 335; "War, Anthem of Labor," *The Survey*, September 16, 1916, 605.

6. "The Social Significance of Arturo Giovannitti," unsigned, *Current Opinion*, January 1913, 25. Giovannitti's poetry collections are *Arrows in the Gale*, introduction by Helen Keller (Riverside, Conn.: Hillacre Bookhouse, 1914); *Parole e sangue* (New York: Labor Press, 1938); *Quando canta il gallo*, introduction by Carmelo Zito (Chicago: E. Clemente & Sons, 1957); and *The Collected Poems of Arturo Giovannitti*, introduction by Norman Thomas (Chicago: E. Clemente & Sons, 1962). Martino Marazzi has recently edited a volume of Giovannitti's poems in Italian also entitled *Parole e Sangue* (Isernia: Cosmo Iannone Editore, 2005) with a selection of poems from his previous volumes.

7. Giovannitti's poems are included for example in Joyce Kornbluh, *Rebel Voices: An IWW Anthology* (Ann Arbor: University of Michigan Press, 1964); Genevieve Taggard, ed., *May Days: An Anthology of Verse from Masses-Liberator, 1912–1924* (New York: Boni and Liveright, 1925); and Louis Untermeyer, *Modern American Poetry* (New York: Harcourt Brace, 1921).

8. See for example Philip Foner, *The Industrial Workers of the World, 1905–1917* (New York: International Publishers, 1965); Patrick Renshaw, *The Wobblies: The Story of Syndicalism in the United States* (New York: Doubleday, 1967); Melvyn Dubofsky, *We Shall Be All: A History of the Industrial Workers of the World* (Urbana: University of Illinois Press, 1969); Mari Jo Buhle, Paul Buhle, and Dan Georgakas, eds., *Encyclopedia of the American Left* (Urbana: University of Illinois Press, 1990); Mari Jo Buhle, Paul Buhle and Harvey J. Kaye, eds., *The American Radical* (New York: Routledge, 1994); and Michael Topp, *Those Without a Country: The Political Culture of Italian American Syndicalists* (Minneapolis: University of Minnesota Press, 2001).

9. Giovannitti, for example, is ignored altogether by Christopher Lasch, *The New Radicalism in America* (New York: W. W. Norton, 1965); James B. Gilbert, *Writers and Partisans: A History of Literary Radicalism in America* (New York: John Wiley & Sons, 1968); and John Patrick Diggins, *The Rise and Fall of the American Left* (New York: W. W. Norton, 1973); and is only cursorily mentioned by Christine Stansell in her *American Moderns: Bohemian New York and the Creation of a New Century* (New York: Metropolitan Books, 2000).

10. Daniel Aaron, *Writers on the Left: Episodes in American Literary Communism* (1961; repr., New York: Columbia University Press, 1992), 62 and 71; and Donald Winters, *The Soul of the Wobblies* (Westport, Conn.: Greenwood Press, 1985), chapter 5.

11. See Nunzio Pernicone, "Arturo Giovannitti's 'Son of the Abyss' and the Westmoreland Strike of 1910–1911," *Italian Americana* 17, 2 (Summer 1999): 178–92; Lucinda LaBella Mays, "Arturo Giovannitti: Writing from Lawrence," in Domenic Candeloro and Fred Gardaphè, eds., *Italian Ethics: Their Languages, Literature and Lives* (Chicago: American Italian Historical Association, 1990), 79–89; Wallace Sillanpoa, "The Poetry and Politics of Arturo Giovannitti," in Jerome Krase and William Egelman, eds., *The Melting Pot and Beyond: The Italian Americans in the Year 2000* (Staten Island, N.Y.: American

Italian Historical Association, 1987), 175–89; and Renato Lalli, *Arturo Giovannitti: Poesia, cristianesimo e socialismo tra le lotte operaie di primo Novecento americano* (Campobasso: Editoriale Rufus, 1981).

12. Mark Starr, in "Omaggio ad Arturo Giovannitti," 17.

13. Mary Brown Sumner, "Arturo Giovannitti," *The Survey*, November 2, 1912, 163; and "The Poetry of Syndicalism," unsigned, *Atlantic Monthly*, June 1913, 853.

14. Pernicone, "Arturo Giovannitti's 'Son of the Abyss' and the Westmoreland Strike," 180.

15. Sillanpoa, "The Poetry and Politics of Arturo Giovannitti," 182.

16. Cited in Ebert, "Who Arturo Giovannitti Is," 1. Giovannitti apparently wrote this for an article in the *International Socialist Review* on the causes of the Italian war in Tripoli.

17. Lalli, *Arturo Giovannitti*, 21–23.

18. Lalli, *Arturo Giovannitti*, 24–31. Cited also in Pernicone, "Arturo Giovannitti's 'Son of the Abyss' and the Westmoreland Strike," 181; and Sillanpoa, "The Poetry and Politics of Arturo Giovannitti," 178.

19. "Psicoanalisi minima," in *Parole e sangue*, ed., Marazzi, 270–71.

20. Giovannitti's *Address to Jury* (Boston: School of Social Science, 1913). Cited also in LaBella Mays, "Arturo Giovannitti: Writing from Lawrence," 79.

21. "Arturo Giovannitti-Cenni biografici," Casellario Politico Centrale (hereafter CPC), Ministero dell'Interno, Direzione Generale di Pubblica Sicurezza, Archivio Centrale dello Stato, Rome (hereafter ACS), busta 2439. Cited also in Pernicone, "Arturo Giovannitti's 'Son of the Abyss' and the Westmoreland Strike," 181.

22. Len Giovannitti, *The Nature of the Beast* (New York: Random House, 1977), 150–51.

23. Untermeyer, *Modern American Poetry*, 286.

24. Mario De Ciampis, "Arturo Massimo Giovannitti, poeta giornalista drammaturgo per la causa dei lavoratori," in "Arturo Giovannitti, Nenia Sennita," Nicola Fiorelli, ed., special issue, *La Parola del Popolo* (July/August 1974): G-9; and Len Giovannitti, *The Nature of the Beast*, 151. See also Pernicone, "Arturo Giovannitti's 'Son of the Abyss' and the Westmoreland Strike," 181; and Sillanpoa, "The Poetry and Politics of Arturo Giovannitti," 178.

25. Cited in "The Social Significance of Arturo Giovannitti," 24.

26. "The Poetry of Syndicalism," unsigned, *Atlantic Monthly*, June 1913, 853; Ebert, "Who Arturo Giovannitti Is," 1; "The Social Significance of Arturo Giovannitti," 24. See also De Ciampis, "Arturo Massimo Giovannitti, poeta giornalista drammaturgo per la causa dei lavoratori," G-9; and Pernicone, "Arturo Giovannitti's 'Son of the Abyss' and the Westmoreland Strike," 182, and *Carlo Tresca: Portrait of a Rebel* (New York: Palgrave, 2005), 50.

27. Max Eastman, *Enjoyment of Living* (New York: Harper, 1948), 399. For critical studies of the 1910s see Van Wyck Brooks, "America's Coming-of-Age," in idem., *Three Essays in America* (1934, repr., New York: E. P. Dutton & Co., 1970); Henry May, *The End of American Innocence: A Study of the First Years of Our Own Time, 1912–1917* (New York: Alfred A. Knopf, 1959); Malcolm Cowley, *Exile's Return: A Literary Odissey of the 1920s* (New York: Penguin Books, 1976); Leslie Fishbein, *The Radicals and "The Masses," 1911–1917* (Chapel Hill: University of North Carolina Press, 1982); Thomas Bender, *New York Intellect* (New York: Alfred A. Knopf, 1987); and Stansell, *American Moderns*.

28. Robert D'Attilio, "Arturo Giovannnitti," in Buhle et al., eds., *The American Radical*, 136.

29. From "O Labor of America: Heartbeat of Mankind," in *The Collected Poems of Arturo Giovannitti*, 2–4. Giovannitti also listed New York (and Canada) as the places where he would prefer to live. "Psicoanalisi minima," *Quando Canta il Gallo*, 295.

30. "New York and I," *The Collected Poems of Arturo Giovannitti*, 5–8, originally published in Italian under the title "La città incredibile" [The incredible city], *Il Fuoco*, March 15, 1915, 8.

31. See Arturo Giovannitti, "Un aneddoto," in Raimondo Fazio, *Scritti politici* (Boston, Comitato educativo sindacalista "Il Proletario," 1948), 44; cited in Lalli, *Arturo Giovannitti*, 78.

32. "The Social Significance of Arturo Giovannitti," 24.

33. Cf. Lalli, *Arturo Giovannitti*, 71–76; Pernicone, "Arturo Giovannitti's 'Son of the Abyss' and the Westmoreland Strike," 182; Winters, *The Soul of the Wobblies*, 99.

34. "Credo," in *The Collected Poems of Arturo Giovannitti*, 85–86.

35. Len Giovannitti, *The Nature of the Beast*, 151.

36. "Arturo Giovannitti," CPC, Letter from the Italian Consul to the Italian Minister of the Interior July 5, 1912, and "Cenni Biografici," August 20, 1912, busta 2439.

37. Topp, *Those Without a Country*, 55.

38. Cited in Aaron, *Writers on the Left*, 22.

39. "John Reed," *The Collected Poems of Arturo Giovannitti*, 126.

40. Aaron, *Writers on the Left*, 10–11.

41. Stansell, *American Moderns*, 3.

42. Diggins, *The American Left in the Twentieth Century* (New York: Harcourt Brace, 1973), 73.

43. Stansell, *American Moderns*, 1; and Diggins, *The Rise and Fall of the American Left*, 94.

44. Quoted in Len Giovannitti, *The Nature of the Beast*, 35.

45. Published in *Il Proletario*, May 1, 1908, 4, later revised and published under the title "La saggezza del mare" in *Quando canta il gallo*, 101.

46. Published in *Il Proletario*, March 17, 1908, 2, later revised and published under the title "Al Caifas di Siviglia" in *Quando canta il gallo*, 163.

47. "Alle due sante, a Luisa Michel, a Maria Spiridonova," *Il Proletario*, March 18, 1909, 2, republished in *Quando canta il gallo*, 46, and 226.

48. Anna Strunsky Walling, "Giovannitti's Poems," *New Review*, 2 (May 1914): 291.

49. "Samnite Cradle Song," *Il Proletario*, April 27, 1911, reprinted in English in *Arrows in the Gale*, 82, and in Italian in *Quando canta il gallo*, 176.

50. Pernicone, "Arturo Giovannitti's 'Son of the Abyss' and the Westmoreland Strike," 184.

51. First published in Italian in *Il Proletario*, May 1, 1911, and reprinted in *Quando canta il gallo*, 157. The English translation, by Paul Italia, is in Pernicone, "Arturo Giovannitti's 'Son of the Abyss' and the Westmoreland Strike," 187–90.

52. Arturo Giovannitti, "Introduction" to Emile Pouget, *Sabotage* (Chicago: Charles Kerr, 1913), 11, 13–14, 22, 25, 36.

53. "The Social Significance of Arturo Giovannitti," 24; Ebert, "Who Arturo Giovannitti Is," 1; and Pernicone, "Arturo Giovannitti's 'Son of the Abyss' and the Westmoreland Strike."

54. "The Social Significance of Arturo Giovannitti," 24.

55. Justus Ebert, *The Trial of a New Society* (Cleveland: IWW Publishing Bureau, 1912), 45; Elizabeth Gurley Flynn, *The Rebel Girl: An Autobiography* (1955; repr., New York: International Publishers, 1994), 134; and Walter E. Weyl, "It Is Time to Know," in "The Lawrence Struggle from Various Angles," *The Survey*, April 6, 1912, 65.

56. Flynn, *The Rebel Girl*, 127–28; and Dubofsky, *We Shall Be All*, 132–35.

57. Flynn, 143.

58. Ebert, *The Trial of a New Society*, 38–40; Nicholas Vanderpuyl, "Intimate Story of Joseph J. Ettor," *Boston Herald*, January 24, 1912; and Dubofsky, *We Shall Be All*, 237.

59. Dubofsky, *We Shall Be All*, 237.

60. Ebert, *The Trial of a New Society*, 38, 69.

61. Ibid., 70.

62. "The Sermon on the Common," in *Arrows in the Gale*, 77.

63. Weyl, "It Is Time to Know," 65–66.

64. "Prison Life of Ettor and Giovannitti," unsigned, *Literary Digest*, September 14, 1912, 461. See also "One Striker Killed; Two Leaders Held," *New York Times*, January 31, 1912, 1.

65. Ebert, *The Trial of a New Society*, 71.

66. See Flynn, *The Rebel Girl*, 146–47; "Acquittal of the I.W.W. Leaders," "Haywood Arrest," unsigned, *Literary Digest*, September 28, 1912, 503; and "Make Giovannitti Candidate," *New York Times*, November 25, 1912, 4. Information about activities in support of Giovannitti and Ettor at Ripabottoni are reported in a letter dated August 22, 1912, from the Prefecture of Campobasso to the Ministry of the Interior, in "Arturo Giovannitti" CPC file.

67. "Haywood Arrest," 502; Flynn, *The Rebel Girl*, 147–49; and Nunzio Pernicone, *Carlo Tresca: Portrait of a Rebel* (New York: Palgrave, 2003), 52–55.

68. James Heaton, "The Salem Trial," *The Survey*, December 7, 1912, 301–4, and "The Social Significance of Giovannitti," 24.

69. Cf. Giuseppe Prezzolini, "Elogio di un trapiantato molisano, bardo della libertà negli Stati Uniti," in "Arturo Giovannitti. Nenia Sannita," G17–G18.

70. "The Social Significance of Arturo Giovannitti," 24.

71. As evidence of Giovannitti's and Ettor's responsibility the state offered the speeches made by them, but they were unable to present any written notes of their statements. The defense countered those accusations by introducing ministers who testified to the innocent intent of their speeches. See "The Salem Trial," 303; and "Acquitted, They Kissed," *New York Times*, November 27, 1912, 1.

72. "The Poetry of Syndicalism," 854.

73. Joseph Tusiani, "La poesia inglese di Giovannnitti," *La Parola del Popolo* (November–December 1978): 95; and Sillanpoa, "The Poetry and Politics of Arturo Giovannitti," 180.

74. Sumner, "Arturo Giovannitti," 165.

75. *Arrows in the Gale*, 21.

76. See Walling, "Giovannitti's Poems," 289, and "The Social Significance of Giovannitti," 25.

77. Tusiani, "La poesia inglese di Giovannnitti," 95; the translation is of Sillanpoa, "The Poetry and Politics of Arturo Giovannitti," 181.

78. Untermeyer, *Modern American Poetry*, 287, and *American Poetry Since 1900*, 279; "The Social Significance of Arturo Giovannitti," 25.

79. *Arrows in the Gale*, 27.

80. For the full poem see *Arrows in the Gale*, 90–95.

81. "Book Review: *Arrows in the Gale*," unsigned, *The Survey*, June 27, 1914, 347.

82. "The Poetry of Syndicalism," 854.

83. Tusiani, "La poesia inglese di Arturo Giovannitti," 94.

84. "Arturo Giovannitti," unsigned, *The Survey*, November 2, 1912, 163.

85. Helen Keller, "Introduction" to *Arrows in the Gale*, 10.

86. Florence Converse, "*Arrows in the Gale*. A Review," *The Survey*, June 27, 1914, 347.

87. Cf. Tusiani, "La poesia inglese di Arturo Giovannitti," 97.

88. Zappulla, "Un poeta che scompare," 4–5. Among the idyllic poems Zappulla lists are "Madre Terra," "Inno all'Uomo Nuovo," "Beethoven," "La Saggezza del Mare," "Il cenacolo," "Un poeta che scompare," "A Mia Madre," and "La Cisterna," all of them published in *Quando Canta il Gallo*.

89. Charles Ashley, "The Poetry of Revolt," *The Little Review*, September 1914, 22.

90. Cf. Untermeyer, *American Poetry Since 1900*, 277.

91. In "Omaggio ad Arturo Giovannitti," 12.

92. Carmelo Zito, *Quando canta il gallo*, xi. The translation is by Sillanpoa, "The Poetry and Politics of Arturo Giovannitti," 183.

93. Winters, *The Soul of the Wobblies*, 84.

94. Ibid., 21.

95. Paul Buhle, "Italian-American Radicals and Labor in Rhode Island, 1905–1930," *Radical History Review* 17 (Spring 1978): 126.

96. "L'autore che non possiede nulla di suo, nemmeno il suo scarso ingegno, se non per grazia del popolo lavoratore, rinuncia ad ogni proprietà letteraria." Front page of *Parole and Sangue*. The translation is mine.

97. See *Il Proletario*, January 25, 1913.

98. "Violent Draper Strike Rocked Hopedale 55 Years Ago," *Milford Daily News*, April 1, 1968; and "Milford History: 1880–1930" both available at http://www.geocities.com/danin-hopedale/draperstrike1913.html. For a full analysis of the strike see chapter 1 of Aviva Chomsky, *Linked Labor Histories: New England, Colombia, and the Making of a Global Working Class* (Durham, N.C.: Duke University Press, 2008).

99. See Steve Golin, *The Fragile Bridge: Paterson Silk Strike, 1913* (Philadelphia: Temple University Press, 1988) and Anne Huber Tripp, *The I.W.W. and the Paterson Silk Strike of 1913* (Urbana: University of Illinois Press, 1987).

100. De Ciampis, "Storia del movimento socialista rivoluzionario italiano," 160.

101. "Che cos'è *Il Fuoco*," and "Giovannitti ci lascia," *Il Fuoco*, May 31, 1915, 5, and June 15, 1915, 2. For a critical study of *Il Fuoco* see Marcella Bencivenni, "A Magazine of Art and Struggle: The Experience of *Il Fuoco*, 1914–1915," *Italian American Review* 8, 1 (Spring/Summer 2001): 57–84.

102. Ninety-three people were convicted with sentences up to twenty years. Cf. Flynn, *The Rebel Girl*, 236–38; and Pernicone, *Carlo Tresca*, 96–98.

103. See for example "March 1919," "When the Great Day Came," "Litany of the Revolution," and "On Lenin's Fiftieth Birthday," all in *The Collected Poems of Arturo Giovannitti*.

104. De Ciampis, "Storia del movimento rivoluzionario italiano," 162; and Giovannitti CPC file, March 22, 1919.

105. "When the Great Day Came."

106. See Massimo Salvadori, "Generazione che passa," and Rosario Dramis, "Il poeta dei diseredati che disprezzò le tirannie," both in "Omaggio a Giovannitti," 2 and 5.

107. Arturo Giovannitti, editorial of *Il Veltro*, August 15, 1924, 3.

108. There are several references to Giovannitti's life in Hollywood, but precise information is lacking. Cf. Rosario Dramis, "Il poeta dei diseredati," in *Omaggio ad Arturo Giovannitti*, 6; and Giovannitti CPC file documents from September 1930–January 1932. The script for the movie has not been preserved.

109. Arturo Giovannitti to Vincenzo De Lalla, August 21, 1948. Vincenzo De Lalla Papers, IHRC522, Immigration History Research Center (hereafter IHRC), University of Minnesota; Len Giovannitti, *The Nature of the Beast*, 26–37, 123–46; and Roma Rieger, unpublished phone interview by Nunzio Pernicone, August 6, 1996 (courtesy of Nunzio Pernicone).

110. Len Giovannitti, *The Nature of the Beast*, 130 and 136. Arturo Giovannitti to Vincenzo DeLalla, February 2 1927. Vincenzo De Lalla Papers, IHRC522,IHRC.

111. See Meredith Tax, *The Rising of the Women: Feminist Solidarity and Class Conflict, 1880–1917* (New York: Monthly Review Press, 1980), 198.

112. Joseph Tusiani, "Arturo Giovannitti as I knew him," unpublished manuscript (courtesy of Nunzio Pernicone), 5; see also his *La parola difficile: Autobiografia di un Italo-Americano* (Fasano: Schena Editore, 1988), 236–37.

113. Arturo Giovannitti to Vicenzo De Lalla, March 23, 1951. Vincenzo De Lalla Papers, IHRC522, IHRC.

114. "Arturo Giovannitti," CPC.

115. Len Giovannitti, *The Nature of the Beast*, 157.

CHAPTER 7

1. Two important, although incomplete, collections of his cartoons are now available at the Immigration History Research Center at Minneapolis and the Tamiment Library at New York University.

2. Cécile Whiting, *Antifascism in American Art* (New Haven, Conn.: Yale University Press, 1989).

3. Randall P. Harrison, *The Cartoon: Communication to the Quick* (London: Sage Publications, 1981), 11.

4. A biographical sketch of Velona can be found in his files in the Casellario Politico Centrale (CPC), busta 5346, Archivio Centrale dello Stato (ACS), Rome. The CPC file, however, contains a few mistakes, most notably his birth date (August 3, 1886, instead of January 18, 1893); his mother's name, which was Severina, not Domenica; and his political affiliation, which was socialism, not anarchism. More precise information can be found in two articles published in *La Parola del Popolo*: "Fort Velona" (December 1958/January 1959): 283–84 and "E' morto Fort Velona" (June/July 1965), 47. Information on his family was provided to me by his son Walter Velona in a phone interview on January 30, 2003.

5. "Fort Velona," 283.

6. Ibid. *La Luce* in turn would be one of the few Italian publications to acknowledge Velona's activism in America. Its October 5, 1947, issue featured a photograph of the cartoonist on the front page with a brief note of thanks for his contributions to the socialist cause. In Girolamo Valenti Papers, Box 2, folder "Fort Velona," Tamiment Library, New York University.

7. "Fort Velona," 284.

8. See "Fort Velona" and "E' morto Fort Velona."

9. Phone interview with Walter Velona, January 30, 2003. See also "Biographical Sketch," Fortunato Velona, CPC, busta 5346, ACS, Rome.

10. Other speakers included Norman Thomas, Jacob Panken, Sidney Hillman, and David Dubinsky. See police record dated May 18, 1933, Fortunato Velona, CPC, busta 5346, ACS.

11. See "La grandiosa protesta operaia contro il terrorismo Fascista," *La Stampa Libera*, April 16, 1933, 1.

12. Diggins, *Mussolini and Fascism*, 131–33; Pernicone, *Carlo Tresca*, 206–8; and John Herling and Morris Shapiro, *The Terzani Case* (pamphlet, New York, 1934).

13. For a detailed account of the events see "Il compagno Antonio Fierro assassinato dai fascisti," *La Stampa Libera*, July 16, 1933, 1; police record dated August, 23, 1933, Fortunato Velona, CPC, busta 5346, ACS; and Vanni Montana, *Amarostico: testimonianze euro-americane* (Livorno, Italy: U. Bastogi, 1975), 124–27.

14. "La piovra bolscevica" (1939?), unpublished article, Fortunato Velona Papers, IHRC2786, Box 1, IHRC.

15. See Velona Fortunato, CPC, busta 5346, ACS.

16. Harrison, *The Cartoon*, 16.

17. Maurice Horn, ed., *The World Encyclopedia of Cartoons*, Vol. 1 (New York: Chelsea House Publishers, 1980), 15–16.

18. Ibid., 16.

19. For biographical information on them see Andreucci and Detti, *Il movimento operaio italiano.*

20. See Donald Dewey, *The Art of Ill Will: The Story of American Political Cartoons* (New York: New York University Press, 2007).

21. For a brief discussion of printing techniques see Richard Fitzgerald, *Art and Politics: Cartoonists of the Masses and Liberator* (Westport, Conn.: Greenwood Press, 1973), 6–9; and Charles Press, *The Political Cartoon* (East Brunswick, N.J.: Associated University Presses, 1981), chapter 2. On the changes in the publishing industry see Christopher Wilson, "The Rhetoric of Consumption: Mass-Market Magazines and the Demise of the Gentle Reader, 1880–1920," in Richard Wightman Fox and T. J. Jackson Lears, eds., *The Culture of Consumption: Critical Essays in American History, 1880–1980* (New York: Pantheon, 1983), 39–64.

22. See Warren Susman, *Culture as History: The Transformation of American Society in the Twentieth Century* (New York: Pantheon Books, 1984).

23. The CPC file indicates that Velona's last name had a final accent (Velonà), a detail that was confirmed to me by his son Walter. However, in America he signed his art without the accent, nor did other sources use it. He probably dropped the accent to anglicize his name, just as he changed Fortunato to Fort.

24. Phone interview with Walter Velona, January 30, 2003.

25. Rebecca Zurier, *Art for The Masses, A Radical Magazine and Its Graphics, 1911–1917* (Philadelphia: Temple University Press, 1988), 55.

26. See Enrico Sturani, *Otto milioni di cartoline per il Duce* (Turin: Centro Scientifico Editore, 1995), xii–viv; and Italo Calvino, "*Il Duce's* Portraits," *The New Yorker*, January 6, 2003, 34–39.

27. *Mussolini and Fascism: The View from America* (Princeton, N.J.: Princeton University Press, 1972), 58–73.

28. *La Scopa*, July 24, 1926, 1.

29. *Il Nuovo Mondo*, February 7, 1926, 1.

30. Nunzio Pernicone, ed., *The Autobiography of Carlo Tresca* (New York: The John D. Calandra Italian American Institute, 2003), 77–68. See also Nunzio Pernicone, *Carlo Tresca: Portrait of a Rebel* (New York: Palgrave, 2005), 18–19.

31. See Didier Musidlak, "Religion and Political Culture in the Thought of Mussolini," *Totalitarian Movements and Political Religions* 6, 3 (December 2005) 395–406.

32. Fama, "Fascist Propaganda in the United States," unpublished manuscript, in Valenti Girolamo Papers, box 2, Folder 50, Tamiment Library, New York University.

33. Seton-Watson, *Italy from Liberalism to Fascism*, 141; Pernicone, *Carlo Tresca*, 132–33; and Digggins, *Mussolini and Fascism*, chapter 8.

34. Roland Sarti, "Politics and Ideology in Fascist Italy," in Edward R. Tannenbaum and Emiliana P. Noether, eds., *Modern Italy: A Topical History Since 1861* (New York: New York University Press, 1974), 68–69.

35. Diggins, *Mussolini and Fascism*, chapters 2 and 3; and Alan Brinkely, *Voices of Protest: Huey Long, Father Coughlin and the Great Depression* (New York: Vintage Books, 1983).

36. Fraser Ottanelli, "'If Fascism Comes to America We Will Push It Back into the Ocean': Italian American Antifascism in the 1920s and 1930s," in Gabaccia and Ottanelli, eds., *Italian Workers of the World*, 185.

37. Diggins, *Mussolini and Fascism*, 78; Vecoli, "The Making and Un-Making of the Italian American Working Class," 53; and Pernicone, *Carlo Tresca*, 127.

38. See for example Pietro Rinaldo Fanesi, "Italian Antifascism and the Garibaldine Tradition in Latin America"; and Antonio Bechelloni, "Antifascist Resistance in France from the 'Phony War' to Liberation: Identities and Destinies in Question," both in Gabaccia and Ottanelli, eds., *Italian Workers of the World*, 163–77, 214–31.

39. Diggins, *Mussolini and Fascism*, 58–73, 78–79.

40. Diggins, *Mussolini and Fascism*, 83–84; and Pernicone, *Carlo Tresca*, 130–31.

41. Gaetano Salvemini, *Italian Fascist Activities in the United States,* edited with an introduction by Philip V. Cannistraro (New York: Center for Migration Studies, 1977), xx, and "Mussolini's American Empire in the United States," in Frances Keene, ed., *Neither Liberty Nor Bread: The Meaning and Tragedy of Fascism* (New York: Harper, 1940), 336–49. See also Marcus Duffield, "Mussolini's American Empire: The Fascist Invasion of the United States," *Harper Magazine* 159 (November 1929): 661–72; and Cannistraro, *Blackshirts in Little Italies*, 14.

42. For information on Trombetta and *Il Grido* see Cannistraro, *Blackshirts in Little Italies.*

43. "Italian Fascism in America," *Il Mondo*, February 1941, 11; cited in Diggins, *Mussolini and Fascism*, 182. See also Salvemini, *Italian Fascist Activities in the United States*, 145–64.

44. Charles Fama, "Fascist Propaganda in the United States," and Ottanelli, "'If Fascism Comes to America We Will Push It Back into the Ocean,'" 182.

45. Christopher Seton Watson, *Italy from Liberalism to Fascism, 1870–1925* (New York: Barnes & Noble, 1967), 141.

46. Salvemini, *Italian Fascist Activities in the United States,* xx.

47. See Gian Giacomo Migone, "La stabilizzazione della lira. La finanza americana e Mussolini," *Rivista di Storia Contemporanea,* 2 (April 1973): 145–85; and Diggins, *Mussolini and Fascism,* 144–59.

48. See Nadia Venturini, *Neri e italiani ad Harlem. Gli anni trenta e la guerra d'Etiopia* (Rome: Edizioni Lavoro, 1990); and Gian Giacomo Migone, *Gli Stati Uniti e il fascismo* (Milan: Feltrinelli, 1980), 350–57.

49. Pernicone, *Carlo Tresca,* 219.

50. Diggins, *Mussolini and Fascism,* 287–312; and Pernicone, *Carlo Tresca,* 220–24.

51. *Il Proletario,* May 1, 1936, 1.

52. Diggins, *Mussolini and Fascism,* 340–52, 404–9.

CONCLUSION

1. See Daniel Bell, *Marxian Socialism in America* (Princeton, N.J.: Princeton University Press, 1973); and James Weinstein, *The Decline of Socialism in America* (New York: Alfred A. Knopf, 1967).

2. I am borrowing the term from Gerald Sorin, *The Prophetic Minority* (Bloomington: Indiana University Press, 1985), 2.

3. Paul Avrich, *Anarchist Voices* (1995; repr., Edinburgh/Oakland: AK Press, 2005), 87–190.

4. Nunzio Pernicone, "Italian Immigrant Radicalism in New York," in Philip V. Cannistraro, ed., *The Italians of New York* (New York: New-York Historical Society, 1999), 89.

Glossary of Frequently
Used Italian Terms

cafone (pl., *cafoni*) Literally a peasant, but by extension someone who is stupid, semi-literate, and ill mannered.

campanilismo Parochialism, excessive attachment to one's native town or village. From the word *campanile* (church bell tower), it refers to the sense of identity and belonging shared by all those who lived within the territory where the ringing of the church bell could be heard.

colonia italiana (pl., *colonie italiane*) Literally Italian colony; the designation Italians used to refer to the Italian immigrant communities all over the world.

compaesano (pl., *compaesani*) Fellow villager.

contadino (pl., *contadini*) Peasant, landless farm laborer hired by the day on great estates.

festa (pl., *feste*) Communal feast.

fuoruscito (pl., *fuorusciti*) Exile, but referring especially to anti-fascist refugee.

italianità Italianness, Italian sentiment or identity; usually referred to culture rather than politics. The term emerged from the *Risorgimento* and in Italian American studies is used to define and locate Italian American identity.

mezzogiorno Literally midday; in Italian, often used to refer to southern Italy.

paesano (pl. *paesani*) Coming from the same village.

prominente (pl., *prominenti*) Prominent, powerful men of the Little Italies. Italian American radicals used this term in a pejorative way, suggesting that such men were corrupt and opportunistic.

Risorgimento Literally resurrection, resurgence; it refers to both the historical period and the political movement that led to the unification of Italy in 1861.

signori The gentry, who owned great landed estates cultivated by poor peasants.

sovversivo (pl., *sovversivi*; feminine, *sovversiva/e*) Subversive; word that Italian authorities used to designate leftist radicals of all political persuasions (anarchists, socialists, syndicalists, communists).

Index

Naselli, consul, 76
nativism, 8, 23, 33, 201
Nazioni Unite, 97, 220
Negri, Ada, 138, 139, 147
Nelson, Bruce, 59, 67
New Orleans lynching, 8
Ninfo, Salvatore, 25, 31
Novatore, Il, 21, 113
Nuovo Mondo, Il, 69, 72, 94, 95–96, 125, 126, 183, 187, 194, 198, 204

Oestreicher, Richard, 43
O'Hare, Kate Richards, 47
Operaia, L', 27, 73, 92
Orano, Paolo, 28
Order of the Sons of Italy, 30, 96
Ottanelli, Fraser, 33, 201, 204

padrone system, 104, 111, 112
Parenti, Luigi, 55
Park, Robert, 69
Parola del Medico, La, 75
Parola del Popolo, La, 34, 70, 119, 224
Pascoli, Giovanni, 139
Paterson Strike, 180
Paterson Strike Pageant, 106, 180–181
Patrizi, Ettore, 202
Pellico, Silvio, 106
Pernicone, Nunzio, 20, 39, 40, 51, 56, 68, 79, 129, 158, 167, 224
Petrarca, Reverend, 78
Pitea, Francesco, 96, 140, 188; personal background and poetry, 151–152
Pius IX, Pope, 46
Pius XI, Pope, 82, 199, 204
Plebe, La, 71, 81
Podrecca, Guido, 78
Pope, Generoso, 77, 202, 204, 216, 220
Popular Front, 33, 100, 188, 194
Pouget, Emile, 167
Pozzetta, George, 53, 77
Prato, Carlo, 130
Presi, Antonio, 29
Prezzolini, Giuseppe, 129
Progresso Italo-Americano, Il, 77, 152, 202, 216

Proletario, Il, 17, 23, 28, 56, 58, 62, 69, 70, 71, 72, 75, 76, 79, 82, 84, 89, 94, 104, 106, 119, 140, 141, 145, 152, 164, 165, 167, 194, 196, 218
prominenti, 37–38, 46, 56, 75, 76, 77, 82, 96, 97, 109, 110, 112, 140, 150, 152, 172, 202, 220
propaganda of the deed, 17
propaganda tours. See giri di propaganda
Protesta Umana, La, 16
Provo, Bartolomeo, 55

Questione Sociale, La (Paterson, NJ), 15, 16, 20, 55, 58, 61, 62, 69, 72, 82, 85, 89, 92, 103, 111, 122, 136, 150
Quintiliano, Luigi, 50, 91

Rabinowitz, Paula, 114
radical communities, 50–51
radical culture: agitprop, 131; definition, 2–3; celebrations, 62; Christian symbolism, 82, 108, 116, 134–135, 141, 163, 171; proletarian and socialist literature, 129–138; picnics, 61–62, 65; poetry, 138–152; theater, 100–108
radical movement, 1–2; divisions, 18, 43, 221; women, 137, 143–144
radical press, 67–71; anti-fascist newspapers, 94–97; attacks against the prominenti, 75–78; circulation, 71–72; function, 68, 75; fundraising, 6–9; governmental repression, 70, 96; ideological fragmentation, 68, 96; style, 72–74
radical theater, 99–128: attendance and frequency, 101–2; anti-fascist plays, 124–127; anti-militarist plays, 115–117; commedia dell'arte, 107; decline of, 128; filodrammatiche rosse (radical theatrical groups), 101; function of, 104; general themes, 107; gender issues, 114; melodrama, 107, 111, 113, 118; proletarian plays, 109, 120–121; romance plays, 122–124; teatro del popolo, 105–106; women's participation, 103–104
Ragionieri, Ernesto, 13
Rapisardi, Mario, 139, 147, 148, 159

About the Author

MARCELLA BENCIVENNI was born in Calabria, Italy, and moved to New York City in 1995 to undertake graduate studies in U.S. history. She received an M.A. from New York University and a Ph.D. from the Graduate School of the City University of New York. Currently assistant professor of history at Hostos Community College (CUNY), she is co-editor of *Radical Perspectives on Immigration*, a special issue of the journal *Socialism and Democracy* (November 2008), and the author of various articles on Italian American history and American radicalism.